This volume is sponsored by
the Center for Chinese Studies
University of California, Berkeley

Communist
Neo-Traditionalism

Communist Neo-Traditionalism

Work and Authority in Chinese Industry

Andrew G. Walder

University of California Press

Berkeley / Los Angeles / London

University of California Press
Berkeley and Los Angeles, California

University of California Press, Ltd.
London, England

Printed in the United States of America

Library of Congress Cataloging-in-Publication Data
Walder, Andrew George.
   Communist neo-traditionalism.
   Bibliography: p.
   Includes index.
      1. Industrial relations—China.   2. Communism—
China.   3. Labor and laboring classes—China.
I. Title.
HD8736.5.W34   1986   306'.36'0951   85-27093
ISBN 0-520-05439-3 (alk. paper)

1   2   3   4   5   6   7   8   9

Chapters 2 through 6 contain material
previously published in the following
publications and revised for this book:

Andrew G. Walder, "The Remaking of the
Chinese Working Class: 1949–1981." *Modern
China* 10, no. 1 (Jan. 1984). Reprinted by
permission of Sage Publications, Inc.

Andrew G. Walder, "Communist Social
Structure and Workers' Politics in China." In
Citizens and Groups in Contemporary China,
ed. by Victor C. Falkenheim. Michigan
Monographs in Chinese Studies, vol. 56 (Ann
Arbor: University of Michigan, Center for
Chinese Studies, 1986). Reprinted by permission
of the Center for Chinese Studies, University of
Michigan.

Andrew G. Walder, "Organized Dependency
and Cultures of Authority in Chinese Industry."
Journal of Asian Studies 43, no. 1 (Nov. 1983):
51–76. Reprinted by permission of the
Association for Asian Studies, Inc.

To my parents
Margaret and George Walder

Contents

List of Maps   x

List of Tables   xi

Preface   xiii

Acknowledgments   xix

1.   Communist Neo-Traditionalism:
     An Introductory Essay   1
     The Neo-Traditional Image of
         Communist Society   2
     Communist Neo-Traditionalism as a
         Type-Concept   8
     Social and Economic Dependence on
         the Enterprise   14
     Political Dependence on Management   17
     Personal Dependence on Superiors   20
     The Institutional Culture of Authority   22
     Précis of the Analysis   27

2.   The Factory as an Institution:
     Life Chances in a Status Society   28
     The Transition to a Communist Pattern   30
     Demographic Problems and the
         Administrative Response   35
     Status Groups in the Labor Force   39
     The Supply and Allocation of State
         Sector Jobs   56
     Social and Economic Aspects of the
         Employment Relationship   59

Labor Mobility and Dependence on
the Enterprise   68

Mobility and Life Chances in the Enterprise   76

The Structured Dependence of the
Enterprise Community   81

3.   The Party-State in the Factory   85

The Party-State and the Working Class   86

The Political Organization of the Factory   88

The "Foreman's Empire" on the Shop Floor   95

The Chinese Work Group System   102

Stalinist and Maoist Mobilization: A
Comparison   113

4.   Principled Particularism: Moral and Political
Aspects of Authority   123

Social Ties in Ideological Groups   125

From Ideological Orientation to
Principled Particularism   130

Biaoxian and the Flexibility of
Rewards and Punishments   132

Worker Responses to Moral-Political
Authority   143

The Substantive Ambiguity of *Biaoxian*   160

5.   Clientelist Bureaucracy:
The Factory Social Order   162

The Divided Workforce as a Social Fact   166

The Official Patron-Client Network   170

Cliques and Factions   175

Instrumental-Personal Ties   179

A Comparative Perspective   186

6.   Maoist Asceticism:
The Failed Revitalization   190

Maoism as a Revitalization Movement   191

Trends in Real Wages and Living Standards 194

The Inequities of Wage Austerity 201

The Emergence of Indulgent Patterns
of Authority 205

The Expanding Scope of Instrumental-
Personal Ties 210

The Decline of Work Groups 212

The Unintended Consequences of
Revitalization 219

7. From Asceticism to Paternalism:
Changes in the Wake of Maoism 222

From Asceticism to Paternalism 224

The Restriction of Moral-Political
Mobilization 227

Recasting the Political Standards 229

The Redefinition of Activism 233

The Changing Role of the Party 235

Continuities in the Pattern of Dependence 237

The Evolving Institutional Culture 238

8. Theoretical Reflections 242

The Structure of Communist Societies 243

Social Stability and Legitimacy in
Communist States 246

The Varieties of Modern Industrial Authority 249

The Evolution of Communist Societies 251

Appendix A: The Hong Kong Interviews:
An Essay on Method 255

Appendix B: List of Informants 270

Bibliography 273

Index 295

Map

A.1.   Location of Informants' Work Experience   267

Tables

1. Urban Population in China, 1949–1982   38
2. Structure of the Industrial Labor Force, 1981   41
3. Comparison of Selected Insurance and Welfare Benefits, by Sector   44
4. Standardized Retail Food Prices in Four Countries   62
5. Yearly Wage Data for State Sector Industry, 1952–1982   195
6. Average Per Capita Income in Urban China, 1957 and 1977   197
7. Average Per Capita Income of Wage-Earning Families, 1957 and 1977   198
8. Urban Household Characteristics, by Income Level, 1980   199
A.1. Size and Level of Administration of Informants' Enterprises   262
A.2. Informants' Work Experience, by Industrial Sector   266

Preface

This book is the outcome of a long intellectual and personal journey, whose turning point was my fieldwork in Hong Kong during 1979 and 1980. When I set out for Hong Kong, armed with a set of questions I had derived from reading secondary literature and the official press of the People's Republic of China, I expected that my interviews with emigres would provide data that would help me to answer them. As usually happens in field research, my conception of the intellectual problems changed, new questions and new perspectives arose, the original questions were discarded as uninteresting or irrelevant, and completely unanticipated perspectives forced their way into my consciousness.

During the course of one year's field interviews with emigre workers, staff, and managers, three arresting impressions were etched deeply into my mind. None of them had been a part of my original conception of the research. The first was the many-sided dependence of workers on their firms and superiors, something far more extensive than knowledge of formal political and economic institutions would suggest. The second was the central importance of stable vertical ties cultivated by party and management among a devoted minority of workers; these loyalties mingle the official with the personal and create a social cleavage widely reflected in the perceptions, interests, and political activities of workers. Third was a system of political incentives that appears on the surface to be based on political appeals and nonmaterial incentives, but which, in fact, is based on a deep-seated particularism in the allocation of material rewards and career opportunities.

I reported these findings in my 1981 doctoral dissertation and in some journal articles published shortly thereafter, but this turned out to be just the beginning of a second stage in my inquiry. What was I to make of these social patterns? Were they just another example of "informal organization" to be catalogued along with the findings of

Blau, Dalton, Gouldner, and the students of Japanese industry or did
they have a deeper comparative significance? Did they comprise a
peculiarly Chinese adaptation of institutions imported from the Soviet Union? Did this adaptation, if it was that, result from a distinctively Chinese cultural tradition or from economic and political conditions peculiar to China? What did I mean by the term *dependence*,
and is the position of workers in China really so different from that of
workers elsewhere? If so, in precisely what ways?

The only way to answer these questions was through comparisons: with Chinese factory life before 1949; with contemporary
and historical practices in other communist countries, with China's
East Asian neighbor, Japan, and with the United States. I had originally thought that China's variant of communist labor relations
might stand in relation to the Soviet Union's as Japan's variant of
capitalist labor relations stands in relation to the United States': one
that stresses loyalty to the firm and management, lifetime employment, and the cultivation of group loyalties. The more I read about
the Soviet Union and Eastern Europe, however, the more I came to
realize that the Chinese features I had thought so distinctive were in
fact variants of generic communist patterns of authority. The more I
read of Chinese factories in earlier historical periods, the more I
was convinced that these patterns were recent developments introduced by communist political and economic organization. The
more I read of Japanese industry, the more I realized that, under-
neath the superficial similarities, there are fundamental differences
with China in factory institutions, group relations, and patterns of
advancement and reward. The more I read of the United States, and
particularly of studies of informal organization in industry, the
more I began to doubt whether the common distinction between
the formal and the informal makes sense in analyzing the phenomenon of party-clientelism. And the more I read of personal networks,
patronage, and political clientelism in other settings, the more I
became convinced that communist labor relations embody basic
structural differences from the patterns described elsewhere.

After my field experience, when I read about other institutions in
China and other communist societies, I frequently detected the
same underlying themes of dependence and vertical loyalties, even
though the authors often did not draw attention to them. I gradually came to view the patterns of authority I had studied in state-
owned Chinese factories as sharing certain generic features with

other communist institutions, and I came to understand these generic features as the outcome, albeit unintended, of basic features of the organization of established Leninist parties and of central planning.

At the same time, I realized that my emerging understanding of communist social organization—stressing dependence, vertical loyalties, and networks of strong personal ties—did not fit well with the prevailing sociological images of communist society. The "totalitarian" image, of which there are now several versions, stresses political repression and formally organized social control—certainly present in the society I studied. However, this view neglects the positive incentives offered to individuals, stressing instead the destruction of social ties, the atomization of society, and the impersonal nature of the loyalty demanded to the party and its ideology. "Group" and "pluralist" images rightly stress the prevalence of conflict, bargaining, and the pursuit of interests despite the party's efforts to prevent it, but they too readily abstract from communist institutions that structure society and political activity in qualitatively distinctive ways, and they use a language of group activity that has limited usefulness. The discussions of "modernization" in communist societies, which stress the erosion of ideological orientations in favor of more pragmatic, nonideological orientations required in all complex industrial societies, address a genuine trend but miss completely the themes that I had come to understand as central. As a result, I decided to present my work not only as a comparative study of industrial authority, but also as an inquiry into the nature of communist society and its pattern of evolution. Stimulated by Kenneth Jowitt's (1983) discussion of the political corruption of the Leninist party in the Soviet Union, I decided, despite my reservations about the misunderstandings the term might elicit, to summarize my perspective with the term *communist neotraditionalism*.

I am less committed to the label than to the concept it represents, which is my effort to conceptualize the distinctive characteristics of communist political authority. Built into the concept is an explanation of how a Leninist party's mass mobilization evolves into neotraditional patterns; there is room in the concept for variation and change through time. Although the concept was designed as an effort to compare and interpret authority relations in industry, it is also relevant to broader questions about the relationship between the communist state and society, the relationship of social mobility to political power, and the politically relevant aspects of communist social structure.

The analysis offered here is based in large part on four sources of information: government documents, both published and internal, pertaining to employee wages, benefits, rewards, and punishments, and the responsibilities of the party in labor relations; official newspaper accounts and statistical compendia; scholarly books and articles published by Chinese social scientists; and over 500 hours of interviews that I conducted with 80 former Chinese industrial employees residing in Hong Kong and, in two instances, New York City.

This last source was by far the most important, and the number of citations do not adequately convey its overall contribution to the study. The interviews, open-ended and ethnographic in nature and at times leading into oral history, were as much a source of orientation and insight as a source of data. Many of the citations in this book are to published documents, but the interviews provided the background that led me to frame the questions and structure the analysis the way I have. And the interviews, by providing a sounder sense of industrial realities than would otherwise have been possible, shaped the way that I interpreted published regulations and other documents and allowed me to see additional implications that I would otherwise have missed. The argument and outline of this book were formed as a result of my field research, but the analysis and documentation were built up over the next several years, as I rechecked interviews and collected documentary materials that corroborated, extended, or modified those gathered in my initial interviews, and then completed a second round of interviews to clear up ambiguities and sharpen and test my conceptualizations. The result is a tapestry of documentation and description in which interview and printed sources are woven together.

I find it curious that emigre interviews often meet the suspicion that they are singularly prone to bias because of the presumed political attitudes of the informants. This is curious not because it should not cause concern, but because similar anxieties are almost never expressed about the systematic censorship and management that shapes the mass media and popular literature, used far more commonly as a source of information on China and other "closed" societies. Having used both sources extensively, I find it odd that people are generally much more confident about our ability to "see through" the biases of the press than the testimony of emigres. The attitudes and perspectives of emigres are more varied than those reflected in the press; their experiences in China, and reasons for leaving, vary considerably; and the bias involved in their reporting, not managed or coordinated by any organization, is less systematic than that exhibited in the state media. Moreover, the interview has an inestimable advantage over the written document: you can ask questions in an interview, probe further after an initial answer is given, and ask for explanations, examples, and clarifications. You do not have to accept the informant's statements at face value; further probing usually supplies information that could support a perspective different from the one consciously held by the informant. The point is not that emigre testimony should not be treated with care, but that the problems presented by this source are, if anything, more manageable than those presented by other sources of information that are commonly used with little more than a ritual nod to the problem of bias.

Direct and sustained observation in Chinese factories, accompanied by unrestricted anonymous interviewing, would help to assess more fully the accuracy of emigre testimony. Although it is now common for Americans to live, work, and conduct research in China, systematic field research among industrial employees has not been permitted. To live in China, develop friendships with Chinese citizens, and enjoy periodic conversations with industrial employees can certainly help one develop a sound body of general knowledge and an intuitive feel for social institutions and behavior. One may also learn a good deal from the brief formal interviews that are now relatively easy to arrange with factory officials. My own experiences on five visits to China, and the longer stays of many of my friends, have strengthened my confidence in the reliability of emigre interviews. Yet none of these experiences amount to sustained and systematic research of the type that is possible in Hong Kong. Until unrestricted access to large numbers of industrial employees for long and anonymous interviews is granted foreign researchers, we will not be able to dispense with emigre testimony.

Even if questions about the validity and reliability of emigre testimony are not so uniquely serious as is popularly assumed, a researcher who relies heavily on them must still interpret such material with care, and the careful reader deserves an account of how the research was conducted, and the "data" interpreted. Appendix A is designed to answer these questions and to address the related intellectual (and not merely methodological) issues. Because this book is only the latest in a long line of studies based on emigre interviews, I do not intend to repeat the now-familiar themes. Rather, I will stress the aspects of my approach that differ from those of my predecessors. I do not conceive of the problems of emigre interviewing through the lens of survey research, in which one tries to anticipate potential sources of respondent bias, minimize it in the design of questions, and mentally or statistically compensate for it. Instead, I view the technique as a special case of ethnography and related field methods, in which the interviews are used to orient oneself to a social setting, develop, test, and refine conceptualizations over the course of the research. Readers interested in the empirical underpinnings of this book are invited to turn to appendix A.

New York City
May 1985

Acknowledgments

It is remarkable how many personal and institutional debts one can accumulate while completing a project such as this. A small army of friends and colleagues have offered their thoughts on this and related efforts, and their cumulative impact has been considerable. I am grateful to one and all. On these pages I will not attempt to name everyone, but I will single out a small number who have contributed in a major way and thank the institutions that helped me to complete my work. My intellectual debts, which are many, are acknowledged in the references and footnotes.

Because this book began as a doctoral dissertation at the University of Michigan, I should begin with the members of my dissertation committee: Martin Whyte, Robert Cole, Charles Tilly, Mayer Zald, and Arnold Tannenbaum. Each took an active interest in my work and contributed significantly to it. Allan Silver helped me sharpen my presentation of "principled particularism" and introduced me to the work of Edward Shils and Vladimir Nahirny that helped me to understand its origins in the ideological orientation. Linda Cook steered me to published and unpublished work on Soviet labor relations in the 1920s and 1930s, and her dissertation on Stalinist labor mobilization during the First Five-Year Plan has allowed me to make the comparisons presented in chapter 3. Several others gave extensive written evaluations of subsequent drafts: Victoria Bonnell, Herbert Gans, Andrew Nathan, Jean Oi, Susan Shirk, and Martin Whyte (again). In Hong Kong, Liu Zicheng skillfully coordinated my interviewing project. He made the all-important initial contacts with potential informants, convincingly explained to them my aims and the nature of my research, and scheduled all of the initial meetings. Wei Zengdu (a pseudonym) served as a language tutor and as a key informant, having worked in industry for over two decades. He took this novice China specialist under his wing and provided an invaluable orientation to China's popular culture and recent history. David Wang and Howard Huang provided diligent bibliographical assistance. At Columbia University, Kuan Hao and Chou Yangshan searched current journals and newspapers for relevant articles about changes in recent years. Several Chinese students with past industrial work experience, who are now studying in the United States, offered their valuable perspectives on some early formulations of my analysis. Two of them consented to lengthy formal interviews. Although these Chinese citizens remain unnamed, they contributed greatly to the testing and refinement of my ideas.

Three research centers provided a work environment during periods in which I was occupied exclusively with this project. The Universities Service Centre in Hong Kong supplied an office and assisted in many other ways during two stays: 12 months in 1979–1980, and 3 months in 1984. I am especially grateful to the centre's director, John Dolfin, who provided limitless assistance and valued friendship. The Center for Research on Social Organization at the University of Michigan provided office facilities during the period in which this book was initially conceived and written. More importantly, it provided a stimulating intellectual environment for people interested in developing social theories through comparative and historical work. The center's director during those years, Charles Tilly, gave generously of his time and insight. The Center for Chinese Studies, at the University of California at Berkeley, provided me with a postdoctoral fellowship and a congenial intellectual home during 1981–1982, a year in which I began to rethink the book's themes and pursue further research.

Several other institutions provided financial support. Fulbright and Social Science Research Council fellowships jointly provided a stipend and travel expenses for the original dissertation research. A National Science Foundation dissertation grant covered expenses related to the Hong Kong interviewing project. The Council for Research in the Social Sciences, Graduate School of Arts and Sciences of Columbia University, provided me with two summer fellowships to complete work on this book; one of these was spent in Hong Kong to complete a final series of interviews. And the China Research Committee, East Asian Institute at Columbia, provided funds for research assistance in New York and Hong Kong. None of these institutions is responsible for the conclusions I have presented here.

Of all the people who provided aid and inspiration, two must be singled out for special thanks. Martin Whyte, an academic advisor who quickly became a valued friend and colleague, was involved in my project from its inception and always gave generously of his time and knowledge. In the year preceding my own field research, I assisted him in his project on urban social life in China, reading and indexing his Hong Kong interview transcripts from the preceding year and trying to develop codes that characterized the scope of people's social and economic involvements with their work units. Since the appearance of the book that resulted (Whyte and Parish 1984), I have belatedly realized that this experience led me unconsciously into an investigation of organized dependence and its social consequences, which forms a central theme of this book.

Since my first trip to Hong Kong, Jean Oi has been a constant research companion, my closest counsel, toughest critic, and most valued colleague. Jean introduced me to the concept of clientelism, which has become an important theme of this book. The concept has oriented her research on the political institutions of China's villages from its inception. Her forthcoming book on village political life will treat, in a different social setting, some of the themes explored here. That our books offer compatible interpretations of Chinese society and politics is a reflection of our close personal and intellectual partnership.

1. Communist Neo-Traditionalism: An Introductory Essay

In the wake of the Chinese and Russian revolutions, the twentieth century has witnessed the birth and maturation of a distinctive kind of party-state, a new type of state-led industrialization, and a novel set of political relationships. Of all the varieties of modern authoritarianism, the communist state has been among the most stable, the most thoroughly organized, the most autonomous from organized interests, and the most complete in its reform of prior political and economic arrangements. These party-states have proven adept at implementing a wide variety of social and economic programs, extracting and mobilizing resources for rapid industrial growth, providing extensive social welfare at an early stage of development, and promoting national military strength. They have at the same time literally called a modern working class into being; and, out of this process of growth and transformation, they have developed, not entirely from conscious design, a distinctive tradition of labor relations.

This is a study of the Chinese industrial working class, its place in a communist political order, and the pattern of authority in which it lives and works. In the People's Republic of China, as in all countries, it is precisely in such organizations as industrial enterprises that social classes meet one another on a regular basis. In a communist state, it is precisely in the enterprise that workers come into contact with party and state officials. Authority relations in the Chinese factory are, therefore, a window on political relationships characteristic of this type of state and society. If one understands how compliance is secured in the workplace, one also understands an important foundation of the national political order. Although this is a study of authority relations in contemporary Chinese industry, and of how and why these relations are different from those elsewhere, it is just as importantly an inquiry into the social foundations of a communist political order. I have labeled this pattern of authority *neo-traditional*.

The Neo-Traditional Image of Communist Society

The neo-traditional image of communist society differs fundamentally from two others that are often perceived as the only alternatives: the images of totalitarianism and group theory.

There has never been a clearer image of communist society than that of totalitarianism. In totalitarian society, the party recognizes no legal or moral constraints on its actions: it strives for total power, total submission, and total social transformation as prescribed by its ideology. Aided by secret police, informers, and a wide variety of institutions designed for political communication and control, the totalitarian party pursues its aims by terrorizing selected elements of the population and keeping the rest in a state of habitual submission bred by caution and fear (see Arendt 1951: chap. 3; Brzezinski 1956; Friedrich 1954; Wittfogel 1957: 137–48; 427–43; Wolfe 1956).

A totalitarian society has two distinguishing characteristics. The first is the nature of the tie between the totalitarian party and its active adherents: it is an impersonal, ideological one, based on an identification that grows out of psychological impulses as much as considered political commitment. It is the nature of totalitarian movements to appeal not to material interests, but to mass psychology: "Large numbers of people do not respond to totalitarian movements primarily from the standpoint of economic calculus; but instead, they respond to the nihilistic tone of totalitarian movements, as an expression of their feelings of resentment against the present" (Kornhauser 1959: 48). This fundamental ideological orientation continues after the movement comes to power: in its attempts to mobilize the population, people are forced into activism in the service of the party. But this adherence, however forced, often results in "hyper-attachments" to the totalitarian elite and its ideology; the overidentification of the true believer. The roots of this identification are psychological: "Since people are given no other choice as to objects of attachment, they must find psychological sustenance in this manner or do without it" (Kornhauser 1959: 62–63; see also Arendt 1951: 158–72).

The second feature is social atomization: the obliteration of social ties that are not directly harnessed to the party's aims. Totalitarian societies recognize no legitimate distinction between private
and public spheres. Allegiances not subordinated to the party are
potentially subversive to its aims. "The core of this imagery is the
atomized society . . . a situation in which an aggregate of individuals are related to one another only by way of their relation to a common authority. . . . That is, individuals are not directly related
to one another in a variety of independent groups" (Kornhauser
1959: 32; see also Friedrich 1954). A totalitarian regime requires
"atomized masses" not only to keep power, by preventing alternative loyalties independent of the regime, but also to ensure that
there are no obstacles to inhibit the total mobilization of the population that is characteristic of totalitarianism (Kornhauser 1959:
62; see also Brzezinski 1955). The terms *alienation, anomie,* and
loneliness are regularly said to characterize this structure of social
relations in pronounced forms (Gerth and Mills 1952: 405–59;
Arendt 1951: 172–77; Wittfogel 1957: 149–60).

Virtually all contemporary writers, beginning with the origina-
tors of the totalitarian image, recognize that communist regimes
gradually reduce their reliance on political terror to rule their populations and that they do not permanently attempt to keep their societies in a state of constant political mobilization (e.g., Arendt
1951: 90–113; Friedrich, Curtis, and Barber 1969). Although
there have been countless explicit discussions of how the image of
the totalitarian "political system" needs to be modified in light of
this evolution (see Johnson 1970), it is less clear how much, and
precisely in what ways, the image of totalitarian society needs to be
altered. Some argue that the declining reliance on political terror
and mass mobilization does not represent a fundamental change,
but merely the greater refinement, "rationalization," and sophistica-
tion of the instruments of political control (Cocks 1970; Dallin and
Breslauer 1970; Kassof 1964). The implication, not always drawn,
is that communist society still reflects social atomization and impersonal ideological ties between the party and its adherents (see
Zaslavsky 1982a).[1]

---

1. Although it is now widely agreed that the original totalitarian image *no longer*
accurately describes communist regimes, there are those, like myself, who argue that
it was never a valid analytical description of *social relations* at *any stage* in the development of communist societies. I take this to be the main thrust of recent social and

One alternative view of communist political systems, however, does project a clear image of a society quite different from the totalitarian one. Many studies of communist political systems insist that, as political terror and mass mobilization subside, there is an accompanying revival of genuine political competition within the framework of political controls—a competition that can be described as *pluralistic* (e.g., Hough 1977). Social groups emerge from the temporary atomization of earlier periods and begin to articulate and otherwise pursue their shared interests. This activity, to be sure, is not formally organized as is interest group activity in liberal regimes, but it is, however, based on group identities and interests (Skilling 1983; Skilling and Griffiths 1970). Although these writers often eschew claims of societal convergence (e.g., Skilling 1970), the concepts and comparisons employed, nonetheless, invite such speculation. Pluralist and totalitarian societies are placed at different ends of an implicit continuum. The more that a totalitarian system "liberalizes" and allows limited pluralistic competition, and the more group politics pervades bureaucratic institutions (one must logically conclude), the less pronounced become the differences between the societies of East and West.[2]

At the core of this image of communist society is an unspoken ontological commitment: "real" political activities are based on *groups* that share common interests, and these groups act through formal political institutions, which often mask the reality of group action. This stance is identical to that of the original group theories about pluralism from which it is derived: the "group" is assumed to be the basic element of politics and operates under the institutional

---

political analyses of the Stalin era, e.g., Fitzpatrick (1978), Hough (1978), and Lewin (1977; 1978). Most research on Chinese society under Mao would, in my opinion, support this view.

2. Hough (1977:14) takes the argument further than others:

> There may not be much difference between stating that the Soviet Union is basically a directed society with a number of pluralistic or semi-pluralistic elements and stating that the Soviet Union is a kind of pluralist society with certain types of restrictions. It is perhaps the difference between saying that the bottle is 55 percent full or that it is 55 percent empty: the difference in tone is greater than the difference in substance.

I am not interested here in the question of *how similar* these types of societies are, but in the logically prior question of whether or not one can gauge similarity or difference with a few scaled attributes (in this case, pluralistic competition).

cover of administrative agencies, courts, legislative bodies, and political parties. Just as the group image of politics in communist society has emerged as a conscious reaction against the totalitarian
image, group theory originally was a reaction to earlier theories
that stressed the formal institutions of liberal regimes: "[Group the-
ory] was a sociological revolt against legal formalism: group interaction constituted the reality of political life operating behind the
formal legal-institutional guises of society and the state" (Almond
1983: 245).[3] Research in this vein focuses on the classification and
description of groups: their identity, boundaries, (presumed) shared
interests, and opportunities to exercise influence on the making and
implementation of policy. The distinctive communist institutions
that serve to organize political activity—the Leninist party and
its subordinate organizations—are not of interest except to the
extent that they provide an opportunity for groups to pursue their
interests.[4]

The neo-traditional image differs fundamentally from both of
these. At the same time, it implies a pattern of genuine evolution
that cannot be described as convergent. The neo-traditional image
shares with the totalitarian one a focus on the distinctive communist institutions that foster organized political control, and it shares
the premise that these forms of organization shape patterns of association and political behavior in distinctive ways. But the neo-
traditional image departs from the totalitarian one, even its latter-
day versions, in several crucial respects. First, though recognizing
the constraints placed on citizen behavior by the system of sur-

3. I should note in passing that proponents of this image often conflate "pluralism" with "group politics." "Pluralism" signifies the fact of competition and conflict over political power, influence, public goods, or policy outcomes. "Group politics" implies that collectivities, united by common interests, are the most important,
if not the only, political actors. Thus we find the heads of bureaucratic agencies, regional leaders, professional strata, and leadership factions all labeled "groups," despite wide differences in the nature of their mutual affiliation and the activities in
which they engage. Janos (1970) provides one of the few sound efforts to bring some
order to this conceptually chaotic field.

4. An outstanding example is Hough's (1977: 125–39) examination of the party,
not as an instrument of organization and control, but as an institution in which
group views are represented to the extent that group members are represented in the
party membership. The nature of the party as an organization and its activities and
aims, however (not to mention how it decides which workers and intellectuals will be
admitted), are crucial in interpreting what membership means in this context. Chapters 3 through 5 present material that can be read as an extended critique of this
approach.

veillance and political control, it stresses the positive incentives offered for compliance. Central to the concept of neo-traditionalism is the notion that, from the establishment of a communist regime, political loyalty is rewarded systematically with career opportunities, special distributions, and other favors that officials in communist societies are uniquely able to dispense. Where the totalitarian image places its emphasis on the disincentives and psychological states created by fear and inbred caution, the neo-traditional image places emphasis on the meshing of economic and political power— on the structured incentives offered by the party.[5]

Second, the neo-traditional image posits a paradox: communist parties do put forward impersonal ideological standards of behavior in their attempt to mobilize society, and these are stressed precisely during the period that the regime attempts to transform radically the existing social structure. But these impersonal standards dictate preferential treatment in return for loyalty and ideological adherence, and standard party leadership practices require the cultivation of stable networks of such activists in all social settings. The totalitarian image captures the ideological intentions and the party's formal hostility to personal ties, but it misses the unintended social consequences of the party's ideological orientation: party branches develop stable networks of loyal clients, who exchange their loyalty and support for preference in career opportunities and other rewards. The result is a highly institutionalized network of patron-client relations that is maintained by the party and is integral to its rule: a clientelist system in which public loyalty to the party and its ideology is mingled with personal loyalties between party branch officials and their clients.[6]

Third, instead of social atomization and the destruction of social ties not subordinated to the party's aims, the neo-traditional image posits a rich subculture of instrumental-personal ties through which individuals circumvent formal regulations to obtain official ap-

5. Research on Chinese society in the 1960s and 1970s has long stressed the positive incentives offered for compliance. A representative sampling is Oksenberg (1970), Shirk (1982), Unger (1982), and Oi (1985), all of whom offer analyses of communist institutions that stress competition for career opportunities, rewards, or public goods. The neo-traditional image is consistent with this work, although only Oi formulates arguments that bear directly on the image I am developing here.

6. This "corruption" of the official ideology and organization can eventually pervade and transform the entire structure of the party and government, as Jowitt (1983) argues in his analysis of the Soviet Union. My discussion is of the state-society relationship, not of the structure of the regime, though the two may well be linked.

provals, housing, and other public and private goods controlled by low-level officials. The party's ideology and organization have always been hostile to these "unprincipled" personal ties, which at one extreme shade into corruption. But the system of political and economic organization, which creates scarcity and leaves so many legal and distributional decisions to the discretion of lower-ranking officials, *structurally* encourages these ties. In sum, instead of the totalitarian image of impersonal mobilization and social atomization, the neo-traditional image stresses a formally organized particularism in the distribution of goods, income, and career opportunities, a network of patron-client relations maintained by the party, and a rich subculture of instrumental-personal ties independent of the party's control.

The neo-traditional image shares with the "group-pluralist" one the conviction that communist societies are pervaded by competition and conflict at all levels, and that people have a variety of means to pursue their interests. Yet it departs from the group-pluralist image in two fundamental ways. First, it does not share its ontology: that the "real" political and social forces are group forces, and that these shape formal political institutions and work through them. The neo-traditional image stresses the "reality" and priority of communist institutions designed to exercise political control: they not only shape political behavior and create a set of genuine political and personal loyalties, but in so doing they shape *social structure itself*. Second, it does not enshrine the "group" as the basic unit of political behavior or group ties as the basic element of social structure. The party organizes social institutions in a way that systematically diverts political activity and individual allegiances away from group identifications. It coopts a minority into networks whose allegiances rest with the party branch, and it implicitly tolerates a wide variety of individuated instrumental-personal ties, even those that border on corruption. Communist institutions exist in continuous tension with group allegiances and activities, but only a narrow spectrum of political behavior can be appropriately fitted to group concepts.[7] The neo-traditional image stresses the social network, not the group, as its main structural concept.

7. An adequate political sociology of communist states, and of their distinctive variety of "pluralism," would require an elaboration of the central tension between group politics and vertical loyalties, and it would involve a conceptual reordering that recognizes the distinction between the identity and interests of social aggregates

Finally, the neo-traditional image is at odds with the idea that communist societies evolve in a pattern that represents convergence with the advanced capitalist societies. Whether this convergence is measured on a continuum that contrasts particularism with universalism, ascription with achievement, tradition with modernity, or totalitarianism with pluralism, the effort to gauge degrees of difference is bound to mislead. None of these concepts adequately characterizes the distinctive social configuration of contemporary communism or allows us to interpret its pattern of change. Instead of an evolution, however partial, toward pluralistic competition and group allegiances and activities, there is an evolution toward a historically new system of institutionalized clientelism; a neo-traditional pattern of authority based on citizen dependence on social institutions and their leaders. Communist societies and economies are indeed "modernizing" in many respects, but as political communities they are becoming more "neo-traditional"; they are transformed *from within* by their patterns of economic organization and the ambiguities of their official ideology and political institutions (see Jowitt 1983). This evolution, moreover, is deeply rooted in the origins of communist institutions: there are no fundamental distinctions between "mobilization" and "postmobilization" stages of development, as far as these core features are concerned.[8] The description of factory authority offered in this book is an elaboration of this neo-traditional image of communist society and an analysis of its origins, stability, and evolution over the decades in the People's Republic of China.

Communist Neo-Traditionalism as a Type-Concept

Although *communist neo-traditionalism* is a term designed to convey an image of communist society, it is also a type-concept designed for the comparative study of authority relations in industry. The concept was not derived from any preexisting theory or ty-

---

and how political activity is organized and the actors defined. Frey (1985) and Janos (1970) would undoubtedly be the place to begin such a task, but this is well beyond the scope of this book.

8. I suspect that I would root these patterns much earlier in the "mobilization stage" than does Jowitt (1983).

pology but was built from elements of the observed reality of institutions and behavior in Chinese industry and refined through comparisons with analogous aspects of labor relations in other communist states.[9] The type includes only those elements that I consider to be the defining ones. Wage policies and other labor relations practices have changed repeatedly in China over the past three decades; but, despite these policy changes, there has been a consistent and enduring set of institutions, structures, and orientations to authority. These *enduring elements* are the ones incorporated in the type. In a similar manner, I have compared these enduring Chinese elements with those apparent in the literature on Soviet labor relations in an effort to distinguish the Chinese from the generically communist. The resulting type is, therefore, stated at a level of generality that allows it to be used to distinguish the common and unique features of the Soviet, Chinese, and other communist patterns, while at the same time providing a framework for analyzing problems and patterns of change specific to China.

Before defining this type, one important caveat: the term *neo-traditional* is used in an analytical, rather than historical, sense. It is not intended to convey a proposition that is a virtual truism—that authority relations in contemporary industry reflect the influence of prerevolutionary cultural traditions. Because all modern societies represent a complex pattern of continuity and change with regard to their traditional social structures and the consequences of industrialization (Bendix 1964), all national patterns of industrial authority are in one sense neo-traditional. The question is why particular institutional and cultural patterns common to a wide variety of premodern and early modern settings (such as personal dependence in craft and early factory production) are incorporated in the modern institutions of some societies, but transformed in others. We cannot explain contemporary neo-traditionalism by referring to cultural traditions, for two reasons. First, a cultural tradition can-

9. Although my cast of mind is evidently Weberian, I do not view my task to be to extend or elaborate on Weber's own work, nor do I attempt a typology that covers all other varieties of industrial authority. I would rather have the subject of my research, rather than Weber's type concepts, be the focus of attention. The term "neo-traditionalism" was suggested to me by a reading of an early draft of Jowitt's (1983) interpretation of the Soviet Union. He offers it as a characterization of the communist party and its system of rule taken as a whole. Here I apply it to the "state-society relationship" alone and develop the concept further through research on a specific institutional setting.

not explain its own continuity (or lack thereof) without resorting
to tautology: the continuity of culture itself must be explained by its
relation to institutional structures that serve to perpetuate it (see
Merton 1968a: 84–86; Stinchcombe 1968: 101–29). Second, we
cannot safely assume that there is a "tradition" with which contemporary social institutions exhibit continuity. In China, as in Japan
(Cole 1971; Gordon 1985), contemporary patterns of industrial authority that might appear at first glance to be traditional in fact
have no precedent in the forms of industrial organization of earlier
periods. The tradition in question did not crystallize in either country until after World War II. Communist neo-traditionalism is a
modern type of industrial authority.[10]

The term *neo-traditional*, in other words, does not signify a social pattern that is not yet "modern." There is no implied universal
scale of modernity. This position has been elaborated both in general terms (Bendix 1967; Gusfield 1967; Nisbet 1969) and in the
study of individual developing societies (Rudolph and Rudolph
1964; Rustow 1965). These arguments need not be repeated here.
Why, then, must we use the term neo-*traditional* at all? The answer
is in the tradition of Western social science itself. In modern social
science, which was born as an effort to understand the profound
social changes in Western Europe during the eighteenth and nineteenth centuries, the term *tradition* has come to be associated with
dependence, deference, and particularism, and the term *modern*
with independence, contract, and universalism (Nisbet 1966). I
have adopted the term *neo-traditional* in order to highlight the contrast with more familiar modern forms of industrial authority that
are notable for their relative impersonality and anonymity, the relative political and economic independence of workers from management, and the resulting prominence of group conflict, bargaining,
contract, and the relatively tight bureaucratic restriction of the personal discretion of immediate superiors. Out of common convention, the term *traditional* communicates these social attributes
more concisely than any other.

10. This argument does not imply that one cannot talk of the impact of "cultural
traditions" in a meaningful way; it simply means that the notion must be used carefully and in a well-defined fashion, and that it should not be invoked lightly to
explain national differences for which one has no ready explanation. Nor does my
insistence on the modernity of this type imply that it may not evolve in unforeseen
ways in the future.

Communist neo-traditionalism is defined by the following elements. First, the employment relationship has several distinctive features, all of which revolve around the fact that employment is not primarily a market relationship, nor is the firm an economic enterprise in the capitalist sense. Labor has many of the features of fixed, rather than variable, capital in centrally planned industry. It is not a factor of production readily separable from the firm; employment does not fluctuate according to the firm's demand for labor, nor does the firm's demand fluctuate with changes in demand for its products. Wages and conditions of employment are not subject to formal bargaining; labor and management are not recognized as separate parties; and wage scales and conditions are set by higher agencies. Employment plays a welfare role: it is a value in itself, and many social services are delivered at the state workplace, so there is a systemic inhibition to minimizing the size of the labor force. But perhaps more directly relevant is a system of planning and budgeting that provides weak incentives to economize on costs of production, including labor. To be more efficient in labor utilization is to have labor budgets cut—to have labor cut is to risk shortfalls in the future. The management orientation to labor is, therefore, to retain it as a fixed element of production in excess of current needs. This provides the economic framework for the evolution of a distinctive set of authority relations in the factory.[11]

A second set of features pertain to the political and economic organization of the workplace. First, the enterprise is a focal point for the delivery of public goods, services, and other material and social advantages that are not readily available from other sources. Second, the party, with its auxiliary organizations in the workplace, strives to eliminate informal political association of workers outside of official auspices, and, because of its organized presence in workshops, it is able to do so under normal circumstances. Third, the discretion of supervisors, relatively unrestrained by enforceable regulations and contracts, is quite broad, and they have considerable ability to influence the promotions, raises, and, more importantly, the degree to which a worker and his or her family may enjoy the many nonwage benefits and advantages potentially supplied by the

11. Contrast Weber's account of the capitalist enterprise (1922: 63–211) with Kornai's (1980) and Berliner's (1957) of the socialist. A comparative analysis of the diverse forms of modern rationality could easily be developed from these materials.

enterprise. Each of these three elements reflects a relatively high degree of dependence, compared with other types of modern industrial relations: economic and social dependence on the enterprise; political dependence on the party and management; and personal dependence on supervisors.

These elements of workplace organization—generic features of modern communism—give rise to several other features of factory political life and authority relations that complete the definition of the type. Each of these elements may take varied forms, but they are all present in the communist factory. First, management attempts to control the workforce and elicit its active cooperation by fostering a stable relationship, clientelist in nature, with a minority of loyal and cooperative workers who are given preference not only in career opportunities and pay, but in access to the many other benefits and privileges available at the factory. Second, these vertical networks of loyalty are marked publicly on a regular basis—highlighting the split in the workforce—and serve to draw the antagonisms of the rank and file, otherwise reserved for management, onto these privileged and cooperative clients. Third, rank-and-file workers pursue their interests in the workplace through their participation in a vigorous subculture of private exchange and mutual support, which sometimes includes petty corruption, in which workers attempt to influence the decisions of individual supervisors and officials with discretionary power over factory benefits.

This type can accommodate wide variations in specific policies and practices designed to improve the performance of workers. Management may stress ideological indoctrination, group persuasion and mass mobilization as the primary tool of work motivation; it may use this tool in a ritual fashion; or it may explicitly reject this tool as a motivating mechanism. Management may stress "distribution according to work" or material reward for performance; it may give this principle no more than lip service; or it may reject it as a bourgeois principle. The state may enforce an austere wage policy designed to maximize accumulation at the expense of worker consumption; or it may switch to a policy designed to satisfy workers as consumers. Management may in some periods stress strict penalties for breaches of labor discipline and publicize their application as warnings; it may honor existing regulations in the breach; or it may explicitly reject such penalties.

Management may stress a clear division of labor and explicit job rules for individuals; or it may foster a group or "labor brigade" orientation in which responsibility is collective. The state may allow or even encourage labor turnover, or it may place tight restrictions on it. The state may encourage enterprises to borrow and adapt foreign labor management techniques; or it may demand the development of nativist and politically pure techniques. The party may literally shove professional managers aside and commandeer the factory for political and production campaigns run according to Leninist precepts; or it may retreat into a cooperative and supportive stance, becoming partly "professional" in its own orientations. China itself has changed its policies and prescribed practices regularly over the past 30 years, and in these respects it has often been at odds with the Soviet Union and the rest of the Eastern bloc. Although state policies and management practices have come and gone, the core institutional features endure.

As an analytical type, communist neo-traditionalism guides comparisons of industrial authority by focusing attention not on these shifting policies and practices, but on two institutional features. The first is "organized dependence" or the extent to which, and ways in which, workers are dependent economically on their enterprises, politically on the party and management, and personally on supervisors. Existing economic and political arrangements and the internal organization of the factory are of relevance to the extent that they foster more or less dependence in each of these areas. The second feature is the "institutional culture" of the factory; the patterns of association between superior and subordinate, the patterns of association among workers, and the strategies employed by workers, given the opportunities provided by the setting, to advance their interests.

Although this book is a case study, it is explicitly comparative in its aims.[12] Communist neo-traditionalism is an analytical type that embodies a comparative argument: the "institutional culture" characteristic of a national tradition of industrial authority varies according to the configuration of dependence experienced by that nation's workforce.[13] In the course of elaborating the Chinese variant

12. Strictly speaking, a case study is by definition comparative, because it must be a case of some phenomenon of which there are theoretically analogous cases. The term has been debased in common usage by its application to studies that are simply descriptive rather than analytical.

13. Industrial sectors are far from homogeneous within nations, a fact suppressed, but not ignored, in cross-national comparisons. When I compare national types, I am referring, unless otherwise specified, to large, modern enterprises in all countries. In Japan and the U.S., they are the large, "primary sector" firms. In China

of neo-traditionalism and its evolution, I will make brief comparisons, primarily with historical and contemporary practices in Russia, Japan, and the United States. Behind the primary aim of these comparisons, which is to illuminate the distinctive features of industrial authority in communist countries, and the Chinese variant of this type, there is a second aim—to sketch the elements of a theory of national diversity in industrial authority.

Social and Economic Dependence on the Enterprise

All workers are dependent on their enterprises for the satisfaction of their needs. This is the material basis of industrial authority; it provides what Weber called "interests in obedience." But the employment relationship and the degree and type of the dependence it embodies vary widely from country to country and, indeed, change markedly in the course of industrial development. Two aspects of the employment relationship define the extent of worker dependence. The first is the proportion of the workers' needs satisfied (or potentially satisfied) at the workplace. This involves, at a bare minimum, the money wage. But, in a variety of contemporary and historical settings, this has also involved the satisfaction of other social and economic needs: health insurance, medical care, pensions, housing, loans, and education, to name only the most common.

The second aspect of dependence, just as important as the first, is the availability of alternative sources for the satisfaction of these needs. This can refer to the availability of employment elsewhere on comparable terms. "Availability" implies not only the existence of

---

and the U.S.S.R., they are large and medium-sized state factories (usually more than 500 people), at the municipal level or higher. We should note that there is less variation in the labor practices in centrally planned economies, because of the uniformity of state regulation and ownership and the lack of differentiated product markets, which serve to make sectors more diverse in market economies. Within any single nation, I would expect aspects of an industrial sector's "institutional culture" to vary according to differences in the configuration of dependence experienced by that sector's workforce—though a more finely differentiated conception of dependence would have to be developed, and the discussion would have to be fashioned to fit a set of institutional realities common across sectors within the nation in question: labor market conditions, union structures, degree and type of government regulation, and so forth. The concept here is a rough one, designed only to differentiate the centrally planned economies from the market economies.

other jobs (something that depends on labor market conditions), but also the absence of legal or political barriers that close off these alternatives.[14] "Alternatives," moreover, need not refer only to employment alternatives; they may just as importantly refer to the availability of outside income or alternative sources for the satisfaction of nonwage needs: pensions, health insurance, housing, loans, and so forth. The greater the proportion of needs satisfied by the enterprise and the fewer the alternatives (either for employment or the satisfaction of needs), the more dependent is the labor force.

In arguing that industrial workers in communist societies are highly dependent on their enterprises, compared to their counterparts in modern industry elsewhere, I do not mean to suggest that a high degree of worker dependence is unique to communism. Such dependence has always been characteristic of industrial paternalism, company towns, and "welfare capitalism" in the American and British historical experiences.[15] Large enterprises in contemporary Japan provide a wide array of benefits for the permanent part of their work force: housing, health insurance, recreational activities, pensions, and so forth. Given the penchant of Japanese managers in this sector to hire these workers at the entry level and retain them for long periods, this makes the Japanese worker dependent on the firm in a way that contrasts with the American pattern.

Geographical isolation may also serve to close off alternatives to workers, both for employment and the satisfaction of nonwage needs, and the use of company stores, payment in company script, and company housing have been employed historically in railway construction, mining, and other industries to create a dependent and disciplined workforce. Perhaps the most common way in which employment alternatives are closed off to a workforce, or a segment

14. Readers of Stinchcombe's (1965) essay on social structure and organizations will recognize the source of the concept "organized dependency" and the way I have reshaped it in the present context. I have also benefitted from Blau's (1964: 118–25) analysis of dependence and power. Cole's (1979: 242–50) use of Stinchcombe's concept to explain some specific differences between Japanese and American labor relations practices spurred me to develop it as a tool for the comparative analysis of China.

15. For accounts of paternalism in eighteenth- and nineteenth-century England, I have relied on Joyce (1979), Pollard (1965), and Smelser (1959). Brandes (1976) describes the early twentieth-century American developments in "welfare capitalism," the dependence engendered by it, and worker resistance to it. Bendix (1956: 99–116) provides an account of paternalist ideology in nineteenth-century England. Burawoy (1983) outlines the lessening dependence of labor in advanced capitalist countries.

thereof, is through ethnic and racial discrimination that coincides with citizenship or other legal restrictions. Foreign migrant workers from impoverished regions provide a dependent labor force in selected occupations in northern Europe and North America (Thomas 1982). The most extreme form of this type of dependence is that of South Africa's system of apartheid, in which black workers are treated as foreigners in their own country, shackled with identity papers and internal passports, and repatriated to impoverished reservations when their employment is terminated.

In communist economies workers are highly dependent on their enterprises, but in a different way. Despite the many nonwage benefits that may come with employment in some industrial sectors in market economies, the employment relation there is primarily a labor market relationship: a specific contractual exchange of efforts and skills for money and other compensation. In a communist economy, employment in the state enterprise is not primarily a market relationship. It is a position that establishes the worker's social identity and rights to specific distributions and welfare entitlements provided by the state. Moreover, the enterprise exercises authority not only over one highly specialized role, but over the whole person: the state factory is a branch of government and, through the factory's party branch, exerts a measure of the state's political rule over the worker as a citizen.

State-owned enterprises not only provide complete health insurance and pensions, they also provide direct medical care in their own facilities or in an attached hospital; they are the main source for housing; they provide loans, subsidies, child care, meal services, and, sometimes, education; and they are an important source for the procurement of certain consumer goods. People who are not employed in the state sector are not entitled to such a generous array of benefits, and not all state enterprises can provide as wide an array—the specific mix varies by enterprise. The enterprise is also a source of certain sociopolitical services peculiar to the communist setting: obtaining official certificates of permission to travel, to take another job, to get local residence registration for a relative or spouse; or interventions with public agencies for housing, for higher quality medical care or medications, or to lessen the punishment for a criminal offense—to give only some common examples.

Along with this broad range of needs satisfied at the workplace goes a corresponding scarcity of alternatives. In some periods in many communist states, changing jobs without official authorization has been effectively restricted (this includes China for most of the period studied here). Even in those countries where the freedom to change jobs is widely established, residence barriers continue to restrict alternatives to certain areas or regions: a resident of Beijing or Moscow may freely get permission to work in the hinterlands (in the rare case that they would desire to), but someone from the hinterlands cannot readily get permission to reside in a large, "closed" city. Alternatives are also few in a second respect: communist economies invest according to planners' preferences, not consumers' preferences. Investment in consumer goods and housing production is assigned a relatively low priority. This scarcity makes the provisions of the workplace even more important. (This is an important contrast with Japan where, even though large enterprises often provide housing and other benefits, consumer markets are fully developed and not characterized by shortages.) For many of the other needs satisfied at the workplace, there are few reasonable alternatives.

Communist countries do vary in the degree of worker dependence on the enterprise, and there are also variations between sectors. Through the late 1970s China was a case of rather extreme dependence: movement between enterprises was tightly restricted; residence controls were strictly enforced; housing and consumer goods were in extremely short supply; and common consumer items and even basic foodstuffs were rationed through the workplace. These shortages and controls have eased in the 1980s, and China's pattern of dependence has moved toward less severe Eastern European norms. Despite these variations, the communist pattern contrasts with that in large Japanese enterprises and, more sharply, with those in the United States.

Political Dependence on Management

A second feature that distinguishes the communist pattern of authority is the political dependence of workers on management. This aspect is defined by organization: by the independent capacity of workers to collectively resist management initiatives in an organized way; and by the capacity of management to resist such worker initiatives in an organized fashion and organize workers' political

18   *Introductory Essay*

activity on their own terms. In this respect, the communist pattern
differs not only from that of liberal-democratic regimes, but from
most other varieties of modern authoritarianism as well.

Standard theories of collective action stress organization among
members of a group as the key determinant of that group's ability to
enforce its interests. These theories stress geographical proximity
and ability to communicate; the homogeneity of group interests;
the ability of a group to develop and protect competent leadership;
and its ability, given the existing legal order, to organize and communicate freely with one another in the pursuit of group aims (e.g.,
Tilly 1978). When examining differences in workers' collective
strength in different industrial sectors or in different Western nations, such a perspective leads to consideration of the extent to
which enterprises are small, geographically dispersed, or isolated;
whether workers are divided by differences in their conditions of
employment or by ethnic, racial, and linguistic barriers; whether
their organizing efforts are hindered by lack of literacy or reinforced by community patterns and common craft traditions; and
whether workers have political rights to organize that are respected
in practice.[16]

"Repression" is an important concept in these theories. It affects
virtually all organizing activity; the ability to communicate and
organize freely, and to protect leaders. Yet the concept has two
meanings that are not often clearly distinguished. It refers, first, to a
political stance, the willingness of the authorities to use a high
quantity of force, which raises the "cost" (in terms of lives and
resources spent) of collective action. In this meaning of the term,
repression has a deterrent effect and influences the calculative behavior of subordinate groups. Repression can refer, second, to an
organized pattern of activity that makes collective action difficult to
undertake in the first place and that diverts it into other forms.
These two aspects have quite different implications for political dependence. A state or an elite that must use a large amount of force
to repress emerging or ongoing collective action exercises less effective control than a state or elite that is able regularly to prevent
organized group action in the first place. The most brutal and vio-

16. A broad stream of research on early modern European social history stresses
the importance of craft organization and community solidarity: Aminzade (1981),
Thompson (1966), Sewell (1980), Dawley (1976), Liebman (1980), Hanagan
(1980), and Shorter and Tilly (1974).

lent regimes are not necessarily the most effective at imposing political control; their brutality and violence is often a mark of a poorly organized and ineffective effort to stem collective action. A workforce that is able to fight collectively for its interests, no matter how unsuccessfully, is less dependent than a workforce that is unable to do so and that must accept the political forms dictated by their superiors.

Communist regimes do not differ from other authoritarian ones in their willingness to use force to repress workers' collective action. Although they have shown little hesitancy in this regard when faced with organized opposition, real or imagined, it is hard to argue that their willingness to use force against organized workers is greater than that of other contemporary authoritarian regimes or even most liberal regimes in past eras.[17] They do differ in their extraordinary ability to prevent organized political activity even from reaching the stage of collective action. The difference is in the political organization of the workplace. The communist factory is laced with overlapping political organizations that serve both to prevent organized opposition and to recruit and coopt members of the workforce. The party organization itself has branches organized in every workshop. It recruits and rewards activists, often through an auxiliary youth organization, to keep the party informed of workers' dispositions. The state security bureau also maintains a branch office, usually staffed by former military personnel, in every state factory of any consequence, and these offices maintain a network of informers in shops. The security office keeps records on suspect workers, but the personnel department keeps its own political dossiers on every worker, and these records move with the worker if he or she changes jobs. A worker who engages in independent political activity, if not imprisoned, will be unable to find work elsewhere, except in marginal sectors. As representatives of the state, communist managers are extraordinarily unified and well organized.

Communist regimes, more importantly, are effective not only in preventing independent organization and activity: they use their

17. The phenomenon that Burawoy (1984) has referred to as the "company state" in Czarist Russia was also partially reflected in some American practices: the hiring of company spies and private police forces by large companies and the virtual identity of territorial governments and militias with large mining and industrial interests in the Western United States in the late nineteenth and early twentieth centuries.

organization of the workplace and their control of rewards to pull workers into political activity that they organize. Any political activity in the workplace must take place within the approved meetings organized by the party and management. Management, in fact, strives to organize all the available political space to preempt independent activity. Loyal citizens are to avail themselves of the opportunities for expression of grievances granted by the state and party; workers must bring up their suggestions and demands as individuals, within this framework. Those who deny this opportunity are literally forced into "conspiratorial" activity and become vulnerable to the legal charge of participating in a counterrevolutionary organization. In this situation, workers are politically dependent on management to a considerable degree. Party and management organize political activity and set the terms and even the vocabulary of political discourse. The extent to which workers' requirements are satisfied depends mainly on the largess of management and the state, not on the collective initiative of workers.[18] Workers can engage in political activity designed to further their interests, either through individual accommodation and cooptation or through an informal pattern of "bargaining"—the "give and take" between management and labor in each factory over the degree of workers' cooperation and the enforcement and interpretation of factory rules. This kind of hidden bargaining is typical of dependent groups that are unable to pursue their aims collectively.[19]

Personal Dependence on Superiors

There is a final aspect of dependence: the extent to which workers are dependent on their supervisors *personally* for the satisfaction of their needs. When supervisors have the ability to hire and fire or manipulate rewards for individuals under them, workers are personally dependent on them to a high degree. When the ability of individual supervisors to hire or fire or manipulate rewards for individuals has been restrained by collective agreements or bureaucratic regulations, the degree of personal dependence is attenuated; pat-

18. The conditions that determine management largess are a separate matter. It can be influenced by the stage of industrial growth, by fiscal and budgetary realities, by the state of international relations, and by efforts of state officials to remedy poor worker motivation.

19. Sabel and Stark (1982), Pravda (1981), and I (Walder 1983) describe this kind of grassroots bargaining, which Weber (1922: 929) calls "amorphous social action."

terns of dependence are more impersonal ("bureaucratic"). This feature determines the extent to which existing levels of worker dependence on the enterprise promote personal dependence within the enterprise.

Early craft-industrial organization is often characterized by a high degree of personal dependence in precisely this respect. In many trades, journeymen and apprentices were dependent on master craftsmen for their jobs and sometimes for their room and board as well (Aminzade 1981). In later eras, even in many "modern" factories, such personal patterns of dependence were to be found in contracting systems dominated by foremen who controlled the production process in the shops and who had wide personal discretion over hiring, firing, and levels of compensation. This "foreman's empire," as Nelson (1975) calls it, eroded steadily in the first decades of this century in the United States under the twin impact of the labor movement and employers' efforts to wrest control over the production process away from the foremen (see Edwards 1979; Stone 1975; Montgomery 1979: 1–31; Nelson 1975: 48–54). The progressive bureaucratization of labor relations resulted in complex regulations and collective agreements governing compensation at specific skill levels, tasks, and grades of seniority, as well as the hiring and firing of workers. The degree of personal discretion that supervisors had in these matters in earlier eras has shrunk to a bare minimum in many large, unionized plants. Instead, one finds a kind of impersonal rule in which complex patterns of pay, promotion, and internal governance are almost entirely shaped by bureaucratic regulation and enforced by factory unions and staff.[20]

In communist regimes, contemporary shop organization did not evolve out of a history of collective conflict and bargaining, nor is it the outcome of management's efforts to wrest control over the production process from foremen-contractors. Instead, industrialization proceeded from centralized state investment and organization, with a new, politically dependent working class being created in the process and with staff management enjoying uncontested control of

---

20. One might be tempted to object that the image projected by the "paternalism" of large Japanese enterprises (and its associated practices) makes Japan an exception to this statement. A closer reading of materials on Japanese shop organization shows that Japanese foremen are subject to staff regulation just as their American counterparts are, even though these staff regulations often embody different principles.

production and personnel policies. As a result, despite the formal
similarity of communist shop organization with that elsewhere—
especially in the technical organization of production—shop foremen and other supervisors maintain considerable discretion in
personnel matters and in many other aspects of the factory's system
of reward and punishment. The communist factory's distinctive pattern of internal political organization also serves to add to the discretion of shop leaders. The workshop is coterminous with the
party branch, and each branch secretary and foreman has wide political and administrative powers in their area of the factory. Shop
officials, relatively free of interference from above and not shackled
by enforceable collective agreements, are in effect brokers that
mediate between staff management and workers. Although they by
no means enjoy the wide control over production and personnel decisions that turn-of-the-century foremen-contractors did in the
United States, the balance of power between staff office and shop
floor, in many areas, tips in favor of the latter.

The "broker" role of shop supervisors is enhanced by another
factor: there are many other distributions, applications, and ap-
provals in the daily life of the communist factory. Shop officials act
as brokers between the factory administration and the workers, releasing staff offices of much of the enormous day-to-day burden of
making these decisions. Shop officials screen requests for factory
housing and special distributions of consumer items. They review
and approve requests for benefits under state labor insurance guide-
lines: vacations, annual home leave, personal leave, visits to sana-
toria, special medications, and welfare and loan payments. Shop
supervisors are also responsible for writing character reports, relay-
ing information to the party and security apparatus, securing permission for workers to travel, and deciding on the application of
fines and other punishments for breaches of factory rules. Shop officials have broad discretionary powers over these matters—things
that are simply not a part of American and Japanese factory life.
The wide discretion lodged in the communist workshop person-
alizes industrial authority to a comparatively high degree.

The Institutional Culture of
Authority

A high degree of worker dependence in each of these three
respects defines a configuration characteristic of modern commu-

nism. Industries in other countries may exhibit a high degree of dependence in any one of these areas, but rarely to such an extent in all three. Large Japanese enterprises often provide for a broad array of workers' needs, but the range is not so broad as in a communist economy: the Japanese enterprise plays no role in providing sociopolitical services, and free markets for housing and commodities in Japan provide alternative sources of supply, even if not always on attractive terms. Authoritarian regimes may be successful in suppressing independent political activity among workers and in channeling them into officially controlled unions, but they do not organize and penetrate the workplace so thoroughly. Individual enterprises, or specific industrial sectors in certain historical and geographic settings, may reflect a high degree of dependence in two or even three of these areas, but no modern industrial sector does. This general configuration of dependence is characteristic of communism because each of the three aspects of dependence is the result of a generic feature of communist political and economic organization: the role of the enterprise in delivering public goods and services in a poorly developed consumer market; the political organization of the workplace and its role in national governance; and the discretion exercised by shop management and party officials in factory administration.

Interpretive comparisons of "types" of authority inevitably return to Weber's preliminary statements. All forms of authority, according to Weber, involve specific normative or ideological claims made by superiors, "ideal" and material interests in obedience, and a characteristic form of conflict shaped by the pattern of authority. These qualities—normative and ideological claims, motives for obedience, and forms of contention—begin to describe what I mean by an institutional culture of authority. But there are other facets to these cultures that Weber's broadly comparative work does not even begin to describe.[21]

The central puzzle of any type of authority is an elusive, ambiguous condition of "consent": an element of voluntary and habitual compliance. Every type of authority involves an element of tacit consent that shades into normative acceptance. Analysts of authority are often split between those who see consent simply as ha-

---

21. Bendix's (1956) classic study of managerial ideology explores the normative and ideological claims of superiors. This is an important aspect of an institutional culture; one that I will not address here, except indirectly.

bituation to power and those who stress the normative acceptance of the claims of authority. I view consent as a less unitary concept. It is a pattern that emerges from a socially structured and highly differentiated pattern of active cooperation, habituation, calculated conformity, and normative acceptance. In other words, people's orientations vary, and it is the structure of these differences and the social relations between people with different orientations that give the pattern of authority whatever stability it may possess. I refer to these patterns as an institutional culture of authority—a summary concept of the conditions that define the structure of consent.

An institutional culture is not simply a shorthand term for patterns of behavior; nor is it a "superorganic" sphere of cultural norms, perceptions, and expectations. Moreover, this concept is not the equivalent of the dependent variables of comparative research on labor relations, for example, permanent employment, loyalty to the firm, lifetime employment, or small group management. Nor is it reducible to a cluster of such variables. It is, rather, a concept fashioned for the comparative (and necessarily interpretive) analysis of factory authority. My comparisons are not of management practices and formal organizational properties, but of the characteristics of everyday life in factory settings that are most often reported by field researchers and social historians.

Stated generally, the four characteristics that define a culture of authority are the structure of social relations in the enterprise; the content and "ethic" of these relations; the practical and ideological claims of authority; and the "give and take" through which managers and workers try to reshape the terms of the tacit agreement that governs labor-management relations. Stated concretely, the communist pattern, of which China's is a variant, is one in which the party cultivates a network of patron-client ties in workshops (social ties that bind a loyal minority to shop officials); in which these vertical ties serve to divide the workforce socially and politically; and in which a subculture of instrumental-personal ties serves as the avenue through which workers pursue their interests as individuals.

Party-Clientelism

The central feature of this institutional culture is a network of patron-client relations that links the party organization and shop management to a minority of loyal workers on the shop floor. These clientelist ties are not purely instances of "informal organization" or personal networks: if they were only this, they would not be of comparative interest. Cliques, factions, and other kinds of personal networks are a ubiquitous phenomenon; they have been described in every imaginable setting, including American and Japanese factories (Dalton 1959; Blau 1954; Eisenstadt and Roniger 1984; Cole 1971). Party-clientelism is not comprised of personal ties that exist separately from the formal organization of relationships and roles: it emerges from standard party recruitment and leadership practices—indeed, it is created by them. The party and management seek to control the workforce and elicit its active cooperation by developing stable ties with a minority of loyal and cooperative workers. Formally speaking, the relationship is impersonal, a form of "principled particularism": the party itself rewards and promotes people preferentially according to the loyalty and service they render to management and party. The networks that result are "objectively" clientelist in structure: they are vertical, between superior and subordinate, relatively stable, and involve an exchange of mutual benefit between the parties involved. Personal loyalties and affectivity between specific leaders and followers do naturally arise in this setting, become mingled with the public, official loyalties, and often result in more privileges and favors than the party prescribes. Yet this personal dimension is not the significant feature of these ties. Party-clientelism is created "from above"; it is an institutionally prescribed clientelist network that has both formal and informal, impersonal and personal, aspects.

This mixed character of party-clientelism is distinctively neo-traditional. It represents a mixture of ideological commitments and impersonal loyalties demanded by the modern Leninist party and the role expectations of modern industrial organization with the personal loyalties characteristic of traditional authority and patrimonialism. It is, therefore, distinct from traditional patron-client ties, built upon personal loyalties, and it is also distinct from cliques and factions that exist separately from the formal organization of roles. (In fact, cliques and factions do often exist within these official networks, and these cliques are aspects of the informal organization of the Chinese factory.) The factions and personal networks described in American and Japanese factories are a different phenomenon from party-clientelism: they are personal, informal, and not a central instrument of labor relations.

The Divided Workforce
as a Social Fact

A split between the party's loyal clients and the rank and file is a direct consequence of these vertical loyalties. The distinction between loyal activists and other workers results in the social isolation of, and antagonism toward, activists, something that splits the workforce and binds activists more closely to the party. Activists serve as a lightning rod for dissatisfaction: they receive any resentment that workers have toward management. Although workers the world over show scorn for members who break rank in this fashion, nowhere else are such mutual antagonisms so permanently institutionalized in routine labor relations. The communist approach to group relations is therefore not, as is often said of Japan (Rohlen 1975), to promote group loyalty and solidarity, but to divide work groups with these cross-cutting loyalties. These cross-cutting loyalties, further, have structural consequences: they define a social boundary just as real as any other category according to which groups may be defined.

Networks of Instrumental-Personal Ties

The last feature is a subculture of social relations that are at the same time personal and instrumental. These social relations—involving the exchange of favors or a reliance on personal connections or petty corruption to obtain a public or private good—substitute for impersonal market transactions in a setting where such markets are restricted and scarcity prevails. They are also the product of a system of distribution in the workplace that is bureaucratic, but one in which officials have wide personal discretion in the application of rules. In communist societies these networks of personal exchange spread far beyond the workplace and pervade every social setting in which the worker may have dealings. Within the factory, workers commonly cultivate connections with factory officials in a position to bend rules in their favor or give them preference in the distribution of housing or other goods. This instrumental orientation in personal relations, referred to as *blat* in Russian, and *guanxi* in Chinese, is not an ethic peculiar to the communist setting. It has predominated in a wide variety of premodern, especially peasant, settings. Networks of instrumental-personal ties thrive in the modern communist enterprise because of the social and economic resources they control, the scarcity that characterizes the consumer economy, and the wide discretion that officials have in interpreting the rules and distributing resources. These instrumental-personal ties are an important avenue through which workers as individuals may pursue their private interests within the factory.

Précis of the Analysis

In the chapters that follow, I describe and analyze the characteristics of neo-traditionalism in Chinese factories. I also specify the ways that the Chinese variant has diverged from the Soviet. Because my purpose is to analyze an institutional framework that has characterized the past 30 years in the People's Republic of China (despite frequent changes in government policy), the approach is analytical and thematic, rather than chronological and topical. Surveys of Chinese labor and management policy abound (e.g., Andors 1977; Hoffmann 1967, 1974), but these surveys are relevant to the central concerns of this book only insofar as they bear on the institutional features I have just described.

Management policies have changed often in China. The First Five-Year Plan (1953–1957), the Great Leap Forward (1958–1960), the period of "readjustment" (1961–1965), the Cultural Revolution decade (1966–1976), and the period of restoration and reform after Mao's death (1977 to this writing) have each brought significant changes from the preceding period. Two of these periods, the Cultural Revolution and the post-Mao reforms, receive detailed attention because they represent opposing tendencies within the framework of neo-traditionalism. Both periods are analyzed not as distinctive bundles of policy (which they are), but as variations on the central institutional themes analyzed in this book.

2. The Factory as an Institution: Life Chances in a Status Society

The state-owned factory in a communist economy is less an economic enterprise than a social institution. Like its counterparts in competitive market economies, it fabricates products from raw materials and employs labor and capital according to a fixed division of labor. But three features distinguish the communist factory. The first is due to the economics of central planning. The private enterprise exists as long as it can maintain its sales on commodity markets, while keeping its costs low enough to make a profit at a reasonable rate of return on investment. The state enterprise, on the other hand, has what the Hungarian economist János Kornai (1980) terms a "soft budget constraint": its financial performance is directly affected by negotiations with state planning agencies over its prices, costs, supplies, capital investment, credit, and taxation. Because its products are required by various bureaus and commercial agencies that use them as supplies for other enterprises in their jurisdictions, local state agencies are indulgent with enterprises in financial difficulties, and there is little real threat of closings or reorganization.

Under the conditions of shortage that characterize these economies, the neo-classical relationship between supply and demand is altered: this is a "resource-constrained" rather then "demand-constrained" enterprise. Demand for inputs is less sensitive to prices, and, in fact, costs tend to be inflated as a rational response. Managerial behavior in these fiscal conditions is commonly oriented to the covert hoarding of fixed capital, inventories of spare parts and materials, as well as labor.[1] This has a fundamental effect

1. This feature of managerial behavior characterizes China just as much as the Soviet Union and Eastern Europe (see Walder 1982). Berliner (1957) and Kornai (1959; 1980), among others, explore this managerial logic in great depth, and Gra-

on labor relations: for Japanese and American managers, labor is a factor of production whose use and cost must be kept to a minimum; for Chinese and Soviet managers, labor is a factor of production whose cost does not restrain demand for it, especially for skilled labor. There are, in other words, fundamental differences in the economic logic underlying labor-management relations in the two kinds of systems.[2]

The communist enterprise is an institution in a second respect. It not only administers for the state its labor insurance and social security provisions, but it directly supplies a wide range of public goods, services, and even commodities that in other economies would be supplied through markets and a variety of institutions and government agencies. More importantly, the enterprise is the primary source of supply for many of these goods and services. The communist enterprise, therefore, plays a direct role in social stratification: instead of workers' life chances being determined by the conditions of labor and commodity markets (as Weber defines them), they are determined to a considerable degree by the ability of the worker's enterprise to provide these goods and services (with wide variations in this regard).

The communist enterprise, finally, is a political institution. As a unit of government administration, it performs a variety of sociopolitical services that are entirely missing in the Japanese and American experiences. The enterprise is the locus of a worker's social and political identity: it provides permission to travel; it handles residency permits for employees and their family members; and it can intervene with municipal housing authorities, the courts and police, and other agencies on behalf of the worker. The enterprise "represents" the worker to state agencies, and the workers' treatment depends on that enterprise's legal status and informal influence.

---

nick (1975) examines various attempts at reform. Reform has not fundamentally altered this orientation in Hungary. There the budget constraint is soft because of bargaining over a wide range of budgetary items, something that has so far been true in China as well (Walder 1985a).

2. In the Soviet Union, this tendency to hoard labor (rather than lay it off, as is the tendency in market economies) has exacerbated and in many respects has helped to create the current labor shortage. In China, on the other hand, a vast labor surplus has made this less of a problem, because overstaffing serves another pressing purpose: to create employment.

The Chinese enterprise resembles the Soviet in each of these
ways, but, because of Chinese demographic conditions and state
efforts to address them, these features and the dependence on the
enterprise engendered by them have been enhanced over the past
three decades. China suffers from a massive oversupply of labor,
while a labor shortage is currently a major constraint on Soviet industrial growth. The Soviet Union has been a predominantly urban
society for two decades and has already passed through the demographic transition. China's population is still 80 percent rural and
still in the midst of this transition.[3] The chronic problem of labor
absorption in both urban and rural areas and the threat that rural
migrants will innundate the cities and overtax housing supplies and
municipal services have compelled the Chinese government to
install unusually strict controls on labor mobility and migration.
Unintended side effects of these controls are a rigid pattern of status
distinctions in the industrial labor force and a degree of dependence
on the enterprise that has been more pronounced than in the Soviet
Union or in Eastern Europe.

The Transition to a Communist
Pattern

That contemporary Chinese patterns are a variant of generic
communist ones is highlighted by a look at prerevolutionary labor
relations. In the China of the 1920s through 1940s, the pattern of
labor relations was not unlike that in many American industries at
the turn of the century: enterprises provided very little beyond a
money wage and in most cases did not even deal directly with workers at all, except through foremen-contractors. The contracting system was widespread, not only in the large textile industry, but in
mining, dockworking, public transport, construction, and tobacco
industries (Honig 1986: chap. 5; Wright 1981; Hershatter 1986:
chap. 6). Labor insurance and social security were virtually nonexistent; housing was provided for some staff members in the
cotton mills, but not for workers (except in remote areas like mining towns). The labor relationship was weak, often transitory: turn-

3. The "demographic transition" is the change from high birth and death rates to
low birth and death rates, which accompanies the onset of modern economic growth.
Death rates fall before birth rates; the longer the period of time before the decline of
birth rates, the greater the "explosion" of population growth.

over was on the order of 50 to 100 percent annually in the major enterprises, and the labor force was subject to wholesale layoffs in economic crises and wars (Hershatter 1986: chap. 3; Chesneaux 1968: 85–86). Industrial paternalism was much less widespread in China during these years than it had been earlier in the history of the United States and Great Britain (see Brandes 1976; Nelson 1975; Joyce 1979). It would be difficult to argue that this aspect of neo-traditionalism in contemporary China has its roots in an earlier Chinese "tradition."

Some might be tempted to suggest that the foreman-contracting system comprises precisely such a distinctive historical tradition. It is indeed true that workers were highly dependent on these contractors for their employment, wage levels, and, in the most exploitative forms, which affected young women workers in Shanghai, for their housing and food in lieu of wages (Honig 1986: chap. 5). But there is nothing distinctively Chinese about a tradition of management through labor contractors and the personal dependence this usually implies. This was the standard form of industrial management in many industries the world over. The American system has been characterized by Nelson (1975) as "the foreman's empire" and chronicled by such labor historians as Montgomery (1979). Its decline in the face of the labor movement (and management's efforts to control the production process and personnel matters) is a major theme of recent labor history and the sociology of work (see Edwards 1979; Jacoby 1984; Elbaum 1984).[4] What is distinctive about the Chinese pattern is not that a tradition of worker dependence on foremen existed; it is that, in China's post-1949 industrialization, worker dependence was transferred to an all-encompassing dependence on the enterprise itself.[5] Reference to a "tradition" cannot explain this divergence of American and Chinese patterns, because the historical tradition in question was largely a shared one.

4. Honig (1986: chap. 4) describes the initial efforts by plant managers to gain control over personnel matters in the Shanghai cotton textile industry in the 1930s; they did not make much headway until the late 1940s.

5. Russia followed a similar historical sequence, although dependence on the firm was more all-encompassing in many industries in Czarist Russia than in China because of the use of dependent rural laborers who were subject to considerable extralegal coercion (see Zelnick 1971). Unlike China, however, there was a period of genuine worker control in 1917–1918 before the Bolsheviks ended it (Sirianni 1982).

Even if China's prerevolution labor traditions were unique, it would be difficult to find historical continuities in the face of the sweeping and systematic changes of the 1950s. Within a brief span of eight years, China's new communist regime not only remade urban industrial production, but began a major transformation of the working class itself. Privately owned enterprises were all transformed into one form or another of state ownership and control. The massive sector of small private workshops was gradually nationalized, and the small shops were physically combined into cooperatives or small state enterprises. The equally large numbers of individual handicraftsmen in cities and towns were either recruited into the new enterprises or grouped, by trade, into handicraft cooperatives. The state rapidly gained control over industrial investment (a control complete by 1956) and poured resources into modern, large-scale heavy industry. And by the end of this period, local governments had gained near-complete control over the hiring and firing of workers (Howe 1971) and created new, uniform wage and incentive policies, ending earlier practices.

The structure of employment in 1949 was characteristic of dual economies in underdeveloped regions the world over. Of the total of 8.9 million employed in manufacturing that year, 5.7 million (64 percent) were self-employed individual craftsmen; another 1.6 million (18 percent) worked in small private workshops that employed an average of only 13 people. Only 1.4 million (15 percent) worked in a sector of industrial enterprises (with an average employment of almost 500) that could be described as modern (Emerson 1965a: 134, 136).

By 1957 these proportions had been almost completely reversed. First, individual handicraft workers, whose presence was initially tolerated and whose numbers in fact grew to 7.6 million by 1954, were rapidly organized by specialty into small handicraft cooperatives. By 1957 only 760,000 of the individual handicraft workers remained. The majority of these people appear to have been absorbed by cooperatives, because the increase in cooperative employment roughly paralleled the decline of individual craft workers (Emerson 1965a: 134).

Second, the small private industrial workshops, which grew to employ 2.2 million by 1953, were rapidly consolidated and transferred to state ownership by 1956. Large numbers of these small shops were combined to form new state enterprises. The number of small private shops dropped from over 134 thousand in 1954 to just over 1 thousand in 1956, while the number of relatively large, modern state enterprises grew from just under 3 thousand in 1949 to almost 50 thousand in 1956 (Emerson 1965a: 136). By 1956, only 14 thousand individuals were still employed in the formerly predominant small private shops, and the next year the category dropped out of official statistics entirely.

Third, as the total number of enterprises gradually declined and the average size of enterprises grew, virtually all new investment was directed into industry rather than handicrafts, and predominantly into heavy industry. As a result, the numbers employed in industrial enterprises as a proportion of total manufacturing employment rose from 1.6 million (16 percent) in 1949 to 7.9 million (55 percent) in 1957 (Emerson 1965a: 134).

In other words, in a mere eight years, China's manufacturing economy was transformed from one comprised overwhelmingly of small workshops and individual craft workers to one in which, for the first time, large-scale and relatively modern industrial enterprises predominated. This process, moreover, took place in a period of unprecedented industrial expansion, especially in heavy industry. Total employment in handicrafts remained roughly stationary from 1949 to 1957, while industrial employment more than doubled (Emerson 1965a: 134). The net increase of almost 6 million in the total manufacturing employment drew on far more than the reserves of individual craftsmen. Most of these former craft workers appear to have ended up in small handicraft cooperatives. This large net increase in employment represents an influx of new entrants to the industrial workforce. Behind the doubling of industrial employment was an even more rapid leap in industrial output. The annual gross value of industrial output grew by a factor of 5.5 during this same period (State Statistical Bureau 1959: 177). China's industrial manufacturing was not only becoming more modern and large scale, it was also expanding enormously as the state began a massive industrialization drive.

The rapid transformation of the structure of employment and patterns of capital investment had a deeper social and historical meaning that is not evident from the relevant statistics. In Western Europe and the United States, social historians increasingly recognize, the industrial revolution, based on modern factory production and a rapid takeoff of growth, was only the last step of a much longer process of craft industrialization in both town and country (Tilly 1981). And even well into this industrial revolution, the modern factory was often organized internally along craft lines, with workers possessing all the relevant skills, organizing and scheduling production, and contracting with management for the completion of jobs (see Montgomery 1979: 9–31; Nelson 1975: 34–54). It was not until after World War I that management commonly attained control over relevant skills; reorganized the production process; asserted its own control over hiring, wages, and production scheduling; and established the managerial bureaucracies that are today associated with the modern factory (Nelson 1975).

By leaping across the craft and early craft-industrial stages of industrialization and directly into the modern bureaucratic factory production (using administrative hierarchies borrowed wholesale from the Soviet Union), the new Chinese regime literally created, almost from scratch, a new tradition of labor relations. Western traditions were decisively shaped by the long conflict between craft unions and management over control of the production process (and over the share of profits accorded each). Although the workers ultimately did lose the contest for control over production, their long conflict with management shaped a tradition of labor relations characterized by collective bargaining, strict job definitions, contracts specifying wages according to complex job grades, and often union control over the hiring and training of new workers (Sabel 1982; Cole 1979: 101–9).

In China, on the other hand, there was never any question of worker control over production after 1949, or even of workers contesting for control. During the 1950s, the small core of skilled industrial workers were swamped by new recruits to industry.[6] Management, therefore, did not need to seize control over the production process and the skills involved: it created the production process and called into being and trained a new mass of workers. The state itself took over the task of hiring and remunerating new workers; prior agreements with regard to wages, apprenticeships,

6. The impact of this large influx can be inferred from data on the age structure of the labor force. By 1955, 75 percent of the employees in rapidly expanding state industries were 35 years of age or younger—few of them could have been employed very long before 1949. In some of the new large enterprises, as many as 70 to 80 percent of the workforce were under age 26. By contrast, more than 66 percent of the employees in private industry, which was not growing but contracting, were more than 35 years old (Emerson 1965b: 14–15).

and hiring were all suspended with the establishment of local labor bureaus and the final wage reform of 1956, which put all workers under the same set of regulations.[7]

Given this pattern of rapid and thorough change, it makes little sense to view emerging patterns of employee dependence as a "cultural survival" of earlier hiring practices in which workers were dependent on individual hiring contractors. There is, to be sure, an analogy between the two forms of dependence, but that does not mean there is a causal connection or even an indirect historical link between the two. Where, in the earlier period, workers were dependent on the "gang boss" alone, in the contemporary era they are dependent on the enterprise as an institution. This latter-day dependence, further, is far more encompassing and stable than the strictly personal forms of earlier eras, in which workers were highly mobile and not at all dependent on any single enterprise. Because many Western societies exhibited similar forms of personal dependence in early periods of industrialization that later gave way to a relatively independent and collectively organized workforce, the existence of similar historical patterns in China cannot logically explain the new contemporary patterns.

Demographic Problems and the Administrative Response

China's demographic characteristics enhanced the pattern of worker dependence on the enterprise that is normally engendered by communist economic institutions. China entered the twentieth century with extraordinarily high population densities in its countryside and a system of agriculture suited to mass poverty. Moreover, it already had a well-developed urban and commercial network. Unlike Japan, Russia, and most Western countries, China was unable to urbanize rapidly without enormous social and human costs. Its situation was like that of other poor Asian nations just beginning the demographic transition from high birth and death rates to low birth and death rates. Its large cities simply could not absorb such a massive and densely settled rural population (see Davis

7. Another part of the eradication of "tradition" during these years was the ability of the communists, in marked contrast with the Nationalists, to destroy rapidly the grip of secret societies and organized criminal gangs over labor in many sectors of the urban economy (see Hershatter 1986; Lieberthal 1980).

1975). Because the population has again doubled since 1949, this situation has not changed despite China's rapid postrevolution industrial growth.

This demographic legacy presented the Chinese Communist party with a twofold problem as it consolidated its rule in the 1950s: massive and persistent urban unemployment and a swelling urban population. Peace and relative prosperity spurred the formation of families and raised crude fertility rates, while improvements in nutrition and health care lowered China's miserable prerevolution death rates (Aird 1982: 176–87). At the same time, peasants were lured into cities by the prospect of industrial employment and dislocated by the process of land reform and collectivization of agriculture. Not until 1956–1957 did the government complete the socialization of urban industry and attain relatively comprehensive control over job opportunities in urban areas, and not until 1955 was the collectivization of agriculture completed, thus setting the basis for control of peasant migration. In the meantime, urban population grew explosively, almost doubling between 1949 and 1957. Uncontrolled migration obstructed progress in bringing urban unemployment under control.[8]

Unemployment could be alleviated (clearly, only in the long run) by addressing three problems simultaneously: stemming migration to cities, reducing fertility, and rapidly expanding employment opportunities through continued industrial growth, especially in labor-intensive sectors. But a temporary and costly detour was taken during the Great Leap Forward of 1958–1960, which concentrated exclusively on a vast increase of industrial employment in a massive mobilization of labor for capital construction and accumulation. Employment in industrial production shot up from 7.5 to 23 million from 1957 to 1958 alone (State Statistical Bureau 1983: 126, col. 1; see also Emerson 1965a: 130), with most of the increase in labor power coming from rural migrants. By all accounts, unemployment was reduced drastically—in Hou's low estimate

8. The urban population increased from 57.6 million in 1949 to 99 million in 1957 (State Statistical Bureau 1983: 103); 56 percent of this increase was due to migration, and the rest to natural increase (Zhang and Chen 1981: 40–41). Hou (1968: 369) estimates that unemployment was between 18 and 31 percent in 1949, and that, despite reductions in the early 1950s, it reached its former levels by 1957. Howe (1971: 39) estimates that, of a total of 1.31 million new entrants into Shanghai's labor force from 1949 to 1957, jobs were found for only 640,000. Migration from rural areas was preventing rapid industrial growth from reducing unemployment.

(1968: 369), from 19.5 to 0.3 percent of the male nonagricultural population. The urban population ballooned under the force of accelerated migration, increasing by 8.2 million in 1957–1958 alone. By 1960 China's urban population had reached 130.7 million, an increase of 31.7 million (32 percent) from 1957 (see table 1), and 90 percent of this increase was due to migration (Zhang and Chen 1981: 40–41; Orleans 1982: 277–85).

When the Great Leap Forward rapidly proved unsustainable, the ensuing economic crisis was compounded by this demographic dimension. Large portions of the reported increases in industrial output were falsified. Much of the actual output was comprised of flawed or useless products that created additional problems for their users. Uncontrolled increases in the wage bill, capital construction, and the ordering of raw materials left the industrial system in financial chaos. Labor productivity shrank, waste of capital and raw materials shot upward, and industrial supplies were exhausted in the initial mobilization. A serious shortage of usable machinery and spare parts, industrial raw materials, and liquid capital to sustain plant operations developed. Beginning in 1960, many factories and shops were closed in a large-scale retrenchment. Manufacturing employment dropped 10 million (almost 50 percent) from 1960 to 1964, and the surplus labor had to be relocated in the countryside (State Statistical Bureau 1983: 126). During the same years, the urban population was reduced from 130 million to 116 million through a systematic, mass program of enforced outmigration (see table 1). The reduction of 14 million in population represents the net reduction due to the excess of outmigration over natural increase—actually, larger numbers were relocated.

With the systematic removal of the surplus population from China's towns and cities, a comprehensive system of residence and employment controls was established and enforced much more strictly than similar controls in the Soviet Union. A complete household registration system was established in urban neighborhoods, tied to rations for grain and other foodstuffs and daily necessities, and coupled with a system of household residency checks by local neighborhood committees.[9] Illegal migrants to the cities would thus be deprived not only of jobs, but also permanent residence and the

---

9. Rationing of cooking oil, grain, pork, coal for cooking and heating, cloth, televisions, bicycles, sewing machines, watches, and furniture remained in effect in most cities into the early 1980s, when it was finally curtailed (see Whyte and Parish 1984: 85–90; Chinn 1980).

Table 1.   *Urban Population in China, 1949–1982*

Year	Urban population (millions)	Percentage of total population	Year	Urban population (millions)	Percentage of total population
1949	57.6	10.6	1966	133.1	17.9
1950	61.7	11.2	1967	135.5	17.7
1951	66.3	11.8	1968	138.4	17.6
1952	71.6	12.5	1969	141.2	17.5
1953	78.2	13.3	1970	144.3	17.4
1954	82.5	13.7	1971	147.1	17.3
1955	82.9	13.5	1972	149.4	17.1
1956	91.9	14.6	1973	153.5	17.2
1957	99.5	15.4	1974	155.9	17.2
1958	107.2	16.2	1975	160.3	17.3
1959	123.7	18.4	1976	163.4	17.4
1960	130.7	19.7	1977	166.7	17.6
1961	127.1	19.3	1978	172.5	17.9
1962	116.6	17.3	1979	184.9	19.0
1963	116.5	16.8	1980	191.4	19.4
1964	129.5	18.4	1981	201.7	20.2
1965	130.1	18.0	1982	211.5	20.8

Source: State Statistical Bureau 1983: 103–4.

right to purchase food. In rural areas, the collectivization of agriculture made possible a related use of food rationing to tie peasants to the land. In order to receive rations from their harvest, peasants had to be present for work in their production teams. They could not be absent from their team and still receive food without their team leader's permission. If one family member was absent, it reduced family income and food allotments (see Parish and Whyte 1978; Oi 1983). The result was a system of residence controls that tied people to rural and urban statuses acquired at birth.

The subsequent growth of China's urban industrial labor force has been due almost solely to the natural increase of the urban population or, more accurately, to an excess of natural increase over net *outmigration* from cities. No sooner were the migrants of the Great Leap Forward relocated in the rural areas by the mid-1960s, than the large 1950s "baby boom" birth cohorts began to reach working age and put renewed pressure on industrial employment. In this period, the policy of relocating urban youths in rural and border areas to keep them out of the urban labor force began (see Bernstein 1977; L. T. White 1978). During the decade after 1965, there was a net outmigration of 5 million youths (16 million relocated, and a reverse flow of 11 million occurred, mostly after 1971). The more rapid urban growth of recent years is due to a large return flow of resettled youths who seek to reclaim their urban status and gain urban employment (Zhang and Chen 1981: 40–41).

An important unintended result of these demographic pressures and of the state's efforts to cope with them in a planned way was the emergence of an unprecedented set of status distinctions in the labor force. In the earliest years of the People's Republic, a generous system of fringe benefits, services, and social security was established for permanent state-sector workers. But the growth of this core industrial sector, which is relatively capital-intensive and produces the vast majority of the nation's industrial output, could not even begin to absorb the urban labor pool. A large sector of relatively small, urban, labor-intensive "collective" enterprises, only partially sheltered by the state's umbrella of benefits, has grown up to meet this need. Various forms of temporary labor are arranged for millions of urban residents without permanent jobs. And millions of rural residents are permitted to work on a temporary basis in urban enterprises and on a more regular basis in the small-scale industries that were increasingly established in the rural areas beginning in the 1960s. Industrial employment as a whole is differentiated into four distinct segments, only one of which, encompassing some 40 percent of the total industrial labor force, receives the full benefits of permanent state employment.

Status Groups in the Labor Force

China's employment structure exhibits a "dualistic" pattern whose general features are shared with a wide variety of market economies. A core, "primary" sector is made up of large, capital-intensive, and modern enterprises, which produce the bulk of industrial output and are able to provide relatively high wages, more stable employment, better fringe benefits, and more generous provisions for social security than smaller, "secondary sector" enterprises. Secondary sector enterprises are usually small, labor-intensive, often use simple technologies, and provide lower wages, less stable employment, and fewer fringe benefits than primary sector firms.

To simply pronounce this pattern of inequality *dualism*, however, would be to miss its most distinctive and, for my purposes, most significant feature. From a comparative perspective, what is significant about this pattern of inequality is that it reflects not the stratified outcomes of labor market processes, but a status order that is conceived and enforced by the state itself. T. H. Marshall defined "status" in a manner applicable to the case at hand, "a position to which is attached a bundle of rights and duties, privileges and obligations, legal capacities and incapacities, which are publicly recognized and which can be defined and enforced by public authority" (quoted in Poggi 1978: 43). China's industrial labor force, reflecting a pattern of stratification characteristic of society as a whole, is divided into several status groups, each of which has its own publicly defined rights to income, job tenure, social security, labor insurance, and housing and residence—each of which, in other words, is legally entitled to a distinctive style of life.

Permanent Workers in State Enterprises

The 27 million permanent workers in state sector industrial enterprises are the only segment of the industrial labor force to participate fully in the welfare state.[10] The benefits they enjoy reflect their importance in the national economy. Although they comprise only 42 percent of the industrial labor force, they produced 75 percent of the country's gross value of industrial output in 1981, and almost all of the heavy industrial output (see table 2). In 1981 their average annual wage, 854 yuan, was almost 40 percent higher than that of the average in urban collective industry and well over twice the average of the other groups in the labor force. Just as important, however, are the many fringe benefits, wage supplements, government subsidies, on-site services, and welfare and insurance provisions that the state provides—an amount whose cash value averaged 527 yuan per worker in 1978 (an additional 82 percent of the

10. The official figures for employment in state industry, according to the State Statistical Bureau (1983: 576–77), include "temporary" workers. I have subtracted 2 million from the state sector figure of 28.6 million to compensate for the temporaries; 2 million is considerably less than the total number of people who work as temporaries in industry at least part of the year (13 million, according to my estimate). Only long-term temporaries are likely to be counted in these statistics; but their numbers are not known.

Table 2. *Structure of the Industrial Labor Force, 1981*

Sector	Total employment (millions)	Percent of industrial employment	Number of enterprises	Average no. employees/ enterprise	Gross value of industrial output (yuan)	Average annual wage (yuan)
State sector (permanent employees) (blue-collar workers only)	32.1ª (26.6)ᵇ	42	84,200ᶜ	405	405 billionᵈ	854ᵉ
Urban collective	14.9ª	18	111,300ᶜ	134	77 billionᵈ	622ᵉ
Rural collective	19.8ᶠ	24	725,000ᶠ	27	58 billionᵍ	374ʰ
Urban temporary workers	@4.0	5	—	—	—	@35/mo.
Rural temporary workers	@9.0	11	—	—	—	@35/mo.

Sources: ªState Statistical Bureau 1982: 106. Includes workers and staff, less estimate for temporaries.
ᵇIbid.: 118. Includes apprentices, production workers, and support workers, less estimate for temporaries.
ᶜIbid.: 203.
ᵈIbid.: 208.
ᵉIbid.: 424. Includes workers and staff.
ᶠEconomic Yearbook 1982: V-94.
ᵍCalculated from data in State Statistical Bureau 1982: 134, 208.
ʰCalculated from data in Economic Yearbook 1981: IV, 56–57. Figure is for 1980 and is an average for all rural collective enterprises, nonindustrial as well as industrial.

Note: Figures for urban and rural temporary workers are estimates based on documents cited in the text.

average wage) (Economic Yearbook 1981: IV, 34).[11] These workers
enjoy virtual lifetime tenure unless they commit a crime or political
offense or are guilty of flagrant forms of absenteeism or irrespon-
sibility on the job.[12] Large and medium-sized enterprises are usually
able to provide them with subsidized meals, housing, medical care,
and many other services and benefits that are unavailable elsewhere.

State labor insurance, available only on a limited basis to workers
who are not permanent employees in state industry, ensures the
security of workers and their families in a variety of life circumstances. Workers are provided paid leave for work-related disorders
at 100 percent of their salary. All medical costs except miscellane-
ous fees are borne by the enterprise, and a lifelong pension of 60 to
70 percent of the salary is paid if disability results. For illnesses and
injuries sustained off the job, the enterprise will pay for all medical
expenses except optional, "expensive" medications, transportation,
nominal registration fees, and meals. For absences from work up to
six continuous months, the worker receives 60 to 100 percent of the
wage, depending on seniority and, after six months, from 40 to 60
percent. Enterprises will also pay one-half the cost of treatment and
medicine for the dependent family members of employees. Retired
workers receive pensions of 50 to 70 percent of their former salary
(increased in 1978 to 60 to 100 percent), depending on their accumulated seniority. If workers find themselves in dire financial straits
due to low family income, the enterprise can provide regular welfare supplements for as long as the problem persists (or they will try
to arrange for the employment of a family member), and in some
cases they can provide the worker with a loan (see table 3).[13]

11. Lardy (1984) estimates that the total subsidies for state sector workers grew
to an average of more than 1,000 yuan by 1983, around 125 percent of the average
annual wage. Elsewhere (Lardy 1983: 163–65), he specifies the composition of these
subsidies and documents their steady growth since the 1950s.

12. Even in cases where enterprises are disbanded by the state because their operations are deemed dispensable, provisions are usually made to transfer workers to
another state enterprise or to provide partial pay while they are unemployed (State
Council 1966). The 16 million employees hired during the Great Leap Forward were
an exception to this policy. Most were returned to the countryside in 1961–1962,
but apparently some longer-term employees were severed as well (State Council
1965). Large numbers of enterprises were disbanded during the 1961–1962 economic readjustment. Collective sector employees do not have the same protections
against layoffs.

13. The labor insurance system is clearly modeled after that of the Soviet Union
(McAuley 1981). The levels of coverage in some categories now differ, reflecting policy changes in each country since the 1950s, but the categories of coverage and principles involved are virtually identical.

These benefits are available uniformly to all state sector employees because they are a fixed portion of the state-supplied budgets of enterprises in this sector. Their benefits are passed directly to the state budget and do not represent a cost to enterprise management, because a fixed proportion of the wage bill is set aside each year for funding these provisions, and the funds cannot legally be used for other purposes. The employees' wages and job tenure are also protected by enterprise financial arrangements, in which permanent employees are part of the "officially authorized size" of the enterprise—something that constitutes the enterprise's budgeted wage bill. Enterprises have little incentive to pare back the labor force. In fact, given budgetary arrangements, they have every incentive to hoard labor and simply pass the costs onto the state budget (the size of the wage bill is the object of negotiations between enterprise officials and planning authorities). State sector workers enjoy such high security, in both job tenure and insurance benefits, because they are sheltered by the financial practices of state planning.

Workers in Urban Collective Industry

Collective sector employees, at least in theory, are not so sheltered. Urban collective industry began in the 1950s as an effort to organize the millions of unemployed people and individual craft workers into handicraft cooperatives—relatively independent undertakings that would absorb labor and produce consumer goods for urban residents. By the late 1950s, the sector began to serve a second purpose: to increase family income at low cost to the state by drawing females into the urban industrial labor force.[14] Since the 1970s, the sector has served a third purpose: to provide jobs for youth who cannot be employed in the state sector. Originally intended as independent accounting units, these collective undertakings were to be responsible for their own profits and losses, outside the protection of the state budget. Over the years, however, many of these cooperatives have grown into full-scale factories, and new generations of cooperatives have been created. Most cooperatives have developed permanent business connections with state agencies or enterprises that now have vested interests in their con-

14. From 1957 to 1980 the proportion of urban residents employed rose from 30 to over 50 percent (Workers' Daily 1981d). The collective sector labor force is currently 57 percent female; the state sector's is only 32 percent female (State Statistical Bureau 1982: 121).

Table 3. *Comparison of Selected Insurance and Welfare Benefits, by Sector*

Item	State sector (permanent workers)	State sector (temporary workers)	Collective sector
Work-related injury or illness	100% cost of treatment, hospital, and travel. 100% wage during treatment. Optional food and medicine, ⅔ cost paid. Registration fee paid by patient	Same as permanent worker while employed, for the period of illness or injury	Varies from full benefits in large collectives to partial coverage in smaller
Work-related disability	Pension 60% former wage until death or recovery. Partial disability resulting in change to lower-paying job: 10–30% of prior wage as supplement, up to level of former wage	No pension for permanent disability. Lump sum 12 mos. wages	Varies according to size of enterprise. Usually partial coverage
Nonwork injury or illness	Fees, costs, medicine paid. Employee pays for expensive medicine, travel, and meals. 60–100% wage up to 6 mos., 40–60% thereafter (amount depends on seniority)	Same as permanent worker, but benefits limited to 3 mos., at 50% of pay	Varies according to size of enterprise. Usually less than state standards
Nonwork-related disability	40–50% wage as a pension for permanent disability	No pension. Lump sum, 3 mos. wage, if not recovered within 3 mos.	Varies, usually lower than state standards
Injury or illness of dependents	Entitled to treatment at clinic or hospital attached to enterprise. 50% cost of treatment and medicine. Expensive medicine, travel, hospital room, meals, reg. fee, exam. fee, and medical tests paid by family	No benefits	No benefits except in large collectives
Death benefits	*Work-related*: Lump sum, 3 mos. pay. 25–50% pay to minor dependents until working age. *Nonwork*: 2 mos. pay as lump sum. 6–12 mos. pay, lump sum, to minor dependents	*Work*: Lump sum, 3 mos. pay. Minor dependents: 6 mos. pay for one, 9 mos. pay for two, 12 mos. for three or more, lump sum. *Nonwork*: 2 mos. pay, lump sum. 3 mos. pay, lump sum, for minor dependents	Varies, usually lower than state standards

Benefits for death of minor dependents	Lump sum ½ mo. pay for child over 10 yrs.; ⅓ mo. for child under 10; no benefit for under 1 yr.	No benefits	Not common except in large collectives
Maternity benefits	56 days leave at full pay (30 days for miscarriage). Prenatal care paid by enterprise, at factory clinic or hospital. 4 yuan supplement on birth of each child. No benefits outside of wedlock	Same as permanent worker, except 60% pay during leave. No benefits for birth out of wedlock	Varies by size of enterprise
Old-age pensions	*Male:* At age 60, with 25 yrs. seniority, and 5 yrs. with present enterprise, 60–90% pay, depending on seniority. If continues work after retirement age, 10–20% pay in addition to full pay. *Female:* Same, but retirement age is 50, with 20 yrs. seniority and 5 yrs. at current job	No pension, except for long-term workers with high seniority	Usually smaller pensions, as % of former wage
Severance pay	Lump sum, based on seniority	None except for long-term workers in one enterprise	None for resignation; in certain circumstances for plant closings
Livelihood supplements	Full eligibility for state supplements	None before six mos. continuous employment, full benefits thereafter	Some enterprises
Paid home leave for distant employment	2-3 wks./yr., depending on distance; full pay. Travel subsidies available at officials' discretion	No paid leave, but leave without pay after 1 yr. After 3 yrs., leave with pay	No provisions
Access to enterprise welfare facilities	Unrestricted	Can be excluded if demand is deemed too high; permanent workers have priority	Unrestricted, but facilities usually limited
Transfer benefits	Moving costs subsidized; insurance covers interim	No benefits	No benefits
Grain price subsidies	Full benefits as dictated by price rises	None before 6 mos. employment	Amount varies by locality

Sources: Based on Planning Commission 1973, esp. State Council 1953, 1964; Fujian Province Price Commission 1966b; and Second Ministry of Light Industry 1966. State Labor Bureau 1980 and Ministry of Finance 1979 consulted for changes made in insurance coverage in 1978.

tinued operation. This sector, as a result, has almost entirely lost its independent character, and, as the enterprises have become stable, often subsidized appendages of state enterprises, employment there has become more secure than would otherwise be the case, especially in the majority of collective factories that now perform subsidiary operations for state sector enterprises (Liu, Wang, and Xing 1980: 23).

In 1981 just under 15 million people were employed in the 111 thousand collective industrial enterprises administered by towns (*zhen*), counties (*xian*), or cities (*shi*). This sector produced 14 percent of the national gross value of industrial output in 1981 in generally small-scale enterprises that employed an average of 134 people. The average annual wage, 622 yuan, was only 73 percent of that for permanent state sector workers. (See table 2.) The regularly budgeted expenditures for labor insurance and fringe benefits are considerably lower than for state enterprises but are not published. Urban collective industry is not under uniform state regulations but is a complex patchwork of administrative jurisdictions with different regulations regarding benefits. Funding for benefits usually is not a fixed proportion of the wage bill or part of fixed allocations in state budgets but in fact depends on the financial success of the enterprise (Liu, Wang, and Xing 1980: 77–80).

The history of this sector helps explain the wide variation in benefits available to workers. The first wave of development in the 1950s was the formation of cooperatives to which former individual handicraft workers and employees of private shops were assigned (see Walder 1984a: 5–10). These handicraft cooperatives, producing light industrial goods and consumer items, and initially averaging 30 employees, were gradually combined to form an array of production cooperatives of varying sizes. By the early 1960s, many were large enough to earn the title *cooperative factories*. Some were placed under the jurisdiction of the Ministry of Light Industry, some under municipal administration, and some under urban districts. These original cooperative factories have grown, combined, and changed jurisdictions ever since (Liu, Wang, and Xing 1980: 4–6). Their average size in 1979 was 374 employees (ibid.: 12).

The second wave of development began in 1958, during the Great Leap Forward effort to mobilize housewives into the labor force by forming "street collectives" and "lane production groups" in urban neighborhoods. These were administered not by district or municipal governments, but by neighborhood committees, the next to the lowest rung of urban government administration (see Whyte and Parish 1984: 22–24). In Shanghai in 1963, these small street collectives averaged 32 employees and were engaged almost exclusively in the hand-processing of small consumer items. But a subset of some 15 percent of these street collectives had already begun to develop into full-scale "street factories," which at that time had an average of 60 employees (Liu, Wang, and Xing 1980: 6). By the mid-1960s, these growing street factories began to perform subsidiary operations for state-sector enterprises, including heavy industrial plants that sometimes donated spare equipment and tools. As they grew and assumed closer ties with state industry, some of the larger street collectives were transferred out of the street committees' jurisdiction and managed instead by municipal district governments. This process of growth is reflected in employment figures: by 1964 street factories in Shanghai averaged 128 employees; by 1979, 224 (ibid.: 8). The street collectives have retained their highly varied characteristics; even as the older ones grew, new, small, street collectives have been formed, in order to absorb the growing numbers of young people entering the labor force each year. A sector that was at first almost exclusively female now absorbs many young males for whom state sector employment is unavailable.

A third and final wave of development is represented by the new factories built and managed by large state enterprises or administrative organs. Beginning in the early 1970s, state enterprises created them to perform subsidiary operations. Local handicraft, textile, light industrial, and even metallurgy bureaus formed them to produce scarce parts or to alleviate processing bottlenecks under their jurisdictions. Since 1978, another important purpose has been to absorb the increasing numbers of unemployed urban youths (Liu, Wang, and Xing 1980: 11–12). They are under the administrative jurisdiction of the enterprise or bureau that establishes them, and they vary greatly in size. Some of the older ones are by now "branch factories," employing over 1 thousand people, and fully linked to the production sequences of a large state enterprise. Others remain quite small and employ only a few dozen.[15]

This complex patchwork of administrative jurisdictions and en-

---

15. This history draws also from my interviews with seven informants who worked in collectives over a period of years and saw their plants grow and change.

terprise sizes makes it difficult to offer general statements about the
fringe benefits available in this sector (see table 3). Some urban collective enterprises under the jurisdiction of state bureaus and ministries receive labor insurance and other benefits that approach those
of permanent state employees. This is especially true in the so-called
"large collective factories" (*da jiti gongchang*), whose employees
enjoy full state sector benefits (Liu, Wang, and Xing 1980: 85).
Outside of this small group of enterprises, benefits vary considerably but almost never approach the level of the state sector.[16] The
funds for welfare and insurance benefits are generated by the profits
of the collective factory itself and are not a fixed portion of the state
wage bill. For much of the past two decades, furthermore, accumulation funds have taken precedence over the welfare and benefits
funds in most collectives (ibid.: 75–81).[17] For many small collectives under street or small town jurisdiction, the benefits available
are only a fraction of those in the state sector, both in number and
size. Just as important, few collective enterprises are able to provide
the services and distributions often provided in the state sector—
enterprise housing, daycare centers, hospitals and clinics, kindergartens, and a wide range of supplements and extra rations for consumer items and foodstuffs (Whyte and Parish 1984: 29–33).

*Temporary Workers in
Urban Enterprises*

Roughly 13 million work in state industrial enterprises on a temporary basis. Some 9 million of these are rural residents whose

16. One of my informants (no. 17), for example, reported that his collective factory, under district administration in a large city, covered only 50 percent of hospital
expenses when he worked there in the 1970s.
17. Funding of benefits in most collective factories is different than in the state
sector, because larger expenditures for wages, larger tax payments to state organs, or
larger contributions to plant reinvestment (accumulation) funds mean that less is left
over for welfare. Another drain on benefits, as well as on the average wage, is that
local officials, especially at the neighborhood and district level, have come to treat
the funds of collective factories under their jurisdictions as a source of payment for
neighborhood amenities and wages for street officials, office personnel, construction
and repair workers, grain office workers, sanitation workers, and night watchmen.
"No show" jobs are created for them in the collective enterprises. Three Chinese investigators estimated that an average of 10 percent of the workforce of collective sector factories in Shanghai were under such an arrangement. Another drain on funds
that would otherwise go for fringe benefits is the imperative to employ neighborhood
youths. The same investigators estimated that 25 percent of the workers of collectives
in one Shanghai district were redundant (Liu, Wang, and Xing 1980: 106).

families also have agricultural income and who are forbidden by law from establishing residence and taking permanent urban employment in all but the smallest towns. For these workers, most of whom work in agriculture at least part of the year, opportunities for temporary industrial employment, in either the state or urban collective sector, provide a major boost for family income, because rural cash incomes are well below urban standards.[18] Another 4 million of these workers are urban residents who have been unable to find regular employment in state industry or who have for one reason or another resigned or been fired from their jobs.[19] Temporary labor is relied on most heavily outside the manufacturing and mining sector that is the object of this study—especially in public works projects, construction, and road-building, where the majority of the workforce on a given project is likely to be hired on a temporary basis. Their numbers have rarely been publicized, in part because the national government may not know how many temporary workers are being employed. Howe (1971; 1973: 107–8; 1974) estimates that the number of temporaries has fluctuated between 10 and 40 percent of the total nonagricultural labor force since the beginning of national labor administration in 1956–1957.

18. Average per capita income in rural areas was 179 yuan in 1980, according to a published survey (Xinhua News Agency 1981). The comparable urban figure was 429 yuan (Xinhua News Agency 1980).

19. Official statistics on temporary employment of any type are almost never published. The standard statistical yearbooks rarely even mention it. The estimate of 9 million temporaries from rural areas is based on a figure published in a recent government document (State Council 1982a) that stated that 9.3 million rural residents were employed on a nonpermanent basis in state enterprises of all types (rural residents who had obtained permanent employment under various guises were explicitly excluded from the figure). The official figure does not include temporary employment of rural residents in urban collectives. If based on local statistics, this figure certainly excludes much of the quasi-legal and informal employment on a casual basis, which usually goes unreported. If we subtract the nonindustrial employment from this 9 million and add the amount of unreported employment, the figure for temporary rural workers in state industry is probably in the neighborhood of 9 million. The estimate for urban residents who work as temporaries is based on a Chinese source cited by Emerson (1983: 4) that states that, of the urban residents in the labor force, 85 percent are permanent workers in both state and urban collective sectors (excluding those in street collectives), 3 percent are employed in street collectives or are self-employed, and 6 percent are unemployed. The remaining 5 percent yields a figure of around 4 million, if we calculate the percentages based on total state and collective sector employment. This should be viewed as a rough estimate. The definition of "temporary worker" among urban residents is complicated conceptually as well, because many shift in and out of street collectives and the "unemployed" category.

In industrial manufacturing and mining, temporaries are less commonly used but still comprise a significant proportion of total employment.

This is a diverse and shadowy group, and government statistics on their earnings, if such statistics exist, are not available. Their earnings differ considerably according to local arrangements. The paths taken to find these jobs and the terms of employment involved also differ enormously. Rural residents may find jobs individually, through private contacts, through private labor brokers, or through officials of their rural production brigades who make contracts to provide village labor to urban industry. The workers may have fixed individual or group contracts, or no contracts at all; they may work in a single place for a week or a season, or stay on for years. Urban residents also work under a variety of circumstances, because each local area works out the details of its temporary hiring system—to the extent that it is regulated it all. Conditions vary widely from the complex, bureaucratic hiring systems of large cities, for example, Shanghai (L. T. White 1978), to the patchwork of informal arrangements in provincial towns in China's hinterland. The bewildering variety of temporary jobs stems in part from the informal nature of the arrangements, which are largely outside of state regulation and planning.

There are a variety of reasons why temporary workers are a necessity in state industry. First, there are many jobs that permanent workers either cannot be spared to do or that they resist doing—particularly heavy labor, excavation work, moving and hauling, and maintenance and cleaning around the factory.[20] Demand for this kind of unskilled labor is generally low and fluctuates only slightly. Short-term temporary workers are hired to do this kind of work and are usually paid with excess labor funds that accumulate in enterprise accounts when permanent workers take unpaid personal leaves or sick leave at a portion of their normal pay. Second, seasonal demands for labor may fluctuate significantly. Heavy industrial plants, especially in metallurgy, experience high rates of absenteeism in the hot summer months. In these cases, urban tempor-

---

20. One informant (no. 8) explained: "If a certain job was being done slowly by the permanent workers, then the leader will call over a temporary worker and get the job done faster. The reason is that if the temporary worker goes slow, he's out of a job. But the permanent worker can take his time, and can refuse to do certain kinds of jobs, and there's nothing a cadre can do except criticize him."

aries, sometimes with industrial skills, will be hired as fill-ins and paid with excess wage funds.

The production process of other enterprises may require a large cyclical expansion of the labor force during a busy season. Sugar refineries, which expand operations during postharvest months, are a leading example. In this case a large number of seasonal workers will be hired, paid from enterprise circulating funds, and entered into the financial accounts as "temporary labor costs." State enterprises also use the temporary employment category to expand covertly the size of their labor force above officially approved "permanent" levels. Temporary workers hired in this way occasionally become permanent employees when the factory gets permission to expand its authorized size.

Finally, when enterprises need to build additions to their plant or refurbish old buildings, there is a need for a labor force to perform the construction work. The formal route is to hire a local state-run construction company to send a team to do the work, but this often requires an unacceptably long waiting period and is expensive relative to privately arranged construction gangs. Instead, large enterprises that have their own "basic construction department" may organize the work themselves and hire a large group of temporary workers for the job. For smaller enterprises or smaller construction jobs, it is standard practice to make contracts with private construction gangs, often from villages near urban areas, to complete the work. If the construction project has been approved by higher authorities and its costs allotted in the enterprise budget, wages for temporary workers are paid from circulating funds allotted for the project and entered into accounts under "temporary labor costs." If the construction project is a small one, arranged informally with construction gangs, and not included in the state-approved budget, the wages are paid out of circulating funds and entered into accounts under false headings, or the village leaders that send the workers are paid in kind with a shipment of pumps, generators, cement, or other materials that are in chronically short supply in rural areas.

Although there is no standard terminology used to describe different forms of temporary employment—people from different parts of the country use different terminology—there are four basic types of temporary employment in state industry. The most common is the "temporary worker" (*linshi gong*). The larger the city,

the more likely these workers are to be residents of urban neighborhoods; in small cities and towns, they may ride in from surrounding villages. In large cities, temporary workers register at
neighborhood "labor service stations" and are allocated through
local labor bureaus. In some neighborhoods, workers are shifted in
and out of small street collectives as demands for temporary workers fluctuate in frequency. Some urban residents, especially in
smaller cities and towns, find temporary jobs through casual inquiries or personal connections. In most cases, they perform jobs that
permanent workers are not assigned to do—cleaning and maintenance, moving and hauling, and other kinds of heavy labor. In some
cases, however, they are skilled workers who perform regular production jobs. They have no fixed term of employment and (judging
by interviews) are usually paid at a daily rate of between 1 and 2
yuan a day. Depending on their skills and local demand for labor,
they can make between 24 and 48 yuan per month. A minority of
skilled temporaries, however, are more valuable and are hired for
longer than a few days or weeks. In some cases they stay for many
years, are paid at a higher rate, and have a good chance, if kept on
this long, of being hired permanently when the enterprise is given
permission to expand its officially registered labor force.[21]

A second kind of temporary labor is the "contract worker"
(*hetong gong*). Contract workers are distinguished from temporary
workers primarily by having a longer, fixed term of employment,
specified in an agreement that is sometimes written, but usually
oral. The agreement may cover several months, a half year, or even
several years. Contract workers usually are village residents, and
the contract is often made not with the individual, but with village
officials. In the system of collective farming that predominated before 1979, contracts specifying terms of employment—renewable
in additional blocks of time—became customary because the peasants had to get permission to be absent from the team and had to
make arrangements to have a portion of the salary paid into the
production team accounts in order to buy work points and earn
grain rations for the worker and his or her family. (Grain was ra-

21. Another variety is the "dependent worker" (*jiashu gong*), a person hired because he or she is a member of a permanent employee's household. This first became
common in the 1970s when pressures to find urban employment were particularly
intense. It was a common way of raising household income in the decade after 1967,
when the wages of workers were virtually frozen.

tioned in urban and rural areas, and rural residents were not eligible to receive grain ration coupons in urban areas; they had to "earn" their grain rations through agriculture labor or "buy out" their labor shares.) These workers are used primarily for heavy labor, particularly on construction projects organized by the enterprise itself. In the 1960s and 1970s, their wages were about the same as the temporary workers', although their net pay was usually lower after deductions by the brigade or team.[22] A variation of contract labor is "rotation labor" (*lunhuan gong*), an arrangement in which a contracted number of workers is maintained in an urban enterprise by a village that assigns peasants to them on a rotating basis.

A third category of temporary labor is hired through an informal system of "outside contract labor" (*waibao gong*). This form of labor is used almost exclusively for excavation and construction work. Arrangements are made between an enterprise and a brigade or production team of a commune for the completion of a job. A lump sum is paid to the leader of the construction gang—if payment is to be in cash—and the team itself distributes wages among members. Sometimes outside contracts are signed with informally constituted construction gangs that work completely outside the legal framework of municipal and rural administration.

A final category of temporary labor is "seasonal labor" (*jijie gong*), sometimes called casual labor (*san gong*). This kind of employment is usually limited to enterprises whose seasonal demand for labor fluctuates widely with the harvest cycle—for example, in sugar refining and papermaking, cotton spinning, grain milling, and the processing of oil-bearing seeds. These enterprises are usually located in suburban or semi-rural areas, and the jobs are arranged either through individual inquiries or through enterprise contacts with rural production teams. Like contract workers, seasonal workers who have rural household registration had to pay a fixed proportion of their wages back to their production team, if they were residents of communes, to ensure continuing entitlement to grain

22. One of my informants reported that contract workers in his factory had to pay 60 percent of their wage to their rural production teams in the 1970s. Since the shift to household contracts in agriculture after 1979, basic grain rations and work points have no longer been used, and these controls over the labor power of rural residents have been weakened. According to interviews conducted in Hong Kong in 1984, rural officials continue to act as labor contractors in some areas and continue to deduct portions of salaries for the collective coffers. Local practices and wage levels now vary so widely that it is difficult to make a valid general statement.

(this practice has abated since 1979). They are paid at the same rate as temporary and contract workers and commonly return to the factory year after year in the slack agricultural season.[23]

The biggest disadvantage of temporary labor is that, unlike permanent workers, job tenure is insecure, and full state insurance and other benefits of state employment are largely denied. Only a minority of temporary workers have been able to attain permanent status in cities. Pensions are usually unavailable, except in rare cases where the temporary employee has worked in the same enterprise for an extended period of years. Accident insurance, hospitalization, and paid sick leave coverage varies widely and appears to be available in some form to most temporaries, but only as long as they are employed. When employed, the extent of coverage is not always the same as that of permanent workers. Temporaries usually enjoy the use of the enterprise meal hall and medical clinic while they are employed but are not allowed to take advantage of enterprise apartments, nurseries, and daycare centers (see table 3). Like employees in collective sector enterprises, temporary laborers must rely either on overtaxed, inadequate urban neighborhood services or on underdeveloped or nonexistent village services for the satisfaction of these needs.

Rural Workers in Collective Town and Village Industry

At the bottom of China's hierarchy of industrial labor are some 20 million residents of rural areas who receive wages in cash (an average of 374 yuan in 1980), and sometimes in kind, for their work in small-scale collectively owned industrial enterprises operated by communes and brigades. (In the early 1980s, the commune's former governmental functions were delegated to a coterminous *xiang* [township government]; the brigade is now *cun*

---

23. Pay levels apparently fluctuate according to local labor needs and appear to have risen considerably in the 1980s. Some have recently reported that casual workers of the towns in the booming Canton–Hong Kong region are currently making as much as 8 yuan a day, a phenomenal amount by past standards. But the economic development of this area is unusually rapid, and the wage rates are probably not duplicated in many parts of the country. There is another large category of temporary workers from rural areas, called *min gong* (a shorthand term for laborers on public works projects). They are used exclusively on road construction, dam building, reservoir excavations, dike construction, and irrigation projects, so they are excluded from the definition of "industrial" adopted in this chapter.

[village].) They work in some 767 thousand of these small rural enterprises, which employ an average of 27 people. These employees produced roughly 10 percent of the nation's gross value of industrial output in 1980 (see table 2). They have rural residence status and do not receive urban grain rations. A minority reside in small towns under commune jurisdiction, or "collective villages" (*jiti zhen*), and do not participate in agricultural production. People with rural residence status are rarely permitted to migrate to cities or obtain permanent employment in the state sector; even marriage to a certified urban resident does not confer urban status. They can participate in these favored urban sectors only as temporary, seasonal, or contract laborers.[24] Positions in local small-scale enterprises, however, are highly valued by rural residents, because this brings a major increase in the family's cash income. And these positions allow the commune member to escape the elements and the drudgery of backbreaking field labor, in an agricultural system that is highly labor-intensive and still largely unmechanized.

Like the urban collectives, this industrial sector is highly varied. Some of the commune enterprises close to major metropolitan areas are small factories that employ hundreds of peasant workers and produce subsidiary products used in urban heavy industry, often on machines provided by the urban enterprise that is their main customer. Others are little more than small shops in which a handful of people are busied weaving baskets from straw, making bricks from local clay, or making bean curd from mashed soybeans. Pay varies considerably as well: some rural enterprises near large cities, especially those in the rapidly developing region adjacent to Hong Kong, have recently been paying their workers wages well above the average for the state sector. Others may make as little as 12 yuan for a full month's work and be paid partly in kind.

24. The restrictions are generally well enforced but are not totally inflexible. Emerson (1983: 8) cites a Chinese author's estimate that 13 million rural residents obtained permanent employment in urban industry between 1966 and 1976. This was out of an agricultural workforce that grew from 244 to 301 million during the same period, an average migration rate of roughly one-half of one percent a year (State Statistical Bureau 1983: 120). Another route to permanent state employment for rural residents is provided by complex informal arrangements surrounding real estate transactions in the suburban rings of cities. Enterprises and municipal industrial bureaus commonly make arrangements to lease land from communes for building factory housing or branch plants. In return they often agree to provide jobs for a fixed number of peasants in the village that is losing cultivable land. They are called "landworkers" (*tudi gong*) in some areas of China.

Although local industrial employment, at whatever pay level, can greatly boost family cash income, in past decades the majority of family needs were met by private agricultural sideline production (livestock, vegetables), grain and other food rations distributed by the production team, and the cash income distributed at the end of the year (Parish and Whyte 1978: 59–71). Since 1979, family farming has taken care of most of their needs. Also, employment in local enterprises can be quite temporary and irregular, depending on the decisions of village leaders, on seasonal labor demands in agriculture and in the small enterprise, and on business trends for the enterprise's products. Many of these rural workers may be able to stay on a near-permanent basis in their industrial positions, but most continue to work in agriculture at least part of the year (Perkins 1977: 216–18). In the system of collective agriculture practiced before 1979, peasants could not be released to work in these local industrial concerns without the permission of their team leaders, and often this permission was obtained only with the understanding that the person would return during the peak harvest season if needed. Even under today's household agriculture, employment is at the discretion of village officials, and the wide array of welfare benefits, services, and insurance provisions provided by state enterprises for their employees is usually unavailable in these factories. The village administration still bears responsibility for welfare matters, and the rural worker's treatment in this respect is at the same level as the average peasant's, which is far below urban industrial standards in every way.

The Supply and Allocation of State Sector Jobs

In the pattern of status distinctions, not only is it difficult for rural residents to find permanent urban jobs, but state sector employment itself has also become progressively more difficult for urban residents to attain over the past two decades. The average size of the age cohorts reaching working age in urban areas each year has increased from less than 1 million in the early 1950s to over 5 million in the early 1980s. During the First Five-Year Plan (1953–1957), an average of 950 thousand young people entered the urban labor force annually, and almost all were provided jobs in the rapidly growing state sector. The figure grew to an annual average of 2 million during the decade after 1966, bringing efforts to divert a total of 16 million youths to rural and border areas (Feng and Zhao 1982: 125–26). By 1977 the ranks of the 3 million urban youths reaching working age each year were swollen by a return flow of resettled urban youths from the countryside (see Gold 1980). As a result, almost 7 million people entered the urban labor force in 1979, and the figure exceeded 5 million for the next two years (Feng and Zhao 1982: 131; State Statistical Bureau 1983: 146). The types of jobs these youths are being assigned reflect the growing inability of the capital-intensive state enterprises to absorb them. In 1980 only 37 percent of those who found employment were assigned to state enterprises, 43 percent were assigned to urban collective enterprises, and 14 percent were given temporary jobs. The employment problem was so severe that the government reversed its two-decades-old hostility to the individual craft and service economy and allowed 6 percent of this total to become "self-employed." Over 11 million of the recent entrants to the labor force remained unemployed (China Almanac 1981: 357).[25]

Given these demographic and economic realities, the entry into secure state sector employment is currently a difficult passage for urban youth and a crucial one in determining their future life chances. Enterprises have some flexibility in hiring new employees, and they preferentially hire two kinds of new recruits when they are given permission to expand their officially authorized roster. One path to state employment is through a period of exemplary performance and skill acquisition as a temporary worker. Despite the general oversupply of labor, enterprises are always willing to hire skilled and experienced labor, which is still in short supply. A small number of temporary workers who have worked in a single enter-

---

25. Official estimates of unemployment in urban China range from 10 to 25 million. Emerson (1983) argues that the actual number is close to the low end of this range. Capital intensity in the state sector dictates labor absorption in the collective sector. It costs an average of 10,000 yuan of fixed capital investment to employ one worker in state industry, and only 2,000 yuan in the collective sector (950 yuan in the rural collective sector) (Economic Yearbook 1981: IV, 34, 56; Feng and Zhao 1982: 130). Statistics on final job assignments from more recent sources do not coincide with those cited above but confirm the downward trend in state sector assignments. According to the State Statistical Bureau (1983: 146), the percentage of new employees assigned to the state sector has dropped from 72 to 62 percent from 1978 to 1982; collective sector assignments have increased from 28 to 33 percent; and the individual sector from 0 to 5 percent. The more recent figures do not mention temporary labor.

prise for several years and who have acquired valuable skills and a
reputation for good workmanship are commonly offered permanent
positions.[26] A second path to state employment is provided by the
common preference that enterprises show in hiring the offspring of
their favored employees. Some large enterprises provide training for
employees' children in their own vocational-technical high schools
and hire them after graduation. Some enterprises in recent years
have been able to fill most of their demand for new workers from
this source (Shirk 1981: 577). There are also legal provisions that
permit retiring employees to designate one of their offspring to replace them. This practice is so important to the families of workers
that rumors about the restriction of this practice in the early 1980s
led to an undesired wave of early retirements for faked medical reasons among highly skilled and valued employees.[27]

Once the enterprise has hired from among these preferred categories, it will turn to the local labor bureau to assign them enough
workers to fill the remainder of their alloted quota.[28] Except for the
college educated, only the graduates of special vocational-technical
high schools are virtually guaranteed employment in the state sector.[29] These graduates, highly sought after for their skill and training, are assigned to workshops as skilled workers and are placed on
the lowest rung of the skilled workers' wage ladder without first
going through the three-year apprenticeship that is obligatory for

26. A series of documents permitted the hiring of long term-temporaries as permanent workers in the early 1970s. They are discussed, but not reproduced, in one
collection of labor and wage documents (see Korzec and Whyte 1981). My informants confirmed that this did indeed occur as the result of the stated policy, but they
also stressed that this was only the most visible instance of a practice that proceeds
continually on a much smaller scale.

27. The practice is known as *dingti* and is described in several secondary
sources: Shirk (1981: 577), Emerson (1983: 11–12), and Korzec and Whyte (1981).
Official regulations pertaining to the practice are summarized in State Labor Bureau
(1980: 32–36). There were many reports in the early 1980s of waves of retirements
touched off in part by rumors of the end of the *dingti* policy; Gu (1981) is a representative one. The rumors turned out to be partly true; *dingti* hiring has recently been
restricted to exclude cases in which the children do not have the minimum qualifica-
tions for employment (Ministry of Labor and Personnel 1983a).

28. A residual preferred category should be mentioned before we move on: jobs
provided for relatives of officials who are in a position to do a favor for the enterprise. This was more important in the 1970s, when colleges were disbanded for a
period and almost all youths sent to the countryside.

29. College graduates are also guaranteed state sector assignments, but only a
small portion of them are assigned to industry, and then as office staff or technicians
(an engineering grade).

all others. (Instead graduates have a pro forma trial period that usually lasts six months.) Some of them may be assigned jobs as "assistant technicians" (*zhuli jishuyuan*), a subengineering grade on the technical-engineering scale that includes skilled maintenance and repair work in the shop or simple technical drawing and other assistance work in technical staff offices.

The remainder of the recruits are drawn from the large pool of academic high school graduates who have failed to gain admission to college and a small pool of youths who dropped out of school earlier. High school enrollments expanded steadily throughout the 1960s and 1970s, increasing more than tenfold from 1957 to 1977. Yet during the same period, the number of postsecondary places increased a mere 70 percent. As a result, only 2.6 percent of general high school graduates now gain admission to higher education (State Statistical Bureau 1982: 441). This has been the group hardest hit by the tightening of state sector opportunities. Unlike students from vocational-technical schools, they have no special industrial training. Some do not resign themselves to a manual job and stay at home or enroll in private remedial classes in order to improve their chances in the next year's college entrance examinations. Most, however, request assignments from the labor bureau and hope that the assignment will be to a state enterprise.[30] In recent years, the backlog of new labor force entrants has caused a wait of up to two years for many of these young people, during which they were officially considered not as unemployed, but as "awaiting work" (*dai ye*).

Social and Economic Aspects of the Employment Relationship

The importance of a state sector job assignment cannot be measured in money; nor do differences within this sector have much to do with differences in wage levels. To a significant degree, the goods and services that define an individual's standard of living are distributed in China not by markets through the medium of money,

30. Recently many urban enterprises have begun to hire workers from this group directly through advertisements and examinations (Ministry of Labor and Personnel 1983a). This has been the common practice for decades in the Soviet Union, where there has been no counterpart to the municipal labor bureau since the early 1930s (Dyker 1981).

but by bureaucracies through direct distributions and legal entitlements. The workplace—through its administration (or general
affairs) department and union branch—has been the central point
of distribution for housing; ration coupons for major consumer
durables, and daily necessities (such as cloth and coal); subsidized
food and staple goods; and the delivery of major social services and
medical care. The enterprise also administers state labor insurance,
welfare provisions, and social security and provides a wide variety
of subsidies, supplementary payments, and even loans (see Kallgren
1969). Like the Soviet welfare system, the Chinese differs from the
American in that it is administered solely through workplaces and
covers only those employed.[31] Attaining the status of permanent
worker in a state enterprise has a significance for a worker's standard of living far beyond what wage differences would indicate.
This system of socialized distribution, further, makes the enterprise
an intense focus of the worker's social life—not so much in patterns
of association and identification as in the daily effort to improve
one's standard of living, obtain valued goods and services, and negotiate crucial life passages.

Average expenditures in the urban family budget indicate the
overwhelming importance of these direct distributions as a component of the standard of living. In 1982, 92 percent of family income
was spent on commodities and daily necessities, and, of the total,
58 percent was spent on food alone (State Statistical Bureau 1983:
495). Only 5.2 percent of the Chinese family budget was spent on
the necessities that comprise 45 percent of the American family's
expenditures and 21 percent of the Japanese family's—housing, util-
ities, transportation, and medical care (State Statistical Bureau
1983: 495; Bureau of the Census 1982: 467; Statistics Bureau
1982: 444–47). These necessities are inexpensive relative to the
United States and Japan, but they are also things commonly deliv-

---

31. Rimlinger's (1968) contrast of the Soviet social security system with the
American holds also for the Chinese. In the American system, the government provides benefits irrespective of status, but on a contractual-contribution basis; various
programs are administered by federal and state governments, unions, and companies
themselves; and the payments, while not used as an incentive tool, are kept to a minimum. The Soviet system provides a much fuller range of benefits, but the payments
are shaped by government planning policy, to spur incentives in important economic
sectors and job statuses; the payments are considered a right, but only for those who
work responsibly (as Rimlinger put it, they are "a reward for loyal performance");
and the state provisions are administered, interpreted, and funded at the workplace.

ered or subsidized by the enterprise. These budget figures reflect enormous state subsidies of state employees' living standards, an amount that surpassed the size of the wage bill by the early 1980s (Lardy 1984: 863). More than one-half of the state workers' living standards, in other words, are the result of direct distributions and subsidies.

Two other factors enhance the importance of workplace distributions and subsidies for individual workers: a rationing and price structure that ensures minimum standards but demands marked frugality to rise above these minimum standards, and the scarcity of virtually all highly valued consumer durables relative to demand. Grain, pork, and cooking oil are the staple food items rationed in most Chinese cities since the 1950s. The rationed amounts cost less than 20 percent of the average monthly wage, but this is a bare minimum standard, especially with regard to balance in the diet: it represents 1 pound of rice each day, but only 2.2 pounds of pork, and 0.5 pound of cooking oil per month (Chinn 1980: 747–49). Urban residents must, therefore, purchase amounts in excess of their rations for nongrain items (the grain ration is usually sufficient) and often at higher prices, especially because consumers are usually forced to go to higher-priced farmers' markets to find the required quantities and qualities of pork and cereal oils. (Since the legalization of farmers' markets in the late 1970s, these supplies have been much more abundant than in the past.) Especially costly in this regard are pork and nonrationed protein substitutes; in terms of hours worked, they are much more expensive as a proportion of earnings than in the U.S.S.R., not to mention the U.S.A. and Japan (see table 4). As a result, almost 60 percent of a Chinese urban family's expenditures are for food.[32]

The frugality exercised in the family budget is also dictated by the prices of consumer goods. In 1979, as a proportion of the average monthly state sector wage (68 yuan), cloth shoes cost roughly 7 percent, a ready-made shirt 13 percent, and a transistor radio from 33 to 67 percent. A one-speed bicycle cost two and one-half to three and one-half a month's wages, a foot-powered sewing machine, just under three months, and a 12-inch black and white television, about seven months (Chinn 1980: 751).

32. In the Soviet Union, the figure is 38.2 percent (Kahan 1979: 285); in the United States, 25 percent (Bureau of the Census 1982: 467); and in Japan, 29 percent (Statistics Bureau 1982: 444–47).

Table 4.   *Standardized Retail Food Prices in Four Countries*

	Retail food prices, in average time worked per kg. (hours: minutes)			
	U.S.A.	Japan	U.S.S.R.	China
Wheat flour	0:05	0:16	0:28	1:28
Milled rice	0:12	0:17	0:58	1:30
Pork	0:54	0:15	2:05	7:55
Chicken	0:15	0:50	3:43	8:45
Eggs	0:16	0:27	2:00	7:30
Vegetable oil	0:16	0:36	2:10	7:17
Cabbage	0:05	0:06	0:09	0:25
Sugar	0:05	0:11	0:59	5:35

Source: Klatt 1983:44.

Because of the marked frugality enforced by rationing and the wage-price structure, small supplements and allowances for state workers, paid in both cash and kind, are of much greater consequence for living standards than might at first appear. For most industrial workers, one set of work clothes and leather work shoes are provided annually. These are items that would cost the worker the equivalent of an average month's wage (Chinn 1980: 751). Many enterprises provide a winter heating supplement, worth around 2 yuan (or an average day's wage) per month, which subsidizes the worker's purchase of the coal used in stoves for cooking and heating in factory dormitories and apartments. In the summer, many enterprises provide what are called "high-temperature supplements" or "cool-drink fees" that are also worth around 2 yuan per month and are to be used to purchase traditional hot-weather drinks (for example, a mixture of water, sugar, and meng bean paste in Hunan Province), or iced refreshments. Other enterprises instead distribute the refreshments directly to the workers.

Workers who live a considerable distance from the enterprise are also eligible for transportation fees to compensate them for tram or bus fare, or simply to compensate them (and supplement the diet) for the extra physical energy expended in bicycling the extra distance to work.[33] Workers who have been assigned jobs that separate

33. Chinn (1980: 750) calculates that in Beijing two bus trips per day of average length (about 0.10 yuan per trip) would cost a resident 6 yuan per month—almost three days' wages.

them from their families can receive travel supplements that cover their train fare and living expenses en route while on annual home leave. Workers who are engaged in hazardous or difficult lines of work—in high-temperature smelting or refining shops, and underground mining, for example—receive regular wage supplements that range from one day's pay up to half a month's. This short list, by no means exhaustive, indicates the range and importance of these direct subsidies, in cash and in kind, for everyday living expenses.

Another important set of state benefits ensure the worker against financial hardships. State labor insurance provisions regarding injury, illness, maternity, and retirement have already been described (see table 3). But there are other benefits of this type: lump sum payments to workers to cover funeral expenses of family members, and extra food ration coupons given to nursing mothers. Families that find themselves in dire financial straits due to a low per capita income can apply for regular welfare supplements that continue as long as the problem persists (the enterprise will usually try first to find employment for a family member). Workers who find themselves in financial difficulty for other reasons are eligible to apply for a short-term loan that does not necessarily need to be repaid (State Labor Bureau 1980: 287–92).

State sector employment brings another advantage independent of subsidies: state workers are in a relatively favored position in the system of socialized distribution. Workplaces are points of distribution for ration coupons not only for highly sought-after industrial goods—sewing machines, bicycles, radios, watches, and furniture—but also for additional coupons for grain and other foodstuffs above the basic rationed amounts.[34] By law, the administration of a state enterprise obtains ration coupons for these items from state commercial agencies and distributes them to employees according to a method of their own determination. But in practice, enterprises regularly engage in "outside the plan" deals with these same agencies or with other enterprises in which they trade products and spare parts in return for goods, which may include ration coupons for, or actual deliveries of, television sets, furniture, or watches. Enterprise officials typically get more than their share of these informally procured items, but my informants commonly re-

34. Before 1979 this was important simply to assure supplies. Now it is important to get better brands and pay low state prices.

ported that some of them were routinely made available to workers as well. By acting as agents for their employees in a bureaucratic system of commodity distribution characterized by shortages, the state enterprise can increase the probability that their workers can buy one of these scarce and valued items and often lower the price, if any, that they must pay.

State enterprises perform the same role in the procurement of foodstuffs. Informal bartering with state commercial agencies or rural communes often brings the enterprise supplies of cured meats, pork, fresh fruit, or vegetables. Many enterprises, in addition, own and maintain their own farms on tracts of land in the suburbs, and sometimes a tract of land is informally allotted to an enterprise by a village in a private agreement of mutual advantage.[35] A total of 1.15 million acres was cultivated by state factories and mines in 1980, and their total product was 500 million kilograms of grain and 1.5 billion kilograms of vegetables (Economic Yearbook 1981: IV, 182).[36] All of this food is outside the urban rationing system, and it is supplied to workers in addition to rationed amounts—either free or at subsidized prices in enterprise meal halls. Many enterprises give free banquets for their employees at the Lunar New Year holiday. One of my informants (no. 72) reported that this routinely included many expensive and scarce items: pork, wine, and fresh fruits and vegetables prepared in regional specialties. Other enterprises distribute scarce foodstuffs directly to workers at holidays, instead of preparing the banquet for them. Again, both in terms of availability and price, the state worker is in a favorable position.

In addition to the direct distribution of commodities, enterprises

35. One of my informants (no. 72) described an informal arrangement between his factory and a commune 10 km. outside his city. The factory was allotted a section of farmland and given help in cultivating rice and melons, and raising pigs. In return, the factory donated machinery to help the commune begin some small factories, provided temporary jobs for some of the peasants, and allowed the commune's peasants the right to cart off sewage from the factory's latrine for use as fertilizer.

36. This yielded an average of 14 kg. of grain and 44 kg. of vegetables for every state employee that year. This was especially valuable in the years before free peasant markets were reintroduced in 1979 after a two-decade hiatus. Then it was a matter of securing supplies of meat and other foodstuffs that were often unavailable; now it is more a matter of convenience and, especially, economy. The Soviet enterprise also delivers an important percentage of foodstuffs directly to workers at subsidized prices or at no cost: a crucial advantage in the consumer shortages of the past decade. In fact, the government began to urge more factories to form "agrarian workshops" in the late 1970s and produce more food for their own employees (see Morton 1984: 13–15).

also provide public goods and services that are not available from other sources. Housing is easily the most important of these. Residential crowding is a serious problem in urban China: each urban resident occupies only 5.6 square meters (State Statistical Bureau 1983: 483).[37] State enterprises currently control 54 percent of the urban housing stock; only 18 percent is still in private hands, and the remaining 29 percent is city-owned (Whyte and Parish 1984: 82). State enterprises currently spend over one-half of all the funds allocated to new housing construction (China Almanac 1981: 540).[38] Large enterprises can also exercise influence with municipal housing bureaus to procure apartments for their employees. The state worker, therefore, relies heavily on the enterprise to obtain larger or newer quarters. Workers' rents are also heavily subsidized and rarely exceed the equivalent of one or two days' pay. Employees who do not live in factory housing but remain in private or municipally owned housing can receive money grants from their enterprises to repair their quarters.

The services supplied by the state enterprise are also highly valued because they are not generally available outside. The services sector has declined steadily since the nationalization of private enterprises and the adoption of a Soviet-inspired model of industrialization. On the eve of the First Five-Year Plan in 1952, the services sector comprised 40 percent of nonagricultural employment. It dropped to 12.5 percent by 1977 and has reached 15 percent in 1982 only after several years of economic reform (calculated from State Statistical Bureau 1983: 126, 134, 137). Most services, instead, are supplied directly by the enterprise. The enterprise meal

37. Housing space actually declined from 1952 to 1978 (see chap. 6) but rebounded in the post-1978 housing boom. The comparable per capita figure for the Soviet Union was 8.6 square meters in 1977 (Morton 1984: 8). In Japan, a market economy where the figure for per capita urban housing space is notoriously low— only 13.4 square meters per capita, compared with 38.4 square meters for dwellers of apartment buildings in the United States (Statistics Bureau 1982: 468; Bureau of the Census 1982: 751, 760)—there is no shortage of housing units relative to demand. In the Soviet Union, the number of new housing units built annually from 1965 to 1975 fell short of the number of marriages by 5 percent (Kahan 1979: 287), while in Japan from 1974 to 1980, new housing units surpassed marriages by 55 percent (Statistics Bureau 1982: 46–47, 236).

38. In the Soviet Union in the mid-1970s, over 70 percent of all housing was state-owned; ministries, through their enterprises, accounted for 70 percent of all expenditures for housing construction (reserved for their employees); and enterprises controlled approximately two-thirds of the housing stock (Morton 1984: 9, 16–17).

hall—standard in all large state enterprises and common in many medium-sized ones—is the most important of these. It usually serves three meals a day and may offer carry-out services—all at subsidized prices.

State enterprises also operate daycare and kindergarten services for the children of families, an important service for the typical family in which both spouses work. Showers and toilet facilities (along with clean towels and free soap) are things that few urban homes have, and many enterprises provide these free of charge. Even haircuts, clothing repair, commissaries that sell household items, and movie screenings are routinely provided for workers at a fraction of their cost outside (and with no waiting in line). And just as for scarce commodities, enterprises are occasionally able to procure tickets to movies and cultural and sporting events for workers that individuals would not be able to buy themselves. The recent resurgence of the individual urban services sector has begun to provide more alternatives than in the past, but at a much higher price.

A final benefit of state employment is the preferential distribution of job opportunities to family members. This preference is expressed in four different ways. Enterprises commonly hire the spouses or children of their permanent workers as temporary employees. This was a practice designed to increase family income under the wage austerity of the 1960s and 1970s; the temporary workers were given the title "dependent workers" (*jiashu gong*) in the official documents that mention them, and Chinese citizens refer to them by that name. Second, many enterprises set up collective sector branch factories whose primary purpose is to provide long-term employment for the family members of permanent workers, thereby solving their employment problem. There were 6,766 of these collective enterprises in existence in 1979 (China Almanac 1980: 293). Third, the children of permanent employees are often shown preference in the hiring of new workers. The children of employees in larger enterprises are often admitted preferentially to attached vocational-technical schools in which enterprises train future skilled workers (Shirk 1981). Even small enterprises do this: in the 1970s, they commonly offered jobs to the children of employees who had been sent to the countryside after high school—thus allowing them to return to the city. All a worker needs to do to initiate this kind of arrangement is place a request with the shop director, usually through a work group leader. The final form this preference takes is the *dingti* practice described earlier in this chapter, in which the worker's offspring serves as a postretirement replacement. This is not only a way to increase family income, it is also a way of passing on state sector status to children. It is, in fact, commonly assumed by both the government and enterprises that the unemployed children of workers are the enterprise's social responsibility. Press articles describing the employment of workers' dependents in a favorable light often refer to this as finding employment for "our unit's" unemployed youth (e.g., Beijing Daily 1981).

The Hierarchy of Life Chances

Not all enterprises can provide all of these benefits to workers, and not all of those that do provide them can provide them in the same amounts. State labor insurance benefits are provided uniformly to permanent employees throughout the state sector, but this is not true for most of the other benefits, especially those that involve informal distributions of goods obtained "outside the plan." Large enterprises, especially those that provide crucial products for ministry, provincial, or municipal plans, are more richly endowed with housing, medical facilities, dining halls, and other amenities that require large capital outlays than are smaller and less important enterprises. Generally speaking, the higher the level of the administrative subsystem in which an enterprise is located, the broader will be the range of fringe benefits and services, and the more plentiful the supply. State enterprises run by national ministries, provinces, and by the large cities, in other words, usually offer more complete benefits than those run by small cities or by counties far from large metropolitan areas. And whatever the advantages or disadvantages conferred by size, location, or importance of product, these benefits vary according to the degree of effort and ingenuity enterprise managers employ in bargaining with bureaucratic agencies or in bartering with commercial agencies, communes, and other enterprises to procure goods that can be distributed to employees.

Although the state sector is by no means uniform with regard to benefits, a much sharper distinction exists between permanent state sector workers and temporary workers or collective sector workers in both city and countryside. All state enterprises provide full state labor insurance and retirement benefits. All but the smallest and most remote state enterprises have at least a dining hall, medical facilities or direct referral services to a local hospital, and provide supplements, loans, distributions in kind, and at least some dormitories and apartments. But only the largest collective enterprises can supply these things: they almost never have factory housing, and they rarely have more than a small first aid clinic. Only the largest collectives can afford dining halls, daycare services, distributions in kind, and other benefits. Differences in the direct delivery of goods and services are just as important as differences in wage and insurance coverage.

This enterprise-centered pattern of social distribution, in its general outlines if not in its details, is one that is familiar to the student of Soviet society: "In the U.S.S.R. differences between plants determine the living condition of workers to a far greater extent than in the West" (Teckenberg 1978: 196–97).[39] The fact that Soviet enterprises offer a wide array of "sociocultural services"—housing, kindergartens, meals, sales of products for home delivery, take-away food, possibilities for workers and their children to go to holiday homes or fishing and hunting resorts, factory schools, reading rooms, swimming pools, sports grounds—leads some to conclude that the life of Soviet citizens is "more centered around the enterprise than the community" (Teckenberg 1978: 196–97; see also McAuley 1981: 221–27; Powell 1977: 281–82). Despite the higher standard of living in the Soviet Union, there are no more alternatives than in China: the services sector has been restricted there as well (see Schroeder 1984).

Labor Mobility and Dependence on the Enterprise

The worker who is able to find employment in the state sector is in a secure and privileged position. In China these assignments are so difficult to obtain and there are so many candidates for the job openings that do exist, that state sector workers in the larger enterprises almost never resign their positions. At the same time, layoffs are rare because wages and benefits are subsidized by the state budget. Temporary workers provide the needed flexibility to meet changing labor demands for construction, transportation, and sum-

---

39. For example, a Soviet worker in an enterprise under a heavy industrial ministry is 18 to 20 times more likely to be allocated a new apartment than a worker in light industry (Morton 1984: 16).

mer fill-ins. Firing for disciplinary reasons is rare. For all of these reasons, there is little turnover in large and medium-sized state enterprises, except that due to retirement, disability, and state-mandated transfers.[40] The individual worker can normally expect to remain in the same enterprise for most, if not all, of his or her working life. This fact is not absolute; a marginal amount of turnover occurs because of job switching, reassignments, plant closings and reorganizations, or politically motivated expulsions.

Job Switching

"Job switching" is a change of workplace initiated by the employee. This is done either by resigning and looking for alternative employment on one's own or by requesting a transfer to a more desirable enterprise. Resignations are rare in the large state sector enterprises—for the simple reason that the state will give an individual one job assignment, but not a second. Someone who resigns from a large enterprise that provides a wide range of services would find it almost impossible to find a comparable alternative. Furthermore, according to state insurance regulations, seniority is lost with resignation. If an employee quits a state sector position—which is quite legal—state sector benefits are lost, and the person must seek work in the collective sector or as a temporary worker (State Council 1957a: art. 8). Quitting a state sector job in such circumstances invariably means a drop in living standards and damage to future life chances—not to mention one's children's chances of gaining state employment. Requested transfers to other state enterprises are also rare, not because there are few applicants, but because the applications made are so rarely acted upon. According to official state policy, transfers will not be granted unless "absolutely unavoidable" (State Council 1957a: art. 1). Even if a worker is able to find another plant willing to take him or her or is able to find a worker at another plant willing to trade positions, the enterprise still must

40. Figures on turnover in China are unavailable, but it is generally known that some industrial sectors experience more turnover than others. Mining, because of the difficulty and danger of the work and its location far from comfortable urban areas, experiences higher turnover. Construction work, outside the boundaries of this sector (all the workforce estimates given so far exclude this sector of 10 million), exhibits considerably more turnover as well and employs high percentages of temporary labor. The entire industrial system exhibited more turnover in the 1950s during the period of rapid industrial growth and administrative reorganization. Turnover became rare after the enforcement of strict hiring and migration controls following the Great Leap Forward.

give its permission before any job change can take place.[41] Such permission is not routinely given, especially if the worker is highly skilled. Transfers are usually made at the convenience of management, not workers.

Job switching in the state sector occurs more commonly in small enterprises with fewer services and benefits and in cases where an individual is dissatisfied with the initial job assignment, usually for geographical reasons. Judging by my interviews, it appears that voluntary resignations most commonly occur among workers under 30 years of age who are dissatisfied with the location of a recent job assignment or an unrequested transfer. Often this dissatisfaction stems from separation from spouse and family—a common problem with labor assignments. Residents of China's large eastern cities who are assigned to faraway jobs in the hinterlands sometimes prefer any type of employment in their hometowns to life in smaller, more backward cities far from their place of origin. One of my informants, a long-time resident of a large city in a coastal province, left a desirable permanent job in a large city in northwestern China because the climate was too cold, the semi-arid location too dusty, and the staple northern cornmeal cakes played havoc with his southern stomach (accustomed to steamed rice). He returned to his native city with the cover story that he "needed to care for his aging mother" and found employment there in a small collective enterprise.[42]

Even in cases where a job and work unit consent are obtained, movement of this sort can be blocked by household registration laws. China's urban areas are sorted into a graded hierarchy, in which the large cities and the desirable coastal ones are almost closed to new residents, while the small cities and towns and the ones in the interior and far to the northwest are more open. One can easily obtain permission to move down in this hierarchy but almost never upward (Whyte and Parish 1984: 17–22). Several of my informants reported that they had to move to join a spouse who was assigned a job in a small city—all attempts to be united in the

41. The enterprise personnel department must agree to this because they hold the worker's all-important personal dossier, without which the worker does not legally exist. A Chinese commentator who argued recently for a weaker attachment of workers to firms called this, quite appropriately, a "system of ownership by the work unit" exercised over the worker (Zhao 1983).

42. Even this transfer required intervention by a bureaucratic organization, the Overseas Chinese Affairs Bureau, which helped this man because his family were Chinese who had migrated from Southeast Asia to China in the 1950s.

large one failed. Others choose to remain separated rather than give up their precious footholds in a large urban area (e.g., Liang and Shapiro 1983).

The important point is that whatever the reason for a job change initiated by the worker—marital concerns, regional affinities, dissatisfaction with a recent unrequested transfer, or something else— it must be a reason pressing enough to outweigh the inevitable worsening of conditions that results from resignation. Job switching is not something done to improve one's life chances in the state sector—it is something done when the prospect of staying is so distasteful that it outweighs the disadvantages of moving.

Reassignments

"Reassignments" are transfers that are initiated by authorities according to their own needs—more common than those initiated by individuals and not always voluntary. It is a happy, if rare, occasion when administrative and individual needs for a transfer coincide. Dissatisfaction with reassignments is, in fact, a leading cause of job switching. Because administrative needs are likely to involve personnel with specific skills, technical personnel are more commonly transferred than workers. This kind of interenterprise mobility may be either temporary or permanent.

Temporary transfers are commonly referred to as "borrowing" (*jieyong*, or *jiediao*) an individual. This occurs when high-level administrative offices require employees with certain skills to perform a job of limited duration—a form of allocative flexibility in an otherwise rigid system. Several of my informants were borrowed in this manner: one was borrowed for two years by a ministry in Beijing to compile a technical standards handbook; another was borrowed for six months by a municipal planning commission to study electrical power consumption in local industry; and still another was borrowed for a year by a municipal scientific and technical commission as a staff advisor. This is a common form of "tethered" mobility: the employee is still officially tied to the original enterprise. All official records remain there, all wages and benefits are still paid out of the budget of the original work unit, and in almost all cases the employee will eventually return (see Fujian Province Labor Bureau 1959). This kind of mobility, however, is usually limited to white collar employees who have rare skills.[43]

---

43. In a large Beijing machine tools factory in 1978, 2.6 percent of the personnel were "borrowed long term" (People's Daily 1978a).

Permanent transfers occur when new enterprises or rapidly expanding ones create personnel needs that can be met only by drawing people from other establishments that are overstaffed and undergoing retrenchment. These transfers take place along the administrative lines of the immediate planning agency. If an enterprise is under the administration of a national machine-building ministry, the transfer will invariably be to another enterprise or to an administrative office within the same ministerial subsystem. If the enterprise is under a municipal chemical industry bureau, the reassignment is likely to be to another enterprise within the subsystem. Permanent transfers rarely cross subsystem boundaries: subsystems try to hold onto workers, just as do enterprises. The smaller the subsystem and the smaller the enterprises in the subsystem, or the more rapid its rate of expansion, the higher the rate of reassignment. Reassignment rates in small industrial subsystems of cities appear to be somewhat higher than others, because a local industrial bureau running a chain of small enterprises will more actively redistribute scarce trained personnel between enterprises as needed. These kinds of transfers are still relatively uncommon for technical and administrative staff and are even more rare among blue collar workers. This is a form of mobility common only for the leading executives and political cadres of an enterprise whose career pattern typically moves them up a promotion ladder that spans across enterprises and subsystems.

Layoffs and Expulsions

Layoffs do occur, but only when enterprises are being disbanded or have suspended operations temporarily. This occurred in the state sector on a large scale only during the retrenchment of 1961–1964 that followed the Great Leap Forward, when some 16 million recently hired workers were laid off and returned to the countryside, and a smaller number of workers of long standing were laid off as well (State Statistical Bureau 1982: 107); and it occurred on a significant, but much smaller, scale during the recent retrenchment of 1979–1981. With the exception of the early 1960s, these layoffs are accompanied either by immediate reassignment to another state enterprise or by unemployment relief while the worker awaits reassignment (State Council 1965; 1966; Central Committee 1964). [44]

44. I spoke privately with a worker in Kunming in summer 1982 who related that about one-third of his coworkers had been idled by a recent retrenchment

In almost all cases of this sort, the local labor bureau actively seeks reassignments, and the workers remain covered by state labor insurance, even if most other fringe benefits end.

"Expulsion," the Chinese term for firing, also occurs rarely, but it does occur. My informants often pointed out to me that there is no such thing as firing (*jiegu*) in China since the revolution, only expulsion (*kaichu*). The distinction they had in mind, which follows that made in official documents, is that the former refers to arbitrary removal or layoff characteristic of capitalism, while the latter is an administrative punishment meted out in response only to flagrant abuses of factory rules or to lawbreakers and political dissidents. Despite the fact that regulations exist that allow expulsion for extreme cases of absenteeism and poor work performance, the sanction is almost never applied for this kind of behavior. It is remarkable that my informants could not recall more than one or two cases of expulsion for reasons related to work discipline, even when they had worked in the same enterprise for decades. "Problem" workers are usually retained by an enterprise and then unloaded on others when the labor bureau dictates that a fixed number of workers must be released to another enterprise (in doing this, the enterprise conserves its valued workers) (Kallgren 1968: 169–70). Throughout the 1960s and 1970s, an enterprise needed the permission of the labor department of their industrial bureau in order to expel an individual for breach of rules. Few enterprises ever bothered to ask, according to virtually all the informants, whether they had occupied management or blue collar positions.

Expulsion for political and legal offenses, however, is more common. Most of my informants could recall a handful of permanent expulsions that resulted from criminal behavior or political dissidence, real or perceived. The two decades after 1956, beginning with the anti-rightist campaign of 1957 and ending with the expulsions and arrests that followed the 1976 demonstration and riot now called the Tiananmen Incident, were characterized by periodic expulsions of small handfuls of workers for purely political reasons.[45] The victims of these campaigns would be sent to labor re-

---

that left them with an unemployment subsidy that was a small fraction of their former wage.

45. The Tiananmen Incident was a large demonstration in the center of Beijing on April 5, 1976. Ostensibly a gathering to commemorate the recent death of Zhou Enlai, it turned into a protest against the policies of the radical faction in the last months of Mao's life.

form camps, to their ancestral villages to become permanent rural residents, or simply left to look for temporary employment. This exception to the "no firing" norm shows how secure state employment really is: unless one becomes a political dissident or commits robbery, rape, or any other crime that requires imprisonment, there is little real possibility of being expelled.

A Comparative Perspective

The Chinese pattern differs from the Soviet in two important respects. First, the Soviet Union has not had a system of job allocation through labor bureaus since the early 1930s, relying instead on local advertisements, word of mouth, and, in recent decades, employment agencies (Dyker 1981: 40–43). Soviet managers consequently do not have the power to prevent a worker from finding employment in another state sector enterprise. Second, the rates of labor turnover there are considerably higher in the state sector than interviews and documents suggest is the case in China.[46] In fact, the average annual turnover rates in the U.S.S.R. have been roughly the same as in the United States. This raises two issues regarding worker dependence on the enterprise: in what sense are we justified in viewing China and the Soviet Union as variations of a single pattern; and in what ways can the Soviet pattern be distinguished from the American in ways relevant to the comparative argument?

The common thread in the Soviet and Chinese pattern is the heavy dependence on the state enterprise, especially the larger ones, for the satisfaction of a broad range of the workers' needs. The voluntary turnover that does occur in China invariably occurs in small

---

46. Köszegi (1978: 307–8) states that in Hungary it is "generally recognized to be perfectly reasonable to change jobs as many as 3 or 5 or even 10 times during a working career." It is not known, however, whether this varies according to the size and resources controlled by the enterprise. Data on turnover in the Soviet Union suggest that it does. In the early 1980s, Chinese enterprises began to hire workers directly through advertisements and examinations, which appears to have opened up job alternatives for workers in small state enterprises and collective enterprises in both urban and rural areas. There is little evidence that workers in large state enterprises have been lured away by these small firms, even when they offer much higher wages, as is now common in rural collective enterprises near large cities. Emigres have reported, and the official press has complained, that workers in state enterprises sometimes retire early (with pensions) to work in these high-paying collectives or take long-term sick leave to do so. But they appear unwilling to sacrifice their housing, benefits, and urban registration to take up these positions. As far as transfers between large state enterprises are concerned, past restrictions on transfers still apply.

state enterprises that provide poor services, among younger workers unsatisfied with their initial jobs, and in geographical areas considered undesirable. This is precisely the pattern in the U.S.S.R., albeit on a somewhat larger scale. Most turnover in the Soviet Union occurs in a large number of small state firms (with fewer than 1,000 people) that employ about 28 percent of the labor force and provide fewer services (Teckenberg 1978: 205–6). In both the U.S.S.R. and Hungary, high rates of turnover are concentrated among the young and unskilled, and much higher rates of turnover exist in Siberia and other remote areas where services, supplies, housing, and cultural life are inferior to the major European cities (see Zaslavsky 1982b). Soviet turnover rates, for example, average only 7 percent overall in European Russia, but they reach 58 percent in areas of Siberia, despite the fact that Siberian wages are much higher than elsewhere (Köszegi 1978: 308–9). This dependence on the enterprise is reflected in the turnover figures: it is precisely in the large enterprises, which provide the best services and housing, where employment alternatives are fewest. China differs from the U.S.S.R. in its tighter restrictions on the mobility of labor; but its lower state sector figures are artificially depressed by the formal exclusion of the small enterprises in the collective sector, where turnover is higher, and by the formal separation of the temporary labor force from the permanent. Neither distinction exists in Soviet industry.

Aggregate Soviet turnover rates are not much different than in the United States, but their structure and social meaning are much different. Turnover averaged 20 percent between 1950 and 1970 in the Soviet Union; 27 percent between 1965 and 1975 in the United States. But these average figures hide wide annual and seasonal fluctuations in the United States: American turnover fluctuates greatly with business cycles; Soviet turnover does not (Powell 1977: 268–69). In most years, layoffs and firings account for the majority of turnover in the United States. In the Soviet Union and the Eastern bloc, surveys show that up to 90 percent of turnover is initiated by the employee (Köszegi 1978: 310). A comparison of these average rates can be misleading: in the Soviet Union, they reflect the harsh geographical conditions of outlying areas and the poorer services supplied by small firms; in the United States, they reflect the layoffs dictated by the business cycle and the sum of personnel practices that vary widely from industry to industry. The social considerations connected with job mobility are the same in China and the U.S.S.R., even if the overall rates differ.

Mobility and Life Chances in the Enterprise

Upward mobility in the state enterprise, unlike common practice in American industry, is not defined by upward movement along a well-defined chain of specific jobs. Many large American firms have devised, often in cooperation with unions, detailed hierarchies in which specific jobs are minutely defined, graded according to skill and pay, and linked into promotion chains. These "internal labor markets" are promotion ladders that can be entered only at the bottom by people being hired from outside; all other positions in the chain are filled internally by people who have spent time in the firm, acquired job-specific skills, and compete for openings when they occur (see Doeringer and Piore 1971). Many large American enterprises have formal bidding systems in which workers compete for the high-rated positions at better pay rates (see Burawoy 1979: 97–104). Some have argued that these job boundaries are artificial creations of management designed to give workers a false sense of advancement and to moderate workers' demands by creating vested interests in a "career" within the firm (Stone 1975; Edwards 1979). Others have stressed that the finely differentiated hierarchies arose as a result of prolonged union-management conflict over the control of production and pay levels, and that they were as much the creation of unions as of management (Cole 1979: 101–13; Sabel 1982). Whatever the causes, the defining feature of this kind of job mobility is a close link between the job performed, its presumed skill content, and the level of pay (whether time or piece rate). Such a close link is entirely foreign to Chinese practices.

In the Chinese enterprise, there is a sharp formal distinction between job promotions (*tisheng* or *tiba*) and wage raises (*tiaozheng* or *ti gongzi*). This has led in practice to a loose link between position and pay. Even more so than in large Japanese enterprises, the most important wage differentials are the result of classifications applied not to jobs, but to individuals, and this classification is little affected by changes in the actual content of work performed. Every worker in state industry is "affixed a grade" (*dingji*) after finishing his or her apprenticeship or trial period. Depending on the general job title (*gongzhong mingcheng*) the worker is given (e.g., fitter, welder, laborer), the grade will be the lowest rung on a pay ladder that may have as many as eight rungs (for skilled work) or as few as six (for unskilled) (First Ministry of Machine Building 1978). In a given enterprise, the differences in pay between skilled and unskilled workers at the same grade are much smaller than the differences between grades within a single classification. The difference between job classifications at the same grade is rarely more than 2 yuan per month, while the difference between grades ranges from 8 to 15 yuan, depending on the levels compared (Hoffmann 1967; and interviews). Changes in job classifications can bring small increases in pay that have more symbolic than economic significance; they are much less tangible than the raises that result from movement up the eight grade scale.

One indication of this loose link between job definitions and pay is a comparatively vague definition of jobs—a characteristic that Chinese pay practices share with the Japanese (Cole 1979: 101–13). In the highly formalized internal labor markets of some American industries, changes from one kind of machine tool to another or changes in the product turned out on the machine tool will bring a different job classification and pay grade. Tasks in Chinese industry, in contrast, are parcelled out informally by work group leaders each day, and no changes in pay rates are connected with them. This casual approach to job definitions is reflected in the simplicity of Chinese job classification schemes. The First Ministry of Machine Building (1978) currently recognizes a grand total of 105 different job classifications, each with 6 to 8 separate skill/pay grades. The comparable manual for the American steel industry in 1945, in striking contrast, recognized over 20,000 different job classifications, each with 30 separate skill/pay grades—and this was after a concerted effort at standardization and simplification in the industry's wage structure (Stone 1975: 64).

Not only is pay only loosely linked with the kind of work performed, but the pay grades assigned to workers—originally designed to reflect skill levels—are also loosely related to actual skill. This is in part due to the design of the pay grading system itself. For the first five years of employment, new skilled workers are given wage raises each year on a predetermined schedule. During each of the first three years, they are paid a monthly apprentice wage that increases by a fixed increment, usually 2 yuan each year. A common wage progression is 18, 20, and 22 yuan. At the beginning of the fourth year, they are given a skill grade of 1, the lowest on the skilled workers' ladder, which usually brings a monthly wage of 30 to 34 yuan. At the beginning of the fifth year, they are given a final automatic raise to grade 2, which usually brings their pay up to 38 to 44 yuan. Once a worker reaches grade 2, further grade raises are possible in most cases only during a national wage readjustment.

Because the grade 2 skill standard for all job classifications, according to the machine building ministry's handbook (and the repeated descriptions of my informants), is merely the ability to perform simple operations without the supervision of an experienced "master" worker, there is a considerable lapse in time between the acquisition of skill and changes in pay. Most workers, except in difficult job classifications, actually reach grade 2 standards before the end of their first year of apprenticeship. And by the end of their fifth year, many are capable of qualifying for standards as high as grade 5 or 6. The enforced slow march through the first five years and the subsequent wait for national wage readjustments thereafter have turned the skill grading system (borrowed wholesale from the Soviet Union in the 1950s) into a de facto seniority system that is similar in superficial respects to the *nenko* system in large Japanese enterprises.

Every seniority system underpays younger workers to some extent, because skills accumulate faster than seniority in the early years of employment. Cole (1971: 72–100) argues that Japanese practices significantly underpay younger workers relative to their actual skill and work contribution, but that this consideration is counterbalanced by the young worker's expectation of regular upgrading in the future. Even within a seniority grade, however, pay in Japan varies according to a skill grade (usually determined by examination) and the job designation (see Clark 1979: 112–25). But in China the link between actual skill and pay is much looser than in Japan, for three reasons. First, wage readjustments are initiated at the national level in China, rather than by the enterprises themselves, as in Japan. Chinese managers, therefore, have had almost no flexibility in rewarding skill acquisition.[47] Second, national wage readjustments have occurred relatively infrequently in China since the 1950s. In Japan, by contrast, almost all workers are given a pay increase each year. Third, and in part because of the infrequency of

47. Recently Chinese officials signaled their intention to allow individual enterprises to readjust wages annually if their profit performance allows it (Ministry of Labor and Personnel 1983b). A similar decision in the early 1960s (Central Committee 1961, art. 26–29) was never implemented on a wide scale.

readjustments, skill has not been an important factor in the decisions to grant wage raises to individuals, and practical and written tests that might guide evaluations have been largely neglected. Despite the fact that the wage system China borrowed from the Soviet Union was supposed to be accompanied by regular grade raises tied strictly to skill levels (Kirsch 1972), China has ended up with a wage ladder that reflects little more than the date employment began.

China's chronic problem of labor absorption, something not shared with the Soviet Union, is largely responsible for this outcome. The high employment–low wage policy dictated relatively infrequent wage readjustments, but the actual degree of austerity practiced for the next two decades was an extreme interpretation of this policy. Some national leaders argued early on, with little success, that wage grades should still be readjusted annually for 20 to 25 percent of the workforce, something closer to Japanese and post-Stalin Soviet practice (Central Committee 1961: 228). The compromise position—one that employees I interviewed had been led to expect in the late 1950s and early 1960s—was that wages would be readjusted every two or three years for roughly 40 percent of the workforce. But, for a number of political and economic reasons, actual practice fell far short of this compromise. Since the completed nationalization of industry in 1956, major national wage readjustments have been initiated only in 1956, 1963, 1972, 1977, 1979, and 1983. According to several of my informants, workers were informed that readjustments were planned in 1966 and 1975, but they never occurred because of political disagreements among Party leaders.

Readjustments that might have occurred in the years from 1958 to 1961 and from 1967 to 1970 were rendered impossible by the financial crises that resulted from the Great Leap Forward and the Cultural Revolution, respectively. As a result, the relationship between skill and pay has been close to nonexistent in many periods; in fact, in the wage readjustment of 1972, seniority was the only criterion. The more frequent wage readjustments since 1977, the reassertion of skill evaluations in principle (though most often honored in the breach), and recent initiatives to allow enterprises to readjust wages annually if they can afford it mean that Chinese practice is changing. Because these principles of wage determination are to be mixed with quotas, bonuses, and piece rates of various types, China's current wage practices are evolving in the direction of the Soviet pattern, in which skill and completion of production quotas have long been mixed with the seniority principle.

In patterns of pay and promotion, Chinese workers have experienced a small degree of what Stinchcombe (1974: 123–35) defines as *career organization*—the sense of progression through a ladder of positions graded according to skill and pay that is typical of the internal labor markets of American industry. But workers do have three other opportunities for career mobility, and each of them involves promotion out of the worker category entirely. In each respect, China's workers experience the same opportunities as their Soviet counterparts. Small numbers of workers can, with the approval of their enterprise leaders, apply to technical institutes or universities and complete an education that will win them subsequent reassignment as technical or staff personnel. More commonly, workers can attend night classes organized by their enterprises, bureaus, or by local colleges, with the intention of passing qualifying exams to be reassigned as assistant technicians in the workshop.[48]

A second career path is into line management. Section heads, shop directors, and assistant shop directors are recruited almost exclusively from among the ranks of the workers. The first step in this career is to become an exemplary skilled worker, if not a model worker, while exhibiting loyalty to management and becoming involved in political activities organized by the party and its youth league. These workers are the ones chosen to be group leaders on the shop floor, and shop leaders are chosen from among these group leaders. This career path may eventually result in a position as a shop director (in a large plant) or even as the head of a staff department (typically general affairs, production, or basic construction) or as vice-director of the plant (more common in small enterprises).

A final path of mobility is a political career. Workers who are particularly active in youth league, union, or party activities and who have proven their loyalty to the party through years of loyal service and activism are occasionally chosen to work in the offices of the union or youth league in the plant or in the offices of the enterprise propaganda department. Shop party branch secretaries

---

48. This was not possible during the austere period from 1966 to 1977, when there was a general freeze on wage raises.

are usually former workers who have moved up in factory political organizations. All of these positions involve reclassification at higher levels of pay on a separate pay ladder for administrative personnel. It also entitles employees to more generous distributions from the enterprise.[49] Party branches continuously select and groom workers for political careers, largely through their union and youth league arms.

Except for small numbers who retrain themselves for technical careers, become promoted into line management, or enter into political careers, "upward mobility" for the blue collar worker means simply the accumulation of years of service, the receipt of occasional increases in base pay through the life course, and continuing enjoyment of the many fringe benefits that the state enterprise has to offer. These benefits increase with seniority and are usually extended as the enterprise grows over the years, adds to its stock of housing and other facilities, and expands the services it is able to offer employees. Aside from one's status within the enterprise, the capacity of the enterprise to satisfy employee needs—something that is by no means equal, even within the state sector—is perhaps the most important determinant of the standard of living and future life chances in urban China.

The Structured Dependence of the Enterprise Community

The dependence of Chinese workers on their state enterprises is a variant of a generic communist pattern, in which labor is treated not as a commodity, but as a political and economic resource, and where enterprises are the primary source for the satisfaction of a broad range of worker needs. The Chinese pattern has diverged from the Soviet in three ways. First, the greater scarcity of food and consumer goods in China and the administrative role of enterprises in past decades in rationing and distributing a wide array of daily necessities and consumer items have broadened the range of needs met by the enterprise and restricted the alternatives. Rationing has

49. This practice, common in Chinese factories, is formally enshrined in the Labor Code of the Soviet Union: "Workers and employees who have successfully and conscientiously performed their duties shall be granted priorities and privileges in the areas of social, cultural, housing, and personal services" (quoted in Powell 1977: 281–82).

not been commonly practiced in the Soviet Union since World War II: Soviet authorities have allowed queues to perform this function. The steady development of consumer markets in the U.S.S.R. since the 1950s, further, has meant that retail outlets, whatever their shortages relative to market economies, do provide an alternative to direct workplace distributions. As the private agricultural and services sectors have revived in China in recent years and as the supply of consumer goods has improved, the importance of rationing has lessened, and the Chinese worker can also enjoy these alternatives, although they are relatively expensive. In these respects, China is now becoming more like the U.S.S.R.

A second Chinese divergence from Soviet patterns is the more rigid barriers to job switching in the state sector and the consequently lower rates of labor mobility. Strict administrative control of job assignments, along with food rationing, has been the Chinese response to their distinctive demographic pressures. But the differences in labor mobility are perhaps not so great as they initially seem. Average Soviet turnover rates are not much lower than the American, but turnover is concentrated in the smallest firms and in remote areas with poor social services. Chinese state sector turnover rates are certainly much lower than the Soviets', but the Chinese state sector formally excludes large numbers of temporary and collective sector workers, whose mobility is considerably greater. Soviet collective enterprises (*artels*) were largely merged with the state sector in the 1960s, and they have not institutionalized a strict status distinction between temporary and permanent workers.[50] Despite these differences, in the Soviet Union, as in China, it is in the large state enterprises with the best housing and other benefits that turnover is low.

The third Chinese variation from the Soviet pattern is the more rigid status distinctions between segments of the workforce. This is the product both of China's demographic structure and its relatively low level of economic development. The state cannot provide full benefits for the entire urban industrial workforce, and it must continue to regulate migration to urban areas tightly. As I have already noted, the distinction between state, collective, and temporary

50. There are small numbers of workers, called *limitchiki*, who are given temporary urban residence permits, usually valid for three years, to enable them to take up employment in labor-short industries (Morton 1984: 5). See also Turovsky (1981: 192–93).

worker is not important in the U.S.S.R. After its rural workforce had shrunk to a minority, the Soviet government in 1971 extended its social security and state labor insurance to all collective farm workers (McAuley 1981: 200). By 1975 the regime repealed the prohibition against the movement of collective farmers and issued them internal passports (Wiles 1981: 28). China's population problem will force the regime to maintain its status distinctions for the foreseeable future.

Dependence on the enterprise is by no means completely foreign to the American experience. The communist enterprise represents the full development of a type of industrial dependence that was more common in the U.S. before World War I, in the brief flirtation with a paternalistic "welfare capitalism"—its most famous expression, the company town. Some large American manufacturers, for a period, actively promoted a model of industrial relations that would undercut unions and worker collective action by offering material benefits and creating dependence on the firm. Some large firms in small towns approached this ideal:

> The relatively small size of the company town, the personal relations that existed between managers and workers, the employee's economic dependence on the company (most company housing leases provided for eviction in the event of a discharge or a strike), and the virtual impossibility of holding a private meeting were major deterrents to concerted action. (Nelson 1975: 94)

This type of industrial dependence and its use as a strategy of control by management gave way under the impact of the union movement after the war. It became more important in large Japanese enterprises after World War II than it had previously been (Gordon 1985), and it has been a central feature of both Soviet and Chinese communist industrialization, where the dependence has taken a more complete form. In China, as in the American company town, this dependence has had an impact not only on workers' collective political capacity, but on the whole texture of authority relationships as well.

The communist version of industrial dependence, however, differs sharply from historical American and contemporary Japanese paternalism. The role of the communist party-state within the enterprise and the political dependence engendered by its characteristic forms of political organization have no parallel in the United States and Japan. Chinese shop floor organization, like its Soviet counter-part, is not content merely to head off independent political activity, it also seeks to mobilize workers' loyalties and discipline them through political organization. In both China and the Soviet Union, the communist party is organized in every workshop, it maintains a regular system of compulsory meetings and political surveillance, and it controls both union and youth league branches in workshops, which act as auxiliary organizations in charge of administering welfare and training selected young workers to be future leaders. Chinese enterprises have introduced some important innovations in this basic pattern: they stress small group organization to a great extent, they articulate a paternalistic managerial ideology that stresses education, verbal persuasion, and the mobilization of peer pressure, and they use a reward system that, for two decades, altered the flow of benefits according to political loyalty mixed with a diffuse sense of moral worth.

3. The Party-State in the Factory

It is impossible to dispute Seymour Martin Lipset's contention that "the nature of working class politics has been profoundly influenced by the variations in the historic conditions under which the proletariat entered the political arena" (1983: 1). Arguably the single most important historic condition is the state: not simply an arena in which politics takes place, it is an organization that directly structures political activity and political relationships, defining and enforcing the legitimate. This is true no less for a liberal-democratic regime than for an authoritarian one, and it is true whether one views the state as a relatively autonomous organization or as a class instrument. This implies, as Alfred Stepan (1978: xii) puts it, that "consolidated modern states should be compared not in terms of whether they structure such relationships, but in terms of the degree to which, and the means through which, they do so."

In a communist regime, the state has a double impact. Not only does it have the organized capacity to shape political relationships and activity more thoroughly than other types of authoritarian regimes; in China and the Soviet Union, the contemporary working class is itself a creation of the industrial drive directed by the party-state (see Walder 1984a). These party-states have not come to power faced with the prospect of defusing a radical and highly mobilized labor movement, as has been the experience of new authoritarian corporatist regimes in Brazil, Argentina, Chile, and elsewhere (see Stepan 1978: 89–113; Erickson 1977; Humphrey 1982). They have in reality created their modern working classes and mobilized them into the political organizations that are grassroots extensions of the party-state itself. In this chapter, I am concerned not with state policies regarding workers nor with related questions about the "class character" of a regime, but with the organizational characteristics that give the communist state the capacity to shape worker political association and activity in distinctive ways.

The Party-State and
the Working Class

Intolerance of independent unions is not a distinctive feature of contemporary communism. Other authoritarian regimes have been able to suppress them in an organized fashion for long periods of time. The distinctive organizational features of the communist party-state are that its cadres are present in every workshop in several capacities and that they strive to incorporate workers by mobilizing them into continuous political activity coordinated by the party itself. In this respect, they present a contrast with authoritarian corporatist regimes in Latin America and elsewhere, which are also noted for their organized approach to their relations with the working class, but which do not have this organizational capacity.

An authoritarian corporatist regime attempts to incorporate a working class by channeling its activity into officially "chartered" associations that are an extension of the government bureaucracy. The state seeks to move away from confrontation with politically mobilized workers by repressing independent organization and conceding to some of labor's demands. In turn, workers are "represented" in official unions by coopted leaders that negotiate directly with government ministries. This has the effect of demobilizing workers and, because part of the bargain is a restriction of political activity, of "keeping effective demand low" (Stepan 1978: 92). The official associations, for their part, are extensions of government ministries that seek to defuse conflict, in part through concessions to labor, but also by actively seeking to reconcile workers to their situation: "interests are taught to, transmitted to, and imposed upon members by associations" (Schmitter 1981: 295).

The defining feature of corporatism is that the state charters private interest groups, "incorporates" them into a stable relationship with relevant branches of the state bureaucracy, while at the same time it defines the legitimate means of pursuing interests to exclude independent and antagonistic political mobilization, which limits workers' ability to pursue their interests.[1] Corporatist regimes differ

---

1. Schmitter (1981: 292) defines corporatism as a system of interest representation in which "constituent units are organized into a limited number of singular, compulsory, hierarchically ordered and functionally differentiated categories, recognized, licensed, or encouraged by the state and granted a representational monopoly

in the degree to which they are imposed from above by an authoritarian regime that makes groups dependent on it or develop naturally "from below" within a pluralist framework, as organized interest groups come to a direct accommodation with relevant branches of the state bureaucracy.[2] Authoritarian corporatist regimes differ considerably in the balance of repression and compromise with which they treat labor.[3] All varieties of corporatism, however authoritarian or repressive they may be, differ from the communist state in one respect: they recognize as natural the existence of private interest groups. Corporatism ideally seeks to manage the associated conflicts for the good of the nation (as it is defined by the rulers); communism seeks to reorganize society in such a way that private interest groups cannot find organized expression or even a clear social identity.[4]

The difference, moreover, is not merely in the intentions and

---

within their respective categories in exchange for observing certain controls on their selection of leaders and articulation of demands and supports." This "chartering" of groups is conceptually analogous to the "estate society" (*standestaat*) that followed feudalism and preceded liberalism in seventeenth-century Europe (Poggi 1978). With regard to labor, it was reflected in the craft guilds in sixteenth- and seventeenth-century London that Unwin (1957) has described. Stepan (1978) offers a stimulating analysis of the history of this tradition of "organic statism," which he finds to continue as an active political ideal among elites in Latin America.

2. Schmitter (1981) distinguishes between "state" corporatism, the kind imposed from above by an authoritarian regime, and "societal" corporatism, the kind that emerges "from below," as organized interest groups develop stable relationships with branches of the government bureaucracy in liberal pluralist regimes.

3. Stepan (1978: 73–75), e.g., contrasts Peron's "inclusionary" stance toward organized labor with Pinochet's "exclusionary" regime.

4. Interestingly, the Chinese Nationalists' approach to organized labor in the 1930s and after 1945 was a "state corporatist" one, judging from Hershatter's (1986) description of the imposed mediation of labor disputes that was part of the Nationalists' effort to deradicalize unions and expunge communist influence in Tianjin.

Yugoslavia is a communist regime that appears to have moved close to the conceptual divide between state corporatism and communism. The regime has come to recognize that group interests are natural and legitimate, yet it retains its organized inhospitability to independent organization in the pursuit of those interests. Instead, officially chartered corporate groups, represented by workers' councils, are the recognized channel for the expression of the enterprise employees' collective interests. Single enterprise strikes have become widely tolerated in fact, if not in law, and there are hundreds each year (Denitch 1981; Comisso 1981). The party also has reportedly altered its organization and powers within the plant so that it plays a diminished role, apparently quite different from that of the party organization I describe in this chapter.

world view of the rulers: it is organizational. A communist regime has an array of organizational structures that supplement government institutions right down to the shop floor; institutions that a corporatist regime does not have. Corporatist regimes place state officials in national and local labor associations, and they place labor leaders on the state payroll. Some even place officials in factory offices to oversee the implementation of state labor policies. Local police agencies may infiltrate the unions and keep perceived radicals under surveillance. A communist regime, however, organizes the factory itself. Propaganda and security departments are active in every factory, along with personnel departments that are subordinate to party committees. The national party is organized in every factory, down to the workshop, and its members and loyal associates dominate leading positions from top to bottom. Communist youth league and union organizations, under the direct control of the factory party branch, mobilize workers to participate in political activities designed by the party. This is the framework of organization that allows communist regimes to neutralize "effective demand" from below, set investment priorities, redistribute wealth, and embark on the rapidly paced industrialization for which both China and the Soviet Union are famous.

The Political Organization of the Factory

The Chinese party-state is represented in the factory by two organizations that shape political relationships and interests right down to the shop floor. The first is the party itself. Every party member in the enterprise is part of an organization that is parallel to, yet separate from, the administrative structure of the enterprise. In a large enterprise with an active and well-run party organization, as many as 15 to 20 percent of the employees will be party members (Richman 1969: 761–62). Rank-and-file party members on the shop floor are organized into a party branch, usually divided into party groups (cells). The heads of these cells are members of the workshop party branch committees. The heads of these branch committees, party branch secretaries, are members of the enterprise party committee. The secretary of the party committee is the top political official in the enterprise. This interlocking network of committees and cells forms a separate hierarchy of communication, command, and discipline. The meetings of the committees and cells are separate from others held in the factory. They can be attended only by party members, and often the information revealed to members in these meetings is not to be revealed to nonmembers.[5] The role that party members play in the factory is described the same way by my informants as it is in party documents: "Every party member should propagate the Party's views, thoroughly carry out the Party's directives, obey Party decisions, complete their responsibilities in an outstanding manner, and use their own model behavior to influence and spur on the masses" (Central Committee 1961: 240).

A group of "activists" or "backbones" is closely associated with the party organization. The party carefully cultivates relationships with these activists and through them extends contol over the shop floor. Activists are people who are positively oriented to the party and who actively do its bidding. Many are members of the communist youth league, which has an organization that replicates, and is directly subordinate to, that of its parent organization. These activists are a minority of the workforce, roughly as numerous as party members themselves, that the party is grooming for eventual membership and often for later promotion to positions of leadership.

The party is able to build and maintain this network of loyalties through its influence over promotions, raises, and other rewards— in addition to its ability to apply punishments to those who challenge it.[6] To screen candidates for promotion and other rewards and to uncover "thought problems" that lead to resistance to party policies, the party must have accurate intelligence on the disposition of individual workers:

5. This is not to say that information never leaks out; such leaks are an important source of political rumors.

6. As a result, the party members dominate and in some periods have had a virtual monopoly on leading administrative positions. This is also true in the Soviet Union and the Eastern bloc countries. Bendix (1956: 355–57) describes an identical situation in East Germany of the 1950s; Bielasiak (1981: 99) cites Russian and Romanian survey data from the 1970s that show not only party dominance of leadership posts, but also party member dominance of all committees and voluntary associations in the workplace. Since 1979 China's party leaders have endorsed the principle that nonparty members should hold offices if they are especially qualified for the post. This is an argument for a modicum of flexibility, not for relinquishing party domination.

Party organizations at every level must keep abreast of the thinking of
the masses in the enterprise, and concretely solve thought problems
among the masses. In the enterprise, various people will need to be
worked on concretely. . . . Distinguish the advanced workers and staff
from the backward, in regard to both the level of their political consciousness and how well they complete their production tasks and work
responsibilities. (Central Committee 1961: 240)

The party employs two institutionalized means of intelligence
gathering and record keeping to help in this task. The first is a
system of surveillance that has both formal and informal compo-
nents. The formal component is the system of regular group meetings in workshops. When workers take part in these political meetings, they are not just talking among themselves—they are talking
directly to the party organization. "Study reports" are regularly
filled out by work group leaders or by activists who are appointed
to take notes:

> The group study leader leads all political study meetings. He sets the
> topics after getting orders from the branch secretary, leads the discus-
> sion, and writes up a report for the secretary on the results. . . . I held
> this position when I was an apprentice. The report sent to the party sec-
> retary includes the notes taken on what everybody says in the meetings.
> If there is no youth league activist in the group, they will transfer one in
> from a group that has two. (Informant no. 64)[7]

In addition, group leaders themselves give regular oral "small reports" (*xiaobao*) to the party branch on the situation in their
groups, which include information on the disposition of individual
workers. If it occurs that an individual, in the course of the work
day, or during a political study meeting, offers a dissenting opinion
that reflects a "thought problem" or reflects an unyielding or skep-
tical attitude with regard to a party policy, this will likely be reported. As the report makes its way up the party hierarchy, it sometimes comes to rest in the personnel department, where it may
become part of the worker's permanent file if the official in charge
deems the matter to be serious.

More informally, workers and, especially, activists are encour-

7. Frolic (1980: 163) offers a similar emigre account of factory group study
meetings.

aged to report utterances and actions of their coworkers that reflect dissent or "thought problems." Some activists "inform on others behind their backs. For example, if we said something in the [factory] dormitory that showed dissatisfaction with the leaders, somehow the leaders would know about it only two days later" (informant no. 50). In political meetings, especially those in which group criticism takes place, the insecurity engendered by informers often spurs workers to reveal more about their own thoughts and actions than would otherwise be the case, because they can never be sure what may already have been reported.

A second mechanism is the system of political dossiers (*dang'an*)— the files kept by the party staff, usually of the personnel department, on every permanent employee except the top leaders. These records contain a complete political history of the employee and immediate family members: class background, occupational status, political punishments, and allegiances before 1949.

> They kept the files in a special room and each year gave [the white-collar employees] a form to fill out on themselves and their relatives. People were afraid to write incorrect information on these forms because [an inconsistency] could be used against us later on. So I kept an extra copy of one year's form in my desk to make sure that the next year I would make no mistakes. (Informant no. 11)

Reports of informers, evaluations made by superiors, serious criticisms, warnings, and other punishments are all recorded here. The dossier stays with the worker throughout his or her life. If there is a transfer or a job change, the file is transferred also. Workers have no right to see their files, and there is a high degree of uncertainty over the eventual consequences of detrimental materials. The files are regularly consulted when reviewing candidates for promotions or raises, and they can even influence applications for housing, the severity of punishments for future transgressions or political offenses, or the selection of targets in political campaigns:

> The biggest political campaign [of the mid-1970s] was right before I left [in 1979]: "Grasp firmly the work of rehabilitation" and "Seriously punish those who have committed crimes." They punished two kinds of people. Those who had committed crimes during the Cultural Revolution and those who were counterrevolutionary, dissatisfied with socialism. This meant talking with foreigners, saying bad things about

China. You would then be given a counterrevolutionary label [in your dossier]. Anyway, they pulled out the dossiers on all the people in the unit, to see whether or not their cases had been disposed of correctly [in the past]. (Informant no. 35)

People who had been declared "rightists" in earlier campaigns, or whose family had been members of exploiting classes, or were closely involved with the Nationalist government before 1949 were especially unlucky in this connection.

When orders came down to criticize a certain type of person, it just didn't do to claim that the factory had no such type of person. So they had to select somebody for criticism, and this usually ended up being the people with suspicious class backgrounds. (Informant no. 8)

They investigated a lot of people [during the "4 cleans" campaign of 1965], in fact, too many, both cadres and masses. They looked into people's files and especially investigated those with bad class backgrounds. In the work groups, we were told to criticize at least two people. In our group we could not find anyone with a problem, so they said to look not just for corruption and life-style problems but also at political thought. They suggested that this would be especially appropriate if the person had a bad class background. They would then be criticized. (Informant no. 12)

Whether or not they have bad class backgrounds or other "historical problems" in their dossiers, workers are acutely concerned to keep detrimental reports out of their files, especially since the future effects of such information are unpredictable. A black mark recorded in a file is usually irreversible and can haunt an individual throughout his or her life.[8]

The second institution, distinct from the party, is the factory security department. It is the local arm of the state public security bureau and is at the same time under the direction of the factory party committee.[9] It routinely acts to "safeguard state property" in the factory, but, in those rare instances when open resistance to authority is offered or when political or criminal offenses are com-

8. Not surprisingly, these dossiers were a major target of attacks by radical groups in the Cultural Revolution. A decade earlier, during the "thaw" of the 1957 Hundred Flowers period, a local Chinese newspaper printed the following criticism of the dossier system: "The personnel department normally acts as a police station, but once a campaign starts, it becomes a court" (quoted in Lee 1982: 19).

9. This was recently reaffirmed by a government decision that restricted the independence of factory security departments (People's Daily 1980).

mitted, the security department is authorized to act. Security departments are not usually staffed by workers who have been promoted from the shop floor and who therefore might have sympathy with the rank and file. Instead, the departments are usually staffed from outside by demobilized soldiers, usually party members, disciplined through years of military indoctrination and regimentation.[10] Their social backgrounds (often from rural areas, where the army gets most of its recruits), experiences, and outlook are quite different from the average worker's. In some factories, security departments have maintained their own networks of informants and "security workers" among employees on the shop floor:

> The security workers (*zhi'an baowei yuan*) were the eyes and ears of the security department. They did basic level investigation work for them. The work of the security department began to increase when Mao started to raise slogans about class struggle . . . each shop had a worker who was appointed "security chief," not a real office position but something done in one's spare time. The "security chief" led all the security workers in the small groups . . . they were not security cadres, just informers. All of them were considered politically reliable and were party members. Did a person say he was unhappy with the food supply? Why is that person expressing opinions about things? The security department would hear reports on these matters and put the material in people's files. . . . It was very scary when people were confronted with things they had said five years before. (Informant no. 64)

Security departments, in addition, can organize their own investigations of suspected employees. They have powers of interrogation and can question friends, coworkers, and relatives about a suspect's behavior. Connected with the municipal branch of the public security bureau, they can trace workers' movements outside a factory or put their homes under surveillance. They are empowered to enact a wide range of administrative punishments for which there are no trials or legal appeals, ranging from putting a worker under a kind of probation known as "political control" to turning them over to a prison or labor reform camp. These measures are not routinely

10. This fact, reported by G. White (1980), was confirmed by several informants: "A major source of cadres for the security department is demobilized soldiers. The army was a training ground for cadres. The security department was always, certainly, led by a demobilized soldier" (informant no. 68). This link with the military sometimes takes on a more formal shape: in at least some factories, the security department recruits workers for military service.

taken, but most workers have seen public security personnel in action at some time in their work experience.

One of my informants (no. 71) had a minor brush with his factory's security department in the mid-1970s:

> Once I told a joke about a fair lady in the "Forbidden City." I was just joking around. The next day, there was an announcement over the public address system: "Zhang San, report to the security department." They wanted to know why I told the joke, what it really meant, who told it to me. Back in those days, if you didn't confess, then things got worse. I said, "it was just a joke, I don't remember where I heard it and I don't know what it means." They looked suspicious, and told me it was about Jiang Qing [Mao's wife, and a leader of the radical Maoist faction]. Two days later, they called me to their office again, and two guys from the Public Security Bureau interrogated me. They told me the joke was a counterrevolutionary rumor aimed at comrade Jiang Qing. They gave me a thorough questioning. They really wanted to know where I heard it. . . . There were other examples too. Once some worker wrote "Down with Mao!" on a poster, and there was a big investigation and a mass meeting about that. Another time a worker scribbled a bunch of characters on a piece of scrap paper. Some security cadre thought he could make out the words "Na-tion-al-ist Par-ty." They launched an investigation.

Not all cases involve such minor matters. Security departments have also responded to genuine protest in a coordinated fashion. One major instance was in 1976, when accumulated dissatisfactions broke out in Beijing (and other major cities) in a two-day demonstration and riot labeled the Tiananmen Incident. Citizens gathered at a revolutionary shrine on a traditional day of remembrance for the dead to commemorate the late Premier Zhou Enlai, a widely perceived opponent of the radical Maoist faction. Security forces attempted to suppress the dissident outpouring of support for him, and a violent riot ensued (see Zweig 1978; Louie and Louie 1981). In the weeks to come, in what has since been described in the post-Mao press as a "reign of white terror," security departments, searching for those involved, carried out investigations in factories and other places of work:

> There were many workers who were upset about the treatment of Zhou Enlai's funeral, and many were involved in the Tiananmen Incident. It's not clear whether they really loved Zhou all that much, but this was a way to protest the restoration of the old policies. Before the Qingming

festival that year, many workers made wreaths at work. At Beijing #2 Steel Factory, they made a steel wreath 20 feet high and brought it to the square. The authorities thought something was going to happen at Qingming, and they told the workers it was forbidden to go downtown. But that day many factories were empty. Later, the security departments arrested a lot of workers, and they interrogated all those who were absent from work that day about where they were, who they saw. The investigation went on for weeks. (Informant no. 71)

The significance of this network of political organization is that it not only makes organized worker resistance and even informal coordination of action difficult, but it creates a cross-cutting organization into which worker activity is absorbed. It provides a sharp contrast with the norm in other industrial regimes, in which the structure of the informal work group is seen to structure the formal organizations as well.[11] This, in concrete terms, is what it means to say that the communist party-state "penetrates" potential interest groups and organizes them in a way that authoritarian corporatist regimes are unable to.

The "Foreman's Empire" on the Shop Floor

The workshop (*chejian*) office is the lowest point in the factory hierarchy at which there is a party branch secretary and full-time staff. It is also the province of the shop director—the equivalent, in small shops, of the foreman. The large shop is divided into a number of work sections (*gongduan*), led by section chiefs who are the equivalent of the foreman. The lowest unit in every shop is the production group (literally, "production small group" [*shengchan xiaozu*]), usually numbering no more than a dozen workers, led by a worker designated as the group leader.

The shop director has full responsibility for production within the shop, and in these matters he or she is directly subordinate to

11. Sabel (1982: 171) says:

The thread with which this strategic pattern is woven is the solidarity of the work group. Without such solidarity, management cannot be forced to concede advantageous work rules; without solidarity, management can bribe individual workers to break the rules that do exist, rewarding them for setting standards of performance that others must follow or for betraying the groups' accumulated knowledge about machines and processes.

the factory production department, its chief engineer, and ultimately the factory director. But, in many other administrative matters, notably in personnel and wage decisions within the shop, in disciplinary actions, in the distribution of fringe benefits and the performance of "sociopolitical services," the shop office has a large measure of discretion. The party branch secretary shares in the exercise of this discretion.

The communist enterprise is usually viewed as highly "bureaucratic" because of the multitude of services and goods it distributes, but the administration of these matters is in fact highly decentralized. In almost all cases, shop officials will either make decisions unilaterally and submit them to staff departments for routine approval or they will make a recommendation that guides the action taken by office staff. This practice relieves department offices of an enormous administrative burden, but convenience is not the sole reason. Without wide workshop discretion in personnel, disciplinary, and distributional decisions, the party organization would be robbed of the resources necessary to exercise political discipline and recruit and reward loyal activists.

This standard communist practice differs strikingly from those in large American and Japanese enterprises. In both these countries, staff departments (and in the case of the United States, unions) have established rules that have removed almost all of the discretion that foremen exercised early in this century in contracting systems. In the United States this loss of foreman control has culminated in the "internal labor market," governed by staff department regulations and voluntary worker "bids" (see Kochan and Cappelli 1984; Jacoby 1984). Indeed, the labor market analogy itself indicates how different things are from the days of the turn-of-the-century foreman's empire. Burawoy's (1983: 593–94) description of the Chicago machine tool plant in which he worked conveys this lack of personal dependence: "Grievances related to the job can be resolved by the employee simply bidding on another job . . . the possibility of bidding off a job gives the worker a certain autonomy vis-à-vis-first-line supervision. If a foreman begins to give trouble, the operator can simply bid off the job to another section."

In large Japanese enterprises, pay and fringe benefits are usually determined jointly by three factors: an automatic seniority grade, a "skill grade" attached to the job performed, and an "ability grade" determined by standardized tests. People are treated differently according to statuses assigned by staff departments. Much has been written about the differences between Japanese and American labor practices, but, from the perspective of communist practice, they share a common characteristic. Despite the fact that Japanese and American staff departments employ different personnel practices, in neither country does the staff department allow foremen wide discretion in these matters. In Japan, not only are the fringe benefits of "paternalism" determined by a status assigned by staff offices, but there is no Japanese equivalent of rationing, "sociopolitical services," or the political career (see Clark 1979: 180–220; Dore 1973: 201–21; Cole 1979: 72–135).

The discretion exercised jointly by the shop director and party branch secretary appears to be a throwback to the foreman's empire of the contracting era of factory production in many parts of the world, including Japan, the United States, and China itself. The analogy is instructive, but there are three differences. First, the communist shop director or section chief does not exercise the authority in production that the contractor-foreman of the past did. Second, the communist foreman does not have an unrestrained ability to hire and fire without answering to factory staff. Third, the communist foreman controls a much wider array of rewards and punishments than did the foreman-contractor of a past era. The dependence engendered by the communist pattern has a different configuration but is much more broadly based. Furthermore, it is just as personal a form of dependence as "premodern" ones.

Wage raises, promotions, monthly and year-end bonuses, and favorable job assignments are the most visible of the reward decisions made by workshop leaders. These decisions are made by the shop director and party branch secretary. They rely on shop production statistics, and especially on the oral recommendations of group leaders or (in a large shop) section chiefs. Sometimes they will convene a committee meeting of shop officials and section chiefs to hear discussions and recommendations. The lists of people chosen to receive these rewards will be submitted to the plant management, often in committee meetings analogous to those held in the shop. The recommendations do not go to the office staff of the labor and wages department, but to ad hoc committees of high-level line management and party officials. Except in the case of wage raises, where the final list may be pared down due to financial considerations, high-level approval is a routine matter. The shop office and branch committee, after all, are the only sources of information that top management has on the candidates.

The shop office makes many other decisions, again relying on the advice of section chiefs or group leaders, who act as brokers in many matters.[12] Final approval of applications for an apartment are made by officials in the general affairs (or administration) department of an enterprise, but these decisions are usually taken on the basis of recommendations of party branch secretaries and shop directors:

> The shop director gives his opinion to the housing office. You see, the application is made through the shop director. The group leader must verify that housing is really needed. The forms are sent up to the shop office, and shop cadres help the worker fill them out. . . . After the application is made, the shop leaders have a meeting to decide if the person really needs housing. . . . They don't always approve the application. They may strongly support you if they like you. (Informant no. 72)

The distribution of ration coupons for scarce consumer durables is also left to the discretion of shop officials, as is the distribution of extra ration coupons for selected staple foods. In some factories, the general affairs department simply allocates a fixed number of apartments, bicycle coupons, or sporting tickets to each shop for them to distribute as they see fit. Through shop officials, jobs can be arranged for employees' children or spouses as temporary workers or as workers in an affiliated collective enterprise. Permission for personal leave and annual leave is granted by shop officials, as is the separate decision of whether to grant leave with pay or, if the leave is for the purpose of visiting a spouse assigned to work elsewhere, whether to grant supplements for travel and meals:[13]

12. As this discussion implies, responsibility and ultimate powers are diffuse. These decisions are supposed to be consensual ones, taken by the leaders of the shop after discussion among themselves, but whether the party branch secretary or shop director has the upper hand, and whether or not they disagree in these matters in the first place, is something that varies with the factories and individuals involved. When the party has politicized factory management, branch secretaries were thrust into the leading position, and pressure was placed on them to exercise discretion according to the party's official political standards. When the party has attempted to depoliticize management, the shop director exercises more discretion. But discretion is there in any case.

13. Regulations regarding eligibility for paid leave are rather complicated, and they lead to many unsolved questions about who is eligible for what kinds of paid leave and what kinds of travel supplements (see State Council 1958).

For applications to visit your family and so forth, you first apply to the section head, and he passes the request up to the shop, and the shop passes it up to the appropriate department for approval. Shop leaders can't really put pressure on workers by refusing applications for things that are spelled out in national regulations, like annual home leave. But for all the things that aren't spelled out in the regulations, the leaders can deny things to people they don't like. (Informant no. 71)

Whether or not to grant a loan or welfare payments to an employee with low family income is also decided by shop officials:

For subsidies and loans, the section leaders have a meeting to decide whether the person really needs it, and how big it should be. They rank people and send the applications up to the top for approval. They can decide how large the subsidy will be. They try to find out about the worker's family situation. . . . Their group leaders give their opinions too. . . . Sometimes people who don't need subsidies get them; sometimes the ones who need them badly don't get large enough ones. There are no fixed regulations, no fixed amounts. It works this way for wage raises too. (Informant no. 76)

If you have an emergency, like a death in the family, you can ask the shop leaders to borrow money, and they decide. . . . The shop uses their control of housing, jobs for relatives, and loans to control workers. For loans, you have to fill out a form, get the group leader's approval, and then the shop leaders have a meeting to decide. You can't just go and apply at the union headquarters. The shop leaders control the applications. (Informant no. 72)

Even the size of the benefits provided by labor insurance regulations can be made to vary considerably according to administrative interpretations of one's accumulated seniority and whether or not one is eligible for specific benefits.[14] Shop officials have a fairly wide range of discretion within the regulations governing many of these benefits. If they are so inclined, they can also expand this range of discretion by taking advantage of confusion or inconsistencies in

14. As Kallgren (1968) notes repeatedly, confusion often surrounds the method of determining seniority, especially if the employee transferred from a collective sector enterprise (common in the 1950s during the consolidation and nationalization of the industrial sector), served in the military, or was subject to political punishment. Many of the documents in the collection of labor and wage documents from Fujian (Planning Commission 1973) were prompted precisely by these recurring questions, e.g., Ministry of Labor (1964). The ambiguity of many regulations leaves considerable scope for official discretion.

regulations, or by simply bending or breaking the rules.[15] In all of these cases, the shop director not only sends recommendations to staff management but, in many cases, actually screens requests. If a shop director or section chief opposes an application or appeal, it will never reach the staff department concerned.

Worker dependence on their supervisors is highlighted by the fact that discretion can be used to punish workers by refusing to exercise it in their favor. Selected individuals can be denied bonuses and raises to which they might otherwise be entitled based on their work performance. Their applications for housing can be ignored. Requests for personal or home leave can be denied, or granted at an inconvenient time, or granted without pay or travel supplements. Requests for certain extra rations, supplements, or loans can be denied, delayed, or only partially met. A desirable transfer can be blocked by denying the employee permission to leave the work unit, or an undesirable transfer can be arranged.[16] Permission for early retirement can be denied, or seniority and eligibility for certain benefits can be calculated in the least favorable way.[17] Permission to marry or divorce, something required of one's work unit, can also be withheld. In a wide variety of ways, supervisors can selectively penalize individual workers.

There are also a variety of administrative punishments that can be meted out to individuals whose behavior transgresses acceptable bounds. The mildest of these is a formal criticism and self-criticism session in the work group—something that may be uncomfortable

15. Many of the documents in the Fujian volume warn officials to follow regulations apparently widely ignored in the past. Informants indicate that most of the rules are not clearly understood by employees, who at any rate do not have a right to see the documents that govern their treatment. This expands the discretion of officials in deciding when to enforce the regulations and when to bend them. Haraszti (1979: 95–97) also notes that Hungarian workers have no right to see their "collective agreements" and recounts an anecdote describing his own efforts to see a copy. He concludes, "Areas of responsibility are vaguely indicated; lines are drawn sharply only when the interests of the company demand it. Within these limits, it is always left to the relevant chief to decide" (ibid.: 96).

16. The worst kind of undesirable transfer—to be "sent down" to a small town or rural area—has been a common punitive sanction against political targets. This involves the loss of housing and urban registration. Sometimes it involves transfer away from family and friends. One million people were "sent down" in this manner as "bad elements" from 1966 to 1976 alone (Zhang and Chen 1981).

17. The most open such practice is the loss of seniority (and therefore deprivation or reduction of pensions and other benefits) for those who are given political labels or who receive other punishments during political campaigns (State Council 1957b; Central Committee 1959; National Labor Federation 1965).

but actually has few more lasting consequences than losing a month's bonus. More serious is a mass criticism or repudiation meeting held in a shop, in which the criticisms are much harsher and which may lead to detrimental material being placed in one's dossier. A worker may also have an official reprimand (*jiguo*) placed in his or her dossier (which definitely affects wage raises and all other rewards). More serious still is a temporary suspension, or being put "under supervision" (*jiandu*) by the plant security department.[18] The ultimate sanctions are expulsion, which means the permanent termination of state-sector employment, or being turned over to the public security bureau for administratively determined sentences of imprisonment or labor reform.[19]

For all of these punishments, there is no formal system of hearing or appeal and no fixed procedure for establishing innocence or guilt. The crucial step is the decision of the shop director and branch secretary to turn the case over to higher authorities. Unless they decide to do so, there will be no formal reprimand, and the plant administration or security department will not become involved. The decision to send the case upward is made after shop officials have discussed the case thoroughly, sometimes interviewing the group leader and the accused. One of the most important factors in their decision is the attitude of the transgressor. Dependent on official judgment in these matters, the only thing that an individual can do to lessen the consequences is to acknowledge his or her errors fully and rapidly, exhibit contrition and show a willingness to reform one's ways. Official regulations, in fact, instruct lighter punishment for those who quickly acknowledge their guilt and pledge to reform.

The most extreme form of shop control over punishment that I have encountered was reported by a worker (informant no. 72) whose factory, during the middle 1970s, ran its own small-scale "labor reform" program on farmland under its control:

18. When an employee is "under supervision," he or she must report to the security department daily and write periodic self-criticisms that report on their progress in correcting their errant thoughts. (All such material is placed in the dossier, along with the security department's evaluation of the material.) At the end of the probationary period (usually six months to a year), the security department may decide, based on the employee's deportment and attitude, whether to end the period of supervision, extend it, or expel the individual from the enterprise.

19. This system of regulations, recently revised, is outlined in State Council (1982b).

The shop head had the power to send you down to the farm for labor if he didn't like you. He sent me there twice—for about one week each time. Some people were sent for a month. The shop director didn't like me. He said I wasn't a socialist worker, but a bourgeois intellectual. He had me criticized in the group several times. . . . If the shop director didn't like you, you were out of luck. The shop director arranged this himself, not the top leaders.

This Chinese pattern of personal dependence on supervisors is similar, at least in its general outlines, to Soviet patterns. The Soviet Union began in the 1930s to use better housing, larger rations, and superior welfare benefits to reward politically loyal and disciplined workers, setting a pattern that has culminated in the contemporary foreman's empire (Barber 1980: 9; Schwarz 1952: chap. 3; McAuley 1981: 219–20). There is suggestive evidence of similar practices, even in the Eastern bloc countries noted for liberal economic reform. Miklos Haraszti's description of the powers of foremen in his 1970s Budapest tractor factory, except for the ability to hire and fire freely, could have been of a factory in Shanghai:

> They are emperors here. They hold us all in their hands. They dole out favors as they see fit. . . . The foreman doesn't just organize our work: first and foremost he organizes *us*. The foremen fix our pay, our jobs, our overtime, our bonuses, and the deductions for excessive rejects. They decide when we go on holiday; write character reports on us for any arm of the state which requests them; pass on assessments of those who apply for further training or request a passport; they supervise trade union activities in the section; they hire, fire, arrange transfers, grant leave, impose fines, give bonuses. Their signatures are essential to authorize any kind of departure from routine. (1979: 86–87).[20]

The Chinese Work Group System

Chinese enterprises have introduced an important structural innovation in this generic communist pattern. The authority of shop directors and section chiefs is parceled out to yet another level of organization—the small group. Soviet and Eastern European

20. Although the dissident intellectual Haraszti was outraged by this perceived violation of socialist ideals, most of my Chinese informants appeared to view the foreman's prerogatives as natural and did not point out this situation as worthy of note unless they had worked under an official they considered especially arbitrary and dictatorial.

work sections are commonly divided into "brigades," which are designated by shop leaders for purposes of socialist labor competitions. But they do not constitute, as they do in China, an intense focus of political and managerial activity.[21] Work group leaders are literally extensions of the section chief and shop director. Appointed by the shop director and party branch secretary because of their loyalty and trustworthiness, they lead their coworkers in a variety of daily tasks. Through their reports and recommendations to their superiors, they exercise a portion of the discretion lodged at the workshop level. The dependence on supervisors common in communist enterprises is, therefore, further personalized in China, because first-level supervision is in fact by a coworker with whom one is in continuous contact.

Group Leaders as Political Brokers

Group leaders are political brokers in the fullest sense of the term. Shop directors and section chiefs ask them to ensure that the group meets all its production quotas, complies with requests for overtime, and carries out such political meetings and activities as the party branch deems necessary. It is through them that management communicates with the workforce. Group leaders relay messages and tasks from above; they also keep shop directors and party branch secretaries abreast of worker responses and moods. Group leaders who perform their tasks well—regularly meeting demands from above and rarely stressing the obstacles facing them or opposition from workers—are often promoted to leadership positions in the section or workshop and reclassified as administrative personnel.

Group leaders must win the cooperation of workers in these tasks, and an important part of this is to keep conflict within the group to a minimum. Chinese work groups perform the latent function of defusing conflict between labor and management over pay and bottling it up within the small group. Workers do not deal with shop management on a regular basis; they deal mainly with other workers who represent management—their group leaders. Because

21. Haraszti's (1979: 66–67) experience was an extreme case of this pattern: "Almost everyone in the section is a member of a brigade. After two months, I learned that I had been attached to the 'First of May' brigade; to this day, I have no idea who the other members are. Twice a year, usually on a feast day, the foreman calls us into his office to let us know whether we have won the right to a special bonus."

pay decisions are made within the group, conflict is usually contained within it. Informants regularly expressed hostility to activists and group leaders but did so less often toward shop and staff management. Both informants and news articles describe arguments within work groups over pay matters but almost never mention group confrontation with line managers. In effect, workers are left to iron out conflicts over tasks and pay among themselves, with group leaders and activists on one side and the rank and file on the other. Group leaders play a crucial mediating role within the group, in effect releasing shop management from direct involvement in supervising the workforce.

Group leaders not only relay demands from above, but they also relay worker requests and applications upward. Group leaders are the workers' primary link with shop management. Group leaders relay evaluations of workers for raises and promotions and often requests for personal leave, paid vacations, home leave, travel supplements, housing assignments, extra ration coupons, loans, relief payments, or permission to travel. For many of these things, decisions are made by the shop leaders in consultation with the group leader, whose recommendation is crucial. Group leaders, therefore, serve as a communications link; they also have a margin of influence over the distribution of many of the factory's resources and benefits. This is the main source of their personal authority:

> Most group leaders can't act like cadres. They don't really have that much power and really aren't that high in status. . . . The power of the group leaders really comes from their ability to report to the leaders above: "He's not a good worker," or "He doesn't listen to orders." That's where their power comes from. The upper levels listen to them. (Informant no. 71)

Group leaders are the lowest rung of shop leadership, are classified as ordinary workers, and usually receive no extra pay for the job. Like others in the group, they hold fixed production posts.[22] The first requirement of group leaders is that they be good at their jobs, experienced, and hard working: if they lacked these qualities,

---

22. Group leaders' precise job responsibilities vary with the production technology. In some factories they are given lighter production tasks and heavier supervisory responsibilities. Although group leaders do not formally get any extra pay for the job, in practice they get the largest bonuses and are the first to be given pay raises and promotions.

they could not keep the respect of their coworkers, nor could they manage to lead the group while completing their own production tasks: "The group leaders are excellent workers, and often they are model workers. They work hard. They come in early and leave late, and oversee everything in the group. The group leaders are crucial. Without them, production would be very hard to arrange. . . . They are often selected model workers and get prizes at the end of the year" (Informant no. 56).

However, group leaders are at the same time considered the representatives of both shop management and the workshop party branch. They are workers who represent the leadership to other workers:

> Sometimes there were meetings after the shift with the shop director to discuss plan completion, tasks, technical problems in production. The group leader's job is to meet with workers, explain things, talk things over with them, find out whether they can work overtime, and so forth. If there are disagreements with workers or expected problems in convincing workers to do something, they work especially hard at these talks. (Informant no. 24)

Given this crucial pivotal role, group leaders are chosen not only for their technical competence, but also for their political reliability and acceptability to the party branch. If they are not already party members, they are at least recognized activists or youth league members who are being groomed for possible admission to the party. They are, therefore, subject to the orders of line managers as well as to the discipline of the party branch.

Typical of the broker role, group leaders must play a balancing game between group members and their own superiors. They must yield enough to group members' inclinations to win their cooperation, but they must also regularly carry out their superiors' directives. Group leaders who become too attentive to worker demands will be replaced or transferred to another group. On the other hand, group leaders who antagonize or alienate their group to such an extent that it leads to chronic arguing or a decline in group performance will suffer the same fate. Group leaders, therefore, will often yield on small issues, occasionally fail to report workers for infractions of rules, and try to convince section chiefs to lower quotas or increase bonuses when it seems opportune to do so. Group leaders will seek to cultivate a loyal follower or two who will provide support whenever needed. They also try to keep conflict within the group to a minimum, often by distributing bonus pay in a relatively equal fashion and avoiding strict job evaluations for raises and bonuses, which lead to the most common conflicts within groups.

Work Group Organization

Work groups perform four functions. First, they are responsible for the routine communication of orders and for organizing production and solving problems on a daily basis: "The group leaders are responsible for receiving the month's task from the managers, and then for planning and arranging (the group's) production . . . they are responsible for making work assignments, teaching workers how to do things, and deciding what to produce on what day" (Informant no. 39).

Daily orders received from the shop office or notices distributed by staff offices are read out to workers in the group meetings held each day either for half an hour before the shift, half an hour after, or both. Preshift meetings are the place where work assignments are made for the day. If problems should arise in the course of work that require more than the half-hour allotted to postshift meetings—a minor machinery malfunction or a recurring quality problem, for example—the group leader will convene a formal "production meeting" (*shengchan huiyi*) or "discussion meeting" (*pengtou hui*) for longer periods after the shift or in the evenings after mealtime. Such meetings may also be held throughout the plant or shop at the instigation of higher levels of management, when they seek resolution of a recurring problem that is common throughout the plant—usually, quality problems or waste of raw materials. Worker suggestions are actively solicited, especially because it is precisely the routine production problems about which experienced production workers are most knowledgeable.

Second, work groups perform a broad range of managerial and record-keeping tasks that are not normally performed on the shop floor in other industrial settings. Although the extent may vary according to the production technology, work groups are usually the basic unit of statistical reporting and accounting. There are two reasons for this. First, materials shortages are chronic in industry, necessitating an internal rationing system for materials that requires an accounting of the use of supplies by each subunit of the enterprise.

As a former plant executive explained, comparing these arrangements with his later factory experience in Hong Kong,

> In China there are many more quotas: for output, quality, use of materials, ordering of materials, and so forth. But in Hong Kong there are no quotas. If you want more materials, you just order them. As a result, there are many more records kept by the small group in China. Materials ordered and received, product quality, output for each worker, materials used, working hours, attendance, and other things are all recorded by the group leader himself. But in Hong Kong the foreman only records the output and quality of each worker and hands it over to the clerk. (Informant no. 5)

China's command economy also requires that enterprise operational plans be split up into quarterly, monthly, and ten-day targets for each subunit of the enterprise, down to the work group level. For most periods, work groups have supplied detailed daily statistics on their output and materials consumption so that staff planners can anticipate imbalances and bottlenecks that might prevent the enterprise from meeting its targets.

As a result, there is a great deal of routine inspection and paperwork within small groups, especially in factories where production is done in batches (such as machine building). Work groups are responsible for reporting their progress in daily production reports, and they must take measures to ensure that their progress is up to the standards set for them. Group leaders rarely perform all of the necessary task themselves—they routinely parcel out duties to different workers in the group, who perform them in their spare time or before or after the shift. Group leaders usually come to rely heavily on the hard-working and cooperative workers who are referred to as the "activists" or "backbones" of the group. These people help fill out daily production reports and check informally on the quality of the product (because below-standard output is not counted toward completion of targets). They help younger workers perform difficult operations and make sure that tools and materials checked out to the group are accounted for. During some periods, particularly in 1957–1958 and 1978–1979, national campaigns have urged enterprises to institute formal "worker-manager" (*gongren guanliyuan*) systems in small groups, where these group tasks are parceled out formally to individuals who are elected by the group and given the titles "statistician," "safetyman," or "tool custodian"—with the object of involving everyone in routine management jobs and heightening their consciousness of managerial problems (see Walder 1981). Formal job definitions are vague in Chinese industry to begin with, and these added tasks are a simple extension of this feature of China's industrial relations.[23]

Third, work groups are responsible not only for ensuring that work discipline is sufficient to meet group targets, but they are also responsible for evaluating worker performance for periodic bonuses and raises. Employees whose slack performance threatens the attainment of group goals will first be talked to informally by the group leader, and, if no change results, the employee will be criticized and called on to justify his or her lax performance in a group meeting:

> If someone's work wasn't good, they did educational work. This was the job of the party organization. They figured if your thought was good, then your work would be good. If your work was not good, then you must have some sort of thought problem. So they would talk to the person: What's the problem? Having family trouble? Money problems? The second step is to criticize the person in the small group. There are all kinds of organizations to apply pressure: the union, communist youth league, and the party members. The third step is to take away the bonus. (Informant no. 44)

Many enterprises will not normally release bonus funds to members of a work group unless the group as a whole meets its targets. In these cases, there is a definite material incentive for other group members to report and criticize lax behavior. Peer pressure operates because the fate of the group as a whole can be negatively influenced by the negligence of an individual. When bonus funds are released to a group, the group convenes a "bonus assessment meeting" (*ping jiang huiyi*)—usually monthly, but sometimes quarterly—to assess the performance of each member. First they decide whether an individual is deserving of a bonus at all, and then they decide how large the bonus will be. When national wage readjustments permit each enterprise to reclassify the wage grades of a fixed proportion of the labor force, work groups will meet after work for as long as it takes to thoroughly assess each worker's long-term perfor-

---

23. These are referred to as "responsibilities to participate in the management of the factory," and they were viewed as "responsibilities" by my informants (see Central Committee 1961: art. 61).

mance and eligibility for a raise. Employees will not be considered for a raise unless their work group first nominates them to shop management.[24]

Finally, work groups are also political study groups, and they are the site for political education, criticism and self-criticism, and the exercise of political control. The number of meetings set aside for these activities varies according to the national political climate, and in fact the content and volume of political meetings have varied enormously over the past 30 years:

> They have not completely abolished political study [since the death of Mao in 1976], although they no longer have a fixed system of political study every Thursday, as they used to. Now when an important document is released, they will hold a meeting to read it. But other than that, meetings are strictly for business. Before the Gang of Four fell [shortly after the death of Mao], we had political study at least four evenings a week. During the high tides of campaigns, we had five nights a week plus one hour on Sundays. For the criticism of Deng Xiaoping in 1976, we met seven days a week, and the meetings went on until 11 P.M. . . . During the period before 1976, it was not uncommon to stop production to study criticisms of Lin Biao and Confucius or study the theory of the dictatorship of the proletariat. (Informant no. 22)

This account accurately reflects the fluctuation in the intensity of political study over the years, but it describes only formal political study. There are more practical, routine applications of group political meetings as well—to make work tasks a political responsibility:

> When introducing tasks, or calling for overtime [often uncompensated or undercompensated], you need meetings to explain the reasons to workers. If they don't do this kind of ideological work, things just won't work out. . . . So the branch secretary's job is a very busy one. . . . He has to continuously combine ideological work with production tasks. (Informant no. 24)

Another worker (informant no. 17) was more clear about how the link between ideological work and production was made, show-

24. In the wage readjustment of 1983–1984, national policy, for the first time, encouraged factories not to use group assessments because of the dangers of conflict and the levelling effects of face-to-face assessments (see Ministry of Labor and Personnel 1983b).

ing how political study meetings often blended with evaluations of
worker performance:

> During the "Criticize Lin, Criticize Confucius" campaign [1974], we
> studied and also had a "high tide of production" campaign. They
> reached the conclusion in the meetings that we should make greater con-
> tributions to socialism, and we were encouraged to increase output. If it
> went down, we would be criticized one by one. They always discussed
> the study documents together with the evaluation of each person's
> work performance.

In addition to straightforward political education and meetings
designed to spur enthusiasm for production, group meetings may
also be called in order to criticize the behavior of one or more members of the group and require them to engage in self-criticism and
pledge to reform. This typically is linked with factory-wide campaigns to enforce work discipline, stop pilferage of supplies, and
so forth:

> If a worker stole materials to make furniture for himself, or if he fixed
> his bicycle during working hours, and the leaders caught him, he would
> be used as a bad example and be criticized by the party cadres at a big
> meeting. In their political study groups, the workers then had criticism
> and self-criticism: "Did you steal something too?" People would say
> things like, "Even though I didn't steal something, I brought my kids
> into the factory to take a shower. This was bourgeois thinking, because
> they aren't covered by state benefits." I would say, "I apologize to the
> party because during work I studied English. Even though I didn't steal
> anything, my thinking is still backward." Someone else would say, "I feel
> sorry because I left the shop half an hour early yesterday" or, "Although
> I didn't steal any state property, I did go to the clinic yesterday pretend-
> ing to have a bad leg, just to get some medicinal wine." . . . Sometimes
> we studied positive models, like Iron Man Wang, the worker from Man-
> churia, "Ah, comparing myself to Iron Man Wang, I feel guilty and un-
> worthy." (Informant no. 72)

Because all social behavior is considered to be indicative of one's underlying political thought, virtually any kind of deviant behavior—
pilfering factory supplies or engaging in (suspected) extramarital
sex, to name two common examples—can have political significance attached to it and be made subject to work group criticism. During the highly charged political campaigns of the Mao
era, these meetings turned into long sessions of group criticism and
confession.

Work Group Incentive Practices

The work group system, virtually universal in state industry by 1957, was not only a structural innovation, but also an attempt to develop a more effective means of motivating workers than the piece rates that were standard in the Soviet Union at that time.[25] During its First Five-Year Plan, China imitated the Soviet pattern. In 1957, 42 percent of its workers were on piece rates (Economic Yearbook 1981: IV, 181–82). By 1958, however, piece rates were almost entirely abolished with the onset of the Great Leap Forward, and they have never been revived on a comparable scale.[26] The Chinese alternative prescribed the use of the political and organizational resources of the party branch to mobilize workers, and the filtering of material incentives through a group framework. The work group system is the product of a deep distrust of the efficacy and desirability of material incentives in the absence of an accompanying framework of political organization and control.

Work group reward systems are a model of administrative simplicity and flexibility. A certain amount of money is set aside out of both planned and above-plan profit, to be distributed to workers and staff as bonuses. Before 1979, this was a fixed portion of the total wage bill—15 percent in the early 1950s and 5 percent after 1958 (Howe 1973: 122). Since 1979, it has been a variable, and often much larger, amount taken as a portion of the factory's retained profits. Bonus funds are usually distributed monthly, and funds not distributed by the end of the year are parceled out as year-end bonuses just before the Lunar New Year holiday. On rare occasions, enterprises will not distribute any bonus funds if the plant as a whole fails to meet its output targets in a given month for other than supply problems. Some enterprises will release bonus funds only to those shops or work groups that meet their targets, or they will release them in variable portions according to the degree of target overfulfillment. Work groups then meet to evaluate individual

25. Piece rates were paid to 73 percent of the Soviet workforce in 1957. After the wage reform of 1958–1960, the percentage dropped to 57.6 percent. From 1955 to 1961, piece rates as a percentage of the wage bill declined from 27.1 to 11.7 percent (Kirsch 1972: 25, 27).

26. Piece rates were paid to 20 percent of China's workers in 1963; they were virtually abolished from 1966 to 1977 (Economic Yearbook 1981: IV, 180–81). They have been revived to the point where 7.6 percent of the wage bill in 1982 was paid out as piece wages.

work performance. The quotas by which individual performance is measured are not the kind of time rates ordinarily set by staff specialists in piece rate systems: they are figures derived simply by dividing up the work group's monthly target into portions that are assigned to each individual.

Work group evaluations of individuals may consider not only work performance, but also performance in the entire range of activities in the group: work attendance and punctuality, attendance at group meetings, activism in political study and criticism sessions, general attitude and cooperativeness, and whether or not the individual has been seriously criticized or disciplined in the work group in the past month. The link of reward with performance is indirect and flexible, and usually is decisively influenced by the impressions of the group leader. In order to motivate workers, however, the group leader must ensure that nonwork criteria do not obscure the link of reward and work performance or violate perceptions of fairness among group members.

Bonuses are usually divided into three grades. The sizes and differences between grades have varied considerably with national incentive policy and from factory to factory. The most common grade is usually the lowest, and the least common, the highest. Most work groups deny bonuses only to those who fail to meet their quotas (a minimum standard) or who have been disciplined within the group in the past month. Year-end bonuses, evaluated in the same fashion, are much larger—and the largest shares sometimes are more than an entire month's salary.

The flexibility of this basic work group pattern has yielded three subvarieties, distinguished according to their treatment of incentive pay. The first, what might be called the "original" work group pattern, is essentially as I have described it so far: group assessments (dominated by the group leader) of all aspects of a worker's performance in the group, followed by an award of a graded bonus. The average bonus is of moderate size, and differences in grades, small. This was the standard pattern in the decade after 1956, from 1978 through the early 1980s, and is still common today. A second type was the "ascetic" Cultural Revolution variety, standard from 1967 to 1977, which abolished incentive pay altogether and attempted to motivate workers primarily through the mechanisms of group evaluation, criticism, and intensified political study and indoctrination.

The third variety is the new "reformed" type, in which incentive pay is to be linked strictly to work performance and attendance (not

political thought), measured, if possible, by objective statistics. The
bonuses are larger than in the original system, and, if government
policy is followed, differences between grades, larger. There is less
emphasis on group criticism and political study than in the original
system, although it continues and is closely linked to production
tasks. This type has been favored by authorities since 1979, and
there is some evidence (discussed in chapter 7) that it was in wide
use by the early 1980s. Although there have been variable approaches to incentive pay, other rewards—promotions, transfers,
housing, and other requests and applications—have been distributed in the same broker-like fashion, on the basis of personal
discretion exercised by shop leaders, during both the Cultural
Revolution and under the current reforms.

Stalinist and Maoist Mobilization:
A Comparison

The Chinese work group system is an artifact of a distinctive
Maoist approach to the mobilization of the labor force. Not only
was mass mobilization pursued more vigorously, more effectively,
and for decades longer than in the Soviet Union, it was also qualitatively different, both in its aims and organization, from early Stalinist efforts at mass mobilization. A brief comparison of Stalinist
and Maoist mobilization is in order—to distinguish the real from
the imagined differences, to explain these differences, and, in so
doing, specify the structural, historical, and ideational elements
that have led to them.

It is widely recognized that mass mobilization in Chinese industry serves to distinguish it from the familiar Soviet pattern. The Chinese concern for political mobilization, "moral" incentives, and intensive group organization on the shop floor are usually taken to be
foreign to "the Soviet model." Two kinds of ad hoc explanations are
offered to account for this presumed Chinese uniqueness. The first
is a psychocultural claim: that Chinese cultural norms are uniquely
group centered and that Chinese communists are guided unconsciously by the Confucian stress on moral tutelage of subordinates.
More concrete is a historical explanation: that the Chinese Communist party, unlike the Soviet, draws on a tradition of leadership
and a set of egalitarian ideals, deeply influenced by the party's experience during decades of administering base areas and prosecuting a
guerrilla war (Andors 1977; Brugger 1976).

*Soviet and Chinese Experiences
with Political Mobilization*

These ad hoc explanations take it as fact that the Chinese attempt at mass mobilization in industry was unique and that it had no counterpart in the Soviet experience. A closer look at Soviet history, however, shows that during the First Five-Year Plan (1928–1932), at the outset of Stalin's "revolution from above," the Soviet party attempted a mass mobilization that bears some striking resemblances to the Maoist. But the approach was abandoned in the early 1930s and repudiated as ineffective. The problem appears to be not one of explaining why the Chinese party employed mass mobilization, but of why the Soviet party was unable to sustain the approach.

The Maoist party cadre would have found a familiar political environment in Stalin's "socialist offensive" of these years:

> The "socialist offensive" was conceived as a revolutionary revitalization movement. . . . It would at the same time complete the politicization of the system by extending party-political control over all areas and levels of decision-making and by infusing the party's activist, voluntarist, and mobilizational norms and methods into all institutions. The Stalinists approached it not as a movement of the party-state over and against society, but as a struggle within society . . . and within the party, between those for and against the advance of socialist construction. Their role as leaders and organizers of the offensive was to identify and vilify the (class) enemy, to mobilize the revolutionary rank-and-file, to heighten mass vigilance, and to direct campaigns. (Cook 1985: chap. 2, p. 7)

Elaborate cultural and historical explanations of the Chinese party's conception of voluntarism, mass commitment, and face-to-face leadership are unnecessary: these elements were central to the early Leninist-Stalinist political culture as well: "The Stalinists believed that they could readily expand the energy and commitment dedicated to collectivist goals by activating these organizations, that their cadre, relying on techniques of saturation propaganda and intensive face-to-face mobilization on the shop floor, could produce broad commitment to the elite's goals" (Cook 1985: chap. 2, p. 15).

Why was this approach to industrial relations, begun with such fanfare at the outset of Stalin's drive for industrial development, dropped after so short a period in the Soviet Union? And relatedly, why was China able to sustain the approach for two decades? A

closer look at the conditions of Soviet industrialization and at the
state of the Russian party organization during the period provides a
stark contrast with China in the 1950s and 1960s and suggests an
answer to the question: turnover was so high that attempts at education and mobilization were rendered futile, and factory party organizations were themselves understaffed and in disarray.

The rapidity of the forced draft industrialization embarked upon
by Stalin in 1928 created chaotic conditions in industry, represented
by, but by no means limited to, the rates of turnover among workers. But these chaotic conditions were rooted in the preceding
period. Throughout the "new economic policy" of the 1920s, industrial turnover had averaged well over 100 percent annually. With
the "leap forward" of the early 1930s, turnover increased greatly: it
averaged 176 percent in all industrial sectors in 1930 and in several
branches of industry was over 300 percent (Barber 1980: table A).
In the course of the 1930s, turnover gradually declined to its earlier
levels, but, despite the imposition of work books (job registration
documents carried by workers) and a criminal law making resignation illegal in 1936, turnover remained extraordinarily high—between 75 and 100 percent, until World War II (ibid.). The targets of
political mobilization were not staying in one place long enough to
listen to the political appeals.

Even more striking was the disarray of Soviet factory party organizations. The high turnover in the labor force was reflected in party
leadership, although it had different causes. In wide areas of industry, party organizations did not exist below the all-plant level: shop
branch and party group organizations were being extended to the
shop floor for the first time just as they were being called upon to
play a mobilizational role. The party was expanding so fast that 43
percent of the total membership in 1932 had only "candidate"
status. Because the party was so weak in rural areas and recruited
primarily among urban residents (preferring industrial workers), a
party member did not have to wait long before he or she was promoted off the shop floor or out of the factory entirely. Many were
sent to rural areas to complete the collectivization campaign; others
were sent to technical schools and colleges to be trained as the engineers and managers of the future. As a result, the leadership of factory party organizations suffered from rates of turnover that were
almost as high as that of the labor force. According to sample surveys conducted in 1930 and 1931, the party secretaries of 20 major
enterprises had held their positions an average of six months;

another sample showed an annual turnover of 150 to 250 percent among enterprise party secretaries; in one city, party branch secretaries and trade union secretaries were replaced monthly (Cook 1985: chap. 5, p. 15).

By 1932 the Soviet leadership reacted to these chaotic conditions by concluding that mass mobilization alone was ineffective in dealing with the serious problems facing industry. The subsequent development of Soviet labor relations should be interpreted as a reaction to the problems of the period: extraordinarily high turnover and severe weakness in grassroots party organizations. They reduced the party's role in management and slowed the growth of the party. Managers were given broader coercive powers to discipline workers and were to use wider wage differentials and piece rates to motivate them. The regime sought to upgrade the skills and education of its managerial personnel. Factories were encouraged to build up a store of goods and collective services that were to be used to attract and hold labor; and access to these scarce goods and services was to be used to discipline the workforce as well. Political campaigns that interfered with the order of production were prohibited (Cook 1985: chap. 6). Thus began the evolution away from the mass mobilization approach that the Chinese would later revive under Mao.

By contrast with the Soviet Union in this formative period, conditions in Chinese industry in the 1950s and early 1960s were highly favorable to the employment of political mobilization. The workforce (described in chapter 2) was highly stable and enjoyed little mobility. The Great Leap Forward had disrupted this stability for three years, but it did not increase interfirm mobility: large numbers of peasants were hired in state firms, and most were later laid off. Enterprise party organizations, compared with their Soviet counterparts of 1928–1932, were extraordinarily stable, well staffed, and well run. Unlike the Soviet party, the Chinese was 4.5 million strong when it attained national power, and it was strongest in the rural areas (Schurmann 1968: 129). A full party organization was established in each enterprise as it was placed under state supervision, and former military and political cadres were sent to organize factories in large numbers (see Lieberthal 1980: chap. 3). They became party secretaries, branch secretaries, heads of propaganda, security, and administration departments, and they headed union and youth league organizations. As new members were recruited on the shop floor, they remained in the factory, because they were not urgently needed elsewhere. And, unlike the Soviet party in 1930, the Chinese already had decades of experience in administering rural areas and controlling and disciplining a mass army with this form of political organization. The same methods were extended to the factory. All of the conditions that undermined mass mobilization in the Soviet Union facilitated it in China.

Yet the case of China is not so readily explained. While organizing factories in the early 1950s, the party, under the influence of the Soviet Union, attempted to adopt the "advanced" Soviet methods that had evolved since the early 1930s in the U.S.S.R. The Chinese did not repudiate this Soviet model until 1957–1958, when it eschewed piece rates, enhanced the party's role, and began to employ group organization as the primary instrument of motivation. We, therefore, need to explain why the Chinese found it difficult to replicate Soviet practices, despite their original intention to do so.[27]

The first problem that the Chinese encountered with Soviet incentive systems is that they were administratively complex and required a large corps of trained labor and wages personnel to continually revise rates and calculate pay, all within the confines of a financial plan. In the Soviet Union, these incentive systems had presupposed an ample supply of technically trained cadres—the training of which the Soviets had emphasized from the outset of their own First Five-Year Plan (Bailes 1978: 188–215). Although China had no shortage of reliable party cadres in the 1950s (the opposite of the early Soviet problem), it did have a severe shortage of trained industrial staff, especially in relation to the demands of the full-blown Soviet management system. The rapid increase in the number of engineers and technicians during this period—from 126 thousand in 1949 to 800 thousand in 1957—was attained only by greatly lowering educational standards. This led to a decline in the average educational level of administrative and technical personnel after the peak was reached in 1953 (Emerson 1973: 50). These edu-

27. This account of the practical and political problems created by the borrowed Soviet labor practices in the early to mid-1950s is based on interviews with a handful of older informants and, especially, on a reading of national and local Chinese press articles on the subject collected in the Union Research Institute's clipping files for 1956 and 1957. I had originally planned a detailed historical analysis of this period before my interests turned to the comparative and analytical. I will draw sparingly on these materials to document partially the argument I am sketching out here.

cational levels, further, were not high to begin with. In 1952, less than one-half of the technical personnel in industry had completed higher education or technical school. As industry grew at unprecedented rates in the 1950s, the shortage of trained personnel worsened, and many enterprises struggled to introduce wage planning of even the most rudimentary kind (see Howe 1973: 119–20). The party could supply growing industry with all the political cadres it needed, but the trained personnel necessary for the latter-day Soviet system were unavailable.

Other problems were created by the rudimentary state of planning and supplies in the 1950s. Piece rates require that output depends on one variable: worker effort. Yet industrial supplies were subject to such chronic shortages and other aspects of plant administration in such an early stage of consolidation that worker output more often varied according to factors beyond their control: for example, shortages of raw materials and the slow delivery of tools from storerooms. Several informants stated that piece rates had to be dropped after a period of months because an unanticipated surge in worker productivity quickly exhausted the meager stores of raw materials and tools and led to serious disaffection among workers who lost income through no fault of their own. These supply problems—typical of the early stages of a planned economy—exacerbated the conflicts that normally develop when labor and wage personnel readjust piece rates.[28] Given this early experience, it is not surprising that none of the older administrators or workers I interviewed perceived piece rates as a desirable reward system.

These administrative problems, however, would have abated with the passage of time, as the planned economy was consolidated and administrative personnel upgraded in the 1960s. The most decisive reasons for the Chinese abandonment of Soviet incentive systems were political ones—not having to do with political ideals held by top party leaders, but with grassroots politics within factories. Soviet labor administration placed the party organization in factories in a distinctly adjunct position, as they had been in the U.S.S.R. since the early 1930s—little more than tenders of a larger technical process of administrative wage determination, over which most party

28. Frequent press reports of conflicts over quota setting indicate that this was a problem. The instability of the rates and the conditions for meeting them generated conflict. Some representative reports: Shenyang Daily (1957), Qiqihaer Daily (1957b), and Yuan (1956).

cadres had little understanding and little control. Because the party organizations were in most cases better consolidated than factory administrations, it made little sense to them that they should not be fully in charge.[29] Moreover, veteran party cadres, many of whom had been awarded factory party posts as a reward for their efforts in the war of liberation, were not willing to be subordinated to new party members of lower rank but with technical training, to the educated "white experts," or to noncommunist professionals, who usually staffed technical and administrative departments.[30]

Piece rates also placed the party organization in an adversary position with workers over matters of pay. They were caught between rate setters over whom they exercised no control and the workers, who they were charged with educating to accept the new political and industrial regime. Veteran party cadres accustomed to leading the masses against the Nationalists and landlords were now placed in a position where, as leaders in labor relations, they drew the ire of workers dissatisfied with administrative manipulations of pay rates. This, in turn, directly undermined the party's efforts to establish political and social control in industry at precisely the period in which they were trying to extend it over a rapidly expanding state sector.[31]

The reaction against Soviet piece rates and the subsequent return to mass mobilization styles of leadership were the result of these ad-

29. In the wide press debate during 1956 and 1957, many party secretaries voiced confidence that they could handle the problems with which executives and staff were struggling; see People's Daily (1956b), and New China Daily (1956).

30. This tension was evident in the many articles that sought (unsuccessfully) to clearly define the respective spheres of authority of party and administration. Mutual recriminations characterized the debate. See Geng (1956), Li (1956), Nie (1956), People's Daily (1956a), and Wang (1956).

31. Factory party organizations attempted to extricate themselves from this position by going on the offensive; blaming administrative cadres for an authoritarian work-style in their manipulation of piece rates, and criticizing them for punishing members of the working class for violating labor discipline. In many enterprises, in a 1956 push to implement "democratic management," party committees organized workers' congresses, whose delegates were political activists, to elect new factory directors—evidently ones that the party would find more pliable (see Workers' Daily 1956; Qiqihaer Daily 1957a). This political critique became official policy with the onset of the anti-rightist campaign of 1957 and the ensuing Great Leap Forward. In coming decades, calls for democratic management were invariably linked with conflicts over the definition of authority of various factory officials. Schurmann (1968: 285–96) traces the debate over the role of the party in these years. Gipouloux (1981) offers the only detailed account of these political conflicts and the position taken in them by workers.

ministrative weaknesses, the political strength of party organizations, and the political conflicts within factories. Egalitarian ideals
derived from the guerrilla experience were drawn upon later to justify the party's leading position. Political organization was strong in
industry; administrative organization was weak. The pattern of
mass mobilization, centered around work groups as an extension
of the political apparatus, drew directly on these strengths and
avoided the administrative weaknesses. Administratively flexible,
the work group system could be easily adapted to any technical
work process. Administratively simple, work groups themselves
evaluated workers for rewards, and this required only that targets
be split up by groups and, within groups, for individuals. Administratively stable, it did not require periodic revisions of quotas and
did not create large fluctuations in worker demand for materials
and tools. Conflict over rewards was directed away from management and the party and was contained within each work group,
where the pay evaluations would take place. The system placed the
party organization, which exerted strong control over the network
of small groups on the shop floor and in offices, fully in control of
labor relations. And, perhaps most importantly, by allowing criteria
other than work performance to enter into evaluations, it gave the
party a powerful lever in enforcing political compliance, and another means of rewarding political activists being groomed for
future leadership positions.

Differing Soviet and Chinese
Concepts of Mass Mobilization

I have so far sought to explain only one contrast between Soviet
and Chinese industry: why the Soviet Union did not sustain its
effort at mass mobilization, while China did. In this account, I left
little room for explanations derived from presumed cultural pre-
dispositions, historical traditions, or political ideals drawn from the
guerrilla and civil war periods. Such explanations bear on the
motives and intentions of people in positions of power, and they
presume these intentions to be different in the case of these two
countries. But, as we have seen, the Soviet party under Stalin began
with similar mobilizational intentions, while the Chinese in fact
sought to adopt the later Soviet model for an even longer period in
the early 1950s. The issue is in fact to explain why the Stalinist
party could not sustain its original intentions, while the Chinese re-

versed their original intention to adopt latter-day Soviet practices. To offer an explanation based on the intentions themselves would be irrelevant. The attempt to mobilize in both cases came from a common legacy of Leninist party organization. As Whyte (1974: 23–45) argues, mass mobilization in China was in effect an attempt to incorporate society more fully into the party organization itself, using standard forms of leadership usually reserved exclusively for the party membership in the Soviet Union. The explanation of Soviet-Chinese differences in this regard must be sought in the conditions that hindered or facilitated mass mobilization in each country at the time that their industrial traditions were taking shape.

There is, however, another important Soviet-Chinese difference to account for. One cannot help but be struck by a subtle, yet important, difference in the way that mass mobilization was defined and practiced in the two countries. Even when their use of mass mobilization was at its height, the Soviets employed it in a relatively instrumental and utilitarian fashion. Workers were mobilized to study the plan, accept and overfulfill inflated targets, form shock brigades, and participate in campaigns to practice economy and improve quality. Linda Cook (1985: chap. 4, p. 34) sums up the aims of Soviet mobilization in a way that fits with most other accounts I have read as "an intensive campaign to propagate the values, habits, and attitudes of an idealized working class culture committed to high productivity, labor discipline, efficient work organization, technical competence and national development."

In a broad sense, of course, this is not fundamentally different from the aims of mass mobilization in China. But something crucial is missing: the utter seriousness with which the Chinese party undertook to educate, resocialize, monitor, and transform the thinking of the masses of workers. One searches in vain in the memoirs of people who worked in Russia during those years for accounts of regular group study or group criticism—even within the party itself (e.g., Kravchenko 1946; Scott 1946). By contrast, these themes pervade similar accounts of Chinese organizational life in the 1950s and 1960s (e.g., Loh and Evans 1962; Tung and Evans 1967). Judging by these and other accounts, criticism and self-criticism meetings appear to have been held only among party members in the Soviet Union and, even then, only occasionally.

To the student of China, the Soviet experience reflects scant attention to the moral and ideological cultivation of workers, thought rectification, and the intensive political education that has marked Chinese industry for decades. True, Soviet factories had and continue to have workshop and section political meetings, and the manifest content and slogans employed bear a family resemblance to those in China, but the purpose appears to be largely to inform, cajole, and pressure. In China, on the other hand, one could say that moral-political remolding was for long periods a goal in itself, in addition to the promotion of production and creation of obedience, and, in some periods, it outranked the other goals.

But the matter is not so simple. The Chinese party appears genuinely to have viewed the moral cultivation of citizens as the only effective way to generate commitment and obedience. Commitments based on other motives are easily changed, perhaps false. Here is where arguments about Chinese traditions have their proper place. As Donald Munro (1977) has shown, Maoist assumptions about human nature and how to foster good citizenship— ideas reflected directly in patterns of leadership and reward—have a long history in Chinese thinking about statecraft. One might argue that the Soviet party was in no position to engage in serious worker education in its early years, while the Chinese party was. But the Chinese party's organizational preparedness did not itself determine how mass mobilization would be interpreted. Structural conditions cannot explain the normative content of Chinese authority. The Chinese interpreted Leninist-Stalinist mobilization in a distinctive way; they infused factory reward systems with a pervasive moral-political content. This system of reward, the exercise of this moral-political authority, and its unintended consequences are the subject of the next chapter.

4. Principled Particularism: Moral and Political Aspects of Authority

The Chinese Communist party's effort to mobilize and incorporate the working class meant that the standards of behavior and thought usually applied solely to party members were extended to the citizenry at large. The broad and sustained application of these standards to the whole population has been a distinctive feature of Chinese communism, and the Chinese have placed their own distinctive emphases on the process of mobilization. The ideological standards for behavior and thought, the demand for unbounded commitment, and the relationships prescribed among people—all are Chinese variations on a common modern theme: social groups whose mutual ties are based on a shared "ideological orientation" (of which Leninist parties are the most famous example). The ideological ties that bind members of such a group are distinct from both "traditional" particularistic or personal orientations and "modern" universalistic orientations. People treat one another as carriers of beliefs; their behavior and action must exhibit commitment to them. The prototypical ideological group is a small, tightly knit association of people who share a deep commitment to a political doctrine.

Any effort to incorporate outsiders who are not already committed, however, inevitably alters the nature of the ideological tie. The group employs indoctrination and education, to be sure, but it must also treat people differently according to the degree to which they manifest adherence to the doctrine. When such a group, like the Chinese Communist party, has the means to place outsiders in a politically and economically dependent position, they can treat people differently by altering the supply of political, material, status, and career advantages. When the group attempts to incorporate outsiders by offering incentives and disincentives for ideological commitment, the "ideological tie" is fundamentally altered. What was in the first instance a mutual orientation among voluntary adherents becomes, in the second instance, the object of a reward system in an organized hierarchy: a distinctive form of "principled particularism." In its attempt to incorporate an entire society through ideological ties, the Chinese Communist party corrupted, from the very outset, the meaning of the ideological tie itself.

A second source of corruption causes "principled particularism" itself to evolve further into more familiar particularistic, or personal, ties. The Chinese factory, like its communist counterparts, leaves considerable discretion to workshop leaders in the distribution of goods and fringe benefits, in wage and promotion decisions, in the peformance of sociopolitical services, and in the application of punishments. The shop's party branch secretary, employing the recommendations of section chiefs and group leaders, acquires even wider discretion in the course of judging subordinates' commitment to political doctrine.

Through time, subordinates are differentiated according to their superior's consistent assessment of their adherence, and the most active adherents receive officially conferred status, advantages, and career opportunities. Because the doctrine is so closely identified with authority, the active display of ideological commitment is in effect a display of loyalty. And because shop officials have personal control over advantages and rely on loyal adherents to run the shop, the stable relationship between leaders and active adherents has a tendency to evolve into personal ties, in which the active loyalty and support of subordinates are rewarded by superiors on a particularistic basis. Principled particularism, therefore, has a tendency, because of its inherent character and the features of communist factory organization, to generate a paradigmatic system of patron-client ties. Through a circuitous route, neo-traditional authority relations, based on particularism and personal loyalties, emerge in a modern organizational setting, the last step in this degeneration of the ideological tie.[1]

1. Given the pattern of dependence in which workers are enmeshed and the wide personal discretion of supervisors, particularism would result even without an attempt to politicize rewards. The point is not that ideological mobilization creates clientelism, but that it cannot escape the imperatives of its setting.

Social Ties in Ideological Groups

Social ties in modern ideological groups are not "personal" in the sense normally intended by the term, nor are they characterized by formal, "depersonalized" role obligations. Members of ideological groups, such as the radical sects among intellectuals in Czarist Russia that Nahirny (1962) has studied, relate to one another in terms of their ideas and beliefs, not in terms of their personal qualities or the specific functions they perform in the group. Ferdinand Tönnies' distinction between "community" (*Gemeinschaft*) and "society" (*Gesellschaft*) has little relevance to these ideological orientations. There is no place for them in Parsons' "pattern variables" (1951), and attempts to place them on a series of "traditional-modern" continua can only lead to confusion. Nor are these ideological orientations captured by Weber's ideal types of "traditional," "rational-legal," and "charismatic" authority, or any "mixed type" composed of them (although they have often been misidentified as a subvariety of charisma). Many analysts have nonetheless attempted to understand the ideological ties of modern communist movements (and their subsequent erosion) with these ill-suited conceptualizations. Because the main task of this chapter is to analyze the Chinese attempt to extend these ideological ties to the broader population and, more generally, to shed light on the evolution and corruption of these ties in communist societies, it is worthwhile to dwell on these conceptual matters before moving forward.

Edward Shils' explorations of social ties (1957) and ideology (1972) clear away the conceptual confusion surrounding the ideological orientation; Nahirny (1962) fashions a conceptualization directly relevant to the original ethic of modern communist parties. In order to highlight the distinctive character of these ideological ties, Nahirny's analysis is developed as a counterpoint to four of Parsons' "pattern variables," which are designed to capture on a series of continua all possible variants of social relationships.

The first point of contrast is with the definition of social roles and the obligations attached to them. Parsons specifies a continuum ranging from the functionally diffuse, ill-defined roles common in premodern societies to the functionally specific, limited, and highly differentiated roles of modern society. Groups bound together by an ideological orientation, however, are characterized by a holistic or "totalistic" definition that does not distinguish between persons and either their roles or beliefs:

> Ideological orientation is *total*—involving a response to the whole person as nothing but a belief-possessed being. Phrased differently, members of ideological groups respond to ideas and beliefs as if these were qualities of persons rather than objects of cognitive or appreciative orientations and, conversely, conceive of themselves as solely the carriers of ideas, not the possessors of various personal qualities. The end result of this orientation is of far-reaching consequence: ideas and beliefs become "personalized," and human beings "ideologized." (Nahirny 1962: 401)

This orientation toward people as carriers of ideas, or the "ideologization" of the self, was a feature that set Lenin's Bolshevism apart from the Marxist social democrats of his day. His famous innovations in the Marxism of the Second International—that the party, not the working class, is the carrier of correct proletarian ideology and that even socialist trade unionists are bourgeois in essence if they work primarily for workers' material improvement— are an expression of this orientation. Where, for Marx, Engels, Kautsky, and Plekhanov, people's viewpoints were determined by their place in the occupational role structure, for Lenin, whether or not a person accepted the Bolsheviks' condemnation of reformist politics and insistence on a tightly disciplined "party of a new type" determined whether the person was in essence "proletarian" or "bourgeois," regardless of their material social position.

The Chinese Communist party not only accepted this orientation in its entirety but developed it further. Perhaps the most commented-on innovation of Chinese Marxism under Mao is the idea that people can become proletarian, regardless of their actual class background, by transforming their thinking in accord with the party's definition of correct thought (Kraus 1981: 89–114; Munro 1977; Starr 1979: 99–116). A pure expression of this orientation is the process of thought reform in which enemies or potential enemies of the revolution undergo an intensive, coercive process of ideological conversion (see Schein et al. 1961). The same practice was applied to American prisoners in China during the Korean war, after which it became known as brainwashing (Lifton 1961). It is also part of the ideal motivation behind the extension of milder forms of small group political study and mutual criticism throughout the population (Whyte 1974).

The second distinctive feature of ideological ties is the emotive, or affective, content in social relations. Parsons specified a continuum running from the "affectivity" of personal relations common in premodern social roles to the "affectively neutral," or unemotional, relations characteristic of many spheres of modern social life. In ideological groups, social relations are neither affective, nor neutral, nor somewhere in between:

> The ideological orientation precludes a direct affective disposition toward human beings. . . . At the same time, it is not an affectively neutral orientation. In fact, ideologists channel all personal passions and emotions on to the collective cause they cherish. Human beings share in this *displaced* and *collective affectivity* to the extent to which they are its vessels. It is thus a profoundly antipersonalistic orientation. (Nahirny 1962: 402)

Not only are emotions and attachments to be focused on the cause, but personal feelings must be exposed and neutralized because they can conflict with commitment to the group and its cause: "They demand that their members obliterate completely the sphere of privacy and lay bare all their innermost feelings and desires" (Nahirny 1962: 400).

A guide for the training of party members, drawn up by the Moscow branch of the Chinese Communist party in the early 1920s, directly reflects this aspect of the ideological orientation:

> Cultivate a pure revolutionary philosophy of life and self-conscious training . . . stand firmly on class grounds. . . . We should absolutely collectivize and adapt our own lives and will to the masses. There is absolutely no such thing as individual life or individual free will. We must strictly criticize our comrades' errors and humbly accept our comrades' criticism. The organization's work is our only work. Aside from revolution, Communist members have no other profession—we are professional revolutionaries. (Quoted in Wilbur 1970: 39)

In a Leninist party, passions and emotions are to be focused on the cause and objectified on the party as a whole. But they are not to be focused on other party members as individuals; instead, members are to see themselves unemotionally as instruments of the party and its cause. Vogel's (1965) classic essay on the party's attempt to transform personal relations in Chinese society in the 1950s perfectly illustrates this aspect of the ideological orientation. Vogel's contrast between "friendship" and "comradeship" captures the dis-

tinction and conflicts between the mutual commitments of personal
relationships and the displaced-collective attachments of party
ideals. When people are required to place their commitments to the
party and its cause above personal affections and obligations, and
when they are required to report their innermost feelings and criticize errant tendencies in others in group meetings, interpersonal
relations are fundamentally changed. Vogel's description of the depersonalized closeness of comradeship is an extended illustration of
this aspect of the ideological tie.

A third contrast is in the orientation toward others. Parsons' continuum places at one end "particularism," the tendency to treat
people differently according to their personal relationship with you.
At the other end is "universalism," the tendency to treat people
according to universal standards of conduct or performance, objectively applied. An ideological orientation, however, is neither particularistic nor universalistic, nor does it lie somewhere in between.
Instead, it exhibits a characteristic called "dichotomy": "It con-
ceives of the social universe in terms of black and white, hopelessly
divided into two irreconcilable parts—one part of it to be collectively saved, another collectively destroyed. Consequently, it gives
rise . . . to two sets of directly opposed rules for approaching and
judging the people" (Nahirny 1962: 402). The continuing effort of
modern Leninist parties, including China's, to distinguish, in
successive periods, enemies from the people; action that reflects
counterrevolutionary intentions from ideologically mistaken ones;
and antagonistic from nonantagonistic contradictions is an expression of this dichotomous orientation. In China, the orientation took
on a bureaucratic character in the practice of classifying the entire
population in terms of their class origin; until the late 1970s, people
were treated accordingly in the legal system and with regard to opportunities for careers and education (see Kraus 1981: 115–41;
185–87).

The final contrast is in the standards by which people are judged.
Parsons places at one end of his continuum "ascription"; the treatment of people according to their inborn qualities: race, nationality,
class, family name. At the modern end of the continuum, he places
"achievement"; judging people according to their performance or
ability to perform in specific role tasks. In an ideological group, the
relevant standard is a third one: "commitment":

> Ideological orientations preclude seeing a human being as a composite of personal ascribed qualities and performances . . . ideologists neither value each other for what they are nor for what they achieve as individual persons. Ideally, they are completely deindividualized and, by renouncing all personal qualities, conceive of themselves as nothing but the carriers of beliefs. To the extent that they do this, the most important criterion is *commitment*. (Nahirny 1962: 402)

People are treated, in other words, according to their exhibited commitment to the belief and aims of the group. The principled particularism analyzed at length in this chapter is a direct expression of this characteristic.

It is often claimed that the social orientations I have just analyzed are well captured by Weber's concept, "charisma" (e.g., Jowitt 1983; Lowenthal 1970). According to this view, the ties that bind a modern ideological movement are a variant of the belief in the extraordinary personal qualities or supernatural powers of a charismatic leader. The belief in the charismatic individual is simply transferred to the infallible Leninist party and its historical mission; the personal cults that have surrounded Lenin (since his death) and Stalin and Mao (during their lifetimes) are simply instances when this basically charismatic orientation has burst to the surface. For these writers, if the beliefs are not focused on a gifted leader, this is an example of what Weber calls "routinized charisma" or what Shils (1965) defines as "office charisma."

I do not dispute the resemblance between charismatic movements and ideological groups, such as the Leninist parties, both of which are bound together by shared beliefs. But I do dispute the conceptual ordering implied. Shils and Nahirny, not Weber, identify the general phenomenon. To the extent that the beliefs of an ideological group are personalized and focused on the extraordinary qualities of an individual, these ties are genuinely charismatic. Charisma is a distinctive subtype of the ideological orientation, not vice versa. All charismatic movements are bound by ideological ties; not all ideological groups are charismatic.

There is a second confusion implied by the application of charisma to a Leninist party. In particular, neither Leninist parties nor the prototypical ideological groups referred to by Nahirny originated in charismatic leadership. They do often develop personality cults around their leaders (usually after being comfortably in power). But these cults are manufactured by party-government propaganda apparatuses and are enforced by the political and economic power of the state. Roth (1968) legitimately questions whether these personality cults are based on the kind of widely held personal beliefs characteristic of genuine charismatic movements or whether they are simply an expression of the personal aggrandizement of modern dictators—an expression of patrimonial rule in modern garb (see also Theobald 1978). Only the cult of Mao Zedong appears to have had genuinely charismatic, not manufactured, qualities—and then only for a brief period of the mass movements at the beginning of the Cultural Revolution and only among certain segments of the movements. To classify Leninist parties as charismatic does violence to the original concept. This point is of direct relevance to my argument, because in this chapter and the next two, I present a view of the evolution of a Leninist party's relationship with society that is an alternative to the common theme of the routinization of charisma.

From Ideological Orientation to Principled Particularism

An ideological group, no matter how closely knit, no matter how intensely committed its members, and no matter how far it isolates itself from the rest of society, must always settle for an approximation of its ideals. When an ideological group, like a Leninist party, grows in size and develops a complex organizational structure that embodies a strict hierarchy of command, the approximation becomes even less perfect. However, when a Leninist party seeks to mobilize an entire society and incorporate outsiders with ideological ties, the orientation begins to change into something else. A turning point is reached when the display of the ideological orientation is made the object of a stable system of reward. At this point, the ideological orientation gives rise, initially, to a distinctive phenomenon: "virtuocracy."

Susan Shirk (1982) defines virtuocracy as a system in which people are regularly rewarded for the display of behavior and attitudes that reflect politically defined "virtue." The difference from the ideological tie is that commitment is rewarded through career opportunities and social status. In the Chinese high schools of the 1960s that Shirk analyzes, students competed not only through academic achievement, but through their emulation of the model of the selfless, committed communist, displayed in their extracurricular activities and relations with their classmates. The emulation was carefully guided, cultivated, and monitored by a network of political advisors and recorded in students' dossiers. The assessment of students' political behavior and attitudes was an important criterion for advancement in the extremely competitive race for college admissions. The virtuocratic principles were mixed with academic performance standards and ascriptive class background criteria.

Virtuocracy is the reward system that embodies most completely the ideological orientation. It is a "pure type": to the extent that virtuocratic standards are applied, they relate to commitment, and commitment alone. But the high school is a special institution: it is designed for the purpose of education and political socialization; students are not engaged in a coordinated task; the student body continually changes; and everyone is involved in a race for upward mobility. In adult work settings, however, other conditions hold. The party is faced with the coordination of a complex task; only a minority can enjoy further upward mobility, and they remain in the organization much of their lives; the workforce may engage in passive resistance and view the leaders with sullen resignation. In this setting, virtuocracy is changed in subtle but important ways: it becomes a form of principled particularism.

Principled particularism differs from virtuocracy in that it is no longer the conformity to ideals of political virtue itself that is rewarded, but the concrete loyalty of workers to the party branch and shop management. It is the relationship, not the moral quality that is rewarded in fact. Party branch secretaries care little for political virtue in the abstract: they need workers who will obey orders, side with management against the other workers, actively cooperate in production and political campaigns, and stay after the shift voluntarily to help leaders prepare posters, statistics, and carry out inspections. True, these are the ways that a worker displays commitment, but this pattern of behavior puts the worker in a long-term, closely cooperative relationship with leaders. The loyalty of the activist worker is rewarded with eventual promotion and with social and material advantages. Because workers are rewarded for their relationship to the party and management, the reward system is particularistic. Because this is not to be a personal relationship, but one formally prescribed by official party standards, the adjective "principled" is warranted. Principled particularism is a mixed type: it has the structural attributes of a vertical patron-client tie, but the content of the tie is the impersonal one prescribed by the ideological orientation. Principled particularism is socially ambiguous and highly unstable: it evolves readily into the personal loyalties of a neo-traditional system of patronage. Only the periodic, militant reassertion of the impersonal, ideological ethic can arrest this corruption of the principles—even so, only temporarily.

Biaoxian and the Flexibility of Rewards and Punishments

Principled particularism, it must be stressed at the outset, is not what is commonly thought of as a moral incentive. Prior discussions of moral incentives in China (Andors 1977; Hoffmann 1974; Bernardo 1977), and in Cuba as well (Bernardo 1971) present this kind of leadership as if the party moves the workforce through moral appeals for sacrifice on behalf of the common good. This is certainly the message of the public appeals made during production campaigns, to which activists regularly respond. What looks like a moral incentive to the distant observer, however, is in fact a system of reward that uses career incentives and the factory's considerable resources to reward "moral" behavior and political loyalty, as defined by party and management, and to penalize their opposite. The rewarded behavior is embodied in the Chinese concept of *biaoxian*, a subjective quality of employees evaluated continuously by leaders and linked to their treatment within the enterprise.

The term *biaoxian* means, literally, to manifest, display, or show; or simply a manifestation or display of something deeper.[2] It describes the broad and vaguely defined realm of behavior and attitudes subject to leadership evaluation—behavior that indicates underlying attitudes, orientations, and loyalties worthy of reward. The vagueness and flexibility of the term is reflected in the way it is used in official documents. Sometimes *biaoxian* refers strictly to the (correct) political thought and activism (in the sense of actively supporting the leadership and the current party line) that an employee displays in political meetings. This is the sense of *biaoxian* expressed in the following passage: "In setting wage grades for newly

2. The term is used as both verb and noun. It is pronounced "beeyow-seeyan."

hired workers, we must carry out well and on a regular basis the assessment of one's politics and work; when setting wage grades, we must do so on the basis of the individual's display (*biaoxian*) of political thought, work attitudes, and level of skill." (Fujian Province Revolutionary Committee 1973: 14)

The term is also used to refer to a realm of individual qualities broader than one's political attitudes and enthusiasm for the regime's policies. For example, one document instructs enterprise officials to set pay rates for starting university graduates according to their "display of virtue and talent (*de, cai biaoxian*) during the period of probationary employment" (Cadre Department, Chinese Academy of Sciences 1961: 73). A still broader sense in which the term is used officially is when it is applied to actual work performance in addition to one's political thought, work attitude, virtue, morality, and other subjective qualities. For example, one document instructs officials to give preferential treatment in setting wage levels to "those with good *biaoxian* in politics and production (*zhengzhi, shengchan biaoxian haode*)" (State Council 1967: 2). Others refer simply to "all aspects of their *biaoxian* (*tamen gefangmian de biaoxian*)" (State Council 1957c: 65), and still others refer, more cryptically, simply to good, bad, or outstanding *biaoxian* (e.g., Fujian Province Revolutionary Committee 1973: 14; 1971: 11; State Council 1957c: 66).

Former employees' discussions of *biaoxian* reflect this loose and shifting definition. They use the term sometimes in the narrowest sense to refer solely to political thought: "Good political *biaoxian* means that a person is patriotic, active during political campaigns and criticism meetings" (informant no. 19). Sometimes the term is used in the broadest (and vaguest) sense to refer to all aspects of an individual's performance. But, in general, the term refers to aspects of one's performance other than actual work. Informants usually refer to two different criteria for reward as if they were distinct: one's work or skill, on the one hand, and on the other hand whether or not one's *biaoxian* was judged to be good (a class of subjective qualities including, in the course of many interviews, work attitude, political thought, helpfulness to coworkers and group leaders, obeying the leaders, and so on).

Biaoxian, as described by most informants, applies in practice to the kinds of opinions, suggestions, and criticisms voiced in meetings; to the extent to which one exhibits an understanding and approval of party policy; to one's willingness to volunteer extra efforts when asked; to the willingness to accept orders without questioning them (the "work attitude" mentioned in the document quoted above); to the ability to maintain cordial working relationships with coworkers and leaders (something referred to as "unity and mutual help" [*tuanjie huzhu*]). Needless to say, if one is criticized for some sort of transgression or if one gains a reputation as someone who contradicts leaders and fails to accept direction, this is poor *biaoxian*. Both official documents and former employees suggest that *biaoxian* encompasses, in effect, compliant and supportive behavior as exhibited in meetings and in day-to-day dealings with leaders.

The centrality of *biaoxian* in evaluations for bonuses, raises, and promotions introduces a marked degree of subjectivity into the process not only because *biaoxian* is a vague notion of individual worth that defies precise definition, but also because one's actual work performance tends to be evaluated at the same time and in the same rule-of-thumb fashion. Wage and labor documents use general formulas to refer to both kinds of evaluative criteria (and these formulas are echoed by informants)—"good work," "high skill level," as well as "good political *biaoxian*," "good work attitude"—while never clearly specifying how these general terms are to be defined in practice. Informants almost unanimously described systems in which work performance was in fact evaluated in a general, rule-of-thumb fashion and in which the overall evaluation blurred together subjective notions of *biaoxian*. Leaders must devise their own working definitions of these qualities, and it is not always clear what proportion of an assessment is comprised of subjective judgments of *biaoxian*. None of my informants, not even the managerial personnel, were ever able to specify how much of an assessment was comprised of *biaoxian* and how much of work performance. They could only list a series of things considered. It makes sense that, in a system where so much is left up to individual interpretation (*biaoxian* is clearly in the eye of the beholder), no precise answer could possibly be given to the question. Some people summed up these rule-of-thumb evaluations as reflecting simply "your relations with the leaders" (informant no. 15), or "whether or not the leaders have a good impression of you" (informant no. 25).

For more than two decades after 1957, *biaoxian* entered explicitly into the evaluations of individuals for monthly bonuses, wage raises, and setting the starting pay scale after an apprentice's or trial worker's probationary period. In each of these cases, the process begins with a discussion within the work group of the individual's work and of all aspects of the person's *biaoxian*. As one document describes a process that applies to promotions as well as bonuses: "The masses democratically assess political and ideological *biaoxian*, labor attitude, and technical skill; the leaders of the unit examine the result and report to the upper levels for approval" (Fujian Province Revolutionary Committee 1973: 14).

The group leader draws conclusions based on the group's discussion and reports the resulting list of nominees to the head of the shop office. Because group assessments often level out differences between individuals, when the shop or office heads meet later in committee with party branch officials to cull the group recommendations and arrive at a final list, they must rely heavily on the group leader's or section chief's personal evaluation of the employees, usually relayed in oral form. These personal evaluations frequently result in alterations of the rankings that emerge from the shop floor. The final lists, therefore, reflect personal, closed-door discussions of the general assessments that leaders make of their subordinates. The decisions of shop-level leaders must subsequently be approved by the top plant leadership, and, in the case of raises, this sometimes results in further changes when party officials and staff from the personnel department find detrimental materials in an employee's file.

The Flexible Determination of Pay Grade Raises

Employees first come into contact with the flexible and politicized factory reward system during their apprenticeship or trial periods:

> After the third year [of apprenticeship], we all wrote summaries of our work experience over the past three years, both politics and work skills. Did we work hard? Were we active in politics? What had we learned? What was our opinion toward our masters, did we respect them? The only apprentices who didn't get promoted had political problems. (Informant no. 50)

In the case of these promotions, the main function of political criteria is largely to screen out deviants, something that informants reported with near unanimity: "If you worked hard, and your political thought is good, then you pass. If you don't make any political errors, then you are assured of passing" (informant no. 8). And the same practice is applied to employees classified as technicians, who are upgraded after one year on the job as "trial technicians": "This was done automatically unless you made a serious political mistake" (informant no. 15).

In wage grade readjustments, the evaluations are equally flexible, but the *biaoxian* standards loom as much more important, because less than one-half of the employees typically can receive an upgrading in these periodic readjustments. In this case, you are not simply ruled out from an automatic upgrading for a bad political showing, as is the case for apprentices. There is a systematic comparison of nonwork attitudes and behavior, and this often ends up as the determining factor in the competition for a fixed number of raises. Except in the period before 1957, when skill examinations were widely administered each year to help determine raises, and in the periods from 1962–1964 and after 1979, when efforts were made to restore skill examinations in many enterprises, there were virtually no measurable standards to limit the scope of *biaoxian* in these assessments.

Some of the older informants remembered the dramatic shift toward *biaoxian* as a criterion for rewards in 1957, a date that coincided with the "anti-rightist" campaign and the effort to universalize small group organization in industry:

> After 1957 the main standard, the first thing they looked at in the readjustments, was your political thought, how active you were in each political campaign, whether or not you supported the Great Leap Forward policies, whether or not you had raised opinions against the party in 1957 [in the Hundred Flowers period]. But before the [1957] anti-rightist campaign they took the best qualified people, whether you were activists or not. (Informant no. 70)

Biaoxian tipped the results of evaluations in two ways: it assured those with an outstanding political showing of an advantage, other things being roughly equal, and it acted to exclude those who had spoken out of line, challenged authority, or exhibited poor *biaoxian* in other areas:

> In fact, people were appraised favorably for reasons other than their work. The people who were evaluated especially favorably were those

nonparty members who were preparing themselves for membership by getting close with party committee members, being active politically, listening to the party's line. These people had a better chance, if things were about equal in other areas. (Informant no. 2)

Usually the raise was based on a mix of four standards: work and skill level, years of experience, relations with others, and the impression of each individual in the eyes of the leadership. This includes political *biaoxian*, which at the time [the early 1960s] meant not telling the truth about the Great Leap Forward, saying it was a success. (Informant no. 21)

In 1963 . . . there were promotions and raises for certain activists and backbone technicians . . . the main criterion, especially if one was a party member, was attitude toward Mao's thought. Whether you opposed the line of the Great Leap Forward and the Three Red Flags, whether or not you had been criticized as a rightist during the 1959 anti-rightist elements campaign . . . were also important standards. If you had a problem in any of these areas, then there was no way to get a raise. You had to say that there really was enough to eat in 1961 and 1962, and not bring up the disasters caused by the Great Leap Forward. In 1963, these were the issues included in whether or not you had good political thought. (Informant no. 53)[3]

Even in the 1972 wage readjustment, which granted raises to the lowest-paid employees only, and strictly according to their seniority, people who had exhibited poor *biaoxian* by making some sort of political mistake were denied raises to which they were otherwise entitled.

The Flexibility of Bonus Assessments

The impact of political assessments on bonuses differed according to the way that work groups practiced their incentive systems, and this varied considerably in different enterprises, in different periods. To the extent that bonuses were distributed in a relatively restricted fashion (e.g., from 50 to 75 percent of the group mem-

---

3. To insist that you had enough to eat in 1960 and 1961 was a supreme act of loyalty. Both foreign and Chinese residents of China during those years have painted vivid pictures of severe hunger in the large cities: the eating of leaves, bark, and the endemic diseases of malnutrition (see Lindqvist 1963; and Liang and Shapiro 1983, for two of the most vivid). Recent Chinese census data show an excess mortality of 20 to 30 million, given what would normally have been expected in those years based on prior mortality rates. These data firmly document the reports of massive (and manmade) famine in rural areas (see Bernstein 1984; Bannister 1985).

bers, as some informants reported) and to the extent that bonuses were given out in three grades that were separated by substantial increments, the monetary advantages of having good *biaoxian* were tangible. But, in situations where almost everyone got some bonus, and where the differences between the sizes of bonuses were small, *biaoxian* was of little monetary consequence except when it was judged to be bad, in which case the employee would be deprived of a bonus completely until he or she reformed.

Regardless of the way bonuses were distributed, *biaoxian* was a regular, important part of bonus assessments:

> In the mine, there was a system of monthly appraisals in the small groups. Everyone discussed each person's performance. First they discussed attendance, then they considered work attitude. They also looked at your relations with other workers. They looked at your political thought, whether you are an advanced or backward element, whether you think of the collective or think of yourself, whether you are satisfied or always complaining. (Informant no. 44)

> The amount of bonus for each person in the group was fixed in a monthly appraisal meeting in the small group, led by the group leader. In these meetings, each person's case was discussed one by one. Workers in the group raised their opinions about the person's *biaoxian*, political thought, whether they came on time, and work attitude. Afterwards there was a discussion and the group leader came to a conclusion that summed up these suggestions . . . in practice, everyone in the group received these small bonuses in equal amounts, except in rare cases . . . almost everyone received one except when they had political problems, or were not active enough in study or campaigns. (Informant no. 1)

In cases where the year-end bonus, a sizable amount paid out immediately before the Lunar New Year holiday, is subject to group assessment (rarely), judgments of *biaoxian* have the same effect. When bonuses were given out equally to all, the effect of *biaoxian*, once again, was to exclude those who had made some kind of mistake: "There was also a year-end bonus. Everyone got the same, usually from 18 to 32 yuan. Some with political mistakes did not get one" (informant no. 3). Even during the decade when monthly bonuses were replaced by an equal supplementary wage paid to all, the evaluation of *biaoxian* continued: "While I worked in the collective factory [in the early 1970s] there were no output quotas at all. [Q: How was worker performance judged?] That was just the problem. They couldn't. They just looked at your political *biao-*

xian. If your relations with the leader were good, then you would be assessed a good worker" (informant no. 57). As in the regular bonus systems, the supplementary wage of this period, at least in some factories, was revoked for bad *biaoxian*: "[The supplementary wage] was about 8 yuan per worker each month, both cadres and workers. If you were absent over 20 days in a month, or made a political mistake, it would be taken away" (informant no. 3).

The Flexibility of Other Rewards

Other important rewards in the enterprise are flexible in similar ways, except that there are no group assessments at the outset. *Biaoxian* is a crucial determinant of job promotions and desirable transfers, even for positions that require technical expertise. In most cases, promotion from the shop floor to an office job is a reward given only to those who have distinguished themselves as loyal activists. These decisions are made by shop directors and party secretaries, often in consultation with the heads of work groups, and the personal recommendation of the group leader, head of the party cell, or youth league branch is often crucial. Manual workers often become clerks or "helpers" (*ganshi*) in shop offices, union and youth league headquarters, and propaganda departments, positions that do not require formal education or technical training. For promotion to group leader or assistant to the shop director, the *biaoxian* standards are even more strict.

Because of their relationships with group leaders and the impressions they make on shop officials and party branch cadres, those with good *biaoxian* often are at an advantage when they apply to enterprise administrative departments for housing, extra food rations, loans, various kinds of paid leave, or employment for spouses or children. For all of these things, the opinion and recommendation of the group leader or section chief influences the action taken by the shop office. My informants were generally convinced that one's success with the plant administration was a function of group leader or section chief support. Those whose *biaoxian* was outstanding had an advantage, while those who had "thought" or "political" problems often ran into problems with the plant bureaucracy as well: "*Biaoxian* also had an effect on who got housing. Those with good *biaoxian* were high on the list. Those who were "bad elements" were low. . . . This one worker with bad *biaoxian* in my group applied, but the shop director didn't want him to get an apartment" (informant no. 72).

The connection between *biaoxian* and benefits is made very clear to workers. It is not considered a corrupt practice by the party, but a principled application of political rewards. Only when discretion is not exercised in this principled fashion, but according to personal affinity, is this flexibility considered illegitimate. Not only is the benefit clearly linked with past behavior, but shop leaders often portray the conferred benefit as carrying an obligation to the party in future behavior:

> If your request is approved, the leaders tell you that your problem is solved now, and this shows how the party is concerned about you and is caring for you. Later, if you goof off at work, the same leader will try to make you feel guilty, remind you of how the party took care of you in the past. Then you say, "I'm sorry, I apologize to the party and will work harder in the future to show how grateful I am." (Informant no. 72)

The Flexibility of Punishments

Biaoxian enters into the flexibility of punishments in a much more complex way. There are at least three different ways that this flexibility enters in. First, as is characteristic of a reward system centered on *biaoxian*, there is a broad array of activities that can be subject to punishment—not only in politics, but in one's personal life as well. Second, there are no fixed rules governing the kinds and severity of punishment to be meted out for specific acts—the relationship is a variable one. And, once one is accused of a transgression, the punishment fits not the "crime," but the person, specifically who they are (their class background and past record of *biaoxian*), and the contrition and willingness to reform they exhibit after they are accused:

> Workers are usually punished for stealing, bad work attitudes and showing up late, absenteeism without leave, and having sex [outside marriage]. There are no set punishments for different things. Having sex is usually treated very seriously, at least a [formal] warning. . . . Chinese people know that sex is serious, they all know because it is traditionally known as immoral behavior. So one kind of standard is fixed in people's minds. They all know what is serious and what is not. (Informant no. 68) [4]

4. I feel certain that there are no written regulations that spell out precisely what constitutes a "life-style" offense, but these standards are nonetheless firmly fixed in the unwritten customary law of the factory.

Some types of behavior, as this person suggests, are treated more seriously than others, and workers generally know what these things are. Generally speaking, poor job performance is not something that moves quickly up the escalating scale of punishments: "For carelessness or violating technical responsibilities, first a self-criticism is written, then it is read to the group. Then the group raises opinions and criticisms about his behavior. Then a report goes to the shop director, who writes a comment on it, usually saying 'his work is usually good, no need for punishment'" (informant no. 64). Generally speaking, violations in the realm of *biaoxian* are those that are dealt with most severely:

> There are morals [*daode*] problems. This includes life-style, sex, cheating others. For morals problems, the first step is self-criticism, second, the shop offers opinions about your case to the factory office, then they decide whether or not to give you a "warning" [*jinggao*]. This is a form filled out by the plant director and the head of the security department. Each one puts his seal of office on it, then it is put in the person's file. It stays in your file all your life. (Informant no. 64)

Regardless of the type of offense, officials in the workshop and above must determine whether the case will be dealt with leniently or harshly. Individuals enduring group criticism are expected to show an attitude of contrition. People on probation, for example, are to be watched carefully to see whether they fully acknowledge their errors and "manifest regret and willingness to mend one's ways" (Ministry of Control 1958: Ministry of Internal Affairs 1964).[5] Assessment of this aspect of attitudes and behavior determines the severity of punishment. In the case cited in these regulations, it determines whether the individual will be restored to permanent employment, continue on probation, or be expelled from the enterprise. This practice is followed for all transgressions, large and small:

> The punishment also depends on the person's attitude after he is caught. The small group has to discuss the person's case, and if the person admits guilt and makes a self-criticism, usually the group will recommend

5. The factory labor reform program mentioned by an informant in the last chapter was originally established to deal with the factory's *biaoxian* problems: "The factory had a small farm out in the suburbs, about 10 kilometers away. The 'bad elements' from the factory were sent there to work, the ones with bad *biaoxian*. The factory security department sent people who stole things, hoodlums. They also had 'labor tempering' . . . they'd send the people out in trucks . . . the main purpose was to reform your thoughts" (informant no. 72).

leniency, and give the person "help" or education. Usually this is enough, because this is embarrassing for a person. But if the person doesn't criticize himself, does not admit his mistake, the group can report the case to the upper levels and give an opinion on punishment. . . . For less serious mistakes, the group has a choice of whether to report it. For more serious things, they have to report it. But, generally speaking, if you confessed and made a sincere self-criticism and were not a repeated offender, they would be lenient with you. (Informant no. 68)

Much also depends, however, on who the offender is. For the two decades after 1957, one's class background was an important consideration when leaders weighed the punishment. The importance of this criterion has fluctuated considerably with China's political climate over the years, but, in the more militant periods, as the following example from the early 1970s shows, the effect can be considerable:

If there were quality problems in the group, we would meet the next day and find out who was responsible. If the family background of the worker responsible was "worker" or "poor peasant," then we would criticize him and this would be considered a small problem. But if his class background was not good, they would turn this into a struggle-criticism session. They might hold an all-workshop repudiation meeting, where we would all yell "Down with Wang," and he would have to confess to receiving orders from his capitalist father or other relatives to sabotage production and socialism. Not until 1974 or so did they gradually stop doing this kind of thing. (Informant no. 56)

Firing, one of the ultimate sanctions available to plant officials, is used only rarely. And when it is used, it is used almost exclusively for matters related to *biaoxian*. As one informant put it, firing occurs "only rarely," and "it almost never happens because of bad work." Instead, it is generally a "legal" matter, "for someone who makes an error in politics or in their social life. It is handled by the security department" (informant no. 8). Another former worker could remember only two firings in his work experience, and both were for "political problems" (informant no. 1). And a third summarized concisely the remarkably uniform responses of informants on this question: "There were no firings unless you got into political trouble or into trouble with public security. The same goes for demotions and wage reductions. There are none unless you make a political mistake" (informant no. 33).

In fact, firings for poor work are so rare that they are not

referred to as "firings" (*jiegu*). Rather, they are so closely associated in the popular mind with political and legal crimes that they
are referred to by the official administrative term of "expulsion"
(*kaichu*).

> There were a few workers who were expelled, usually for disrupting
> public order or committing crimes. Wounding someone or killing them,
> speculating, gambling, these are things you can be expelled for. Also
> there were a number of people who were expelled for political mistakes.
> These people usually went to jail or labor camps. They do not expel
> workers for bad work. This would be called "firing," and they do not
> fire workers in China. (Informant no. 68)

> The units just didn't have the right to fire people or take away their
> wages. But if someone got into political trouble and was sent to a labor
> reform camp, this was equal to being fired. (Informant no. 35)

> There is basically no firing for bad work in China. For stealing, counter-
> revolutionary activities, large-scale corruption, they have public secu-
> rity. After they take you away to labor reform camp, that's not really
> firing by the factory. For bad work, the treatment is education. No one
> was ever fired from my factory for bad work. (Informant no. 55)

Symptomatic of the flexibility of punishments, and the often
moralistic overtones of *biaoxian*, was an example of a type of firing
that was mentioned spontaneously by informants with a frequency
that was disturbing—especially since so few could remember any
cases of firings for other than serious political or legal crimes. This
type of case evidently involves little more than a double standard
applied by the older males who typically run factories: "One female
apprentice was fired for her life-style. She hung around with young
guys on the streets, had loose morals, and got pregnant. They fired
her" (informant no. 54). In an almost identical case, an apprentice
got pregnant but made the fatal mistake of acting defiant instead of
ashamed when criticized. As a result, the shop leaders refused to
permit her to register her marriage. As an unmarried woman, she
was not entitled to maternity leave, so she was fired near the end of
her pregnancy for being absent from work (informant no. 57).

Worker Responses to
Moral-Political Authority

Principled particularism, designed to encourage the development
of deep political loyalties and commitments, stimulates instead a

deeply calculative orientation to authority. This is true for the genuinely committed as much as for the apolitical rank and file. Workers
are well aware that the behavior and attitudes they manifest in the
course of participation in daily work group meetings, small group
political study and mass meetings, and everyday encounters with
leaders are systematically monitored, evaluated, and linked to their
treatment. They are also well aware that shop leaders have clear
goals in mind when they initiate a meeting that workers are required to attend: resolution of specific production problems, increases in shop productivity, criticism of undesirable behavior and
attitudes, or communication of a political message or new policy.
Because both the quantity and quality of participation is regularly
evaluated and linked to rewards, employees find it necessary—
whether they genuinely agree with the authorities on the matter or
not—to develop a strategy to manifest properly compliant behavior
and attitudes. As Vogel (1967) has shown, one cannot sit idly by
and consent through default. A steel worker described the realities
that encourage the adoption of a calculative orientation:

> Workers commonly raised opinions. In fact we were encouraged to par-
> ticipate and had to say something, or we might be criticized for not rais-
> ing opinions. The group leader listened to the opinions, and he usually
> discussed them. The advantage of this system is that it always keeps pro-
> duction on everyone's mind. Everybody knew what the situation was.
> But the disadvantage of the meetings is that you can't be dissatisfied or
> express dissatisfaction with decisions that have been made or methods
> already being used, or in political matters. [If you do] they will then
> criticize you and send a report to the party secretary. Then the leaders
> know and will form a bad impression of you. (Informant no. 59)

A minimum of active participation is expected, and there are
definite boundaries of acceptability in the content of the opinions
expressed. An engineer from a chemical plant, referring specifically
to the political meetings of his office work group, described the rules
of the game in a similar way:

> You can't oppose the leader's suggestions, or you will be criticized. Yet
> you can't keep quiet if you disagree. If you keep silent, the group leader
> will point you out, and direct criticism at you, and try to get you to
> express an opinion. So, basically speaking, you have to approve. You can
> become an activist, volunteer to speak, and approve actively. Or you can
> just go along. But you can't do this quietly, or you will still be criticized.
> (Informant no. 2)

Another major reason for the development of a calculative orientation is that many of the topics of the political study sessions are obscure and far more closely related to factional disputes in the top reaches of the party than with the daily concerns of employees. Yet participation and correct opinions are nonetheless demanded. A young worker's recollection of the early 1970s indicates the texture of the political campaigns of the period:

> There was the "strike one, oppose three" (*yida sanfan*) campaign and the "criticism of Lin Biao and Confucius" campaign. Confucius wanted to "restore the rites" and so forth. There was the criticism of *Water Margin* (the seventeenth-century Chinese novel). The leader of the peasant uprising wanted to surrender, he was a "capitulationist." Mao's instruction was to criticize this book, so we all studied it. Then there was the "study the theory of the proletarian dictatorship" campaign. We learned that it was necessary to carry out a comprehensive dictatorship over the bourgeoisie. There was the "oppose the rightist restorationist wind" [which included] the criticism of the "three poisonous weeds"— a document on scientific and technical work, and two others. We criticized these [documents] for advocating the "theory of the productive forces." After the Tiananmen Incident, they changed this to a criticism of Deng Xiaoping. Then there was the criticism of the Gang of Four. This one was different. The Central Committee sent down real documents and materials in addition to [the usual newspaper] editorials. . . . This was the last political campaign [before he left China in 1979]. (Informant no. 50)

A calculative strategy is required not only because the subjects of political study are often abstract and sometimes nearly incomprehensible to the average worker, but because a current campaign may likely contradict the previous one. It was precisely in the period when politicized rewards predominated that the party line fluctuated most frequently. In the passage quoted above, the 1977–1978 "criticism of the Gang of Four" campaign completely reversed the line of the 1976 "criticism of Deng Xiaoping" campaign, and it in fact presaged the rehabilitation of Deng Xiaoping (his second) and his eventual emergence as the most powerful leader in China after 1978. And the 1973–1974 "criticism of Lin Biao and Confucius" campaign followed, after an interval, the death of Lin Biao, who, before his ill-fated 1971 military coup attempt, had been Mao's designated successor and the second most powerful leader in the country. In both these cases of complete reversals in the party's line, not only were previously worshipped officials heaped with calumny, but their previous political stands were twisted into their opposite. Thus, Lin Biao and the Gang of Four were immediately found to have opposed Mao and his thought for many years, where in fact every factory employee knew that, months previously, they had been counted among Mao's staunchest supporters.

In short, a calculative orientation is demanded by the environment, precisely because the definition of "good political thought" shifts with the political winds: "When they said 'good political thought' in 1977 they meant something different from before. They were rehabilitating a lot of people and were trying to do away with the influence of the Gang of Four. So the measure of good politics was your attitude toward the new direction of modernization" (informant no. 53). Whether an employee is truly committed to the party and its current definition of socialism, indifferent to it, or inwardly opposed, a calculative orientation is necessary. The demands of a reward system centered on *biaoxian* touch all employees equally, regardless of their true loyalties and commitments. This is especially true of the loyal activist, for whom simple commitment is not enough. The activist must always monitor shifts in political line to make sure that his or her active public displays are not the wrong ones (see Oksenberg 1970). Ironically, it is the truly committed who must be the most calculating in their display of commitment, because they are the ones who speak up first, and at greatest length. If they make a single mistake, they may ruin their standing in the party's eyes. This is something that matters most deeply to the truly committed activist. Through several political shifts, the calculativeness may begin to adulterate the commitment; genuine moral commitment may shade into unthinking dogmatism or cynicism.

Daily life in a politicized reward system requires the development of a conscious and calculative "presentation of self." Erving Goffmann (1959) has shown how such a "presentation of self" unconsciously pervades everyday social encounters in our own society. In China this presentation of self (presentation is, in fact, one possible translation of the term *biaoxian*) is conscious, continuous, encouraged, and explicitly evaluated by authority figures. This imbues participation in meetings and other public encounters with authority figures with the substance of ritual. A skilled worker summarized the essence of this public ritual by referring to the literal meaning of the term *biaoxian*: "The whole thing is a performance. You learn very quickly to make these performances and not say what you really feel. . . . *Biaoxian* is an important word. It means 'show.' It depends not on what you think, but on what you show to others" (informant no. 56).

Individuals adopt a variety of orientations in this kind of environment. They range from active and committed compliance to ritualistic conformity. Although there are many subtle differences in individual responses, these orientations generally fall into two major groups: active or competitive orientations, those designed to display conformity with the party's highest behavioral standards; and passive or defensive orientations, those designed to meet the party's minimum standards.

Active-Competitive Orientations

I have defined the "active-competitive" orientation in terms of the behavior these people display, but not in terms of their presumed motivations and beliefs. It would be a distortion to portray activists as being motivated solely or primarily by the calculation of material or career interests. It would be just as much of a distortion to portray them uniformly as the selfless, morally committed citizens their behavior might outwardly suggest. My informants, former activists and nonactivists alike, usually distinguished the truly committed from the unprincipled careerists, and reserved for the latter a special disdain. Not only do people's motives vary, but the motives of most individuals are probably ambiguous. There are so many different kinds of rewards for activism—career and material advantages, officially conferred status, moral approval and recognition by the party—that it is difficult to say which is the most important.

The matter is even more complicated: it has long been recognized that people who adopt values as an act of identification with a higher status reference group will often hold these values deeply (see Merton 1968b: 344–47; also Stinchcombe 1968: 108–10). Those who make it because of their action in accord with these beliefs, in other words, are likely to become deeply convinced of their validity.[6] We must also be mindful of the costs of an activist orientation in

6. Bialer (1980: 41–42) suggests that this sociopsychological mechanism gives the Soviet elite an intense and deeply felt adherence to the party's values and standards, instead of the shallow and ritualistic expression that one might expect.

terms of time, effort, the self-denial of many of the pleasures of personal life, and, as I detail in the next chapter, social isolation and hostility from other workers. It is, therefore, prudent to assume that the motives of activists vary and are often ambiguous, even in their own minds. But they are uniformly strong. Only highly motivated and competitive individuals will pay the costs and strive to distinguish themselves from their peers in meeting the party's moral-political standards.

The fact that activists are rewarded, whatever their true motivation, makes activist behavior a social phenomenon riddled with contradictions. One particularly balanced and insightful informant (no. 71) summed up concisely the conclusions I had drawn from scores of earlier interviews:

> The most common reward [for activists] is promotion to group leader or some other position in the section or shop office. But there are also rewards that come with the status of getting into the youth league and the party. The material things aren't always in the minds of the activists. There is glory in being an activist. But of course activists are always the first ones to get wage raises. And there are other kinds of rewards. For example, it's easier to find a girlfriend if you're an activist, and the same thing goes for getting a wife. It's also easier to get housing. . . . But the real incentive is that this is the first step on the road to becoming an official. If you aren't already a youth league member by this time, you join. After you become a group leader it's easier to get into the party. Joining the party and the youth league is itself a step toward becoming an official in people's minds, anyway, because it leads to promotion later on. There are also some, a minority, who simply are very able and have a strong sense of responsibility. They want to serve the people, and they are committed to the factory. They just do it out of a sense of duty, naturally. Usually all of these motives are mixed together . . . you can't really say they do it just for the money. In my opinion, the most important motive is a combination of wanting to join the party and youth league and of becoming an official later on.

My informants regularly described a variety of activist "types." There was the ambitious, fast-talking careerist; the young and naïve do-gooder; the loyal, hard-working, but relatively apolitical, "advanced producer." There were also mature and committed individuals who internalized the state's ideology as their moral guide:

> Some activists . . . really believed in Mao's thought and did things according to their beliefs and principles. . . . They do these things because

they think it's right. That's why they report on others. . . . They are like the heroes in the stories of old. They don't care if they have friends or not. They put themselves at a distance from others. You can say they're too upright. (Informant no. 71)

Political activists seek to display an unerringly positive attitude of support toward party policy and the initiatives of leaders. They are generally young; almost all of them become members of the shop's Communist Youth League branch. Activists of middle age are rare for the simple reason that successful activists become leaders or are promoted to office positions; unsuccessful activists usually give up the orientation by their 30s if their efforts have gone unrecognized. The hallmark of an activist is that he or she interprets leadership messages and responds in the correct ways. In political study meetings, this means not merely reading articles or listening to people recite them, but thinking of ways to comment on them and to apply the messages in them to the situation in the small group. The orientation involves a vocal approach in meetings and the demonstration of loyalty to power holders in a number of ways.

An activist listens closely to the speeches of enterprise officials when the tasks of the campaign are explained at mobilizational meetings involving an entire workshop. As a youth league member, he or she may already have received briefings and instructions at separate meetings of that organization. Then, in the work group meetings that follow, activists are the first to respond to the party's message. In a production campaign, activists are the first in the group to volunteer for unpaid overtime or to exceed quotas by large percentages, thus putting pressures on other employees to do the same: "There was no basic overtime wage, although some factories gave small overtime supplements. . . . Generally, people were to work overtime because it was a political responsibility. The young communists were willing to be activists in overtime work because they wanted to join the party. They wanted to be chosen as advanced workers" (informant no. 24).

Activists also volunteer for special duty, often in groups referred to by the Soviet term *shock brigade* (*tuji dui*):

If there is a leak in the pipes somewhere or if something is broken and needs fixing right away, the party will get the youth league to mobilize the young people to do it real fast. For example, if they're digging some foundations or tunnels, workers will go very slow and complain about the conditions. So they'll hold a shop meeting, criticize the workers, and then give the job to a shock brigade of activists, and they'll stay up all night and do it in half the time. They work like crazy. Then the party secretary will call another meeting and criticize the workers again, saying "you workers complain about conditions. You have no revolutionary feelings. These young boys did your work for you overnight!" (Informant no. 72)

When self-criticism is required, activists are the first to make a speech about their own shortcomings and how they will reform in the future. The activity has competitive overtones, what Whyte (1974) calls "competitive selflessness":

The activists needed the criticism meetings. This is how they show how pure and honest they are in front of the party. Even if they don't have any bad thoughts, they confess anyway to appear honest. The activists enjoyed this and tried to find things to criticize themselves for. One activist had been writing reports to the party secretary for two years, trying to get in. One day he ran into the party leader's office in a great hurry to turn in 15 yuan he said he found in the street. They said, "Wow! He's a real Lei Feng!" [a model worker famous for his selflessness] and had a big campaign to study and praise him in the factory. He became a model for the whole city, they even sent a newspaper reporter to interview him. As it turned out later, the guy had turned in his own money. His wife lived in the countryside, and wrote a letter to his leader to complain that he hadn't sent her any money for two months. . . . When the leader questioned him about this, he confessed. (Informant no. 72)

Political activism does not merely require saying the right things in meetings. It requires an enormous investment of time, energy, and effort. Activists attend not only the usual round of factory meetings; they help organize them and prepare for them. They have their own separate youth league meetings after hours. They stay after work to prepare the wall posters displaying production figures and political slogans that are ubiquitous in the Chinese factory:

A girl from my school class was sent to the factory the same time as me. She immediately began to establish her activist character and became involved in the campaigns run by the propaganda department—all of those political campaigns of the 1970s. . . . She accumulated more experience and became more familiar with the members of the department. They all knew her by name, and knew who she was. Eventually she was even sent to other shops to help run campaigns, write posters after work, and so forth. She helped arrange cultural performances in the factory; meetings, posters. She did all the organizing. On National Day, she would organize a program where all the shops would give a performance of some kind. (Informant no. 71)

Activists provide a large reservoir of unpaid labor that is at the disposal of workshop leaders, youth league and union organizations, the party, and the propaganda department. The commitment of long hours after work takes away from one's personal life; this is one reason why most activists are young and single.

"Backbones" are a type of activist who displays commitment in a less vocal, less overtly political manner.

> There are also activists who are not interested in politics, and who don't rely on personal relationships either. They don't report on others. They work hard and listen to orders. They attend and listen at political study, but they don't speak up that much. They can get some promotions, but they don't get promoted very far without good political *biaoxian*. (Informant no. 71)

The term *backbone* conveys the function these people perform for leaders. They are the reliable experienced employees on whom leaders can always count for help. Backbones are usually highly skilled, veteran workers; they are good at their jobs. They support party policy in their utterances in meetings (which tend to be shorter than those of the young activists) and in more tangible ways as well. They volunteer to stay after work to perform extra tasks; they counsel younger workers who are having problems on the job; they try to convince the rank and file of the correctness of party policy; and they run errands for their supervisors and, in general, put themselves at their service.

An activist orientation has other costs that cannot be measured in time and effort. One has to endure negative peer pressure from the rank and file and other psychic tensions:

> When activists are teased and attacked, they don't retaliate. They expect this as part of the burden of being an activist. Being an activist is tough. You always have to struggle and compete, especially with the other activists. Now I wasn't an activist so I can't say for sure, but relations between activists seemed very competitive. . . . The life is tough. That's why many drop out of the competition after they reach their goal of joining the youth league. (Informant no. 72)

One important psychic tension is in interpersonal relations. The activist is always forced publicly to "draw a line" between himself and other workers. Loyalty is to the party and its principles, not to friends and coworkers. This makes it difficult for activists to win deep friendships among their coworkers. An activist who sides with friends against the party can ruin a long-standing record of loyalty and service. The dilemma can be a difficult one:

> I got along really well with this activist who was my group leader. I would help him out and give him soap because he was poor and had a lot of kids. But he was still an activist, and he sold me out once. Once I stole coal bricks from the shop and hid them in our dorm room. He turned me in when the leader found it and demanded to know who had done it. But he felt bad about it and was too ashamed even to look at me after that. He couldn't even speak to me. We couldn't room together after that, and he moved out. I felt sorry for him. (Informant no. 72)

There are, finally, no guarantees that one's efforts will win recognition and reward. A minority of activists do fail:

> Sometimes activists are criticized by the party leaders because they have very high standards of conduct. Sometimes the party leaders decide they don't like a certain activist. Then it's really sad, because they don't get any support, either from the workers or the leaders. One roommate I had for a while was a real activist. Every single night he wrote a self-criticism to send to the party. But the branch secretary just laughed at him. He cried every night. He always told me how hard it was to be an activist, and that I should never try to become one. Sometimes I really had sympathy with the activists because they really had it hard. (Informant no. 72)

Despite these difficulties, activist orientations do have considerable rewards. Activism is the path to promotion and party membership. The party cultivates activists through a certain period of time under the tutelage of a member before their entry into probationary party membership (Martin 1981: 7–9). From the activists' perspective, this is a period of testing during which loyalty to the party and its policies must be displayed without faltering. As one decidedly nonactivist worker (no. 56) observed, "There is a saying for this in China, 'Those who can sing a lofty tune can move up in the world.'" Activists who receive glowing evaluations of their *biaoxian* and the personal sponsorship of their superiors for party membership are those who are likely to become work group heads, assistant shop directors, or officials in the union, youth league, or party branch.

Passive-Defensive Orientations

Only a minority of employees can be successful activists. The rewards for competitive orientations can be given to a limited number of people: the number of promotion opportunities, in particular, is small. The personal costs, further, can be a powerful deterrent. Because of this, the majority of employees approach organized political life less as an opportunity than as a hurdle to be negotiated.[7] These employees adopt defensive orientations intended to avoid the "mistakes" that bring a curtailment of rewards, punishment, or the subtle forms of victimization known colloquially as being made to "wear small shoes" (*chuan xiao xiezi*). For these people, participation in factory politics is a game in which there are few tangible rewards but many potential hazards. This defensive orientation is perfectly epitomized in a statement made by an emigre to another researcher (Falkenheim 1978: 22): "If you don't grasp politics, politics will grasp you" (*bu zhua zhengzhi, zhengzhi jiu zhua ni*).

The first rule of this defensive posture is that risk taking is to be avoided. "Safe" responses must be ascertained before venturing to speak out. Nonactivists respond to the messages put forth by leaders only after seeing how the activists respond or after watching the reaction of leaders to the initial responses of other workers. Once the desired response is clear, the nonactivist will stay as close as possible to the orthodox view and carefully word the statement to avoid criticism: "For political study we just did what we were supposed to do and finished with it. Workers at other kinds of meetings would often raise suggestions about problems that the group leader brings up. Many didn't bother. Suggestions were stated, and the leaders listened. There was never a situation where people opposed one another's suggestions and argued about it" (informant no. 18). The same calculation applies to volunteering for unpaid overtime, making self-criticisms, or expressing opinions on national political issues or problems in the plant:

7. This was clearly not the case in the high schools studied by Shirk (1982), where the proportion of activists in the student body appears to have been much higher than in factories.

We had campaigns to criticize Lin Biao and Confucius, and to criticize Deng [Xiaoping]. We had study meetings, read the documents. . . . There were meetings every day after work for two hours, except for Saturday, Sunday, and Wednesday. We just did a pro-forma (*xingshi de*) job. Why would we want to criticize Deng? We liked him! But if we didn't criticize him, and didn't speak up, we would be criticized ourselves. So we just gave a pro-forma criticism, and we didn't really believe what we were saying. We would mouth slogans that we read in the newspapers, or copy the newspaper documents when it was time to write essays. . . . When the Gang of Four fell . . . we criticized the Gang of Four, of course. We had no choice, just like before. (Informant no. 48)

No matter how seemingly irrelevant the topic, or lengthy the exercise, the employee must maintain at least a minimum of attention in order to be able to manifest the proper attitudes:

We studied editorials and politics. Very dull. They talked nonsense. Sometimes we had to give speeches if the leader called on us. This was the most tiresome thing of all. My friends and I would talk for one to three minutes, but the activists would go on and on. . . . When we had to write essays, we just copied the editorials word for word. When we talked we said exactly what the editorials said. We didn't dare say what was really on our minds. . . . We didn't dare fall asleep either, because we would be criticized. We just sat and listened. (Informant no. 50)

A former section chief reflected on his difficulties in running political study among his workers:

We handled political study very simply. We just read the material in *People's Daily* and *Red Flag* aloud to the workers. Then we explained to them what the terms meant, what the general point was, and answered their questions if they had any. Workers generally were very uninterested in all this. Very abstract, hard to understand. Hardly anybody ever spoke up. Often they had trouble staying awake. (Informant no. 76)

Not surprisingly, nonactivists seek to avoid this task if possible. "Most workers used all kinds of excuses to get out of political study. We used to joke about people with sick families: one week their father was ill, the next week their mother, and so on" (informant no. 71).

The defensive orientation is one learned through daily experience on the shop floor. The institutional culture and its rituals, once learned, become second nature to employees.[8] One informant, a skilled worker, described a personal learning process that was perhaps more difficult than usual because he was an overseas Chinese who had migrated to China in his early teens:

> In my first two years in the factory, when I was a worker in the shop, they often had meetings where the shop leader would give a speech that went something like this: "Recently, there have been many people in this shop who have been concerned very little about production and quality. This reflects the influence of the class enemies!" This was common [during that period: 1969–1970]. (Informant no. 56)

The worker was at first puzzled by this approach. To his mind, as he recalled later, inattention to production and quality had nothing to do with class struggle, and everything to do with concrete problems that bothered workers. His own experience suggested that most of the workers in his section, women who had families to care for, could not manage all of their family chores because of the meetings after work. This led to inattention on the job. A more direct approach to the problem, it occurred to him, would be to curtail meetings, let workers go home immediately after the shift, and allow them to direct their thoughts at the factory completely to their work. One day, when his group leader was criticizing one of his coworkers in this way, he decided to make his suggestion:

> At that time, I was just out of school and still did not understand the country and its politics very well. So one time I raised my hand and said, "Look here, if you use this people vs. the enemy contradiction in talking to people all the time, you'll never get anywhere." . . . The group leader then turned to me, pulled out a copy of the little red book of Lin Biao's quotations, and read a quote that went something like this: "Politics is nothing more than class struggle." Then the other workers in the group turned around and criticized me, even the woman I had defended, reading some other quotations. I was criticized a bit. I felt that if I continued [to insist on the point raised], I would soon be made the object of "class struggle." After the meeting, one of the older women in the group came up to me and said, "Look, you just got out of school and came out into society. You don't understand things yet. It would be better for you just

8. Shirk (1982) and Unger (1982) show that this process begins in school, although the degree of activist competition varies according to the place of the school in the academic tracking system.

to talk less and work more, say the things you have to say and be done with it." You can imagine how I felt . . . I didn't speak out like this at meetings anymore. (Informant no. 56)

"Say the things you have to say, and be done with it" sums up the routine approach of those who have adopted this defensive orientation. Those who stick closely to it can avoid the potential hazards of public politics in the shop and maintain the goodwill or at least the neutrality of supervisors: "One attitude toward study and criticism is: well, we have to go along, even though we hate it; we know everyone is lying, but we have to go along so we don't leave a bad impression. Why get in trouble over this petty stuff?" (informant no. 72). The orientation is designed to shield nonactivists from deeper intrusions of public politics into their lives. The party's line and its leadership may change completely, but the rules of the game remain the same:

> After the fall of the Gang of Four [1976], there were changes on the surface. . . . But in reality there were no major changes. . . . The party committee still runs things according to its wishes. All of this rehabilitation of people from the 1950s . . . workers don't understand the meaning of this too well. All they know is that they still have to smile and agree with everything the party says and only then can they go about their own business. (Informant no. 57)

Many employees, therefore, come to view organized political life as the domain of the competitively oriented people who seek advancement, and they withdraw from public politics to the safety of a facade of compliance. The goal of the nonactivist in this public arena is simply to avoid standing out from the rest of the group, to avoid becoming "isolated," as many put it. If others in the group, usually beginning with the activists, volunteer to work unpaid overtime, the nonactivist follows suit to avoid standing out. If others in the group are criticizing a group member, the nonactivist joins in to avoid having his or her silence interpreted as dissent. If others in the group are volunteering to spend their only day off at a mass public rally to celebrate the anniversary of the founding of the party, the nonactivist follows the tide. To fall out of line, to be noticed and singled out for criticism, is to be isolated from the group. When one is cut off from the group in this way, not only social and psychological pressures are applied, but material rewards and punishments are brought into play as well. In the worst case, one will be singled out as someone with poor *biaoxian* and will soon find punishments applied and various aspects of one's livelihood affected.

This orientation, I should point out, is not unique to China nor is it the result solely of the two-decade infusion of moral-political standards into factory reward practices. A similar shop-floor culture exists in Soviet bloc countries, despite incentive systems that focus on the fulfillment of production quotas rather than the display of moral-political virtue. The same workshop pattern of political organization and activism is there focused on the relatively depoliticized matter of production. Haraszti's articulate statement of the nonactivist's perspective is strongly reminiscent of the statements quoted above:

> Nothing can stop the factory newsheet—in its clumsy jargon of enthusiasm—from calling an increase in productivity "the victorious achievement of output totals." . . . Such articles—the habitual sideshows of [labor] competition—along with the photographs of the winners, and so on, get a cold reception from those who bother to read them at all. "Clowning" they call it, even when it's their turn to be among the victorious, or when they have to play the rules of the game and make a commendation to the editors of the brigade journal. They gladly leave all that to the good boys who want a political future and are laying the basis of a career. . . . The situation is an embarrassing one: everyone is aware of the ridiculous and undignified role he plays in this charade; its seriousness is ensured by the foreman, silent and attentive, but always very much in evidence. Everyone knows that before the brigade meeting he and his cronies have already decided on the commendations, and no one mistakes the meaning of his silence. (1979: 69–70)

It is apparent that it is not the militant assertion of moral-political virtue that creates these dispositions. It is the product of the political dependence of the workforce and the foreman's control over the distribution of resources. No matter how militantly the Chinese party asserted its moral-political standards, it could not escape this structured pattern of ritual and passivity. The result is a political culture that has been described by Jowitt as typical of Marxist-Leninist political regimes: a "split posture, one of public compliance on the one hand and private avoidance, skepticism, or rejection on the other," one embodying "a cultural disposition that (is) highly calculative toward the political realm, a posture of complying publicly in order to protect and preserve one's private domain" (1974: 179).

Variations and Their Significance

These competitive and defensive orientations have been described not in order to create stereotypes of employee behavior, but to show the calculativeness involved and to draw the single most important analytical distinction between types of orientations. Activists and nonactivists do not always behave automatically in the same way, and they do not always comply mechanically and ritualistically with the same degree of intensity. Rather, their behavior is flexibly adjusted, within the boundaries of competitive and defensive orientations, according to the employee's calculation of the consequences of certain behavior in variable settings and political climates. "Political atmosphere" (*zhengzhi qihou*) is the key feature of the workplace environment according to which employees adjust their behavior (see Whyte 1974). In a "strict" political atmosphere, the stress placed on orthodox public definitions of *biaoxian* is greater; the utterances and behavior of employees are monitored more carefully and are more likely to be given political significance; the range of opinions that can be expressed openly is more narrow; and the pressure applied for all employees to exhibit an activist demeanor is greater. In a "relaxed" political atmosphere, the opposite is true: orthodox public definitions of *biaoxian* are less strictly enforced; employee utterances and behavior are monitored less closely and are less likely to be given political significance; the range of opinions that can be expressed is broader; and the pressures to exhibit an "activist" demeanor are much less intense.

The strictness of political atmosphere and, therefore, the extent to which ritualized competitive and defensive behavior is employed vary according to three contextual factors. The first is the type of meeting involved. Routine production meetings invariably have a more relaxed political atmosphere than routine political study meetings, and routine political study meetings invariably have a more relaxed atmosphere than meetings called to single out victims for criticism and punishment for deviant political attitudes. The second factor is the tenor of national politics—something that is apparent to all through their political study meetings. The periodic advent of political campaigns brings in its wake a marked tightening of a factory's political atmosphere. Some periods of rule have been notable for their relaxed political atmosphere, absence of major political campaigns, relative deemphasis of orthodox political definitions of *biaoxian*, and relative stress on actual work performance in reward systems. Other periods have been notable for their extreme emphasis on orthodox definitions of *biaoxian* and their militant emphasis on political loyalty; for example, mid-1957 to 1959 and late 1966 to 1972.

The third factor is the organizational setting itself. It is only among the permanent employees of large and medium-sized state enterprises and the large collectives that a strict political atmosphere can be maintained. Only these enterprises have a broad range of rewards to distribute, retain most of their personnel almost permanently, and have fully developed party organizations and networks of activists. Smaller collective enterprises rarely have an organized party presence, "activism" figures less prominently in their reward systems, they wield fewer rewards, and their labor force has a higher rate of turnover. These smaller enterprises, judging by the description of informants who worked in them, are not able to maintain a strict political atmosphere that successfully induces an "activist" demeanor from employees.

Employees, therefore, calculatively adjust their behavior according to their perception of the political atmosphere or, in other words, according to the demands placed on their behavior at that place and time. In a routine political study meeting, during a period with a relatively relaxed national political climate, workers reportedly knit, whisper among themselves, and even doze off during the long-winded, formulaic, and unenthusiastic speeches of leaders and activists. If the average employee says anything, it is in the most mechanical, sometimes desultory, fashion. By contrast, in the politically charged atmosphere of a major campaign, where the rhetoric indicates that victims may be singled out for criticism and punishment, the demands placed on individual *biaoxian* are at their strictest. Activists give emotion-charged speeches; nonactivists make convincingly sincere responses. Tension, nervousness, and sweaty palms are the order of the day, and nonactivists make full efforts to present ritualistically the proper facade of agreement. In short, the behavior typical of competitive and defensive orientations ebbs and flows with the changing political tides that shift the boundaries placed on behavior by currently enforced definitions of *biaoxian*.

The Substantive
Ambiguity of *Biaoxian*

With their ability to sum up group evaluations, to submit personal evaluations of subordinates for bonuses and raises, to pronounce on a subordinate's *biaoxian*, to decide when to report a criticized infraction to the plant administration, and to decide whether or not to support a subordinate's request for housing or other benefits, group leaders, section chiefs, shop directors, and party branch secretaries can amass considerable personal authority. Even without the flexibility afforded by the intrusion of *biaoxian* into rewards and punishments, Chinese shop leaders have much broader discretion, over a wider range of decisions, than their counterparts in Japan and the United States. The politicization of rewards in the Chinese factory simply enhances the tendency, already ingrained in the structure of communist factory organization, to create a marked personal dependence on leaders: "If you are assessed well by the leader, you will do well. If a leader has a bad impression of you, it is hard. In some ways, things are run by the concept 'will of the leader' (*zhangguan yizhi*)" (informant no. 62).

Biaoxian is an ambiguous concept. So far I have described only its official, "public" definition: employee conduct during campaigns and political meetings, their "work attitude" and political loyalty toward the leadership and the party line. But my description of its evaluation on the shop floor suggests that there is an irreducible personal, "private" aspect to the act of assessing *biaoxian* as well. There is clearly more to *biaoxian* than simply making a public display of orthodox political virtue. One has to make a personal impression on the people who do the evaluating. In practice, employees who are unfailingly helpful, cooperative, and courteous in dealings with leaders make a more favorable impression on them and tend to receive better evaluations. Employees quickly learn that an uncooperative or critical attitude toward their supervisors rapidly leads to a bad impression and unfavorable evaluation, no matter how vocal and orthodox the employee is during a political meeting. Conflict with supervisors leads to unfavorable evaluations. Good evaluations are more likely when the employee maintains an agreeable attitude in the face of authority figures, agrees to run errands, take attendance, put away tools after the shift, and generally build up a pool of goodwill. From their own perspective, supervisors are concerned just as much with having subordinates who are helpful, courteous, and obedient as they are with having subordinates who mouth the correct slogans in meetings. It is in fact the former who are more helpful to the supervisors on a daily basis—it makes their jobs easier. Activist behavior inevitably involves a relationship with leaders, one in which the active loyalty and support of a minority is exchanged for status, career opportunities, and favorable treatment in other areas. Party rule in factories, even when the orthodox, public definitions are militantly asserted, is based on a network of patron-client ties.

5. Clientelist Bureaucracy: The Factory Social Order

The Chinese concern for the moral and political education of the workforce, institutionalized in small group organization and in a reward system centered on the evaluation of *biaoxian*, comprises a distinctive variant of generic communist institutions. But the moral-political ethic that the party seeks actively to foster proves elusive. The attempt to revitalize and extend the ideological tie through the use of rewards and career incentives itself injects a calculative element into the display of commitment. Just as importantly, the concept of *biaoxian* is itself ambiguous. On the shop floor, commitment to the party's ideals is displayed through loyalty to the party organization. In principle, loyalty is displayed toward the party as a whole and the abstract ideals it represents, but in practice it is displayed through loyalty to the officials who represent the party in the shop. Because of the close working partnership and mutual dependence of shop officials and activists, this official relationship is easily mingled with personal loyalties. When shop officials exercise their discretion in pay, promotion, and distribution to reward their loyal followers—something that is legitimized by the notion of rewarding *biaoxian*—these ties take on some of the characteristics of "traditional" patron-client ties.

When I speak of a Chinese variant and point out the inherent tendency of principled particularism to evolve into a neo-traditional system of patronage, I am not suggesting that the moral-political rewards cause these patterns of patronage or that patronage is part of what is distinctive about the Chinese variant. The inherently ambiguous and unstable system of moral-political mobilization evolved into a system of clientelism that is also characteristic of the Soviet Union and other Eastern bloc countries. This pattern is the result of structural features common to all communist factories: the workers' economic dependence on the enterprise; political dependence on party and management; and, most important, the wide discretion of shop officials over promotion, pay, direct distributions, and sociopolitical services. It matters little whether activists are to be rewarded broadly for their display of communist morality or, as in the Soviet Union and East Germany during the periods described by Bendix (1956) and Cook (1985), in a more narrowly instrumental sense for their voluntary performance in "shock brigades." Both are a form of principled particularism—only the principles vary in interpretation and content. Nor does it matter that mass mobilization through the party organization gives way to a strategy of work discipline that stresses individual responsibility and reward, and stable, "depoliticized" factory administration (as has been true of the Soviet Union since 1932, with the partial exception of World War II, and in China since 1979). The pattern of dependence is not fundamentally changed: the discretion of shop officials is intact, and the actively loyal minority continue to benefit from their status as the clients of the power structure.[1] China's distinctive approach to mass mobilization, pursued vigorously in industry for most of the two decades after 1957, could not escape the tendencies inherent in the organized dependence of workers.

The generic pattern of principled particularism originated in Soviet industry in the 1930s, as the party sought to discipline the workforce by offering selective access to factory benefits and resources. The Soviets formally enshrined this principle as the doctrine of "preferential access" (*l'got i preimvshchestvennoe snabzhenie*), and it was elaborated into a system of supply and service bureaucracies (Cook 1985: chap. 5, p. 35). Party resolutions in the early 1930s specified privileges for loyal workers—defined formally as activists in production campaigns:

> Workers and technical personnel who show themselves to be the better producers (shock workers and participants in socialist competition), who do work of high quality, and also those who work for long periods at a given enterprise, who introduce valuable proposals and innovations, are to be given incentive by the granting of priority in allocation of apartments, sending to universities and technical schools, vacation homes and health resorts . . . and priority supply of deficit products. (Quoted in Cook 1985: chap. 5, p. 34)

1. I return to this topic in chapter 7, where I examine changes in the period since Mao's death.

Family members of shock workers were also to be given preference in employment at the same enterprise, entry into courses of study, apprenticeships, universities and technical schools, and priority access to kindergartens, nursery schools, supplies from closed distribution networks, and permission to eat in better meal halls (Schwarz 1952: chap. 3; Cook 1985: chap. 5, p. 35). This is the historical origin of institutionalized patronage in the communist factory. The Chinese did not depart fundamentally from this pattern, except to link privileged access more broadly to workers' moral and political attributes.

In this chapter, I describe three distinctive features of the communist factory's institutional culture and analyze their significance from a comparative perspective. The patterns I describe are Chinese. Just as the Chinese modified Stalinist mobilization in a distinctive fashion, so may the patterns I am about to describe reflect distinctive emphases that are the result of the peculiar characteristics of Chinese industry, the party's history and traditions, its postrevolution experience, and, more broadly and ambiguously, the history and culture of China's long civilization. Published studies of factory institutions and social relations in the Soviet Union and Eastern Europe do not permit careful comparisons, but they do suggest that these features are shared ones, and that they distinguish the modern communist pattern from the modern capitalist pattern, whether of the Japanese or American variety.

The first of these features is the division of the workforce along vertical lines, a social cleavage that is just as real and, in fact, more salient in the consciousness and actions of workers than horizontal distinctions based on skill or pay. In the last chapter, I described the different orientations toward authority that distinguish the activist minority from the adaptive rank and file. In this chapter, I speak of the relations between activists and the rank and file; the social antagonisms directed toward activists; and the ways that these antagonisms are reflected in social relations in the factory. My aim is not merely descriptive. I intend to show that these antagonisms have structural consequences: they bind activists more closely to their patrons for personal and moral support, deepening the personal aspects already inherent in this vertical relationship.

The second structural feature is the stable relationship between shop leaders (and sometimes the leaders of certain staff offices) and activists. I have already described the working relationship between activists and leaders and alluded to the rewards that accrue to successful activists. In this chapter I elaborate the features that make this a patron-client relationship: particularly the ongoing exchange of loyalty for advantage, the personal aspects of the relationship, and the tendency for workers to apply to it the same terms that were used to describe patron-client ties before the revolution. The significance of this pattern of patron-client relations is not that personal ties still exist in the "informal" organization of the factory alongside the formally prescribed roles. Their significance is that communist factory organization constitutes a clientelist system, in which these pervasive ties comprise a network that is officially sponsored as part of the prescribed role structure of the organization. These clientelist ties are a central institution through which authority is exercised; they are not an incidental or supplemental aspect of official institutions.[2] To buttress this point, I describe two types of cliques or factions that exist either within the official clientelist network, or separate from it, which are based purely on personal loyalties and which are the functional equivalent of informal organization.

The third feature of the factory's institutional culture is the network of instrumental-personal ties through which workers, primarily nonactivists, pursue their interests by attempting as individuals to influence the decisions of their superiors. These ties range from the favors expected of factory officials with whom one has a long-standing personal relationship to a type of gift giving that amounts to little more than ceremonialized bribery. These instrumental-personal ties are a pervasive feature of Chinese (and Soviet) social relations; they extend well beyond the factory to life outside and often characterize the citizen's dealings with retail outlets and various local government offices. In recent years, they have been the subject of wide publicity and criticism in the Chinese press and in satirical literature, but they have been well entrenched for decades. I limit attention to those relationships in the factory and, of those, only the ones between workers and people in an official capacity to grant a favor: shop leaders, factory doctors, and officials

---

2. On this point I diverge from the emphasis of Eisenstadt and Roniger (1984), who equate clientelism with the element of institutional relationships that is purely personal in nature. Party clientelism does not fit well within their scheme, and its comparative significance is surely not that personal relations are intermingled with official leadership relations.

in the office that distributes factory apartments.[3] These ties are a part of the informal organization of the enterprise. They flourish, despite official hostility to them, because of the role of the work-place in distributing goods and services and in making decisions that greatly affect workers' lives, and because of the wide discretion left to workshop and other officials in these matters. Their signifi-cance for the exercise of authority is that they provide an avenue through which nonactivists can pursue their interests, gain a sense that they have "beaten" or "mastered" the system, and in some cases get "one up" on the activists, who are otherwise advantaged. Perhaps more importantly, this activity reinforces a tendency to-ward individual, rather than group, action among workers. Work-ers, in effect, compete with one another for a limited number of goods by approaching officials as supplicants.

The Divided Workforce
as a Social Fact

By referring to the distinction between activists and nonactivists as a "social fact," I am pointing to a status difference among work-ers that is just as "real" as any division based on skill, pay, or ethnicity in the workforces of other countries. In the communist factory, the distinction is easily the most politically salient social-structural cleavage. On the shop floor and outside of work, this social cleavage is marked by general resentment and open antag-onism toward activists and by their social isolation from the rank and file.[4] There is a family resemblance, to be sure, between these social antagonisms and the peer pressures routinely placed on "rate-busters" in American factories and described in well-known studies of human relations in industry (e.g., Roy 1954). It would trivialize the phenomenon, however, to understand these antag-onisms primarily in this light. The crucial difference is that these are not peer pressures in the communist factory at all, but antagonisms between two distinct groups in the workforce. The antagonism dis-

3. I will not describe instrumental-personal ties between white collar staff and leaders, among leaders at different levels, or instrumental-personal ties among work-ers, because these do not bear directly on the authority relations examined here.

4. Bendix (1956: 417–33), in his study of East German industry in the 1950s, was the first to analyze the "isolation of the activists" (his term).

played toward activists is a reflection of a deeper social fact: that activists have sided politically with the party and management, that they have entered into a special relationship with representatives of the party and act routinely against the interests of the group as a whole, and that they will eventually become leaders themselves.

The most direct cause of the deep resentments that workers harbor toward activists is the habitual practice of informing or making a "small report" (*xiao bao*), something actively encouraged by leaders:

> Most activists were shunned by ordinary workers. We didn't want to run into them. They were always reporting on people for saying things, sleeping on the night shift, and so on. Activists were hated by the others because they played up to the leaders and the party. . . . They talked secretly to the leaders, and that's why they're hated. Even though it was secret, you knew it was happening because when a meeting was called, the leaders already knew what was going on. (Informant no. 71)

One interesting side effect of the resentment toward activists, hardly incidental to the exercise of authority, is that it deflects antagonisms away from the party and management and focuses them onto other members of the workforce. I have already described how small groups bottle up conflict, by causing workers to compete within it for rewards. This is a broad expression of the basic pattern of "divide and rule." In reflecting on my interviews and after subsequent rereadings of the transcripts, I have been struck by how often my informants expressed antagonism toward activists and how rarely similar feelings were voiced toward leaders above the level of the work group. One of my later informants (no. 72) spontaneously offered the conclusion I had reached after many earlier interviews: "In reality, the workers didn't hate the party leaders as much as the activists who reported on them."

Not all activists are resented with equal intensity. In chapter 4, I described various types of activists. Not surprisingly, the activists for whom special animosity is reserved are the ones seen as aggressive careerists, who ingratiate themselves personally with leaders. These are the activists that are most likely to report on others:

> There are different kinds of activists, and they have different relations with average workers. Those who cultivate personal connections with the leaders are hated the most. It is considered unethical to curry favor

with leaders this way. . . . People usually accept the promotion of someone who does good work. But they still don't like the activist who is seen
as trying to become an official. (Informant no. 71)

The antagonism toward activists is expressed most commonly in
their general social isolation: "You can see it when people leave the
plant and go home. Ordinary workers walk in groups and talk
among themselves. At the bus stop, nobody talks to them. Of
course, activists aren't too willing to talk with ordinary people either. The feeling is mutual" (informant no. 71). The social isolation, as these sentences imply, is not wholly the result of the hostility
of the rank and file. Activists hold themselves aloof from many activities on the shop floor: "The way you can tell if someone is no
longer an activist is whether they join in with the other workers
when they stand around and curse the leaders. When they're an activist, they don't take part, they avoid it. But, if someone's no longer
an activist, they enter in too. That's how you tell he's one of the
workers again" (ibid.). The feeling of mutual isolation and distrust
is so deeply rooted that it is difficult to eradicate, even after an activist tries to return to the fold: "There are some activists who give up
after a while if they are not successful. But generally speaking, it's
impossible to go back to being just a common worker and a member of the masses. You've already paid a high price. People's opinion
of you changes" (ibid.).

Social isolation is not the only expression of this division in the
workforce. Open antagonism and even physical intimidation are
not unusual:

> They treat you like the party's slave, or dog. So you feel lonely. Some-
> times [the activists] cry because of all the pressure. The workers are
> really tough on them. They'll say, "You ass kisser! Why don't you give
> your wife to the party secretary to screw!" I saw this happen once, and
> the guy just started crying. (Informant no. 72)

> It was common for workers to do things to activists. We made fun of
> them. Barbs were very common. We would tell an activist, "Hey! Lao
> San is sleeping! Better go tell the section chief!" Also, some of the
> tougher guys would bully them, slap them on the head and insult them.
> . . . The peasant-workers often threw away their clothes or burned
> them, trashed their lockers, or slugged them. The peasants did this a lot.
> They're direct and tough. The rest of us didn't do these things, but we
> still didn't mind it too much. Sometimes we felt bad for the activists. It's

hard to tell who's right and who's wrong sometimes. Most of the bullying goes a bit too far. Burning up their clothes is really bad because cloth
is rationed and expensive. And after all, activists sometimes were only
doing what was right. They weren't always being scoundrels. (Informant
no. 71)

There are limits to the harassment of activists, but they do not
come close to prohibiting it. The line is drawn at physical injury, at
which point the shop leaders get involved. But, even in these cases,
there is no real punishment if the injury is not serious: "If someone
hit an activist real good and bruised him up, they might call a meeting and criticize the guy. . . . But this didn't always work out too
well . . . the guy would secretly be considered a hero in the minds of
the workers. . . . So bullying can go too far, but there's no serious
punishment for it" (informant no. 71).

All of these cases of intimidation refer primarily to younger
activists, ones that do not yet hold any position of leadership. Activists that have already become group leaders or that hold a position in the youth league or union organization have a higher status
and are more closely protected by their direct association with
leaders. After a worker enters the party, a physical attack, much less
a sarcastic insult, is considered a grave political matter; it is an af-
front to party leadership. Party members are off limits. That leaves
the younger activists in an exposed and highly vulnerable position,
the only available outlet for the expression of antagonisms. Aside
from the occasional mass meetings mentioned above and articles in
Workers' Daily that criticize the phenomenon in periodic bursts,
the practice appears to be widely condoned by factory officials.[5] It
may be that this is tacitly considered a rite of passage that all potential party members must endure: part of the "testing through hardship" and "arduous struggle" from which hardened candidates for
party membership will emerge. Indeed, in the light of the way that
activists are required to "draw a line" between themselves and other
workers in the most public of ways, one wonders whether this is a
conscious design of the party organization.

Whether consciously intended by party leaders or not, this pattern of social isolation and hostility has the effect of binding the activists more closely to shop leaders. Once they start down their

5. One such recent burst was in Workers' Daily (1982a; 1982b; 1982c).

path, activists become highly dependent on shop leaders for personal and moral support: "As an activist, you have to choose between supporting the party and the other workers. So there's no longer any trust or affection with the other workers. . . . But the shop director would always support the activists and try to make them feel better. They call meetings to tell the workers to stop attacking and sabotaging the activists" (informant no. 72). This is the origin of the personal bonds that exist between successful activists and leaders: once one's coworkers withdraw their friendship and trust, this emotional support must come from the superiors to whom activists have committed themselves:

> If you are trusted by the party, you feel happy, even though other people might hate you. This is a psychological thing. You feel important, like a big man. If you're not trusted by the party, you're not trusted by the nation. You feel lonely if the party doesn't trust you. [But if it does] it makes you feel great. You talk with a deeper voice, you feel confident, strong, and stand up straight . . . you feel proud. Even though the masses may play jokes on you and start rumors, and fight with you, you know these fools are just stupid. You know the party supports you. (ibid.)

This is just one aspect of the patron-client relationship that develops between activists and shop leaders: trust and emotional support. Before I consider the other aspects of the relationship, I should emphasize the connection between it and the "social fact" of the divided workforce: these social antagonisms drive the activist into deeper identification with and loyalty to their official patrons.

The Official Patron-Client Network

The relations between leaders and activists have generally been analyzed under the rubric of "leadership methods"; rarely have they been considered as a stable relationship that comprises a core element of communist social structure. These relationships have a social depth, in both emotional and material terms, that has not been well understood. The result is a highly cohesive clientelist network, radiating from the party committee, comprised of strong ties that mingle personal loyalties, institutional role performance, and material interest.

The most visible aspect of these relationships are the services that activists perform for the leaders. Activists work closely with their group leaders and section chiefs. They not only support leadership initiatives in the ways already described, but they are also the ones who help leaders fill out reports, take attendance, and order materials and tools. Their help is crucial in allowing group leaders to perform their jobs well and to be evaluated favorably by their own superiors in the shop and party branch: "The group leaders know who the backbone elements in the group are, and they rely on them. These were the people with good work habits, maybe party or youth league members, who could be relied on and were easy to get along with. Group leaders turned to these people for advice and help in arranging the group's work" (informant no. 41).

Former group leaders refer to activists and "backbones" as the "reliable ones" (*kekao de*), people with whom they share a sense of "trust" (*xinren*). In the course of their long after-hours volunteer work, activists also come into contact with shop officials, not only the branch secretary and shop director, but various assistants in charge of the youth league, propaganda work, and union. Many of them eventually develop a close personal familiarity with one or more of these officials in the course of their work with them. Activists that display extraordinary commitment and ability in organizational matters—usually only a handful from a single workshop— will be introduced to officials in factory staff departments or offices that work under the direction of the party. The factory's union office, youth league headquarters, and propaganda department are especially dependent on the volunteer work of capable activists. After-hours work eventually leads to close familiarity; before long, the staff officials will begin to ask the shop director to "borrow" that worker during working hours; and the final step is to transfer the worker permanently to the department staff (the same sequence occurs in promotions to shop staff positions). Between the initial introduction and the eventual promotion, there will be several years in which the activist has a special relationship with the leaders of the department involved.

There is, therefore, an element of exchange to the relationship. Group leaders, section chiefs, workshop leaders, and certain staff offices depend heavily on the support of activists to lead successfully both production and political meetings in the group; the activists and "backbones," in turn, receive consistently favorable evaluations of their *biaoxian*, and the rewards this entails. A former factory executive (no. 55) described how the reward system looked from the top down:

> Of course, they assessed people in small groups [for raises], and politics was a major criterion. But these so-called group assessments were only superficial. The real decisions were made by the plant director in consultation with the party and shop directors. They made the decision and had a fixed percentage limit. In the small groups it was the backbone elements, the activists, who were assessed for raises. The decision is really already set, and everybody in the group knows it. Only four out of ten will get it, everyone knows. So the discussion is just for show.

This special relationship between leaders and their loyal followers does not just bring the advantages of these officially prescribed bonuses, raises, and promotions, but also the informal distributions that characterize the natural economy of the enterprise. It is in this sense that these vertical ties most closely resemble traditional patronage relations:

> Personal loyalty (*yiqi*) can lead to advantages for all the people who are officials or all those who are connected with them. The higher you are, the more the advantage. There aren't all that many advantages for ordinary activists who have not yet entered the party. But there certainly are for group leaders. An example is housing. They have quotas for the number of apartments to be distributed in each shop and section. Each level then distributes them. . . . They get down to the section level, and then it goes to the group leaders. If they don't need it, it is offered to the activists. Often the party branch secretary will make a suggestion to the section chief about who really should get something. If the group leader doesn't need it, then he will suggest someone that he shares loyalty (*yiqi*) with, usually his activists. Housing allocations like this took place only once in a while. More common was the distribution of bicycles, radios, sewing machines. . . . There are so many things distributed this way I can't even begin to describe them. Work clothes. They will get a batch in once a year and distribute them free to certain people. Lumber is another. This is very valuable and hard to get. You use it to make furniture, which is very expensive . . . watches, nightstands, sofas, beds, wardrobes, the factory distributes all of them. They aren't available on the market, or at least they weren't back then. You needed ration coupons for all these things, or at least for the better brands of bicycles like "Fly-

ing Pigeon." . . . Of course, the leaders get most of this stuff. The higher their position, the more they get. But some of it gets down to the activists and workers. (Informant no. 71)

In addition to this informal "trickle-down" distribution that follows the lines of personal loyalty, officials may act as patrons by intervening with other factory offices on behalf of their people:

> If you have good relations with the party, the secretary will tell the head of the general affairs department to think over whether he should give an apartment to you. Of course, the head of the general affairs department has to think it over. He wants to maintain good relations with the party secretary. So all the party secretary has to do is say a few words, and it will be done. If you have good relations with him, things will be fine. (Informant no. 76)

The practice of patronage is not without its limits. Not all items are always distributed in this fashion. One limit is the conflict that open favoritism can cause in shops. If it appears that the distribution of a certain item will cause serious ill will in the shop, they may seek to distribute it through need or by lot:

> The factory will get a certain number of watch coupons, give two or so to each shop, and tell them to give them out as they see fit. Then they ask who wants them. Of course, everyone does. Sometimes this can lead to conflict. Sometimes the section chief or group leader decides. Sometimes they have to talk things over with the ones that aren't chosen after he decides. Sometimes workers will try to get close with the group leader and talk him into it. Others argue and fight, and give them a hard time until they give in. Often group leaders have to go on *biaoxian* alone. Sometimes they just take turns. . . . For a real hot item like a bike, the problems are more serious. Everyone needs these, if not for themselves, then for their relatives. (Informant no. 71)

Another limit to the practice is voluntary. Many activists, taking seriously the image of the selfless communist, will refuse advantages from time to time. They may also consider their relations with the other workers and seek to defuse their hostility by leaving some items for them:

> Now it's true that activists get first pick of the things given out, but often they can't bring themselves to accept it. They're supposed to be selfless and serve the people. So sometimes for moral reasons they refuse. They

may take into account the needs of others in the group as well. . . . Even
the activists who could have first choice often take themselves out of the
running because they want to keep a reputation as a selfless activist.
(Informant no. 71)

There are limits to the selflessness as well. The well-intentioned activists may refuse items for themselves, but it is more difficult for
them to resist pressures from their family members for distributions
they may urgently need. No matter how regularly activists refuse
advantages, in the long run, greater advantages will accrue as they
are promoted upward in the hierarchy of patronage and privilege.
To refuse current privilege is simply to delay it.

Even entrance into the party is often imbued with the ethic of
patronage. To be admitted as a party member, an activist must have
detailed personal recommendations from two members. This is usually from one of the candidate's immediate superiors and from one
higher-ranking party member with seniority, who has received
strong assurances of the candidate's worthiness (see Barnett and
Vogel 1967: 27–29; Lewis 1963: 106–7). There follows a period
of cultivation by someone assigned by the party branch to "develop" the candidate under his or her personal tutelage:

> Sometimes they recommend youth league activists for party member-
> ship. To join the party, you write an application to the party committee.
> Then they send a special person to be your "godfather" to have heart-to-
> heart talks with you at least once a week, and you give your heart to the
> party. You have to tell this person your true thoughts. He is a party mem-
> ber, sometimes the head of the youth league branch. This is a person you
> already know. Maybe he recommended you for membership. . . . He
> is very close to you. This is a person you should give gifts to. (Informant
> no. 72)

The personal aspects of the relationship, finally, are reflected in
the language that informants use to describe them. Several terms
arose regularly in the course of interviews on the subject: *ganqing*
(feeling or affection), *yiqi* (personal loyalty), and *renqing* (human
sentiments). These terms cannot be used to guide our analysis,
because they are popularly employed in an inconsistent way: not
everyone uses them and those who do will not always impart them
with the same meaning. But they are an important piece of evidence
about the meanings that people attach to these relations. All of
these terms were applied to traditional patron-client ties in an ear-

lier period of Chinese history. One of these concepts—*ganqing*—is of particular significance, because it was analyzed at length by Morton Fried (1953) in his study of patron-client relations in the polity and economy of a county seat immediately before 1949. The concept is almost identical to that employed by many of my own informants.

Although these vertical ties of loyalty in today's factory share these cultural features with traditional patron-client ties, this is far from a traditional system of patronage. The networks of loyalty have a personal aspect, but they are mingled with the impersonal ethic of commitment of a modern Leninist party and with the role demands of formal organizational practices. The relationships are cultivated as a direct result of the leadership policies and practices of the communist party organization, even though the intention is not to create a neo-traditional clientelist system.

Cliques and Factions

The official patron-client network that characterizes party rule in factories mingles the formal with the informal; personal loyalty with loyalty to the party and its principles. It is a core element of an institution that is organized along clientelist lines. It is not, however, equivalent to "factions" and "cliques": vertical networks of personal followings that are in conflict with other such networks. These are a separate phenomenon. Factions and cliques exist to some extent in the informal organization of all institutions. Because the party exercises a form of clientelist rule, China's factories are especially prone to factionalism within the official clientelist network: whenever factory officials are seriously at odds with one another, they may head separate personal followings and engage in a form of competition for factory resources and benefits that may border on open conflict.[6] Factionalism was especially prominent during the Cultural Revolution, when the leadership of the party was split, stimulating political rivalries below (see Nathan 1973). However prominent factions may be, there is nothing sociologically distinctive about them in the Chinese setting, as is the case for the official clientelist system.

---

6. Factional conflicts in factories are portrayed vividly in the short stories of the author Jiang Zilong (1979), himself formerly a skilled machinist.

Factions and cliques represent a divergence from the party's network in the same way that informal organization diverges from the
formal in studies of American industry. A factory engineer described the functioning of these ties in the following manner:

> This was a normal situation in factories, called factionalism (*paixing*).
> . . . One's actual power depended on these kinds of ties. A vice-director
> transferred into our factory had a difficult time getting his orders carried
> out because he had no connections. It took a long time for him to build
> up these connections before people would listen to his orders. Friend-
> ship facilitated the carrying out of orders, kind of a way of helping out
> your friends by carrying out their requests. This was called being a
> member of a group (*banzi*), or an informal group of friends like this. If
> the member of a group needs something, others carry out orders more
> quickly than those of other people who weren't in the group. (Informant
> no. 2)

Because factional networks are founded on the exchange of loyalty and mutual assistance, one of their main functions is to make
sure that rewards go to the "right people." A former secretary to an
enterprise director, who was intimately familiar with the process of
promotion, put it this way: "Of course there were connections
(*guanxi*), friendships, people pulling up their own people. It is hard
to get things done otherwise. Sometimes the masses realized what
was going on when they saw someone promoted who wasn't really
fit for the job. . . . The leaders naturally wanted people who would
listen to them" (informant no. 44).

The masses were more than just sometimes aware of this phenomenon. They widely perceived these factional ties as comprising
the main avenue for advancement. A young worker (no. 33) explained, "This affected who got good job assignments, promotions,
and transfers up to the company offices. Factionalism mainly came
out in personnel matters. Each faction in the leading group would
pull up its own people." A mechanical draftsman (no. 25) put it in
the same way: "The youth from one faction were given preference
in promotions. . . . Generally, these kinds of connections (*guanxi*),
not ability, were the major way to get promoted, get a good job
assignment, and so forth." A skilled machinist (no. 34) echoed
this awareness: "The connections (*guanxi*) between people in factions proved to be important when it came time for promotions
and transfers."

These factions, especially during the Cultural Revolution in the late 1960s, were sometimes lined up on opposite sides of open political conflicts, but they existed both before and after this period without being identified by allegiance to any political line. Informants defined factions not according to their political beliefs, but according to their shared interest in mutual support and mobility:

> During the 1970s, there were still factions in "thought" [*sixiang*], but no [factional] organizations. They also had friendships and connections that built up, and also some animosities, gaps between people. This had an influence on the positions people were promoted to, and whether or not they were promoted to leading positions. . . . These kinds of factional ties showed up during the 1970s in almost everything, and it continues today. It shows up in work assignments and assessments for raises and bonuses in work groups. In the top leadership, it means promoting your own people and pulling them up with you. You can't really say these factions are defined by political viewpoints. They're defined by ties of mutual interest (*liyi guanxi*). (Informant no. 8)

The factions predated the Cultural Revolution, at which time they became involved in open factional struggles. But the conflicts of that period, according to many informants and, indeed, according to contemporary Chinese novels and short stories (e.g., Jiang 1979), added to the animosities felt between competing factions in the period that followed in the 1970s.

These factions represent the informal side of the official clientelist network; when they come into open conflict, they represent its breakdown. But there are other varieties of personal followings in the factory that are entirely separate from the official network. In a small number of factories, personal followings develop around highly skilled veteran workers who have played a role in training large numbers of apprentices. These veteran workers, who often started to work in the 1940s or 1950s, usually occupy the highest wage grades and are highly skilled. They occupy a special position on the shop floor. In most cases, they are not party members. It would be face-losing for someone of their age to behave like an activist. They have trained many apprentices over the years, many of whom have long since been promoted to group leader, section chief, or workshop head. They already have high wages, their children have in most cases left home, so they do not have pressing needs to be met by the enterprise. Because of their seniority, their valued skills, their role as the former "master" of many of the workers and even some of the leaders, and their economic independence, they are relatively aloof from organized political life. They have a strong sense of personal dignity, and, according to former followers among my informants, they exude a sense of moral authority.

These masters develop personal followings among their current or recent apprentices, and exercise a benign and patriarchal authority over them. (Former pupils who have become activists or leaders may be indulgent toward them, but they have new loyalties and cannot be entirely trusted by the former master.) These are relationships based almost entirely on personal, affective ties; masters do not have rewards to distribute. They build on the teacher-pupil relationship in a traditional manner. They invite young apprentices to their home for dinner; they mediate disputes and try to resolve marital discord; they will make applications and requests to the shop leaders on behalf of their apprentices; and they show concern for their young followers' personal lives by introducing potential marriage partners to them:

> The old master has authority because of his high morals (*daode*) and because he takes care of his pupils like a father. They watch out for their own. He stands up for his followers in front of leaders. For example, if a worker is in trouble for leaving early and later argues with the group leader about it, the master will help him out. He'll rush over and say, "Enough! Enough!" and calm down the leader, give him a smoke, tell him to sit down and relax. Then he'll back up the worker's story, and say, "If you want to criticize somebody, criticize me." It doesn't matter if you were lying to the group leader or not, you could have been out gambling, but the master will still back you up. Maybe later on he'll ask you where you really were. So workers naturally support these guys. (Informant no. 72)

In return, the master receives a kind of immunity from group criticism, he is given considerable respect and "face," and he is regularly given small gifts, usually on important holidays, more valuable for the respect implied than for their material value.

Because of their considerable personal authority, masters who have been able to cultivate large and cohesive followings are a force to be reckoned with in workshops. Shop leaders, in these cases, have to work through or around masters, coopt, or manipulate them, in order to ensure that their orders will be followed.

The old masters controlled their workers. . . . Workers will do anything their master says, but not necessarily for the party leaders. So the party leaders are very polite and respectful to the masters, always asking for their opinion and so forth. . . . Different masters have different followers, they each had their own clique (*pai*). . . . Each master has pride in his technical ability and his ability to lead his workers. Sometimes they try to outdo one another. . . . A good party secretary knows what the situation is, and uses one clique against another in order to rule them. . . . If you're smart you can control them this way. (Informant no. 72)

These informal cliques are the equivalent of those described by Melville Dalton (1959) and Cole (1971); they are a pure case of the type of phenomenon correctly labelled "informal organization" in other work settings (Blau 1954; Gouldner 1955). Their significance for this book is that they provide an analytical contrast with the party's official patron-client network and reinforce my argument that party-clientelism is not merely a case of informal organization, but a distinctive structure that combines the formal and informal.

Instrumental-Personal Ties

The final distinctive feature of the factory's institutional culture is the informal "natural economy" of personal connections through which workers (and all other employees) regularly pursue their interests. These relationships are popularly referred to in China by the term *guanxi*. The term means, literally, "relationship" or "connection," but in this context it refers to an exchange relationship that mingles instrumental intentions with personal feeling. The concept is by no means culturally unique: the terms *blat* in Russia, and *pratik* in Haiti refer to the same type of instrumental-personal tie (Berliner 1957; Mintz 1966). *Guanxi* is not a sociologically precise term: in common usage, it refers to instrumental-personal ties that range from strong personal loyalties to ceremonialized bribery.

At one end of this spectrum is the type of relationship conveyed by the term *particularism*. This involves showing favoritism toward people with whom one has a preexisting personal tie. In this kind of relationship, the personal element is predominant, and the primary motivation is the affective aspect of the tie. The term *ganqing* (feeling), often applied to stable patron-client relations, is also applied to this strongly personal form of *guanxi*. This type of relationship is governed by normative considerations; chief among them being the dictum that having personal affection for someone means that you are willing to do something for them, and they for you. The instrumental and the personal are fused; if one fails to help a friend, one becomes socially embarrassed: it is a face-losing situation. This normative element is predominant; the person who grants the favor does not benefit directly from his or her actions.

At the other end of the spectrum is the type of relationship that amounts to ceremonialized bribery. This involves a straightforward exchange of favors for material gain or a compensatory favor. The personal element is at a minimum; often these are relatively impersonal transactions. The primary motivation is the instrumental aspect of the direct exchange. This kind of relationship is not normatively governed, although there is a certain etiquette involved that shields the harsh instrumental realities of the transaction. The person who grants the favor benefits immediately and directly, usually before the favor is granted. The only thing that separates this from the publicized cases of corruption is the limited values being exchanged. Within a factory, in matters involving workers, the values are invariably small. But the principle is the same as in legally defined cases of corruption: the use of one's position for personal gain.

Between these extremes is a type of relationship that might be termed *target cultivation*. In this kind of relationship, someone purposefully cultivates a relationship with someone in a position to benefit them. The cultivation takes place over a relatively extended period, through the giving of small gifts and the performance of favors. There is nothing expected, or asked for in return, at least for the time being. The purpose is to cultivate personal familiarity and feeling, but this is for the purpose of future advantage. The personal and instrumental aspects of the relationship are more equally balanced than at either extreme. Both sides benefit more or less equally, although the exchange is neither immediate nor direct. The relationship is normatively regulated, because a person who accepts gifts and favors from another accumulates social obligations, but the instrumental exchange of advantage, being relatively balanced, is also an important motivation for both sides. In the factory, this is the kind of relationship into which workers most commonly enter.

All of these types of instrumental-personal ties are analytically distinct from the kind that characterizes the official patron-client network. From the official perspective of the party, these are all cases of corruption; an unprincipled particularism. This is not the way that officials are supposed to use the discretion inherent in their powers of office. The party continually warns against "putting *ganqing* before policy" (*yi ganqing daiti zhengce*). The patron-client relationships that link activist workers with the party organization, on the other hand, are viewed as entirely legitimate, despite the fact that they often embody strong personal loyalties. These patron-client relationships develop out of the leadership practices of party and management; they emerge from the principled particularism of the official reward system. Whereas patron-client ties represent the mingling of the public and private, orthodox and personal, *guanxi* is a purely private and personal relationship. Despite the fact that *ganqing* may refer both to instrumental-personal ties and those of a patron-client variety, the significance of this purely private variety is different.

Instrumental-personal ties are less stable than the patron-client variety. They do not overlay the formal leadership ties that radiate out from party branches. They can arise between individuals who are not in a superior-subordinate relationship and indeed may arise between people who are barely acquainted. It is to this type of relationship that Chinese apply the colloquial terms *la guanxi* and *gao guanxi* (pull or work connections). When the connection works, it is said that the person has "gone through the back door" (*zou houmen*) or that someone has "opened up the back door" (*kai houmen*) for them—a usage that clearly implies the formal illegitimacy of the relationship. An activist is not said to "pull connections" with his or her superiors: the preference they regularly receive is the fruit of the public, official reward system and comes out of their regular cooperation in publicly defined activities. Furthermore, they do not need to cultivate connections in the ways that the nonactivists do. It is when something other than an official patronage relationship is employed that people say that the "back door" has been employed. For people who adopt a defensive orientation, this kind of relationship is an important way to pursue interests in the shop. Some activists may cultivate instrumental-personal ties, but when they do so they are employing a relationship distinct from the patron-client relationship they may enjoy with their immediate superiors.

Shop directors, department heads, cafeteria employees, factory doctors, officials in the general affairs department—virtually anyone in a position to hand out favors, grant leaves, give work unit permission for further education, marriage, and other things can be a target for cultivation:

> This kind of thing, using human sentiments (*renqing*), is common. . . . This sort of practice influences everything, including raises, bonuses, and promotions. There is always a provision for "ideological thought," or "attitude," so these kinds of considerations enter in. There are two sayings about this in China: "Human sentiments are greater than official certificates" (*Renqing dayu zhengming*), and "One (common) ancestral village is worth three official seals" (*Yige laoxiang dengyu sange tuzhang*). These sayings are very accurate. (Informant no. 35)

One important target of cultivation in the 1970s was the factory doctor. They are empowered to write sick leave certificates that enable workers to take paid leaves up to six months in duration.

> After eight years in the factory you get sick leave with full pay, with no limit on the length of time, especially if you are on good terms with the clinic doctors who must sign a form releasing you from work. That is why doctors live well in China, because so many people give them gifts. People just want to be on good terms with them. They also do housework, repairs, do labor for them, and give them gifts of food and clothing. Volunteering labor is important because in China you have to make your own furniture, carry coal, and so forth. So people are willing to do work like carpentry for the doctors. Doctors have all they could want, despite the fact that their wages are about the same as us technicians.[7] (Informant no. 7)

Several factory doctors confirmed this description of the cultivation of connections, and they also distinguished between different shadings in the quality of the *guanxi* involved. Some kinds of *guanxi* are cultivated steadily over a long period of time and often develop into relationships that entail some human feelings (*ganqing*) between the parties. Other kinds are more short term, directly instrumental, and initial attempts at cultivation are close to the expected favor. The more distant the favor working and gift giving is from the favor expected in return, the more likely the *guanxi* in-

---

7. Volunteer labor is apparently an important part of such ties in Hungary as well. Haraszti (1979: 84) mentions in passing that a worker in his section regularly repaired the foreman's personal car (auto service and parts are notoriously difficult to secure in the Eastern bloc); in return, his wife was given a highly paid inspector's position in the section.

volved includes *ganqing*, and the less likely is it to appear as crudely instrumental on the part of the supplicant and as corruption on the part of the one who grants the favor:

> If the person had good relations (*guanxi*) with the doctor, they would just tell him at the beginning that they needed a rest, had family problems, and such. . . . The method usually worked, because they have good relations with the doctor and the doctor had *ganqing* with them. (Informant no. 46)

> People would use personal connections to get a few days of sick leave without really being ill. Good friends of doctors can get sick leave certificates for their other friends without these friends ever having to come in and see the doctor. But you have to have pretty good relations (*guanxi*) with the doctor to manage this. Sometimes this was accompanied by gifts to the doctors, but these are not directly connected with any particular favor or request. What these gifts are depends on the person's ability. If you have a relative in the countryside, you can give the doctor eggs or vegetables. If you are a skilled worker, you offer to do things in his home—painting, repairing, carpentry. But these favors are usually accepted from people who know the doctor fairly well. So every worker wants to befriend a doctor. Everyone is nice to the doctors. (Informant no. 61)

> The method is not usually to give gifts or money, but to open up the back door (*kai houmen*) for the doctor. This means that the doctor receives special treatment in return for special favors later on. For example, if you have a relative who works in a department store, you can make sure that the doctor is at the top of the waiting list for books, food items, and appliances that are hard to buy. (Informant no. 14)

In those cases where people do not already enjoy *guanxi* with a target, they might attempt rapidly, even aggressively, to build up a relationship by offering favors, giving gifts, or using an intermediary:

> There were ways of going through the back door. If you don't know a doctor personally, you ask for the help of a friend who knows one. Then the friend can introduce him to the doctor and help him establish good relations. It was very common for doctors to receive favors from workers. Apples, oranges, candy, small things worth no more than 2 or 3 yuan or so. Doctors also got free repairs from workers who came to work in their homes. On occasion, they would give you grain ration tickets, but doctors didn't always need these. . . . I had no use for these things personally. When I was offered them, I refused. But people would

insist anyway and send things to my house. Some of the other doctors accepted these things almost as much as the leading cadres. (Informant no. 46)

Another important target is the official in the general affairs department responsible for allocating factory apartments. In this case, nonactivist workers, even those actively opposed by their shop leaders, may circumvent the shop by "going through the back door":

If the shop office doesn't approve your application, you can still go through the back door. This one worker who was not approved by the shop leaders because he had bad *biaoxian*—he really knew how to give gifts and use the back door. He got housing faster, and it was a much better apartment than the two workers approved by the shop leader. . . . [So] it's not always connected with *biaoxian*. You give gifts to cadres that run these things. Cigarettes, good ones. Sugar. Because economic conditions were so bad then [1970s], people used their ration coupons to buy things for cadres. Kerosene, sesame oil, even bicycles. All these things were scarce, and they were given to cadres in the housing office. Tickets for basketball games or Peking opera too. This is very open. You walk into the office and ask about your housing assignment. The cadre will say, "Ah, there are so many people in line, what can I do?" You say, "Hey, there's a basketball game coming up, want a ticket?" He says, "Yeah, make it two!" Then you bring him sesame oil later on. Of course, he'll never say that he'll give you an apartment for this, but after a while he will suddenly find an empty apartment, give you the keys, and cross you off the waiting list. You really had to do this to get a place. The waiting list didn't mean all that much. I had a friend who was too honest and never gave anything to the cadres. We all laughed at him behind his back and said he was real dumb. Three years and still no apartment! (Informant no. 72)

Not everyone can employ this strategy. It requires a certain kind of personality and a certain degree of social self-confidence. Many workers simply disapprove of this way of doing things and refuse to lower themselves. Many are too timid or simply do not know how to cultivate people.[8] There is a definite strategy and style involved in the successful cultivation of an official:

8. In Liu Xinwu's short story "Overpass" (Siu and Stern 1983: 30–89), the main character, whose family is being torn apart by arguments created by their crowded living quarters, regrets that he is unable to cultivate connections and is teased by a rather obnoxious friend who used them to obtain larger quarters for himself.

This is a very deliberate thing. You have to make it seem like it isn't a bribe. It is a very subtle art. You can say, "I don't need this anymore, just let me leave it in your office for a while." It's really a gift, but on the surface it doesn't look like it. It's a delicate and complicated matter. . . . It's like a down payment that obliges the person to do you a favor later on, or lose face. . . . Of course many people think it's wrong, but it still goes on.[9] (Informant no. 71)

The cultivation of instrumental-personal ties may even take place within the workshop itself, although it is limited there by the fact that workshop officials seek to reward their loyal activists first. There it is limited to the short-term, primarily instrumental exchange: "To get out of political study or a shop meeting, you need the permission of the group leader. To get out of a shop meeting, you need the shop director's permission. So you might just give the group leader a few cigarettes, and that might increase your chances. At the section or shop level, cigarettes won't work. There you send a gift" (informant no. 71). There is an important limit to this type of cultivation: it is generally effective only for those favors that are within the power of an individual to grant. Wage raises, bonuses, and promotions are usually committee decisions or must be approved at several different levels of the factory. In these cases, to have one person on your side will not be sufficient (especially because public loyalty to the party organization is a competing criterion). The cultivation of *guanxi*, therefore, centers on the factory allocations and sociopolitical services that are controlled by individuals.

This aspect of the factory's institutional culture has received wide publicity in recent years. A major party rectification document specified the "back door" in housing and other workplace allocations as a major cause of low morale and lack of confidence in the party (Xinhua News Agency 1983). One model factory director authored an article in which he declared that these practices must end—people in his factory had become too accustomed to manipulating *guanxi* to get higher bonuses, raises, and larger housing quarters; it was destroying morale and willingness to work hard (People's Daily 1979). Another factory director was praised for returning all of the gifts given him by subordinates at the Lunar New

9. A nearly identical account can be found in Liang and Shapiro (1983: 253–58).

Year festival (Workers' Daily 1982d). And *Workers' Daily* sponsored a symposium on the subject in 1981, asking readers to send in letters on the topic of whether the phenomenon was caused by material shortages or a breakdown of public morality.[10]

No matter how vigorously party leaders seek to curtail this corruption of official institutions, they will fight a losing battle unless they reshape the institutions themselves. Instrumental-personal ties may represent a weakening of the moral fiber of the citizenry, but they are just as much an outcome as a cause. As long as enterprises distribute so many goods and perform so many services, as long as supplies are short, as long as workers are dependent on them, and as long as factory officials have such wide personal discretion in these decisions, the thriving subculture of instrumental-personal ties will be hard to eradicate.

Despite the party's official hostility to this aspect of the institutional culture, these ties have a certain stabilizing effect on authority relations. Ordinary workers who do not receive the preference given activists still have a widely condoned avenue to pursue their interests in a way that does not challenge authority. This kind of social action, despite its "corrupt" status, is much less of a concern to the party than is coordinated action among workers, and it is not treated in the same harsh manner. Workers may "beat the system" by defensively exhibiting outward compliance, while working for individual advantage behind the scenes. When they win at this unofficial game, they may gain a sense that they have, for once, bettered the activists. This systematic opportunity to use the back door reinforces the passive and adaptive stance of most workers and serves more deeply to ingrain the tendency for individual, rather than group, action.

A Comparative Perspective

Every organization, whether in China, the Soviet Union, Japan, or the United States, has an informal organization that is distinct from the structure of its formal roles. This has been axiomatic in the sociology of organization for decades. The significance of the mate-

---

10. The symposium was initiated by an article in December 1981 and was followed by dozens of short essays and letters to the editor over the next two months, covering entire pages of some issues. One of the most interesting sought to specify the social basis of the phenomenon (Workers' Daily 1981a).

rial presented in this chapter, therefore, is not that "communist institutions do not operate in the ways they are designed"—surely this is true of every real world organization. From a comparative perspective, these patterns are significant because they reveal distinctive aspects of the authority relationship in a communist factory. Two of the patterns I have examined—the division of the workforce and the subculture of instrumental-personal ties—are distinctive aspects of informal organization. Another pattern—the official clientelist network—is an institutional amalgam of what we normally think of as the formal and informal.

The division of the workforce between activists and nonactivists has its counterpart in the peer pressure toward "rate-busters" and others oriented toward management in American industry. Yet it would trivialize the phenomenon to understand it in this light. In no other industrial setting is this distinction cultivated so consciously as a central part of management policy; the rewards so broad and so explicitly tied to cooperativeness; the distinctions so publicly displayed in meetings and after-hours work; and the divisions systematically cultivated as a form of political rule. In the communist factory, this social distinction is as salient and the antagonisms related to it as prominent as any divisions of the workforce based on skill, pay, or ethnicity in other countries. It is, in fact, a prominent status distinction directly related to the exercise of political power in a communist society.

The clientelist network that links activists to the party and management also has no parallel in the United States or Japan. To be sure, there are cliques in American factories, and patron-client relations (*oyabun-kobun*) often develop between workers and their supervisors in Japanese firms (Cole 1970: 196–204). These are informal social relations based on personal loyalties. Their direct counterparts in China are the factions and cliques of personal followings that I have examined in this chapter. The official patron-client network, however, emerges not from personal affections but from standard Leninist organizational practices, themselves the descendants of an earlier ideological orientation. Principled particularism is the formally prescribed practice of the party; loyal followers are regularly cultivated and rewarded. Personal ties may arise, but they infuse an official, formally organized network, which is already formed on the basis of broader political and ideological loyalties and a collective affinity for the party, what it stands for,

and its membership as a whole. In point of fact, the distinction between the formal and informal, in which the universalistic and affectively neutral inhabit the formal and the personal and affective
inhabit the informal does not appear to be designed with this kind
of structure in mind. One could argue that the clientelist network
fuses the formal and informal. But it is probably more accurate
to say that it is neither, but a distinctive structure for which the
formal-informal contrast has little relevance—just as the "ideological tie" is not captured by Parsons' pattern variables.

The pervasive subculture of instrumental-personal ties, described
by many students of the Soviet Union (Gitelman 1984;
DiFranceisco and Gitelman 1984; Morton 1980),[11] also has no
close parallel in either American or Japanese industry. In neither of
these market economies do enterprises satisfy directly a broad
range of needs or perform sociopolitical services. In large Japanese
enterprises, which satisfy many more needs than is common in the
United States, shop and staff officials do not have the wide personal
discretion that their Chinese (and Soviet) counterparts have. Economic conditions do not support such a subculture in the market
economies: in Japan and the United States, commodities exist in
abundance; money is the scarce item. Networks of instrumental-
personal ties in China and the Soviet Union comprise a kind of natural economy that one normally associates with precapitalist barter
economies, low levels of technical development, and poor transportation and communication networks. To be sure, the type of exchange relationship implied by the Chinese term *guanxi* exists in all
social settings, but the natural economy of such ties, essential to the
procurement of goods and services, is a distinctive feature of the
communist factory setting.

These relationships may appear traditional to us, but we should
not confuse them with the dependency relations that existed in the
past. Personal dependence in industry, particularly with regard to

---

11. E.g., Henry Morton (1984: 12) writes:

The Soviet Union is a "society of connections"; who you know may well determine how well you are housed, what food you eat, what kind of clothing you
wear, and what kinds of deficit goods (from quality tape recorders to re-
frigerators) you can obtain. It is not simply a question of money . . . more important are one's connections because there are so many commodities and services
that money alone cannot buy and that can only be obtained as favors, to be paid
back immediately or at some future date.

hiring and compensation, which was controlled by contractors, was widespread earlier in this century.[12] But this kind of personal dependence has existed in virtually all countries at early stages of industrialization. What is notable about the Chinese pattern is that, after these traditional forms of personal dependence eroded, new forms of dependence were created in the modern enterprise. In the United States and in many other Western nations, particularism, affectivity, and diffuseness evolved in the factory setting toward (a by no means perfect) universalism, affective neutrality, and specificity as modern social roles were defined. In China, dependence has been transferred from individual foremen to a more all-encompassing modern dependence on the enterprise and the party-state. Particularism and other characteristics of traditional social roles have become firmly embedded in the modern enterprise itself. Because these patterns are rooted in a specific modern type of economic and political organization, and not simply in a low level of economic development, there is no reason to assume that they will gradually disappear as China modernizes in other respects.

12. The relations between workers and foremen before the revolution, described by Honig (1986: chaps. 4, 6), were marked by exchanges that were in fact the equivalent of what I have called instrumental-personal ties. Potential workers were hired after cultivating connections with foremen by giving them gifts of food and money or performing labor services around the house. The practices were continued in order to keep the job: gifts were regularly offered at New Year's and other holidays, and the foreman's birthday. Some pledged a godmother/godfather relationship with their foreman. In this way, workers ensured job security and good treatment. These patronage relations, unlike party clientelism after the revolution, were built "from the bottom up" through the cultivation of foremen by workers. Party clientelism was created from the top down, and, though it does involve a personal dimension, it does not sanction this type of corrupt exchange, nor is it based upon it in fact.

6. Maoist Asceticism: The Failed Revitalization

The drift toward a stable pattern of clientelism and a subculture of instrumental-personal ties was well advanced by the mid-1960s. These developments were viewed with concern by many party officials. The growth of personal loyalties was making the system of political mobilization less responsive to national leaders and, therefore, less effective as a tool of economic development. At the same time, the wide discretion given leaders in evaluating *biaoxian*, even in the calculation of incentive pay, had obscured the link between reward and work performance. Growth in labor productivity had almost halted since the late 1950s, despite large investments in capital improvements (Field 1983). Many national leaders felt that factory party organizations and the work group system were not effectively motivating workers and needed to be changed.

One group of national leaders felt that the answer was reform. In their view, work groups were not effectively motivating workers because they were not providing clear-cut material incentives for individual effort. The incentives were being blunted by the tendency for groups to level payments and by the intrusion of *biaoxian* into work assessments. As did Soviet leaders after 1931, these leaders urged a closer link between reward and performance, especially with regard to bonuses and wage raises. It made little sense to them that incentive pay was not tied to output and output alone, and they saw political pressure as an increasingly outmoded motivational tool. These leaders urged reforms in factory incentive systems that parallelled those that had been widely discussed in the Soviet Union since the mid-1950s and that had begun to be implemented there in 1965 (see Schroeder 1973). They sought to disentangle work incentives from the bureaucratic and personal vagaries of work group evaluations, depoliticize bonus and raise assessments, and provide clear-cut individual rewards for output.

Maoism as a
Revitalization Movement

These ideas—and many related ones—were anathema to Maoists, who occupied a position on the left of China's political spectrum. They had a fundamentally different diagnosis of slackness in industry and offered a radically different cure. They acknowledged that the corruption of the instruments of political mobilization caused slack work performance, but, more importantly for them, the phenomenon was a cause for alarm in itself. Slack work performance was just a symptom of an overall political degeneration of the party apparatus—the exchange of public for personal loyalties, the corruption of orthodox definitions of *biaoxian* by private ones. To their way of thinking, these trends were associated with a turning away from Mao's pure political vision. A shift toward clear-cut material incentives, in their view, would only make matters worse. It would only serve to accelerate the corruption of the political apparatus and the degeneration of orthodox loyalties. By the eve of the Cultural Revolution, China's Maoists had come to interpret the call for reform as expressing the class interests of corrupted party cadres and revisionist leaders throughout the system.

The Maoist alternative to reform was revitalization. Public loyalties were to be revitalized; the private and personal, criticized and repudiated. Orthodox definitions of *biaoxian* were to be militantly reasserted in practice. Enterprise officials who lacked moral adherence to these orthodox values were to be purged, criticized, and reeducated. New leaders, loyal to these orthodox values, were to replace them. The material incentives that supposedly served to corrupt the motivations of leaders and workers alike were to be abolished. The political atmosphere intensified: political study meetings were lengthened and became more frequent, and they promoted an ethic of asceticism and sacrifice. The work group system was transformed into a purely political apparatus. Already implemented much more thoroughly in Chinese than Soviet industry, the Cultural Revolution carried the distinctive Chinese interpretation of Leninist organizational principles to their logical extreme.

Although Maoists claimed to be the only progressive, forward-looking, and revolutionary elements in the party, their answer to the drift in party organization was essentially conservative and backward-looking. Like other moral revitalization movements, the

Maoism of the Cultural Revolution blamed social problems on the degeneration of fundamental values (in this case, the ideological orientation analyzed in chapter 4). Their answer was not to change the system of political mobilization that inevitably drifted into private loyalties, but to attack the orientations and loyalties that were a symptom of this drift. This is why Maoists, in their effort to revitalize the ideological orientation, put such an emphasis on political education and thought and so militantly reasserted orthodox party values. There was, indeed, a certain logic to their position: only extreme and continuing political pressures could shake up the apparatus and break through the deeply entrenched web of personal loyalties. But the logic was flawed: as a revitalization movement, Maoism treated the symptom rather than the cause. The structure of the political apparatus of factories itself generates calculative political orientations and clientelist ties. Even if the changes favored by Maoists were carefully considered and implemented flexibly (which they were not), the effort was bound from the outset to be self-defeating, because the causes of the drift were still embedded in the basic political institutions that Maoists sought to restore and revitalize.

With the onset of the Cultural Revolution in late 1966, several changes were made in factory incentive practices. They remained in effect until shortly after Mao's death late in 1976. Bonuses linked to work group appraisals of individual performance and *biaoxian* were abolished, and workers were paid instead a fixed "supplementary wage." The periodic readjustment of wage grades after group assessments was also discontinued (Fujian Province Labor Bureau 1966). With the abolition of pay incentives came a corresponding reemphasis of political mobilization: political study meetings were intensified and lengthened, political atmosphere became more strict, and workers were expected to undertake their tasks with a resolve that reflected a heightened sense of responsibility to the nation and the revolution.[1]

During this period, Chinese industry came to the attention of a number of Western observers who viewed it as the embodiment of collectivist and egalitarian values—a system whose existence pro-

---

1. Much more happened in factories during the Cultural Revolution, of course, but those events are beyond the scope of this analysis. I discuss only those changes that are directly relevant to the problems of central concern here.

vided a lesson for the capitalist West because it demonstrated the viability of these values in practice (Andors 1977; Bernardo 1977; Hoffmann 1974; Riskin 1973). In retrospect, it is easy to find fault with this portrayal. Not only was this altered version of the work group reward system not a success, it helped usher in a marked decline in virtually every aspect of work discipline and performance as well as an unmistakable deterioration of the work group itself. But this portrayal is faulty in a second, more important sense. The practices of this era were less collectivist and egalitarian than they were militantly ascetic in their opposition to any motivations other than pure political loyalty, and relatively insensitive to the material needs of workers. In some respects, as I argue in this chapter, the Maoist version of factory life was less egalitarian and collectivist than the earlier one.

Maoist asceticism, as it was interpreted in factories during the 1960s and 1970s, is, therefore, a poor test of anyone's theories about the viability of collectivist and egalitarian practices in modern industry. Not only were these values poorly reflected in actual practice, but it was a messy social experiment; there were too many uncontrolled variables. A number of independent conditions separately undermined work group morale. The enforcement of a wage freeze in the name of equality inadvertently created new forms of inequality, as generations aged in a frozen wage structure. The abolition of group bonuses took away the incentives for a thorough assessment of coworker performance and undermined the link between individual performance and collective income. The decline of real wages and the worsening of the housing shortage eroded individual morale. Political factionalism and a threatening environment toward professional managers created strong disincentives for the enforcement of work discipline and arrangements for productivity. Under these conditions, any kind of incentive scheme was bound to fail. More importantly, however, these factors intensified workers' economic dependence on the enterprise; made the privileges of client-activists more pronounced and more resented, leading to widespread cynicism about the collectivist and egalitarian rhetoric; and intensified the "corrupt" pursuit of advantage through instrumental-personal ties. The failure of the Maoist attempt at revitalization thoroughly discredited the practice of moral-political mobilization and set the stage for the reforms of the 1980s.

Trends in Real Wages
and Living Standards

Perhaps the most important single factor in the failure of Maoist revitalization is the material effect of asceticism: workers were not merely asked to be frugal, but their wages and living standards suffered. It is beyond dispute that China's state sector industrial workers enjoy a much higher standard of living than agricultural laborers and that they are distinctly advantaged compared with industrial workers in other sectors. It is also beyond dispute that there have been substantial improvements in worker income levels and social welfare since 1949. These improvements, however, were largely accomplished by 1957, and for the next two decades real wage levels declined and living standards stagnated.

From 1957 to 1977, average real wages in state industry declined by 19.4 percent (see table 5).[2] Most of this decline, further, took place during the decade under examination. The decline in real wages in state industry was 16.5 percent if measured from their pre–Cultural Revolution peak in 1964. The decline was so prolonged that the average real wage in 1977 was even lower than it had been in 1952 (table 5). Despite efforts to raise industrial wage levels since 1977, as of this writing real wages have yet to return to the levels attained in 1956 (table 5). These figures, not released until five years after the death of Mao, put the militant Maoist stress on sacrifice for the collective good in a new light.

Average housing space for urban residents declined by almost the same percentage. In 1952 there was an average of 4.3 square meters for each urban resident. By 1978 this figure had declined to 3.6 square meters, a reduction of 16 percent (Zhou and Lin 1980). This trend was the result of the low priority attached to new construction for social, rather than productive, uses. In the five-year plan preceding 1957, 9.1 percent of the annual investment in basic construction was for housing. In the twenty years that followed, the figure was cut to an average of 5.4 percent (State Statistical Bureau 1983: 339). The increased overcrowding that resulted was compounded by the equally low priority assigned to investment in the

2. This decline was not the result of wage cutting, as was the case in the Soviet Union from 1928 to 1948. The average wage declined because wages were frozen for veteran workers, and new workers were added to the workforce at the lowest pay scales.

Table 5.   *Yearly Wage Data for State Sector Industry, 1952–1982*

Year	Nominal wage (yuan)	Cost of living index (1950 = 100)	Real wage (1950 yuan)	Real wage index (1952 = 100)	Real wage index (1956 = 100)
1952	515	115.5	446	100.0	81.7
1953	576	121.4	474	106.3	86.8
1954	597	123.1	485	108.7	88.8
1955	600	123.5	486	109.0	89.0
1956	674	123.4	546	122.4	100.0
1957	690	126.6	545	122.2	99.8
1958	526	125.2	420	94.1	76.9
1959	514	125.6	409	91.7	74.9
1960	538	128.8	418	93.7	76.6
1961	560	149.6	374	83.8	68.5
1962	652	155.3	419	93.9	76.7
1963	720	146.1	493	110.5	90.3
1964	741	140.7	527	118.2	96.5
1965	729	139.0	524	117.5	96.0
1966	689	137.3	501	112.3	91.8
1967	701	136.4	514	115.2	94.1
1968	689	136.5	505	113.2	92.5
1969	683	137.8	496	111.2	90.8
1970	661	137.8	480	107.6	87.9
1971	635	137.7	461	103.4	84.4
1972	650	137.9	471	105.6	86.3
1973	640	138.0	464	104.0	85.0
1974	648	138.9	467	104.7	85.5
1975	644	139.5	462	103.6	84.6
1976	634	139.9	453	101.6	83.0
1977	632	143.7	440	98.7	80.6
1978	683	144.7	472	105.8	86.4
1979	758	147.4	514	115.2	94.1
1980	854	158.5	539	120.9	98.7
1981	852	162.5	524	117.5	96.0
1982	864	165.8	521	116.8	95.4

Source: Nominal Wage and Cost of Living Index, State Statistical Bureau 1983: 490, col. 2; 455, col. 2. Other columns calculated from this series.

maintenance of existing housing stock. By 1978, according to official standards, over 50 percent of the housing stock was in "poor repair," and over 10 percent, "dangerously" so. Another 10 percent consisted of makeshift shacks. Over one-third of all urban households were classified as "overcrowded." The current official conclusion, echoed repeatedly by my informants, was that "this urgent situation brings serious hardships into people's lives, and seriously affects production, work, and study" (Zhou and Lin 1980).[3]

During the two decades (1957 to 1977) in which the average real wage and housing space declined considerably, per capita real income in urban areas appears to have increased by around 25 percent, a modest average annual increase of 1.25 percent (table 6). This improvement, in spite of the decline in the average wage, was entirely due to a 60 percent rise in the rate of participation in the urban labor force: in 1957, 30 percent of urban residents were employed; by 1977, around 50 percent (Workers' Daily 1981d). This was accomplished, in part, by curtailing migration from the countryside to the cities and by the relocation of some 17 million urban residents in villages after the early 1960s (see chapter 2). Although the urban population grew by only 15 percent during these two decades, employment in the state and urban collective sectors almost tripled (State Statistical Bureau 1982: 105). Most of the increase in labor force participation represents the increased absorption of women into the labor force, especially in the collective sector.

These aggregate changes made it possible for urban families, through planning, effort, and some sacrifice, to increase their per capita family income by a significant (but modest) amount over the years of austerity. By finding employment for both spouses, delaying child-bearing and reducing family size, and by having children of working age delay marriage and contribute their income to the family, per capita income for the family could be increased. The increasingly tight housing situation led children to marry and live with their spouses in their parents' homes. Household composition, as a result, showed a marked increase in the number of employed adults; this is what caused per person family income to increase. According to the results of sample surveys recently published in China (but

3. Liu Xinwu's short story "Overpass" (Siu and Stern 1983) provides a vivid description of the emotional strain and conflict that cramped housing created within families.

Table 6. *Average Per Capita Income in Urban China, 1957 and 1977*

	1957	1977
Urban population (millions)	99.0	115
Percentage employed	30	@50
Employed urban population (millions)	29.7	55.2
Average industrial wage (yuan/yr.)	690	632
Avg. real industrial wage (yuan/yr.)	690	540
Real per capita income (yuan/yr.)	207	259

Sources: Urban population, table 1. Percent employed in urban areas, *Gongren Ribao*, June 25, 1981, p. 1. Employed urban population calculated from above rows. Average industrial wage and real wage, table 5. Real per capita income, calculated from above rows.

whose representativeness is unverifiable and, therefore, should be taken only as a rough indicator of trends), the average number of dependents per wage earner in urban families declined from 2.3 to less than 1 from 1957 to 1980 (Economic Yearbook 1981: VI, 25). If we calculate changes in per capita income from this survey data, we get a larger figure than that derived from population data: it would have increased by roughly 45 percent from 1957 to 1977, or an average annual increase of 2.25 percent (table 7). Whether the actual figure is closer to 25 or 45 percent, virtually all of this increase is due to the adjustments made by families. What separates prosperous urban families from the poor today is not the average wage of the employed family members, but the proportion of family members employed (table 8; and State Statistical Bureau 1983: 493).

These adjustments created strains that took their toll on worker motivation. Many informants named this as a source of declining performance on the job in the 1970s, as have most recent analyses published in China. The account of a middle-aged technician (no. 6) was typical: "Workers and cadres both had poor work habits . . . workers purposefully took their time at work. This was not because workers talk with one another and consciously plan a slowdown (*daigong*). It is an attitude problem caused by many material problems in daily life." The "material problems" were described by this same technician, whose words were echoed, at least in part, by most of the other informants:

198   *Maoist Asceticism*

Table 7.   *Average Per Capita Income of Wage-Earning Families, 1957
           and 1977*

	1957	1977
Average family size	4.37	4.30
Avg. no. employed family members	1.33	2.20
Dependents per wage earner	2.29	1.10
Average nominal wage (yuan/yr.)	690	632
Average real wage (1950 yuan)	545	440
Average per capita income (1950 yuan)	166	218

Sources: Family data: Economic Yearbook 1981: VI-25; *Nanfang Ribao*, Nov.
8, 1979, p. 1. Wage data: table 5.
Note: Avg. family size figure for 1977 is actually 1980 figure; avg. no. employed
family members and dependents per wage earner for 1977 are actually 1978
figures.

The first material problem was the wage problem. So many workers
stayed at the same pay level for many years. . . . There were no wage
readjustments for over ten years. . . . If you graduated and began work
in 1965, you probably wouldn't get a raise for twelve years. . . . This is a
big problem because a man's family situation changes greatly from the
time he first begins work. When he's young and single, he's a grade 2
worker. Ten years later, he has a wife and kids, and is still grade 2. . . .
My own wages did not change from 1964 to 1977. . . . This was not so
great a hardship for me because I got married late, and my wife worked
too.

A second technician (no. 20), who had lived at the opposite end of
the country from the first, echoed his account:

For a long time there was no change in wages for most people despite
changes in their family situation, the addition of wives and children.
This had an effect on people's attitudes toward work. It showed when
they showed up late, left early, worked slowly, chatted during work
hours, pretended to be sick, and frequently asked for personal leave.
They didn't lose wages for any of this. This was not such a big problem
in the 1950s and early 1960s. Gradually it became more serious
after that.

The worsening housing shortage was also a commonly cited
reason for declining morale: "The second material problem was

Table 8. *Urban Household Characteristics, by Income Level, 1980*

Household per capita disposable income (yuan/mo.)	Percent of sample in stratum	Average wage of household wage earners (yuan/mo.)	Salary earners per household	Persons in household	Percentage of household members employed	Average number of dependents per household wage earner
Above 50	9.3	71.2	3.0	3.5	85	0.17
36 to 49	30.2	64.4	2.9	4.2	68	0.46
26 to 35	37.0	63.5	2.4	4.6	51	0.94
15 to 25	21.4	61.9	2.0	5.0	40	1.54
Below 15	2.1	62.4	1.3	5.3	25	3.05

Source: Xinhua News Agency 1980.

housing. Some people's housing problems were not solved, so it influenced their work. This happens when workers have children, but
can't get assigned to larger quarters. This is common" (informant
no. 6).

Even those families that were able to increase their per capita
family income during this period were still faced with short supplies
and rationing for a wide range of food and consumer items. Rationing of most staple foods (save vegetables and fruits) was in force
during this period. Private marketing of peasant produce was illegal
before 1978. Supplies above rationed amounts were difficult to
obtain, and black market prices were often prohibitive. Daily
household necessities were also in chronically short supply, if not
rationed—coal for cooking and heating, matches, toilet paper, furniture, clothing, and metal cooking utensils are common examples.
Major consumer items that were highly sought after—watches,
foot-powered sewing machines, bicycles, televisions—were also rationed and were often simply unavailable, despite the fact that they
were usually priced at several months' wages:

> Third, there is the commodity supply problem. Major goods are ra-
> tioned and the supplies are fixed—grain oils, sugar, pork, fuel, cloth . . .
> the (rationed) amounts are basically enough. It's just that it is set at a low
> standard of living. The only way to increase your supplies is by the free
> market, but these prices rise year by year. Or you can go through the
> back door, and use personal connections with friends and relatives, or
> use your high personal status. (Informant no. 6)

> Material incentives have limits because, even if you have a lot of money,
> commodities are still hard to buy. There were constant shortages of
> minor articles. This was especially bad in 1976 and early 1977. There
> were shortages of matches, cooking pots, bowls, and other things. So
> some people still find bonuses uninteresting because it is hard to buy so
> many things. The situation with commodities got a little better during
> 1978–79, but still there were a lot of things that were hard to buy. (In-
> formant no. 2)

Chronic shortages and the barriers presented by rationing made
shopping a time-consuming preoccupation. Families were required
to shop vigilantly to take advantage of supplies when they arrive.
This was especially a problem for the many households in which
both spouses worked. The strains associated with shopping itself
would become an important cause of increased absenteeism in
the 1970s.

One of the reasons why these livelihood problems were reflected directly in worker motivation is that, during this period, there were no formal channels through which to voice complaints, and such complaints were considered politically suspect. Before 1966 enterprise trade unions served a welfare role and were an office to which workers could apply for relief of acute livelihood problems and voice concern over problems in their daily life. But trade unions were disbanded in 1967 and were not formally reconstituted until 1974. An electrician (no. 58) explained:

> Before the Cultural Revolution workers could bring up their livelihood problems—housing, food, and pay—with their shop union representatives. Or they could bring them up with the party branch secretary when he came down twice a week for chats with workers to find out about livelihood problems. But after this time there was no union anymore, and the branch secretary was in political trouble. Workers could not bring up these livelihood issues. It was said to reflect bourgeois thinking.

One charge brought against trade union officials during the Cultural Revolution was that they had stimulated "economism" among workers by being too indulgent to their material needs and by laying insufficient stress on political discipline and loyalty to Mao's thought. As a result, precisely during the period in which livelihood problems became most pressing, there was no formal outlet for the expression of such difficulties, and such expression was politically stigmatized. "Problems with material life" became expressed primarily through the conscious withdrawal of work efficiency.

The Inequities of Wage Austerity

Wage austerity not only contributed to the stagnation in workers' living standards, but the burdens of austerity were distributed in an unequal and highly inequitable manner. The wage freeze simply fixed existing inequalities in place, and, as the workforce aged for more than a decade at preexisting rates of pay, the hardships were much heavier in some age groups than in others. The workers most seriously affected were not, of course, the oldest and highest paid, but the workers who had entered the labor force from 1958 to 1966. Workers who had begun work before 1956 occupied the highest grades, level 4 and above, and were paid from 65 to 100 yuan a month. Those who began work after 1956 had opportunities for raises in 1963 and 1972, but they had begun at the bottom of the new national pay scales, and opportunities for raises were much less frequent than before 1956.[4] Those who entered from 1958 to 1963, depending on the length of their apprenticeship period, usually had not worked long enough to qualify for the 1963 readjustment; those who missed out in 1963 had to wait, along with the 1963–1966 age groups, until 1972 for their first raise. Therefore, most of the employees who began work during this period stayed at the low pay grades they were initially given for a minimum of 5 and a maximum of 15 years, before being moved up one grade, either in 1972 or 1977.

The long wait for this age group was compounded by the fact that the same employees were, by the 1970s, in the middle of their childbearing years and were those most likely to have large and increasing ratios of family dependents to wage earners. Because they were at the same time among the lowest paid, these workers were the most likely to have low and declining per capita family income. These were the workers most likely to fall into the low income groups described in table 8. Children were present in the home, but they were not yet old enough to begin to contribute income (note that the middle and upper income classes in table 8 average well over two wage earners per family).

Wage austerity, in fact, was much more burdensome for the age groups that reached middle age in the late 1970s than it was on others. These were the people commonly mentioned in interviews as supporting growing families on a fixed income and suffering most from the acute shortage of housing space. The text that accompanied the release of the household income survey on which table 8 is based singles out the age groups that began work between 1958 and 1966 as having notably higher dependency ratios and notably lower per capita income, and as still suffering the effects years later (Xinhua News Agency 1980). Ironically, they were the ones—not the older, higher paid employees who often had children of working age—who sacrificed the most for the changes made by Maoists in the name of equality.

4. The general policy after the late 1950s, according to many informants, was not to promote workers to a grade higher than 5. Wages had been much higher in the private enterprises transferred to state ownership in the mid-1950s, and their veteran workers received "retained wages" (*baoliu gongzi*) that supplemented their new state pay grades by an amount that matched the old wage level.

The youngest, lowest paid workers, who were hired after 1966, fared almost as poorly. They were affected both by the wage freeze—they would not become eligible for a wage raise until 1977—and also by the abolition of bonuses. When bonuses were abolished, workers who were on the job by 1966 received a fixed monthly "supplemental wage" that usually amounted to 5 yuan. Workers who began work after 1966 were prohibited from receiving these supplements and, naturally, bonus income as well.[5] This change amounted to a demotion of one pay grade for the entire post-1966 generation, since 5 yuan per month is almost equivalent to the difference between grades at that level. Compounding this was the widespread delay, caused by the political turmoil and purges of factory leaders from 1967 to 1970, in automatic apprenticeship promotions and the automatic promotions from grade 1 to 2 for skilled workers after one year on the job. The breakdown of factory administration during these years cost young workers money. The wage readjustment of 1972, which was explicitly limited to the lowest paid workers and to those whose automatic promotions had been delayed, has sometimes been portrayed by Western observers as an effort to bring about greater wage equality by raising only the lowest paid. In reality, this readjustment was a partial measure to alleviate the hardships imposed on those who had not already received their rightful raises and who had lost income with the abolition of bonuses.[6]

Older workers viewed the plight of these younger ones with some sympathy. As one veteran technician (no. 62) noted about the switch to the supplementary wage: "This made things difficult for the workers with lower wages, because they didn't have a chance to increase their income with large bonuses. The people who already had a high basic wage were living comfortably." An older construction worker (no. 27) sympathetically viewed the impact of wage difficulties on the personal lives of young workers: "After four years on the job, workers still made only 35 yuan, and they were already

5. This policy is spelled out firmly in Political Department (1971). One informant (no. 62) reported that in his factory a two-step system was used. Workers who had finished their apprenticeship before 1967 were given a full supplementary wage of 5.9 yuan, and those who were still apprentices in 1967 were given half the amount. Younger workers received nothing.

6. The documents related to this readjustment make clear that this was the only reason for the raises, which were to be restricted to those at the bottom rungs of the wage ladder.

thinking about getting married. But there was no way to support a family, so they lost their activism in work and couldn't even think about love." The only strategy that workers in this age group could pursue to maintain their standard of living was to delay marriage, find an employed spouse, and delay childbearing.

Because the burdens of wage austerity were distributed unequally, and because wage inequalities were in some ways increased by these policies, employees widely perceived the situation as highly inequitable. Middle-aged and younger workers, who are always underpaid relative to older workers with seniority—especially when the raises are not frequent—found their expectations of rising income through the life cycle grossly violated. It is this common expectation that provides for work motivation in seniority systems and makes the wage inequalities for similar kinds of work palatable (Cole 1971). And the inequalities, as well as the perceived inequities, were considerable. Workers with 10 and, sometimes, close to 20 years of service were often still rated at grades 2 and 3, making the same or almost the same as workers with much less experience who were automatically set at grade 2 after 1 year at the lowest grade. Somewhat older workers who had entered the workforce only 5 years before them, however, might be making almost twice their salary. Workers in this position sometimes felt that their years of loyal service were going unrewarded. Whether the criterion for judgment was seniority, ability, or actual work performed, many felt this to be unfair.[7] One middle-aged technician (no. 6) explained:

> So many workers were stuck at the same pay level for so many years. This means that workers of different abilities are at the same pay grade. So how can a worker put out effort in this situation? There were also cases of apprentices getting the same pay as their masters after only one year of training. Also workers of different abilities, performing different jobs of different importance and levels of responsibility, were getting the same pay.

A younger skilled worker (no. 18) expressed the same problem as a distinction between the young and old: "Generally speaking, older

---

7. We should also keep in mind that relatively small pay differentials often have important symbolic and motivational significance. Lawler (1973) argues that pay raises motivate primarily because of the psychic rewards attached to them. One of my informants (no. 2) repeated Lawler's conclusion when he said, "Some said that 10 yuan a month was nothing to work hard for, but others wanted the highest bonuses for purposes of reputation. So in a way you can say these 'material' incentives are more 'moral' than anything else."

workers worked harder than younger workers, who didn't have much motivation. One of the reasons is that the older workers might make 70 to 80 yuan, while younger workers doing the same work would get about half that. They felt the difference in pay was too large, and unfair." Wage austerity, in short, created new kinds of inequalities and a widespread perception that the principles of income distribution were unfair.

The Emergence of Indulgent
Patterns of Authority

An increasingly demoralized labor force was not the only cause of deteriorating work discipline in the 1970s. Management was itself part of the problem. Out of a mixture of indifference, fear, and considerable demoralization of their own, and knowing that they could not attack the source of the problems by raising wages or restoring prohibited bonuses, they did little to enforce work discipline. In the years from late 1966 to 1968, most factories were so disrupted by political battles, the purge of factory administrations, and shortages of raw materials and tools that work discipline was not noticeable as a problem. The years from 1968 to 1971, when most factories were under the rule of military officers, were marked by a series of purge campaigns that struck workers as well as office personnel. The political atmosphere was so tense and the possibility of being declared a class enemy for violating labor discipline so real, that work discipline still met minimum standards.[8] Work discipline became a major problem after 1971–1972, when the reconstituted party and government began to push for a full restoration of industrial production, and military officers were withdrawn from factories. Management became a major part of the labor problem in these years.

First of all, there were few incentives for managers to enforce rules and press to keep up labor discipline. There were no bonuses for managers; financial criteria used to judge enterprise performance were loose and themselves rarely enforced; and labor productivity was not a major constraint on the fulfillment of plans, especially when compared with the more pressing problems of en-

8. This was easily the most repressive period of labor relations since 1949. Three separate purge campaigns struck workers as well as managers, both for their past histories and for their activities as participants of mass movements during the Cultural Revolution.

suring supplies of materials and parts and their prompt delivery. These factors were not unique to this period—in fact, they previously characterized China, and most other Soviet-style economies exhibit a certain indulgence on the part of managers with regard to enforcing work discipline.

This characteristic indulgence was greatly magnified by other factors—to such an extent that work discipline at times was barely enforced at all. A large percentage of factory administrators had been criticized at mass meetings from 1966–1968, held in makeshift isolation cells for months and sometimes more than a year, and were thereafter demoted to menial tasks in the shops. Almost all other factory administrators had spent periods ranging from several months to several years "voluntarily" engaging in reeducation through labor in the workshops, doing the jobs of ordinary workers.[9] When these administrators finally began to return en masse to their administrative positions after 1971, they faced a political environment that was not supportive of the strict enforcement of factory rules. Factional disputes in the capital pitted the proponents of Cultural Revolution Maoism against officials who sought to restore earlier methods of administration in order to improve production. The question of how much one should restore the earlier methods of management—including bonuses, quotas, inspection systems—was a contentious political issue. The Maoist faction argued that their opponents sought to "restore capitalism" and lead China back down the road to ideological revisionism. Many of the political campaigns during this period were designed precisely in order to discourage this "revisionist" stress on the "productive forces."[10] The fact that many new administrators had risen to their positions during the Cultural Revolution assured that there were many who were willing to denounce "revisionists," should the opportunity occur in a political campaign.[11] An engineer (no. 2) observed:

9. Virtually every informant who had held a white collar position had worked on the shop floor during this period, and they all said that this was something that almost everyone in their position was required to do. Those accused of political crimes simply worked there longer than others or were sent to labor camps.

10. When, as was common during this period, a party editorial warned against attempts to "reverse correct verdicts" and to undermine the "newborn things" of the Cultural Revolution, everyone in the factory knew the practices associated with these slogans and was put on guard.

11. This is a major theme in the short story "Manager Qiao Assumes Office" (Jiang 1979). The editorial preface to the new punitive regulations for factories (see

Leaders didn't have much power [then], and they were afraid to exercise the power they did have. This was mainly because they had been criticized during the Cultural Revolution, and also because workers had gotten into the habit of ignoring their orders. Also, Mao's quotation was on everyone's mind: "There will not be only one Cultural Revolution, but several; one is needed perhaps once every five years." So everyone was careful not to do things that could be seen as "taking the capitalist road."

A personal aide to an enterprise director (no. 44) explained her boss's dilemma during these years:

There were no problems with work activism in the early 1960s. . . . You could say that this period was the best for worker activism on the job. Only during the Cultural Revolution and afterward did things become a mess. . . . After the Cultural Revolution . . . you could see things had changed. Women would wash clothes on the job and mend their worn cloth shoes. Why? Because the leaders were still paralyzed, they had been accused of being "capitalist roaders." They didn't dare discipline workers. Anyway, no one would listen to them if they tried.

A man who had headed his factory's production department and who had been acting factory director for several years during this period (no. 23), described an identical concern:

There were real problems with quality of work and attendance. I knew of workers who just came to report in at various times of the day, then rode off on their bicycles. This was a very serious problem. You couldn't punish them. After the Cultural Revolution a cadre didn't dare punish a worker. Workers were considered revolutionary. A cadre who did this would be out of luck when the next campaign came along. . . . No one wanted to be struggled against and then get sent to do farm labor. No one wanted to be accused of putting technology in command or of taking the capitalist road.

A copy clerk (no. 47) who had worked in the factory director's office observed the same thing: "Leading cadres were afraid to handle production too well; they didn't dare grasp it too firmly. They stuck to politics because it was safer. If they were afraid to grasp production, they were just as unwilling to urge the workers to

State Council 1982b) refers to the fact that managers were made to fear the accusation that they were "turning the spearhead of struggle toward the masses."

work hard and come in on time." Plant officials therefore had their
own strategy for survival, and this included turning a blind eye
toward violations of labor discipline.[12]

There were, after all, a limited range of incentive tools at the disposal of managers. Bonuses and raises were prohibited, and most
managers realized that income was the core of the problem. Punishment of recalcitrant workers was too risky politically. Only political
study and periodic production campaigns that were replete with
political slogans were safe management methods. But these methods had their limits, as one worker (no. 18) recalled:

> Basically people just did not meet their quotas, and there was no punish-
> ment for this in wages or otherwise. . . . At times management would
> run a production campaign, and cadres would come down to the shops
> to do ideological and mobilizational work. When this occurred workers
> worked harder. They were not willing to be so lax at work when the
> cadres were right there. But when the cadres were not there to watch,
> things got more relaxed again.

A technician (no. 3) concurred: "They tried often during this period
to remedy the problem with political education and study, reading
Mao's quotations that said you should work hard. But its effect was
not that great. There was really nothing they could do about this
problem until 1977. . . . Not until then could raises be tied to work
performance." Through these limited means, managers could safely
pressure workers periodically to speed up—especially before the
end of a reporting period for plan completion, when officials from
state or party organs came for an inspection tour or when foreign
delegations were scheduled to arrive for a visit. At these times,
managers could temporarily pressure workers with increased supervisory presence and political work. A shift supervisor who was in
charge of several work groups in a large and well-known textile mill
(no. 54) related:

> The cadres had things they could do, but they could not fire anyone or
> deduct wages. They had to rely on criticism in meetings. They would

12. As two informants put it: "Managers were afraid after 1966, and they didn't
dare fire contract workers. They didn't want to be criticized for following the 'theory
of the primacy of the productive forces'" (no. 41); "Leaders didn't criticize workers
for bad work because, first of all, they were a little afraid to, and second, it was
useless anyway" (no. 42).

usually use a "learn from Daqing" campaign.[13] When a work team came to inspect the plant, or when foreign friends came, everything was suddenly cleaned up, everyone was at their posts and working hard. But all of this was false.

Prohibited by political inhibitions and their concern for their careers, managers were, therefore, limited to the use of measures that were only temporarily effective. Feeling buffeted by political forces beyond their control, their hands tied by politics, managers began to exhibit the same symptoms of demoralization as workers. If they would not be allowed to use effective methods, then why should they worry about the results? Why press for more efficient factory operations when it could only lead to real trouble? Flagging managerial motivation and lack of responsibility became a key part of the overall problem, as an office worker in a coal mining enterprise (no. 13) observed:

> The cadres knew this [slack work discipline] was a problem, but they were pretty so-so themselves. Cadres knew that to be too hard-working would risk "putting production in command" and having a [bad political] label put on you [and entered in one's file]. This was called the "theory of putting production first." The mine lost money every year. They lost about two yuan for each ton of coal mined. The state set a target on the loss rate per ton, but the mine "overfulfilled" this target too. It still didn't matter. They were given supplementary funds, and the leaders were never punished for this.

A metal worker in an auto plant (no. 57) seconded this assessment:

> Right up to 1978, workers came late, asked for a lot of sick leave and were absent without leave, dragged out jobs, went out in the middle of the day to go shopping, and so forth. The leaders just didn't worry about it. The leadership was in disorder anyway, and they were only interested in holding meetings. They figured it was all the state's money anyway, so why worry about it.

During these years, the factory's institutional culture took on a new feature. Management developed an exaggeratedly indulgent pattern of leadership with regard to the enforcement of work disci-

---

13. Daqing was a model oilfield that served as the object of numerous emulation campaigns to speed production, cut costs, and improve quality. Most production campaigns of the 1970s took this name.

pline. Many workers, recognizing clearly the new elements in the rules of the game, adjusted their behavior accordingly. Political attitudes were still monitored closely, but, with the exception of periodic production campaigns, there was little impetus from the factory leadership to have work groups apply pressure. The prescribed administrative punishments for violating work discipline simply went unenforced. Output quotas for individuals, if they existed, had not been revised in years. Group criticism and political education were the only tools used in work groups, and these had been rendered ineffective because the bonuses and raises that had been linked to them no longer existed.

The Expanding Scope of Instrumental-Personal Ties

The changes in reward systems during this period, coupled with the long policy of wage austerity, had an unintended, yet logical, consequence: the natural economy of instrumental-personal ties took on greater importance in factory life. With housing shortages becoming more acute, the wage freeze and abolition of bonuses creating serious hardships for certain age groups, and shortages of commodities and foodstuffs continuing, competition for access to these goods and resources was intensified. Enterprise officials, with their ability to satisfy (selectively) requests for new apartments, extra ration coupons, loans, and relief payments, became the logical targets for this competition. Because wage policies had severed pay from work performance, one could not try to satisfy these needs through hard work. One way for workers to satisfy their increasingly pressing needs was to pursue them more aggressively by cultivating instrumental-personal ties with people in a position to confer favors. (Activists still received preference for these things as clients of the power structure.) Wage austerity affected factory officials as well, and their chief means to satisfy their own families' needs was to use their powers in exchange for favors or gifts. From both below and above, there were heightened incentives during this period to drive people into the natural economy of instrumental-personal ties.

A personal aide to an enterprise director accurately summarized the accounts of many informants when she (no. 44) explained:

Workers could use all kinds of methods to get around regulations. After the Cultural Revolution, there was a back door for everything, and it became very serious. . . . Before the Cultural Revolution, things were generally run according to strict procedures. . . . [Q: Why did the situation change after the Cultural Revolution?] Conditions were like this: wages were low, material things were scarce. So people used whatever advantage they had, given their position in society. . . . [People] were willing to exchange favors with others and cultivate *guanxi* to live easier, and for mutual advantage. [Q: Didn't this kind of thing occur before the Cultural Revolution, too?] Of course . . . you can't say that it didn't occur at all. It's just that before the Cultural Revolution it was on a smaller scale, and less open. . . . But after the Cultural Revolution this became much more widespread, much more open, and used commonly in everyday situations. People say that after the Cultural Revolution, "*ganqing* replaced policies" [*yi ganqing daiti zhengce*].

Factory doctors, targets for attempts to establish *guanxi* by workers who wanted several days, sometimes weeks, of paid sick leave, also noticed a marked upsurge in this activity during these years: "There were ways of going through the back door. . . . It was very common for doctors to receive gifts and favors from workers. . . . This was always a problem, but before the cancellation of bonuses in 1965 it was not widespread. It got worse gradually after then, especially during and after the Cultural Revolution, right up to 1978 [when I left China]" (informant no. 46).

The proliferation of this petty (and sometimes not so petty) corruption, and the explanation for it, has been a topic of many newspaper editorials and short stories in China since the death of Mao (see chapter 5). The relevance of this phenomenon for this study is not only that Maoist wage and incentive policies exaggerated this standard feature of communist factory culture, but that it had consequences for worker morale as well. The time and effort expended in the cultivation of these connections took time and energy away from one's work post. When other employees saw that target cultivation resulted in preferential treatment for some, this led to further demoralization. And since, in a systemwide sense, the increased volume of rewards distributed through instrumental-personal ties decreased the volume distributed through the official reward system, this further weakened and corrupted the formal system of rewards and eroded incentives to work. A disgruntled factory director who had his article-length complaint published in *People's Daily* (1979) summarized the consequences for worker morale perfectly: people are rewarded for wasting working hours building *guanxi* with officials in the housing office, and the hard-working employees get angry when they see these people getting preferential treatment.

The Decline of Work Groups

There were, therefore, five different, although interrelated, factors that contributed to a marked decline in worker performance in the early 1970s. The first factor was the abolition of bonuses and the end of readjustments linked to evaluations of performance. This completely severed the link, already somewhat indirect due to the concept of *biaoxian*, between work performance and reward at both the individual and the group level. The second was the decline of real wages and housing space, and the general stagnation of living standards in the two decades after 1957. The third was the inequity inherent in wage austerity, which intensified hardships for certain age groups, distorted the wage structure, and created greater inequalities and a deeply felt sense among workers that wage distribution was neither rational nor fair. The fourth was an emerging pattern of indulgent leadership on the part of an increasingly demoralized managerial corps, whose initiative was bound by political prohibitions and factionalism. And the fifth was the increasing importance of instrumental-personal ties for the satisfaction of needs, something that not only diverted efforts from work responsibilities, but also led to resentment on the part of those who did not benefit from the practice. The result has been documented in statistics on labor productivity (Field 1983), but these statistics do not tell us about the effects on shop floor experience: "Workers' thinking was unsettled. There was a common problem of dissatisfaction with wages, so workers would drag out their jobs, and slow down the pace. This problem, called *daigong* [slowdown], was very widespread. . . . People put in the time but didn't put out the effort" (informant no. 23).

The political campaigns of the period also contributed to the problem. Active resentments built up over the false accusations, constant criticism, and occasional victimizations involved: "There were poor relations between cadres and masses. The political campaigns and accusations that often turned out later to be false made people hold anger in their stomachs toward cadres. If they hold anger in their stomachs, they won't work hard" (informant no. 47). Political campaigns contributed to the problem, further, simply because of the time and energy they occupied:

> Right up to 1972 we had political study every day. You might think that workers would be too tired to study after the shift, but work in China is not like work in Hong Kong. Workers work much more slowly, because political study is tiring, and there are continual livelihood problems, like not getting enough to eat, and not being able to get enough of certain kinds of commodities. (Informant no. 4)

> The common attitude during the 1970s was that you would get the same amount of money whether you worked hard or not, so why bother? They tried to stimulate worker enthusiam with slogans, but it didn't work. Worker attendance fell, they left early, sneaked off during work hours, stole things, slowed down. It was very serious. Worker enthusiasm and discipline was much worse in the 1970s than in the early 1960s. But the problem in fact began earlier, after the anti-rightist campaign of 1957. With each political campaign, workers became less enthusiastic. The purpose of the political campaigns was to stimulate production, but the effect was just the opposite. When they ran all these campaigns, they forgot that it is a worker's nature to work, not study Marxism-Leninism, discuss, and criticize. (Informant no. 31)

The widespread disaffection among workers and staff in factories affected virtually all aspects of work performance: attendance, tardiness, work intensity (depending on the degree to which the work process allowed workers to control their own work pace), attention to quality, attention to the condition of machinery and tools, and so forth. A veteran skilled worker (no. 18) described the situation in her semi-automated workshop:

> Generally speaking, people were dissatisfied with their wages. They felt they were too low, but they could not go to another factory to get higher wages. It was all the same, and there was not much you could do. [Q: Did this influence people's work?] Yes . . . some would leave early, and arrive late. Others wouldn't pay very close attention to instruments they were supposed to check. So quality fell, and this led to a waste of materials. This was for regular production work. There were other kinds of workers, like repair and maintenance workers, who would just take their time repairing things. They would use two hours when one was all they needed, and then they didn't fix things very well. Generally people slowed down and didn't pay very close attention to what they were doing. This repair work was very important, because the machinery al-

ways needed some sort of repairs, and often there were halts in production because of this. So when the repair workers came late and worked
slowly, the damage to production could be great. In our kind of [semi-
automated] shop, these were key workers, so they needed to be prompt
and hard-working.

Sometimes this disaffection resulted in small but open acts of insubordination: "Workers would also refuse to do certain kinds of
work because they were stuck at low pay grades. If asked to do a
relatively skill-demanding job, they sometimes would refuse and
say, 'Give it to a grade 5 worker!' This happened" (informant no. 3).
Still another result often described by informants was a form of passive resistance to leaders, a studied lethargy in following orders and
maintaining time discipline when supervisory personnel were absent. As a young worker (no. 35) put it: "Workers would listen to
orders all right, but they would take their time following them.
They would not take the initiative to do things unless they received
a direct order."

The most common manifestation of this disaffection was a work
pace and a style of life in factories that was extraordinarily relaxed,
with plenty of spare time for socializing, attending to personal affairs, or simply resting. A shift supervisor from a large textile factory (no. 54) recalled a situation that had repeatedly frustrated him:

> Things went very slowly in factories. Work efficiency was very low.
> There was a lot of unproductive time during the day. But they did finish
> the quotas because quotas were set conservatively. They were set conser-
> vatively because the leaders were fond of exaggerating and declaring that
> all the targets were 100 percent fulfilled. The workers knew just how
> much it took to finish and would pace themselves and do no more. They
> would set aside time for washing clothes, repairing their bicycles, and
> sleeping. It was easy to find a place to sleep in a big factory where no
> one could find you. . . . People on the night shift slept on the job. They
> had quotas but didn't want to fulfill them. Whether they finished or not
> was all the same to them.

This work pace, and the comfort associated with it, was something
that emigres often described in nostalgic terms after their initiation
into the frantic work pace in Hong Kong factories and sweatshops.
Ironically, it was the most tangible benefit of socialism during the
period, as a shop technician (no. 56) recalled:

Workers in China couldn't subscribe to *Reference News*[14] like I could, but they would get ahold of copies and read about foreign countries. They often felt that factory work in America was too fast-paced, and that life in factories there wasn't very comfortable. But they felt they were fortunate in China's factories, where life could be so comfortable.

Some of this behavior was designed to reclaim time and material goods from the enterprise in a situation where compensation was perceived to be insufficient. One theme stressed repeatedly by informants was the increased appropriation of raw materials from the plant to make household articles that were strictly rationed or unavailable. Employees of machine shops were especially fortunate, because they had access to metals, sometimes rare stainless steel, and could fashion them into cooking utensils. Several former machinists reported that this practice, which had always existed to some degree, increased noticeably during the 1970s. A skilled worker from a plate glass factory (no. 8) described a similar situation:

> There was a serious problem of workers stealing glass for use in the home. This always had happened, but it became more serious around 1975. Management knew about it, but they didn't know what to do. . . . The intention of the workers was to supplement their wages with things taken from the plant, since their wages were low. A saying for this is: "If you lose out in the system, make up for it outside" (*Tinei sunshi, tiwai bu*). In their homes people did not have much furniture, and they could use the glass to make tables and desk tops. It was very useful. They also had fire-resistant glass that was very useful for cooking around the home.

Workers also reclaimed time from their enterprises for their personal use, especially in a situation where they were frequently required to stay after the shift, or to return to the enterprise in the evenings for political study. A machine-shop technician (no. 56) explained:

> Workers often finished their quotas early and did their own personal things. This was the biggest problem with China's factories in the

14. *Cankao Xiaoxi* (Reference News) is a daily compendium of translations of foreign news service reports that is distributed to work units in China, but not circulated openly (see Rudolph 1984).

1970s. . . . They would wash their clothes with factory soap and water, go find a friend and talk for thirty minutes to an hour. Also, they would go to the collective showers of the factory, clean up, use the toilet. They don't have showers and toilets in most houses. So they get their clothes and themselves all cleaned up, and, by the time the shift is over, they can go straight home.

The most effective way of reclaiming time for personal use, while at the same time completely withdrawing work effort, was to take paid sick leave—a practice that grew into a major problem in the 1970s. Generous labor insurance, coupled with the lax enforcement of plant regulations, made this a popular and effective method of withdrawing effort. State sector employees (and some collective sector employees) can receive paid sick leave for a period of up to six continuous months. Depending on their seniority, they receive from 60 to 100 percent of their salary during these periods. All that was required to receive these benefits was a signed certificate from a factory doctor (or from a doctor at an affiliated hospital) prescribing a period of recuperation. Before the Cultural Revolution, work groups normally penalized excessive use of sick leave by placing a limit, usually two or three days a month, which, if surpassed, would disqualify the individual from receiving a bonus during the month. With the abolition of bonuses and the move toward a supplementary wage for pre-1967 employees, sick leave became a relatively costfree way for workers to withdraw effort. The greatest limit on the practice was the inability of the employee to obtain the required doctor's signature.

In virtually all industrial systems, turnover and absenteeism are the two things that are tied most closely with worker dissatisfaction (Lawler 1973). In Chinese industry (for reasons explained in chapter 2), voluntary job changes are almost nonexistent. Absenteeism, therefore, became the chief means through which this dissatisfaction was expressed. A skilled worker (no. 7) explained:

> People eventually began to take advantage of sick leave. After eight years in the factory you get sick leave with full pay, and there are no limits on the amount of leave, especially if you are on good terms with the clinic doctors who must sign a form releasing you from work. . . . This abuse of sick leave began in the middle of the Cultural Revolution and continued until very recently when work attendance was connected with the new bonuses. Often attendance rates were as low as 70 percent. People

used sick leave for their personal business. Both workers and staff did this, but workers did it more, because staff had more freedom . . . they can slip out to do errands for one or two hours, unlike workers.

A doctor from a factory hospital (no. 14), who became intimately familiar with sick leave trends in the course of his daily office hours, offered reflections on this period that are consistent with those of the worker and technician quoted above:

> Before 1977, workers knew that whether or not they came to work, they would get the same pay. So during the period of the Gang of Four . . . this problem increased. . . . This was especially a problem with workers who had more than eight years of seniority. They would get full pay even if they took six months' sick leave per year. But workers with less than eight years' experience got full pay only for injury leave and had part of their salary deducted for sick time. So the younger workers usually asked for long leaves only if they had serious problems. [Q: Why did workers do this during these years?] On the one hand, there was no one checking them or applying penalties regularly during these years. On the other hand, wages were low and hadn't changed for a long time, so workers would very quickly ask for sick leave if they had the chance.

Extra leave time, it should be remembered, was often necessitated by the social trends of this period. With a six-day work week, study meetings several evenings each week, chronic food and commodity shortages, and the emergence of two wage earners per family as the norm, finding time for household chores and shopping became a major concern. A staff technician (no. 7) who had a husband and children to care for described this common situation:

> With an eight-hour day and political study later, when do you have time for family shopping? . . . There are no refrigerators, so you have to shop every day for vegetables and meat. Stores unfortunately held the same hours as factories . . . so people were always busy, there was no rest. There is a saying: "There is no Sunday, only a seventh day to the week" (*Mei you xingqi tian, jiu you xingqi qi*). It means that there is no time to rest. This was a real burden on people, and it affected their attendance and work.

Interestingly, these accounts indicate that many workers felt they could improve their livelihood and standard of living more by staying at home than by going to work.

In this situation, factory doctors became pivotal figures. Their signatures were crucial in securing paid sick leave. Not only were instrumental-personal ties cultivated with doctors to receive these forms, but two other methods were used increasingly during the period. The first was to fake an illness. One doctor (no. 14) reported:

> How can you tell if a person is really sick or just faking? It is difficult, because there is a whole range of seriousness in illness. Is someone slightly ill, faking, or seriously ill? You can give an examination, but usually you come up with no clear symptoms. But the worker still insists he feels sick, and may ask for two or three days off. Sometimes, I would check with the shop foreman first in really doubtful cases, and sometimes I would cut the request down to one day. What changed after 1977 is that workers stopped asking for sick leave for common colds and minor discomforts, coughs, and intestinal problems.

If this first strategy did not work, the worker might then try a second: argument and intimidation. Another factory doctor (no. 16) explained,

> There were fewer workers asking for sick leave during the periods before 1966 and after 1977. During the ten years in between, workers asked for sick leave more often, often faking illness and arguing with us over the number of days of leave we gave them. When they argued, we usually just signed the form because the worker might accuse us of being a stinking intellectual who didn't serve the workers, the peasants, and the army. . . . During these ten years, workers usually asked for more leave than we gave them at first. But before this period and after, they hesitated to take more than two days, even if we offered it, because after three days there would be no bonus.

This entire pattern of decline in worker performance, work discipline, and attendance is symptomatic of a parallel erosion of the effectiveness of work groups. Group criticism, earlier used with some effectiveness to induce lagging individuals to keep up, was much less effective when there were no tangible rewards or sanctions connected with it:

> For bad work performance and bad labor attitude, before the Cultural Revolution they could not fire you, but they could reduce your bonus and criticize you in a meeting or in wall posters. The only difference after the Cultural Revolution was that there was no bonus to be taken away. If you worked, fine. If you didn't work, that was fine, too. They did

still have the criticism, but after the Cultural Revolution it was possible not to listen and get away with it, since there was no real difference anyway. (Informant no. 36)

The criticisms were rendered doubly ineffective by the pervasiveness of lax discipline. When only a few individuals are lagging behind, criticism might be effective. When a large percentage of the workforce is doing so, the criticisms are rather empty. And, because group pay no longer varied with group performance, there was no moral basis for collective peer pressure on laggards who held back the group: you were no longer letting down your coworkers.

Passive orientations, as a result, shifted subtly from the convincing presentation of compliant behavior and attitudes to the mere avoidance of expressing politically proscribed opinions. Passiveness and even open disinterest became more common in group meetings. A growing gulf emerged between the behavior of activists and nonactivists, who were more sharply differentiated by the rewards available to them. This led to growing animosity toward activists who appeared as opportunists and careerists. Activists, in short, became increasingly isolated from the rest of their (increasingly demoralized) groups, and they lost the ability to influence group behavior in the ways they had been able to when work groups were intact. Mutual evaluation and criticism became an empty ritual. Group evaluation and criticism of performance became more infrequent as the decade progressed and more concerned with the selection of model activists for honorary awards that helped launch political careers. Political meetings continued and, in fact, increased in number, but they were characterized by a widening gap between activists and nonactivists. Work groups no longer operated in the ways that they had in earlier years.

The Unintended Consequences of Revitalization

The Maoist attempt to revitalize work groups not only failed to achieve its aims; it actually intensified many of the problems it had set out to correct. Work groups themselves deteriorated badly; petty corruption and other forms of personal exchange actually intensified; worker orientation to the political system became, if anything, even more calculative than before; and all aspects of work performance declined considerably. To be sure, Maoist revitalization efforts were not carried out in the most favorable of circumstances. The decline in real wages and stagnation in worker living standards would have sorely tested any conception of work groups. The material hardships, inequalities, and inequities that accompanied the wage freeze were a result less of the central Maoist principles than the manner in which they were interpreted in practice.

However, the central Maoist conception of moral revitalization was itself deeply flawed. Revitalization speaks not to the root causes of systemic drift, but to its symptoms. The degeneration of the system of political mobilization was inherent in its very structure: in its principled particularism, in its favored treatment of activist-clients, in its demand for political loyalty, and in the wide personal discretion necessary in the exercise of its rewards and punishments. In militantly reasserting a purer version of the basic pattern, Maoists were doing nothing more than recreating the conditions that had originally led, according to their internal logic, to personal loyalties, calculative involvement, and corruption. The only way out of this vicious circle was to change workers' moral and political orientations, but the more Maoists attempted to do this through a politicized reward system, the more they recreated calculative involvements and intensified political cynicism.

In stressing Maoism as a model of collectivism and egalitarianism, some writers have presented it as something it was not. Chinese industry during this decade, in fact, represented an effort to substitute centralized, bureaucratic mobilization of a labor force for material rewards of any sort. It was an effort to offset severe wage austerity and a stagnation of living standards with heightened demands for sacrifice and an ideology that stressed class struggle and revolutionary asceticism. The factory did not represent a collectivist and egalitarian community in which there is a tangible link between individual performance and group welfare; where participation in the community is voluntary and not coerced; or where there is a tangible improvement in collective welfare directly connected with group efforts. The entire exercise was driven forward and manipulated by a distant, faction-ridden bureaucracy whose concerns were far removed from those of the direct participants. Cultural Revolution–era Maoism was a peculiar manifestation of collectivist and egalitarian values; in many ways, it ran counter to them. The irony is that Maoism succeeded in undermining the politicized reward systems that were supposed to be its essence and served primarily to reinforce the evolution toward neo-traditional social forms.

7. From Asceticism to Paternalism: Changes in the Wake of Maoism

> Methods of enterprise management that are modeled
> after the patriarchal family system, or after medieval
> practices or the ways of Genghis Khan, cannot possibly
> sustain a lasting rise in production. Militaristic
> methods and political incentives can, it is true,
> motivate workers over the short term; but as time
> wears on this approach is doomed to failure. . . .
> Management principles modeled on the feudal
> patriarchal system are a step backward from
> capitalism; they constrict people, inhibit them, and
> block their abilities and potential. It should go without
> saying that socialist modernization gains nothing
> from this.
>
> (Liu 1983: 7–8)

In his characteristically outspoken style, the writer Liu Binyan delivers an indictment of Maoist methods that reflects the official assumptions behind China's recent reforms. The long Chinese experience with moral-political mobilization and the damage wrought by the Maoist attempt at revitalization have had a final unintended consequence: to spur China's post-Mao leaders to consider fundamental reforms. The industrial failures of Maoism were far more serious than the shortcomings attributed to Stalinist methods in the Soviet Union after the Soviet leader's death. Even the leadership faction that deposed the Maoist Gang of Four in late 1976—most of them also former supporters and beneficiaries of the Cultural Revolution—recognized the need for immediate changes. A wage readjustment was announced within months and began in late 1977. Incentive pay was revived. The party mobilized for an intensive modernization drive; propaganda shifted from class struggle to the struggle for production. Plans were announced for the expansion of housing and a rapid improvement in living standards.

By the end of 1978, as party leaders purged during the Cultural Revolution regained the upper hand, economic policy took an unexpected, innovative turn. Instead of a simple restoration of the status quo ante, the party embarked on a course of reform. By 1979 this had led to the virtual decollectivization of agriculture and the revival of independent peasant marketing of produce (Shue 1984). In industry, a less well-defined series of experiments and reforms in planning, finance, and incentive practices appeared by the end of 1984 to be moving in the same direction as Hungary's "New Economic Mechanism" (Walder 1984b, 1985a; Field 1984).

It is well beyond the scope of this book to chronicle the progress of industrial reform.[1] My concern is with institutions and behavior, not with discrete bundles of policies and their implementation. Moreover, these reforms are still in progress, perhaps still in their early stages. But it is well within the scope of this book—indeed, it is imperative—to indicate the impact that the reforms, taken as a whole, have had and are likely to have on the factory institutions and patterns of authority that are my central concern. From a comparative perspective, these reforms recapitulate a transition earlier made by the Soviet Union after Stalin, away from enforced sacrifice and austerity and toward an economic model that seeks sustained improvements in citizen welfare. China's version of this transition is made more interesting by the simultaneous reform of basic Soviet-derived institutions.

By the summer of 1984, when research for this study was completed, important changes in patterns of authority had already taken place.[2] The austerity of the Cultural Revolution decade, and indeed of the entire 20 years after 1957, has been decisively reversed. Not only has the Maoist concern for moral-political revitalization been repudiated, but, for the first time since the mid-1950s, political organization and mobilization are no longer central tools of labor motivation. As a result, the concept of *biaoxian* has been redefined, and its application in reward systems, restricted. The phenomenon of activism, and the definition of a model activist, has been reshaped. The party's role on the shop floor has been restricted and reformulated, and its orientation toward the workforce changed.

All of these changes have greatly altered the daily experience of

1. It is also beyond the scope of this book to analyze the impact of these policies on work motivation and industrial efficiency, because these are tangential to my analysis of authority relations. I have addressed this question in separate publications (Walder 1984b; 1983).

2. This chapter is based on my reading of the press and other Chinese sources and on a final set of highly focused interviews in Hong Kong in summer 1984.

factory life for China's workers, and they require some amendments
to some of the description and analysis of previous chapters, which
are based on policies adhered to in the 1960s and 1970s. However,
these changes have occurred within a framework of strong institutional continuity. The pattern of organized dependence that characterizes employment in the state enterprises has not changed significantly. The economic dependence on the enterprise has diminished,
but only in relation to the extreme forms characteristic of China
since the late 1950s. The role of the party organization on the shop
floor has been modified, but its organizational integrity in the shop
is intact: it still claims a monopoly on all organized activity, and it is
no more tolerant of independent political action than before. The
shop director exercises his personal discretion more independently
of the party branch secretary, and he is now urged by his superiors
to use it to promote production, but the contours of the "foreman's
empire" and the personal dependence involved have not been challenged by reform initiatives. The official concept of activism has
changed, and the bundle of rewards for activism has been altered,
but shop leaders still cultivate ties with activists and reward their
loyal clients preferentially, and the division between the leaders' clients and the workers is still a central cleavage in the workforce. As I
describe the changes of recent years—some of which are striking
departures from past decades—I portray them as the latest Chinese
redefinition of the generic "neo-traditional" pattern, not as a departure from it.

From Asceticism to Paternalism

The most striking departure from the Maoist decade, and indeed
from the entire period after 1957, is the party's changed stance
toward the living standards of workers. No longer demanding extended sacrifice from the population, whether in the ethic reflected
in public propaganda or in the hard realities of investment priorities, the party has made a strong commitment to consumers'
needs. Indeed, the ability to satisfy these needs has become a self-
imposed standard of the party's legitimacy. This historic shift, like
the one begun in the Soviet Union in the mid-1950s, marks the end
of the period of "primitive socialist accumulation" that characterized early Stalinist industrialization, in which historically unprecedented percentages of national income were reinvested in industry.

China's transition, however, has been, at least initially, much more rapid and vigorous than the gradual improvements marked over the past decades in the Soviet Union.

The most striking change has been in wage policy. Virtually frozen from 1963 to 1976, with only a small 1972 readjustment, nominal wages were raised for almost one-half the workforce on three separate occasions from 1977 to 1984. Additional wage increases followed the restoration and rapid expansion of bonuses (see Shirk 1981; Lardy 1984). In the six years after 1977, nominal wages in state industry increased by 37 percent, real wages by 18 percent (see table 5). By 1982 state sector workers received an annual average of 160 yuan in bonus pay, an amount equal to more than two months' average salary (calculated from State Statistical Bureau 1983: 490–91). Increased inflation has eaten into these advances, but real wage levels have nonetheless quickly returned almost to the previous high watermark of 1956 (see table 5; also Lardy 1984).

A series of related changes have helped ensure that there are more goods and services on which to spend this income. The decollectivization of agriculture in favor of household farming has not only greatly increased agricultural productivity, it has improved the delivery of foodstuffs to the cities: private farmers' markets have sprung up throughout urban China, and supplies of vegetables, fish, and pork have greatly improved in quality and quantity. The legalization of a petty trade and service sector in the cities has also improved the delivery of goods and services: the number of service and trade establishments tripled from 1978 to 1982, and the number of service personnel doubled (State Statistical Bureau 1983: 483).

Industry has also been reoriented to produce more consumer goods. Growth rates in heavy industry were three times that of light industry from 1949 to 1978. From 1979 to 1982, output in light industry grew by 50 percent, heavy industry, only 9 percent (State Statistical Bureau 1983: 217). This shift permitted a 26 percent increase in total per capita purchases of consumer goods in urban areas from 1978 to 1981 (Xinhua News Agency 1982). Through 1982, urban ownership of television sets increased eightfold over 1978; bicycles, 45 percent; watches, 97 percent; sewing machines, 72 percent; and radios, 62 percent (State Statistical Bureau 1983: 508). With increasing supplies, the ration coupon system was discontinued for most of these commodities.

The housing shortage, long a symbol of the suffering of the urban resident, has also been addressed with new vigor. State expenditures on housing construction have increased almost fivefold, from the 1958 to 1977 average of 5.5 percent of the national construction budget to 25 percent in 1981 and 1982 (derived from State Statistical Bureau 1983: 339). More new urban housing was built from 1978 to 1984 than in the first three decades of the People's Republic (State Statistical Bureau 1983: 357; Lardy 1984: 862). By 1982, urban per capita housing space reached 5.6 square meters, finally surpassing the 1952 level of 5.2 (State Statistical Bureau 1983: 483).

More directly relevant to the central concern of this book is the role that state factories have played in the more consumer-oriented regime. State enterprises are still the leading builders of urban housing.[3] In the course of financial reforms, they have also gained control, for the first time, over significant percentages of their profits, and they have allocated a large percentage of these retained funds to bonuses, direct distributions, and the expansion and upgrading of factory housing and services. In the earlier regime of austerity, enterprises had control of a small, fixed portion of their wage bill to fund factory benefits, and, in a situation of extreme scarcity, the small distributions of rationed commodities obtained through both legal and informal channels loomed as very important. Political study and calls for sacrifice were a central part of management's orientation to the worker. This orientation has now shifted to an explicit paternalism, and managers view large wage and bonus increases and sustained improvements in factory amenities as central tools of labor relations. This orientation is reflected also in state subsidies and fringe benefits for state workers: the total subsidies and benefits doubled from 1978 to 1983, while nominal wages increased by only one-third (Lardy 1984: 862–63).

In this regard, the change from the 1960s and 1970s is striking. Both emigres and current news articles report a party and a professional managerial corps newly concerned with workers' welfare, making it an important preoccupation of shop meetings and annual workers' congresses. All improvements, of course, are officially celebrated and given wide publicity within the factory, and sometimes

3. In 1981, over 60 percent of national expenditures for housing construction were spent by state enterprises from their own funds (Workers' Daily 1982e).

in the mass media. New blocks of apartments are the most celebrated of accomplishments, but improvements in the factory's other services are also highly valued. One informant reported that his factory's meal hall—long a source of worker complaints—greatly expanded, improved its service, and increased the variety and quality of the food. They accomplished this by building a storefront open to the street, hiring professional cooks, and turning part of the meal hall into a profit-making restaurant open to the public. The profits from the business side subsidized services for workers.

The press has been filled with similar reports in recent years: expansion of factory housing, giving money to workers for renovation of their current apartments; improvements in the variety and quality of produce from the factory's farmland; employment for more workers' children in newly created branch collectives; the expansion of daycare and kindergartens; the establishment of new repair services for workers' families; the purchase and delivery of coal for apartment and dorm residents; free clothing repair services for single workers—the list is seemingly endless (e.g., Workers' Daily 1981c, 1981e, 1981f). One factory reflected its concern for its employees' personal lives by setting up a matchmaking service for its bachelors (Workers' Daily 1981b). This last example, seemingly trivial, is emblematic of the decisive post-Mao shift from asceticism to paternalism. Whether or not the increase in services is as fast as recent news articles suggest, it is clear that the provision of collective services and benefits is now a central part of a new paternalistic approach to labor relations. The state enterprise continues to play a central role in the delivery of these free or highly subsidized goods and services.

The Restriction of
Moral-Political Mobilization

The shift from asceticism to paternalism is closely linked to a second change: the end of a labor strategy centered on moral-political mobilization. Workers are no longer asked to sacrifice for the sake of class, party, or nation; they are to work for their own material well being. If all work hard and benefit according to the revived Soviet principle, "To each according to his labor," the nation as a whole will be enriched. The corollary is an ethic of individual work responsibility and individual reward and punishment—of the type employed in the Soviet Union beginning in the early 1930s. This shift has had an enormous impact on the symbol of Chinese moral-political rewards—the concept of *biaoxian*. At least in its political and attitudinal elements, *biaoxian* is no longer regularly evaluated in work groups, and it is no longer explicitly linked to wage raises and bonuses.

The notion that material rewards should not be linked solely with work performance but should also be used to reward proper socialist attitudes among workers did not die easily. In the late 1970s, there were still many among China's elite who found it difficult to abandon this long-established principle, despite its repudiation by the new leadership.[4] Nor did factory managers and party branches readily discontinue the practice. A three-year propaganda campaign, beginning in late 1978, waged a battle against the continued use of "soft" criteria for bonuses and raises. Managers and party organizations were told that "good politics," "activism in study," "being a good youth league member," or, even more vaguely, being a "good person" had no proper place in bonus assessments (e.g., People's Daily 1978b). By the early 1980s, managers were being told that the best criteria were "hard" ones that could be calculated based on production statistics. The customary group assessments could be discontinued if such hard measures could be devised. By late 1983, this effort had finally made a deep impact on shop floor practices—the emigres interviewed in summer 1984 generally agreed that *biaoxian*, strictly interpreted, no longer played an important role in bonus and raise decisions.

Although there has been a clear decline in the salience of *biaoxian*, there has just as clearly not been a corresponding rise in the officially favored "hard" criteria, except on paper. Official publications continued to lament the weak link between performance and pay into late 1984, and emigres confirm their complaints—that bonuses are distributed relatively equally, even when they are linked with shop output figures, and that wage raises are usually given out based on seniority or leaders' general impressions. Two factors contribute to this continued "softness": the workers' pronounced tendency to dispute assessment standards, argue, and engage in slowdowns when bonus grades have been highly unequal and when group assessments are linked to raises (leading to a managerial de-

4. See Bao (1981) and the exchange between Sun (1979) and Qian (1981).

sire to avoid the problem), and the continuing weak incentives for managers to increase labor productivity.[5]

Official statistics on the distribution of bonus income reinforce this picture. The percentage of the state sector wage bill comprised of time wages decreased from 85 percent in 1978 to 64 percent in 1982, but incentive pay of all varieties still comprises only 18.5 percent of the wage bill. Most telling is the fact that only 7.6 percent of the total is paid as bonuses directly linked to output (as piece rates or above-quota premiums) (State Statistical Bureau 1983: 491). By contrast, almost all Soviet incentive pay—averaging 25 to 30 percent of the wage bill in the 1970s—was paid as piece rates and premiums (Chapman 1979). An important point is indicated by these trends: as orthodox political standards are no longer enforced and as "hard," nonmanipulatable criteria fail to emerge, the personal discretion of shop directors, section chiefs, and group leaders may well increase.

Recasting the Political Standards

Although political standards are no longer used to mobilize and motivate the workforce and no longer influence incentive pay, it is far from the case that there are no longer any explicit political standards for behavior or that workers' conformity to them is no longer a factor in their treatment by the enterprise. It is easy to conclude that political standards are less important than before, but this conclusion would tell us little about what the remaining standards are—and it might leave the mistaken impression that there remain only residual standards with which workers must conform. These standards, to the contrary, are still explicit and enforced systematically within the enterprise. The problem is not to gauge the degree of importance of such standards, but to conceptualize the new standards as they have been recast by the party. This point is of central importance for the interpretation of changes in Chinese society since the death of Mao, but it is of general theoretical importance as well: it is at the center of the debate about the evolution of communist society after the initial "mobilization" or "totalitarian" phase of their histories.

It is accurate to say that shop authority has been depoliticized

---

5. This is a short summary of a much longer analysis (see Walder 1983).

compared with past years. But, as soon as we use this term, we must define it. In this context, depoliticization has a specific and limited meaning. The first of three aspects in which shop authority has been depoliticized was outlined in the preceding section: bonuses and raises no longer depend on political *biaoxian*, and the application of these standards in work groups is no longer intended as a direct motivational tool. The second aspect of depoliticization is that political discrimination against people in certain ascriptive categories is no longer official policy. Because the party has repudiated the Maoist emphasis on "class struggle," employees who are descended from or related to rightists, counterrevolutionaries, landlords, capitalists, former Nationalist officials, and so forth are no longer to be discriminated against as part of official policy.[6] The third aspect, one less apparent than the first two, is the redefinition of *biaoxian* itself. It, too, has been depoliticized, but in a specific and limited sense.

It is probably more meaningful to say that *biaoxian* has been less depoliticized than deideologized. The distinctive Maoist emphasis on beliefs and ideological commitment has diminished, along with the end of the effort to mobilize the labor force by incorporating them through ideological ties. When one speaks of *biaoxian* today, one is no longer referring primarily to public adherence to abstract doctrine, but to concrete loyalties to the party and management in the factory. And central to this loyalty is work performance (although much more is implied). In the past, it was assumed that, if one's political thought was correct, good work performance would follow naturally: therefore, the Maoist emphasis on indoctrination and politicized rewards. Now the party assumes that, if one's performance at work is outstanding, this in itself is strong evidence of good political thought. This equation, and the reversal of past em-

6. One informant (no. 22) related :

In 1979, with the relaxation of party leadership, they got rid of the pre-1949 class labels and took all bad material related to them out of the dossiers. Their class designations were changed to their present occupation. This was true for landlords, rich peasants, capitalists, traitors, spies, rightists, and so forth. All these labels are gone. So there is no more discrimination of this sort in promotions and school admissions.

Interestingly, the commentary that announced the end of such discrimination (Workers' Daily 1979) said that *biaoxian* would be the most important criterion in judging citizens' political loyalty, not their class background or the political records of their relatives. In essence, this is a switch from an ascribed to an achieved status.

phases that it implies, is made easier by the party's redefinition of its current task: no longer the prosecution of class struggle, it is peaceful economic modernization (Organization Bureau 1983: chap. 1). *Biaoxian*, in short, still signifies loyalty, but it no longer attributes special qualities to an ideological adherent. Adherence to generalized beliefs is sufficient.

The party's ideological orientation has declined, but it still spells out an elaborate framework of general beliefs from which citizens cannot dissent in public discourse. Group political study continues on the shop floor. It is no longer an incentive device, nor is it held as frequently as in the past. The content of the materials studied has also been deideologized: where Mao's writings were filled with allusions to class struggle, the works of Deng Xiaoping (studied in factories and offices in the early 1980s) stress socialist modernization and the correct attitudes and political viewpoints required for the task. But the current study materials, though less ideological, are no less political. They spell out the duties of citizens, their proper behavior (and not just on the job), and they prescribe the correct attitudes that citizens should hold toward issues of concern to the party. And such study meetings are still seen as an important tool in the exercise of power:

> We still had political study three days a week for two hours to read editorials and documents. There has been a lot in the past five years [up to 1984]. We had a campaign against factionalism about 1979 or so, against followers of the Gang of Four. There were several campaigns against corruption and waste. In 1983 they had the "spiritual pollution" campaign. It was pretty serious. They interfered with the way you dressed, what you read, and your life-style. (Informant no. 77)

The "spiritual pollution" campaign, while extreme by post-Mao standards, is nonetheless a perfect example of the redefined political standards of the post-Mao era. This was not a campaign to revitalize ideological commitment but to curtail "unhealthy" social phenomena: in this case, the adoption of bourgeois life-styles and attitudes, especially among young workers and highly educated staff. Factory party secretaries organized meetings to criticize the adoption of Western fashions and the popularity of foreign music and literature. Young workers with long hair, tight-fitting jeans, and T shirts with English logos were criticized in shop meetings and made to write self-criticisms. People who owned tapes of popular

music from Taiwan, Hong Kong, and the West were required to register them with the party organization and to turn in certain forbidden titles:

> They had a meeting and an investigation to see if workers were listening
> to tapes from Hong Kong and Taiwan, or reading dirty books and going
> dancing at night. They read out the [campaign] document at a mass
> meeting. Every small group had to register the things they had at home
> that might be polluted. The lists were sent to the party committee, and
> they decided whether you had to erase your tapes or destroy the books,
> or whether you could keep them. They also had study meetings to op-
> pose spiritual pollution. . . . It had a big impact, all these habits stopped
> for a while. If you didn't stop, the branch secretary would call you in for
> a talk. (Informant no. 80)

Although this campaign was rapidly curtailed (see Gold 1984), it
illustrates a broader point: the political standards have been recast,
but the party continues to define acceptable behavior and political
attitudes:

> They don't use *biaoxian* as a standard as clearly as in the past. But it's
> still there. There's still the "four upholds."[7] If you don't violate them
> openly, there's no problem. But, if the party secretary doesn't like your
> thought, he would have a bad impression of you. Since everyone knows
> how to say what is necessary, it doesn't matter anyway. (Ibid.)

Why, if *biaoxian* is no longer a regular part of bonus and raise
evaluations, do employees still have an incentive to conform, especially when the political atmosphere and threat of repression is considerably less serious than before? We should realize that, though
bonuses and raises are no longer paid according to a formal procedure of ideological grading, those who are singled out for violating
political standards are regularly deprived of bonuses and raises. But
the more important answer is that *biaoxian* has not been repudiated as a standard for rewards other than bonuses and raises. In its
recast form, it remains central to virtually all the promotions for
which workers are eligible and to the entire range of factory distributions and sociopolitical services.

7. The "four upholds" comprise the political standards that currently define, albeit vaguely, the forbidden areas of political expression. Citizens in principle are free
to air their opinions and criticisms, but they must continue to affirm the socialist
road of development, the dictatorship of the proletariat (now called the people's
democratic dictatorship), the leadership of the Communist party, and the principles
of Marxism–Leninism–Mao Zedong thought.

The Redefinition of Activism

As *biaoxian* has been recast, activism has been redefined. Just as *biaoxian* has become deideologized, the activist is no longer defined by his or her adherence to doctrine:

> Back then, political *biaoxian* was number one. But that was just an empty concept, how much you talked in meetings. Not anymore. Most important now is whether or not you work hard. Those false and empty words don't get you very far these days. (Informant no. 76)

> Now if you work hard, they say you have good thought. Good thought is automatic now if you work hard and become an "advanced producer." They don't even talk about political activists that much anymore. Now they talk a lot about "advanced producers." (Informant no. 77)

The "advanced producer"—the honorary term given to the most common type of model worker—typifies the current definition of the activist. The activist in China has become more like his Soviet bloc counterpart, as defined by Reinhard Bendix (1956: 403) in his study of East German industry: "'Activist' is party jargon for all workers who exceed previously established work norms."

The fact that the activist, as well as the initiatives of management and party, have become deideologized and more production-oriented does not mean that activism no longer has political content. The cultivation of activists is still central to the exercise of power in the factory. An advanced producer is not merely someone who overfulfills production quotas. Implicit in this concept is the earlier notion of deference and loyalty to shop leaders. The loyalty of the activist is still clearly with the party and management, not with the workers. The activist now does not dispute new disciplinary regulations and their enforcement, but becomes a model of work discipline. The activist does not dispute new quotas or argue about bonus and raise assessments, but diligently overfulfills the quotas, thereby showing that those who object are shirkers. The activist does not collude with other workers in resisting new management initiatives regarding overtime, sick leave, and bonus assessments, nor does he participate in soldiering designed to bring management around to the workers' viewpoint. Instead, the activist alerts management to brewing problems, seeks to convince workers to comply, and acts to help the implementation of management initiatives.

As was the case in years past, activists must also participate in extensive after-hours voluntary work. Where in the past this was likely to be an ideological campaign, today it is more likely to be a production campaign. The workshop office, the youth league and party branch, the union office, and the propaganda department still depend on the after-hours volunteer work of activists. Daily and weekly production and quality statistics must be calculated, and charts drawn up to publicize the performance of sections, groups, and individuals. Notices, wall posters, and slogans regarding factory regulations and job performance must be drawn up, duplicated by hand, and posted around the factory. Youth league branches still meet to coordinate their responses in the next day's study or production meetings. Cultural performances, films, and other activities still must be arranged and staffed. The activities are more production-oriented than in the past, but activists still take part in the same broad range of after-hours activities.

Activists, in short, still manifest the most active loyalty to their superiors in the shop, assist them in the performance of their duties, and side publicly with leaders against the rank and file. As before, they form the pool of candidates eligible for promotion to leadership positions, on or off the shop floor. This does not conflict with the party's new stress on skill and ability as much as one might at first imagine. In the first instance, the party's policy is to promote people who have skill and ability, not to promote the most skilled and able: "They no longer want amateurs leading professionals. They now want people who are qualified to lead work in departments. But this doesn't mean they appoint the person who is best at the work. It means they now want someone who knows something about the work. They still want people who obey the party" (informant no. 80). This informant was speaking of the new situation in technical staff departments, where the conflict between loyalty and skill would presumably be at its sharpest.[8] The conflict is far less on the shop floor. There are few technical requirements for the positions for which workers are eligible. To be a section chief or a member of the workshop staff requires basic literacy, knowledge of the

8. An increase in the demand for technical training and genuine ability does not necessarily lead to a reduction in the demand for political loyalty, except in the extreme situation in which the politically loyal and the able are mutually exclusive groups. As levels of overall training and education increase and as incentives for skill acquisition upgrade the workforce, the party and management may preferentially select the most loyal without sacrificing ability (see Walder 1985b).

production process, and leadership ability. Less rigorous standards apply to all of the promotions still controlled solely by the party organization: in the youth league, union, and propaganda department offices. For all of these positions, the most important qualification is still a record of consistent loyalty and commitment.

The Changing Role of the Party

The party organization, as many of the changes already described suggest, has begun to alter its role in the factory. My discussion of changes in activism and the definition of *biaoxian* indicates a deeper shift in the party's self-definition. Recognizing the failure of the long Maoist effort at revitalization, it no longer defines itself as an ideological group nor seeks to discipline its members and society through ideological ties. Members are no longer to be bound by their total commitment to a sacred doctrine, but by their civic loyalty to the nation and the party. To use Shils' (1957) terms, the ties that bind party members have evolved from the "sacred" ideological ties of past years to "civil" ties or a sense of patriotism and civic duty. This serves as a basis for cooperation with elements outside the party who in the past were not considered carriers of proletarian consciousness, but who may share this patriotic consciousness.

Because of this official change in its self-definition, the party no longer takes such a pronounced "exclusivist" stance toward the rest of society: its membership is not so sharply differentiated from nonmembers. This shift is characteristic of the erosion of the ideological orientation: "The sharply defined boundaries become eroded. The members cease to define themselves exclusively by their ideological qualities . . . distinctive ideological elements fade into a ceremonially asserted formula" (Shils 1972: 32). The party no longer takes an antagonistic stance toward staff experts and other professionals in the factory hierarchy; it is to unite with and support all social elements that are able to serve in the current task of modernization.

As this exclusivistic definition has eroded, so has the party's impulse to oversee and interfere with the daily operations of the factory's professional management. Party committees have been ordered not to interfere in the day-to-day operations of the factory —and emigres report some real changes in this regard. Party committees may no longer commandeer the factory and its personnel for a political or production campaign; they may no longer inject extraneous ideological considerations into incentive programs; they may no longer interfere in the factory director's staffing decisions (on his own professional staff); and they may no longer intimidate the professional management in matters of work discipline.[9] In the workshops, the shop director's duties have been more clearly differentiated from the branch secretary's, and the secretary's influence over shop management decisions has declined. Ideally, the branch secretary will become a supportive protégé of the shop director.

The party organization's new mandate is to serve the factory management, support its decisions and activities, and help create conditions that promote productivity:

> Party organizations in enterprises should actively support directors in exercising their authority in giving unified direction to production and operations, guarantee and supervise the implementation of the principles and policies of the party and the state, strengthen the party's ideological and organizational work in enterprises, improve their leadership over the trade unions and Communist Youth League organizations, and do effective ideological and political work among workers and staff. (Xinhua News Agency 1984: K13)

The deployment of the factory party organization has changed more than its organization and daily activities. Its form of organization is virtually unchanged: it continues to staff its panoply of offices internally; it continues to cultivate loyal activists for positions of leadership in the shop hierarchy, youth league, union, and propaganda departments; and it continues to organize such study meetings as the party headquarters may order and such production campaigns as the factory managers define. More than in the past, it plays an important role in ironing out dissatisfactions related to matters of pay. Sudden drops in bonus income, public evaluations for wage raises, or a tightening of factory regulations have in recent years often provoked passive resistance or open arguments within groups, and party organizations must swing into action to override opposition through intensive meetings for "ideological work" (see

9. These are statements of official policy intentions; the realities of power in each factory make generalizations about actual practices hazardous. Much depends on the informal balance of power of different leadership cliques and the relationship between the plant director and party secretary: e.g., how long each has held the post and their respective backing from above.

Walder 1983). Finally, the least obvious but most fundamental role played by the party—and the one that serves to distinguish communist from corporatist states—has been completely unaltered. Despite all the changes in its self-definition, its stance vis-à-vis professional management, and its deployment in the factory, the party organization still acts systematically to prevent organized group activity among workers, except that promoted by the party itself.

Continuities in the Pattern of Dependence

Of the pattern of organized dependence that defines communist neo-traditionalism, only one—economic dependence on the enterprise—has been reduced significantly. The organized capacity of the party to place workers in a politically dependent position has not changed, although the party's role in the factory has. The shop director still heads a "foreman's empire": wide discretion over job assignments, promotions, bonuses, wage raises, punishments, distributions, and sociopolitical services. The shop director no longer shares this discretion with the party branch secretary to the same extent as before, and his decisions are to be guided by consideration of performance and ability, not by *biaoxian*. Shop directors have begun to employ production statistics and skill examinations to guide them in the exercise of their discretion, especially in matters of incentive pay. Therefore, the exercise of discretion will appear less arbitrary than in the past. But they still retain as much personal discretion as before, especially in promotions, distributions, and sociopolitical services, where the relevance of production statistics and examinations is limited.[10] Not until this discretion is lodged in staff offices, as it is in large American and Japanese enterprises, will this personal dependence on shop officials be significantly altered.

The workers' economic dependence on the enterprise has changed more significantly from the pattern described earlier. The increased supplies of food and consumer goods, the gradual easing

10. E.g., informant no. 75 said: "Now you must be good at your work. You can't just rely on your speaking ability to get promoted anymore. . . . But this is [only] the policy. At the basic levels they don't really do things this way. They said you were supposed to promote people according to ability, but in reality they choose people because of personal relationships."

of rationing, and the opening up of a private trade and services sector in cities have provided alternative sources for the satisfaction of many needs. Workers are no longer completely dependent on their enterprises for the direct delivery of many foodstuffs and consumer goods. Yet, a number of other changes have offset this erosion of economic dependence. First, the state enterprise, especially the large ones, have sought actively to improve their services, supply of housing, and increase their informal distributions. Second, the goods and services provided outside the enterprise, especially in the new private sector, have been hit hardest by price inflation and are usually much more expensive than comparable state goods and subsidized factory services, most of which are supplied at a small fraction of their actual cost (see Lardy 1984). They are an expensive alternative. Third, the privileged protection of the state sector worker with regard to insurance and benefits has continued on an enhanced scale: state expenditures on benefits financed through the state labor insurance system increased by 170 percent from 1978 to 1983, while the number of state employees grew by only 18 percent (Lardy 1984: 862). As the extreme scarcity of the past has eased, the state enterprise is no longer the primary source for the distribution of ordinary consumer goods, but its employees still depend on it for the highly subsidized satisfaction of a broad range of their needs—from housing to grain price subsidies.

The Evolving Institutional Culture

The main outlines of the generic institutional culture of the communist factory have endured in the 1980s. A minority of loyal activists are still maintained as the clients of the power structure. With the lessening of scarcity, nonactivists have, in effect, been given a "square deal"—they can now more readily receive consumer goods and housing. The sharp distinction between the treatment of activists and nonactivists, which was so invidious in the austerity of the Maoist era, has softened. Activists are no longer so deeply scorned, in part because they are increasingly perceived as earning their status through hard work, in part because their advantages no longer contrast with the deprivation of nonactivists. This does not mean, however, that the division between client-activists and workers is no longer a social fact—the informal persecution of activists continues as before, perhaps made sharper in recent years by the growing importance of incentive pay and the perception that activists now harm the pay packet of the other workers by inviting managers to raise quotas.[11] The subculture of instrumental-personal ties continues to thrive as well, and the recent party campaign against it leaves the impression that it may have expanded further with the lessening of ideological pressures.

But other aspects of the institutional culture of authority, in its Maoist version, have changed. A number of these changes parallel those that have taken place in the Soviet Union since Stalin: an increased emphasis on workers' living standards; a growing depoliticization, or deideologization, of the management of factories and of the party's self-definition; and a corresponding emphasis on tacit consent to party authority rather than active ideological commitment. Where the mobilizational approach sought to roll over resistance through political pressures, selective victimization, and the distribution of material rewards according to political activism, the current paternalistic approach mixes firm and consistent demands for obedience and an emphasis on loyalty (as reflected in job performance and voluntary work) with elaborate displays of concern over workers' material life. These are two versions of the same pattern of authority.

Out of the Maoist era has emerged another new facet of the institutional culture: an amorphous pattern of negotiation between management and workers within the factory that Sabel and Stark (1982) label "hidden bargaining." This pattern is "socially amorphous" because it is unorganized and does not work through the formal articulation of interests. Rather, workers react to management actions and policies through slowdowns and covert acts of insubordination and resistance. Management responds to these worker actions and usually attempts to anticipate and avoid them. Such communication as occurs takes place in sections or groups, through the reports of activists or the expression of gripes outside of meetings.

This amorphous pattern of anticipation and reaction has always characterized factory authority, even during the period of mass mobilization. But a new development has given these informal negotiations greater importance: the factory now has much greater

11. See the recent accounts of the persecution of model workers in *Workers' Daily* (1982a; 1982b; 1982c).

control over its revenues and their distribution as incentive pay. For the first time, workers can influence the distribution of a large bonus fund and the factory's policy regarding wage raises and promotions. In the exercise of their recently enhanced autonomy, managers must deal with their workforce in a way that is functionally analogous to more formal collective bargaining. Some of the recent behavior of management—especially their overpayment of bonuses—is clearly attributable to this informal negotiation (see Walder 1983). This pattern of negotiation, however real, remains socially amorphous, unorganized, and coexists with all the formal and informal institutions I describe in this book. Without organization, amorphous social action is limited in its effectiveness: it represents "friction" in the system, not a political initiative. It must not be interpreted, as some of its analysts suggest, as the emergence of group politics.[12]

The changes that I interpret in this chapter have a broader significance: they are a case study of institutional change in what has at times been called the "postmobilization phase" of communist political development. One of the enduring debates about the nature of communist societies has been prompted by precisely this transition. In the Soviet Union, it was marked by the relaxation of police terror; in China, by the relaxation of the party's ideological orientation; in both, by the evolution toward paternalism. How fundamental a change this represents has been subject to different interpretations, and the concepts that have guided investigations have usually been a series of unrelated continua: the *degree* of universalism and achievement in the reward structure; the *degree* of political repression; the *scope* for free expression; and the *extent* to which the party seeks to respond to consumers' needs. The problem with a continuum is that there is no standard calibration: where some have found the emergence of a kind of pluralism, others find "totalitarianism without terror." My interpretation of China's evolution since Mao, as viewed from the shop floor, involves the use of a type concept, and the conceptualization of qualitative variation in the elements of that type. I would be tempted to conclude that my

---

12. Although, as Pravda (1981) argues, genuine group politics may emerge, as in Poland, if the government experiences an economic crisis that forces managers to take a hard line against workers in all areas, leaving virtually no slack for informal negotiation.

interpretation lies somewhere between the ones just mentioned, but that would only reinforce the misimpression that a continuum is involved. As I interpret them, there have been more complex and significant changes than a partial relaxation of political controls—the party's self-definition and deployment have changed, *biaoxian* and activism have been redefined, and there is more informal negotiation over wages. But these changes have occurred in a context of strong institutional continuity; they represent a new version of the generic communist pattern, not its erosion.

8. Theoretical Reflections

In this book I have illustrated a theoretical statement about the nature of communist societies with a study of industrial authority. The comparisons have sharpened my conception of the differences between Chinese and Soviet institutions, but they have also convinced me that they share the same underlying pattern. Much further research needs to be done to test the applicability of this neo-traditional image to communist regimes other than China's and to social settings other than industry. I have been able, through brief comparisons with the Soviet Union and other Eastern European countries, to document the generic pattern of dependence better than I have been able to document the generic institutional culture. I have found evidence of a subculture of instrumental-personal ties in the Soviet Union, but how this actually works in the factory is still unclear. And, though I have established basic similarities in party organization, in "principled particularism," and the allied notion of "privileged access," no study of Eastern European factory life exists in English that shows how all of this actually operates in workshops or addresses the nature of the vertical ties between workers and shop officials. I nonetheless feel sufficiently confident of this suggestive pattern of evidence to offer the general statements I have made in this book. I hope that others will seek to test, refine, and correct them with research of their own.

In this final chapter, I specify some of the broader implications of this study for theory and research on communist societies. The first set of implications is for the study of the class relations and social structure of communist societies; the second about theories regarding the stability and legitimacy of these regimes. A third set regards the type of industrial authority analyzed in this book: the ways that it is structurally distinct from that in other settings and whether this type of authority is part of a master process of bureaucratization that appears to be characteristic of modern industrialization. And the final set of implications is about evolution and change in communist societies.

The Structure of Communist Societies

Although not an explicit theme of the preceding chapters, the analysis of authority relations in industry has direct relevance for efforts to understand social stratification and class relations in communist societies. I have examined, in its institutional setting, the exercise of authority over an industrial working class or, more abstractly, the political relationship between capital and labor. In a capitalist setting, this would involve the relationships between labor on the one hand, and the private owners of capital and their paid white collar executives and managerial staff, on the other. In the communist setting, authority is exercised by a class of petty officials—salaried enterprise administrators and party cadres—who control capital owned nominally by the state and who use this capital "in trust." When I have examined "authority in the workplace," I have simultaneously examined the essentials of a class relationship central to communist civilization.

My examination of this class relationship, however, points to the importance of some social-structural principles rarely hinted at in prior examinations of the social structure of these societies. When political sociologists have examined social stratification, it has invariably been for the purpose of defining the boundaries between social groups by specifying as precisely as possible differences in income, standards of living, and mobility opportunities for both individuals and their offspring (e.g., Lane 1982; Parkin 1971). This pervasive interest in defining group boundaries is inspired by an implicit concept of social structure as a constellation of groups and a definitional-deductive approach to the relationship between social structure and politics. To understand political allegiances and the social basis of conflict as well as stability according to this approach, one must first define distinct groups based on common income and consumption patterns, occupational and educational characteristics, and opportunities for upward mobility. The approach is deductive: once groups based on common characteristics are identified, one deduces (or sometimes simply guesses at) political interests, attitudes, and allegiances. This approach has guided efforts to understand the place of intellectuals in society, to determine the social sources of regime support, and indeed has guided virtually all efforts to identify the "group" basis of conflict and policy making in communist regimes.

My approach has been quite different. It has not been guided by the identification of groups and the definition of boundaries between them, nor has it been deductive in nature. Instead, I have looked at the relationships between members of different groups, and have not deduced individual interests and orientations based on group characteristics. I have grounded this analysis of political orientations and interests, instead, in data about the political orientations and relationships themselves. When I have referred in this book to social structure, I have not meant a collection of groups, but instead, as Radcliffe-Brown (1952) puts it, a pattern of "actually existing social relationships": to social networks rather than groups.

This difference in approach to the study of social structure is of more than theoretical interest: it leads to a different understanding of political orientations, allegiances, and social conflict, precisely the phenomena that people have sought to illuminate with a "group-deductive" approach. The preceding chapters indicate the difficulty faced by any attempt to deduce the "group" interests, orientations, or political allegiances of workers, no matter how finely one differentiates them by skill, pay, or industry. No matter what their current income or skill level, worker political orientations are determined by their adoption of active-competitive or passive-defensive strategies. Every occupational group or stratum, no matter how defined, is divided by the social distinction between activist and nonactivist that pervades everyday life. The activists are linked to the petty officials in the enterprise by well-developed networks of communication and command, and by a clientelist relationship with superiors in which loyalty is exchanged for future career opportunities and privileges. Every social group, in other words, is riddled with cross-cutting networks of allegiances that are central to the exercise of power. Information about group characteristics, boundaries, and their inferred interests, no matter how complete, cannot tell us anything about these networks and allegiances. We need data about behavior and relationships, not about group characteristics.

If these social networks are so central to political allegiances and

orientations, then they should be reflected in the workers' own perceptions of their interests, and their political self-identification. We
have already seen, in chapter 5, the pronounced social gulf between
activists and nonactivists that occasionally surfaces in open antagonism and even physical violence. There is a pronounced feeling of
"us" versus "them" characteristic of relations between these two
groups of workers. Each of the two political groups, further, reacts
to political campaigns in a different way: their perceptions, strategies, and overt behavior distinguish them publicly from one another. The most dramatic evidence of the importance of these network allegiances in dividing groups against themselves emerged in
the factional allegiances that split workers during the Cultural
Revolution of 1966–1969. At the outset of the movement, workers
divided into two antagonistic factions: a "royalist" faction supportive of the party leadership in the enterprise, and dominated by
party members, activists, and model workers, and a "rebel" faction
made up of disgruntled nonactivists victimized by the system in the
past, political dissidents, and frustrated activists whose careers had
been jeopardized by a single political mistake or soured personal
relations with superiors. These networks provided the fissures along
which state workers divided during the Cultural Revolution.[1] Network, not group, is the structural principle that shaped this political behavior.

Group theorists view the subjects of concern in this book simply
as leadership practices and reward systems, not as aspects of social
structure. But in a communist society these leadership and reward
practices have definite social-structural consequences. They create
and maintain stable networks of identification and allegiance. These
structures are just as "real" as those based on common income levels, occupation, skill, and education. Indeed, in the social setting I
have analyzed, the network allegiances are in many ways more
"real" than the group ones. Communist society may indeed contain
groups defined by their common characteristics, and it is undeni-
ably valuable to know about them. But, if we wish to understand
how political rule is exercised or the sources of political stability, we
must start with a realization that all of these social groups are di-

---

1. I spell out this argument more fully in Walder (1986), and I am currently
working on a book that will explore the social basis of mass political activity among
workers and other groups in this period.

vided by enduring network ties that create conflicting interests and loyalties, are clientelist in content, are continually cultivated and reinforced with social activities and material exchange, and lead ultimately to the organization of the ruling party itself.

Social Stability and Legitimacy in Communist States

This analysis of workplace authority relations has not been framed solely as a study in industrial sociology for an important reason: Chinese workers relate to plant officials as employees, but at the same time they relate to these state functionaries as citizens to their government. When workers routinely comply with party and managerial authority, they are also consenting to the political authority of the state. This allows us a different perspective on long-standing questions about the social sources of political stability and about the nature of political legitimacy and consent in communist regimes. These questions are usually approached either as a matter of gauging public opinion, the effects of media control, political indoctrination, and appeals to nationalism (Inkeles 1950), or through the study of social trends as they affect key social groups: trends in standard of living, the supply of goods and services, material expectations, opportunities for education and upward mobility. This aggregate picture of publics, analogous to group approaches to social structure, is an indispensable part of the puzzle. But this study of the integration of a working class into a communist state as it occurs at the site of integration, shows that citizen consent (and the legitimacy of the regime) is also a socially structured phenomenon. It grows directly out of complex patterns of interaction in everyday life. And a central feature of this pattern of relationships is a party organization that works tirelessly and systematically to maintain this structure of consent.

The first, and perhaps most important, structural source of consent is the network of clientelist ties that links the activist minority to the party and management. This not only provides a bedrock of positive support among key workers, but it divides workers as a group (often shifting antagonisms away from management and toward the activists themselves) and provides a structural barrier to concerted worker resistance. The party reaches out to the citizenry through constantly cultivated patronage relationships, in which active support and loyalty are exchanged for mobility opportunities, material advantages, and social status. This exchange relationship is not an impersonal one: factory leaders have considerable flexibility in rewarding activist-clients, they work closely with them, come to know them well, and intervene personally on their behalf with higher authorities. In this relationship, the institutional and personal aspects are closely intertwined: public loyalties to the party and the orthodox versions of its ideology are subtly mixed with private and personal loyalties to one's leader-patron.

A second structural source of consent is the diffuse web of purely personal relationships through which most individuals—not just activist-clients—can bend rules in their favor or circumvent formal channels of rationing and application making. This has the effect both of giving the average worker the sense that he or she has "beaten the system" through individual, not collective, action and of reinforcing a propensity to retreat from coordinated group action and indeed from "politics" in general. Burawoy's (1979) ethnography of work in an American machine shop portrays consent as something that emerges from an elaborately structured "game" on the shop floor. A complex legal framework of workplace governance, with individual appeals to grievance committees and individual bidding on job openings, gives the workplace a sense of legitimate due process, while the individual machine operator works at breakneck speed, trying to "make out" individually in piece rate systems. The worker that plays—and wins—according to these structured rules of the game, Burawoy argues, will not be one likely to question the system itself or engage in collective action to change it.

An analogous game operates in the very different setting of the Chinese factory. Systematically demobilized as a group, and facing a reward system that penalizes the voicing of genuine criticisms of conditions and of group demands, workers can beat the system without being coopted by it through the cultivation of purely personal relationships based on petty corruption or the exchange of favors. Workers who "make out" by playing the game in this manner are funneling their efforts into individual action motivated for personal benefit. The real satisfactions of beating the system are not the most important source of consent to emerge from this "game": workers who focus their attention onto these matters will be less likely to think about abstract issues of justice and equality in a political way; they exhibit routine compliance and an unfocused acceptance of the political status quo because they know there is always the possibility of winning a personal exception to formal rules. This focusing of individual efforts onto private and personal matters, and the apolitical mentality that it reinforces, might appear as a detrimental outcome to those who interpret formal political institutions literally, but it is in fact an important (if unintended) source of worker consent and routine acceptance of the status quo.

A third structural source of consent, and especially of legitimacy, is the practice of paternalism by the enterprise. The extraordinary job security and benefits, the goods and services distributed directly by the state enterprise in a situation of scarcity that affects other sectors of the workforce more severely, is an important source of acceptance of the system (see also Connor 1979; Fehér 1982). This sense of acceptance is enhanced to the extent that enterprises go out of their way to procure extra ration coupons, material for housing construction, and foodstuffs for the cafeteria. Indeed many managers do this habitually in order to boost morale and win the cooperation and goodwill of their workers—and they are always sure to remind "their" workers of this generosity in mass meetings and at annual congresses of workers and staff. The negative reaction of several of my informants to the fast work pace, low job security, minimal insurance and benefits characteristic of factory work in Hong Kong (often expressed in terms of moral disapproval) convinces me that paternalism is an important source of regime legitimacy in China.

This structural perspective on consent reveals a far more complex and subtle pattern of authority than that suggested by a formal system of party mobilization that demands unquestioning loyalty to a rigidly orthodox official ideology. Even for committed activists, the object of loyalty is ambiguous. It is both public and private: activists are loyal both to the party as an institution, and to their superiors as patrons. They work for the good of the nation as defined by the party, but they also reap considerable personal benefits from their acts of selflessness and personal sacrifice (although sometimes the benefits are deferred until later in their careers). Even in the continually reenacted ceremonies of *biaoxian*, in which activists are expected to express positive support of the public and orthodox definitions of party ideology, the content of the ideology, or its current practical interpretation, is distinctly secondary to the act of expression itself. When activists engage in public displays of approval, they are siding publicly with the party, taking a stand that isolates them from other workers and often earns them enmity as well. It is a ritual not because it is meaningless, or the act of loyalty empty and formalistic. It is a ritual in the deepest social meaning of the term: it publicly marks activists from the rank and file; it reaffirms the personal loyalty of the party's clients; and, by forcing the activist to publicly side with the party instead of with coworkers and friends, it binds them ever more tightly to their patrons in the leadership. Activists deprived of social support from their coworkers become more dependent on their patrons for this support and approval. The social consequences of this ritual are real.

This pervasive personalization of party rule—in the clientelist nature of party-activist relations, in the diffuse web of personal ties used for individual advantage and mutual support, and in the practice and ideology of paternalism in the enterprise community—could properly be viewed as a corruption both of the formal system of party mobilization and of its official ideology. Definitionally, this is characteristic of political corruption the world over, and it was certainly viewed as corruption by Maoists who sought to revitalize the party organization and its ideology during the Cultural Revolution. But, in an unintended way, this partial "corruption" of the system promotes social stability by creating personal loyalties and obligations among a minority of workers that run parallel to formal leadership ties, and by encouraging the rest to withdraw from politics and political thinking into private and individual pursuits hidden by a facade of conformity. This complex web of personal loyalty, mutual support, and material interest creates a stable pattern of tacit acceptance and active cooperation for the regime that no amount of political terror, coercion, or indoctrination can even begin to provide.

The Varieties of Modern Industrial Authority

There can be little doubt that the factory regime typical of the contemporary Chinese enterprise is "bureaucratic," at least in one sense of the term: the size of the administrative structure and the scope of its powers. Like the bureaucratic managerial hierarchies that emerged from prior subcontracting systems in the United

States early in the twentieth century, Chinese management completely controls hiring, promotion, and wages, and it defines careers and the succession of jobs that comprise them. Also like their bureaucratic American (not to mention Soviet and Japanese) counterparts, Chinese managers control the conception, pace, and execution of work itself; they draw up these plans in white collar staff offices; they have proprietary control over skill and its acquisition; and they design jobs for workers with job-specific skills. And in some ways, especially in the scope of administrative powers, the Chinese firm is much more bureaucratic than the American. Management control over mobility, residence, and the direct supply of a wide array of goods and services gives Chinese administrators powers that no American or Japanese manager can contemplate. In this regard, the Chinese managerial bureaucracy encompasses a number of functions that are handled by commodity markets or by separate public and private institutions in other countries.

However, in another important, Weberian sense of the term, Chinese management hierarchies are only partially bureaucratic. The content of the social relations and roles embedded in the organization are incompletely impersonal; rewards are not tied solely to performance of formal functional roles; the authority of the individual is by no means distinct from the authority of the office; formally rational means-ends calculation does not dominate the behavior of supervisors. The often decried consequences of bureaucratization in the American workplace—the treatment of workers as interchangeable cogs in a production process, the impersonal character of authority, the alienating lack of personal interaction among coworkers, and the extreme stress on productivity—are not characteristic of industrial life in China.

The point of this last observation is not merely that Chinese industry represents a deviation from the ideal type of bureaucracy formulated by Weber. Certainly every researcher of real world bureaucracies has found a number of such deviations. This is not at all surprising—Weber, after all, called his an "ideal" type for a reason. The point, instead, is that Chinese industrial hierarchies, viewed from the perspective of the way that authority is exercised in them, are approximated by a different ideal type of authority. When personal ties and understandings enter into the reward of persons, this is not a deviation from formally universalistic standards of evaluation, but from the principled particularism of reward practices.

Formal reward systems demand evaluation not simply of performance of role tasks, but of an entirely separate realm of individual behavior, attitudinal orientations, and personal loyalties. The ideal type of political community that is closest to Chinese industrial bureaucracy is not Weber's "bureaucracy," but his "patrimonialism"; the type of authority is not his "rational-legal," but his "traditional." What is significant from a comparative perspective about Chinese industrial bureaucracy is not that it deviates from the ideal type of bureaucracy, but that it represents the integration of patrimonial rule with modern bureaucratic form. This is precisely why I (along with Jowitt) describe this modern institutional setting as "neo-traditional."

The point of this argument, further, is not merely that clientelist patterns have been discovered or that the informal organization of the Chinese enterprise is larger in scope or analytically "more important" than in comparable organizations elsewhere. Every organization has its pattern of informal personal relationships, and clientelism exists in some form in a wide range of historical and institutional settings. When I apply the concept *clientelist bureaucracy* to the Chinese enterprise, I am pointing to a structured pattern of particularistic rule that has both formal and informal dimensions. These clientelist networks have a definite personal aspect, but they operate in conjunction with well-developed and officially prescribed institutional roles. They elicit personal loyalties, but these loyalties grow up out of the regime's effort to create public political loyalties. What is notable about this pattern is not that there is a personal and informal side to the organization, but that the entire complex of formal and informal, public and private relationships represents a form of particularism that is at the very core of this type of industrial bureaucracy.

The Evolution of Communist Societies

A full appreciation of the character of this type of authority affords us a different perspective on the evolution of communist societies than that commonly reflected in studies of their modernization. By far the dominant motif is that of the decay of the mobilization system, based on Leninist principles, because of the demands of economic modernization, which require the increasing adoption of Western bureaucratic organization and modern technologies. In this view, the dominant trend is one in which Leninist patterns of organization—demanding allegiance to a unitary ideology, political loyalty, and the mobilization of efforts to concentrate on party-defined tasks—give way to more familiar forms of modern bureaucracy in which the ideology becomes an ornament, in which job performance is stressed, and administration becomes routine. Looked at from the perspective of technique and form, one sees convergence under the impact of modernization.

This study of bureaucratic authority, though not a study of the problems of administration, identifies another aspect of this trend of evolution away from classic Leninist organization: one that alters the way we interpret patterns of change. We have seen that Leninist forms evolve, by their own logic, into a form of clientelist rule. The particularism remains embedded in "decayed" Leninist institutions. Maoists recognized this trend with tragic clarity: they publicly censured as "capitalist" the trappings of rational-legal bureaucracy, but their proposed remedies reflected a realization that the Leninist forms were being corrupted from within. That realization led to their failed effort to revitalize the public and orthodox spirit of these Leninist forms. The failure of this revitalization reflects not the triumph of the "demands of modernization" for rational-legal bureaucracy, but the inability to halt this evolution toward a stable, "corrupted" form of organization. The implication is that there is a particularism in these institutions that does not melt away with the demands of industrialization. The tension between particularism and universalism, between affective and instrumental action, is deeply entrenched and is resolved not by the erosion of the "traditional," but by efforts to combine demands for loyalty with demands for performance in ways not seen in modern Western civilization. In other words, we are not witnessing a single process of bureaucratization, but more than one; and these types of bureaucracy evolve along separate, and not necessarily converging, paths.

This statement should not be surprising. Few of the social conditions that Weber specified in his *Economy and Society* as leading to the peculiar rationality of Western capitalism, subsequently embodied in its modern bureaucracies, have characterized China since the revolution (see also Anderson and Anderson 1978; Delaney 1963). These conditions—the freeing of labor from social and legal encumbrances to land or social institutions; the existence of labor as a commodity bought and sold freely on markets; the universalization of labor and commodity markets and their associated money ethic and the consequent ability to rationally calculate costs and act to minimize them; and the universalization of the profit motive that embeds formally rational means-end calculation more deeply—are instead conspicuous by their absence. On the contrary, in China labor is tied to the enterprise, labor and commodity markets are weakly developed, and the enterprise is a budgetary arm of the state whose existence and prosperity are linked weakly to capital and labor efficiency. China's revolution has succeeded in creating a type of modern civilization that is profoundly anticapitalist. The type of bureaucratic authority analyzed in this book is one of its defining features.

China's revolutionary leaders did not set out to create neo-traditional patterns of authority exercised by a clientelist party. On the contrary, theirs was a vision of politically pure commitment to national purpose and principled social discipline. But, due to their planned response to intractable demographic and social problems and the unintended consequences of these new institutional forms, this vision translated into a different reality. In this process of trans-lation, Marx's historical vision of a working class that arises collec-tively in the course of capitalist industrialization to contend for and seize their share of power has given way to another: one in which a powerful party-state calls into being a working class that is, from the outset, dependent politically and economically on their enter-prises and the petty officials who operate them. The political and cultural consequences of this development defy categorization along the conventional spectrums of right and left, reactionary and progressive, traditional and modern; they comprise a historical development that we have only dimly begun to understand.

Appendix A

The Hong Kong Interviews:
An Essay on Method

Methodological discussions of emigre interviewing are usually influenced, either consciously or unconsciously, by the logic of survey research. This is understandable, because these discussions are invariably touched off by the obvious violation of the basic tenets of sampling theory. Emigre populations are, after all, self-selected rather than randomly sampled, and there is every reason to suspect that the principles of self-selection make emigres an atypical subgroup, especially with regard to their political attitudes (see Whyte 1983:68–70). But, for many research topics and styles of interviewing, the survey research model and its logical approach to the problem of reliability and the drawing of inferences are conceptually and practically inappropriate.

Emigre Interviews as a Field Method

The survey research model has proved fruitful in studies that have been devised as surveys or quasi-surveys. Some scholars have designed and administered questionnaires to emigre populations about their attitudes or political activities and, carefully avoiding inferences that would be unwarranted given the nature of the sample, have interpreted them in illuminating ways (Inkeles 1950; Inkeles and Bauer 1959; Gitelman 1977; Falkenheim 1978; Nathan 1985). Other have coded transcripts of semi-structured interviews and used their tabulations on family life, employment, income, social mobility, neighborhood organization, village customs, and other subjects as a substitute for a field survey (Parish and Whyte 1978; Whyte and Parish 1984; Whyte 1983:73; Parish 1981). This strategy requires a standard list of questions, even when responses are open-ended. When one is able to specify in advance the concepts appropriate to the study and operationalize them in units of measurement, the survey model is directly appropriate. In these instances, set questionnaires and tabulations of frequencies are vital operations.

However, in many instances they are not. This is because interviewing research can also be an open-ended process of discovery in which one encounters unexpected insights and new kinds of "data," and in so doing redefines the concept of the research problem itself. This is not due to any lack of preparation on the part of the researcher; it is part and parcel of field research, whether carried out "on site" or solely through interviews. For many kinds of research questions, one simply cannot develop adequate questions without having first familiarized oneself with the social setting by living there or doing preliminary interviews as a means of orientation. Some settings are too foreign to our own experience and culture to permit this; some concepts, like authority, are not amenable to ready operationalization; some areas of research are virtually uncharted. Most social scientists in fieldwork expect their concept of the research to change during its course: it is a sign that one is learning something.

If the concept of the research changes in its course, then the survey model and its prescriptions for handling the problem of reliability through the design of questions and formalized rules about drawing inferences are of little help. In this case, one is not engaged in gathering data in response to fixed questions that are based on concepts already operationalized and well understood. Nor is one putting a preexisting theoretical model to a test. Instead, the questions evolve and are revised, the focus of the inquiry narrows over time, and one develops, tests, and refines new concepts and explanations in the course of research. How, then, is one to assess the reliability of the data? The same way that other field researchers do, but with an eye to the peculiarities of emigre interviewing.

The intellectual and methodological problems of emigre interviews parallel those of fieldwork, though there are some important differences. The most important is the ability, in field research, to interview many people about the same event or institution, and check these with personal observations: a method of "triangulation" that allows the researcher to come to well-grounded conclusions. In emigre interviewing, one cannot rely on one's own observations to check what one is being told. Only in rare cases (e.g., Chan, Madsen, and Unger 1984) will the researcher in Hong Kong find more than one person from the same social unit, and so it is difficult to get more than one report on the same event or setting (see also Becker and Geer 1969).

But these differences from the classic style of ethnography are not so complete as they at first appear. In some respects, they yield advantages for the Hong Kong interviewer. First of all, most of what ethnographers do in the field is comprised of interviews, and even most of the observations one makes must be interpreted through interviews:

Fieldwork, despite the best intentions of the researcher, almost always boils down to a series of endless conversations intersected by a few major events. . . . The information as recorded by the fieldworker is then primarily talk . . . not only because this is what occupies the vast majority of the ethnographer's time but also because . . . understanding the concrete activities taking place in the field is grounded largely upon what members have to say about what such activities mean to them. (Van-Maanen 1983:43)

Further, there are always parts of the social system that a fieldworker can never penetrate because of his or her status as an outsider. Informants are the only source of information on these inaccessible areas and for accounts of events in the past (Zelditch 1962:572). Interviews done outside the setting of interest, though not supplemented by direct observation, are, therefore, not a radically different research operation.

These differences with field ethnography can bring both advantages and disadvantages. For example, one does not have a number of informants from a single setting, but a number of informants from a single type of setting. One cannot use the method of "triangulation," as it is commonly practiced in fieldwork, because people are not talking about the same institution and the same events. But one can still compare reports about similar types of settings on the same topics and perform triangulation at a somewhat higher level of generality—less reliable for specific events, but not less reliable for general structures and social behaviors. In fact, this last point is an advantage: because the informants are drawn from a large number of similar settings, the findings are more readily generalizable than those obtained in conventional field ethnography.

The crux of the problem of emigre interviews is that, unlike the ethnographer in the field, one has a set of informants who are self-selected in the sense that all have chosen to leave their homeland. One, therefore, runs the risk of getting only one perspective, and a distorted one at that. This problem is not unknown to the ethnographer. In the field, there is always the danger that one has tapped a certain faction in the setting and has become identified with one's key informants or with authority figures who gave permission to conduct the research, thereby cutting oneself off from other perspectives and definitions of the situation (Kahn and Mann 1969).

How does one compensate in the field? By interviewing people with different statuses and positions, and searching out those with manifestly different viewpoints. Is this impossible when working among emigres? By no means. First of all, this is far from a uniform population. I interviewed line managers and workers, employees of different generations and different pay levels, skilled and unskilled, intellectuals and the functionally illiterate, and, more to the point, former political activists and people who avoided political involvements. These people had widely different reasons for leaving China: some left because they detested the regime, some left because of poor career opportunities and the low standard of living, some left because their spouses were determined to leave. And people had manifestly different political and social viewpoints: some yearned for liberal political freedoms, others had only a vague idea what these freedoms are or felt they are far too permissive; some thrived in Hong Kong's capitalist economy and culture, but many felt threatened and alienated by it; some were happy to be out of China, but most missed it deeply and felt out of place; some rejected communism, but most were critical only of certain leaders and their excesses. Just as in field ethnography, one must use these manifest differences and compare accounts when interpreting the interviews (McCall 1969).

How does one know that informants are "telling the truth"? This, again, is a standard problem faced by fieldworkers (Dean and Whyte 1969). Informants often lie to the fieldworker, or, more accurately, they often give self-serving interpretations of events and practices (VanMaanen 1983). The first rule for assessing an informant's reliability is whether he or she can be expected to know what they are reporting on (Dean and Whyte 1969: 110–12; Zelditch 1962: 572–74). The factory is a single setting, but it is made up of many different social worlds. The shop floor is not the shop office; the design department is not the party committee. Is the informant reporting on a setting in which he or she worked? Is the informant reporting on the motivations of others? If reporting on an event, was the informant present or did he or she hear about it? Every response of interest should be followed with further questions to find out how the informant knows what he or she claims or why they have offered a certain conclusion or opinion. Responses to these questions—their depth of detail, consistency, and clarity—can strengthen or weaken the interviewer's confidence in the reliability of the informant (McCall 1969: 133–36).

One must also compare on a continuous basis the information an informant gives on a certain topic with what others have said, and pay close attention not only to what they say, but who they are and how they say it. One example from this research is the description informants gave of political activists. People who had not been activists, often those who were also demonstrably critical of the political system, regularly exhibited hostility toward activists and portrayed them as unprincipled careerists primarily interested in promoting themselves at the expense of others. Yet others who had not been activists, while admitting a distrust of them, would admit that their motives were often upright and patriotic. Some informants who had formerly been activists portrayed their activism as a pragmatic career choice that involved considerable hardship and personal sacrifice: others laid their activism to the patriotism and idealism of their youth. In this case, I was able to gauge the range of motivations of activists, and I gained a sense of the tensions in the relations between activists and other workers, and their perceptions of one another and themselves. But I noted something else: regardless of the informants' former status or manifest attitudes, their descriptions of the concrete activities of activists, the rewards for activism, and the relations between activists and leaders were fundamentally in agreement. These are the kinds of comparisons, wrought from the detail yielded in follow-up questions, that the interviewer uses to judge the reliability of an informant and to draw conclusions. The problem, really, is not so much how to tell if an informant is telling the truth, but how to reconcile the different "truths" that informants present.

Continuously to compare is continuously to retrace the same ground with different people, to continue to probe in search of verification, but, more importantly, in search of that new piece of information, new perspective on a subject, or the newly revealed dimension to a problem that generates a rush of new follow-up questions and reshapes what one previously "knew." One searches for insights and conceptual refinement just as much as for information or data (see Glaser and Strauss 1967; Glaser 1969). As these insights and clarifications reshape one's conception of the research, the questions evolve, and the study is focused in new ways. One becomes confident of one's understanding of some subjects when the same account is relayed again and again in unvarying form; these questions begin to drop out of the inquiry. Time is budgeted to cover areas in which one still does not have full confidence.

The answer to the problem of informant reliability, therefore, is that one pushes for as much detail and clarity as possible, that one constantly compares the accounts of different informants, that one endlessly covers familiar ground, and that one remains sensitive to who the informant is, and how he or she says something. This involves the cultivation and exercise of judgment, something that one can only acquire in the course of the research. Because the data are not a set of responses to standard questions, the problem of reliability cannot be addressed through the logic of survey research. The data are complex and variegated, and one must delve into this complexity and variety in order to assess their reliability. The result of such a study is a conceptualization of social processes, or a new theoretical statement, that is grounded directly in research (see Merton 1968c). It is up to future researchers to put the results of this research to more rigorous tests of their own devising: they will have the advantage of a preexisting model to elaborate, test, and refine (see Barton and Lazarsfeld 1969).

Emigre Interviews in Hong Kong

I have completed 232 interviews, totaling 532 hours, with 80 former employees of Chinese industrial enterprises. The initial 70 informants were interviewed in Hong Kong between November 1979 and August 1980. Two informants were interviewed in the United States during 1983 and 1984. And the last 8 were interviewed in Hong Kong between June and August 1984. Interviews with the last 10 informants were much more focused on questions that had arisen in the analysis of the initial materials; they were designed to resolve the uncertainties encountered in writing the first draft of this book. Because I asked more pointed questions about topics that had become of central interest, quotations from these last informants figure prominently in the text.

This study is the first to employ interviews with a large number of Chinese industrial employees. Not until the mid-1970s were appreciable numbers of urban industrial employees able to emigrate to Hong Kong, and not until the late 1970s did they emigrate in enough numbers to make a large interviewing project possible. This increasing emigration was touched off by America's diplomatic recognition of China in December 1978 and by the subsequent relaxation of China's emigration laws, designed in part to gain "most favored nation" trading status with the United States.

In the late 1960s, those who were interviewed by scholars in Hong Kong were properly labeled refugees. The overwhelming majority of them had escaped illegally across the Hong Kong border, by water or land, often after a number of unsuccessful attempts. Not until 1973 were appreciable numbers of people permitted to emigrate legally. The number rose gradually during the 1970s, until 1978 and 1979, when the number of people emigrating annually to Hong Kong through legal application nearly tripled, rising from 25 thousand in 1977 to 70 thousand in 1979 (*South China Morning Post*, July 7, 1980, p. 1). By 1984, when I returned for a second set of interviews, one-tenth of the population of Hong Kong had emigrated from China since 1978 (*Far Eastern Economic Review*, Feb. 16, 1984, pp. 11–12).

This gradual shift from refugee to emigre has altered the types of people available for interviewing, and the ways that these people can be located. The illegal escapee is usually young, from the countryside, and almost exclusively from the province of Guangdong, which borders Hong Kong. Before being integrated into Hong Kong society, they register with international relief agencies or live in resettlement camps. Foreign scholars locate them through contacts with these agencies. The legal applicant, by contrast, is most often middle-aged, from urban areas throughout the country, and often possesses higher education and specialized skills. Emigres find jobs readily with their education and skills, and are more quickly integrated into Hong Kong society. They usually emigrate from Hong Kong to other countries by applying to foreign consulates with the assistance of overseas relatives and, therefore, do not normally register with resettlement programs.

The first consequence of this shift from refugee to emigre is a marked change in the work experience and geographical origin of the informants. Of the 93 people interviewed by Whyte in 1969, only 7 had emigrated legally; their average age was 29, and only 10 had lived in provinces other than Guangdong (Whyte 1974: 258–63). Reflecting the difficulty of finding people with experience in urban institutions other than schools, Whyte was able to locate 14 former workers but was unable to locate any who had industrial work experience in a large urban state enterprise. By contrast, of the 80 people I interviewed in 1979, 1980, and 1984, all but 6 had left China through legal application, their average age was just under 40 years, and almost two-thirds had worked in provinces other than Guangdong. Reflecting the urban origins of the legal emigre, 55 of them had worked in modern state sector enterprises that employed more than 500 people, and 34 of these 55 had worked in enterprises that employed more than 1,000 (see table A.1).

A second consequence of the shift from refugee to emigre is a change in the method of locating potential informants. Before the late 1970s, Hong Kong researchers located their informants through contacts with resettlement agencies and through friendship networks within the refugee community. I did not find it necessary to use resettlement agencies or to rely extensively on friendship networks. Instead, I found that I was able to locate more suitable informants than I could possibly interview by placing classified advertisements in Hong Kong newspapers.

Locating and Selecting Informants

On four separate occasions, I placed a short classified advertisement in the employment section of two Chinese-language dailies, *Cheng Bao* and *Xingdao Ribao*. The advertisement specified that a foreign scholar needed help on a temporary, part-time basis in completing a research project on the Chinese economy, and people with work experience in mainland industrial enterprises should apply. Each time that I placed the advertisement, I received 50 to 70 inquiries by mail. Those who had the appropriate work experience were ranked according to the kind of work specified in the letter. I ranked most highly those who had attributes that were valued but relatively rare: those who had held leadership positions in workshops, people who had worked in large, heavy industrial plants, who had worked in the same enterprise for a decade or more, and who had worked in provinces other than Guangdong. Those ranked lowest were the young, those who had only worked for a few years, and those who came from nearby Guangdong province. I selectively interviewed those ranked in the top two-thirds of the list, making sure that the eventual pool of informants adequately represented different geographical areas, industries, and types of enterprises.

Table A.1 *Size and Level of Administration of Informants' Enterprises*

Level of administration	1–100	101–500	501–1,000	Number of employees 1,001–2,000	2,001–5,000	5,001 +	Unknown	TOTAL
State sector								
Province or ministry		6	11	10	7	8	2	44
Municipal		9	8	7	2		1	27
District (municipal)		1						1
County		10	2					12
Town		2						2
Collective sector								
Municipal		3	1					4
District (municipal)		1	1					2
Street (municipal)		1						1
County	1							1
Town	2							2
TOTAL	3	33	23	17	9	8	3	96

A research assistant who was a Canton native and fluent in both Mandarin and Cantonese made the initial telephone contacts. He explained my identity, the nature of my research project, and the type of work involved. Those who were interested made appointments to speak with me personally. I used this first visit to explain more fully the nature of the interviews, the topics I would ask about, and the uses to which my research would be put. In order to put potential informants at ease and to create an initial rapport, I answered any questions about myself, my sources of funding, my sponsoring organizations, and what I intended to write on returning home. In so doing, I often had to explain why a young American would bother to come halfway around the world to study such a topic, and this in turn led to discussion of American university life, my own career motivations, and how I got involved in this topic in the first place. My responsiveness to questions about me, especially personal ones, was crucial in building a sense of familiarity and trust. I explained that the interviews would be completely confidential: I would not keep records of persons' names, nor would I publish material in such a way that would make it possible to guess individual identities. No tape recorders would be used, and I would take handwritten notes. No one else would be present during interviews (except during the first month, when my research assistant helped with translating). Informants (though not the ones in the United States) were paid a fee equal to $3 American per hour (in 1984, $4).

When the visitor was satisfied on all of these counts and consented to the interview (a small number declined at this stage), I established the person's general career history—type of work, type and size of enterprise, location, years employed, pay levels and years given promotions and raises. This helped me plan detailed questions for the next session and confirm that the person actually had industrial work experience. If in subsequent interviews I suspected that a person may not have had the experience claimed, I asked detailed questions about pay grading systems or the physical layout of the workplace. People without genuine experience could not have given detailed answers to such questions. After my first few weeks of interviews, people who did not really have the work experience they claimed became easy to detect. This occurred rarely, but I did eliminate a handful of people on this account. Once I was satisfied that the career information was accurate, and the informant appeared at ease, I made another appointment to begin the formal interview.

The Interviews

The formal interviews were not based on fixed questionnaires but were semi-structured sessions that varied considerably in length and content. I began the project with a tentative interview schedule, but it was revised and expanded greatly in the course of the research. Informants unfailingly illuminated additional, sometimes quite unexpected, dimensions of factory life, and this meant that new questions inevitably arose in the course of an interview. Through the months, my working list of questions evolved considerably according to the new dimensions that were continually brought to light. In addition, informants had different work experiences and personal inclinations. Production workers, staff technicians, and line managers see quite different aspects of factory life and cannot generally be asked the same set of questions. A production worker knows the physical work process and basic-level shop organization; accountants know the financing of the enterprise; production engineers know the production planning process. Individuals also differ considerably in the kinds of things they remember, and in the kinds of things they are able to communicate effectively. Some are able to describe vividly the texture of interpersonal relationships and the tone and nuance of encounters with authority, but do not remember clearly rules and regulations regarding monetary compensation. Others can recount regulations and formal procedures in great detail, but are totally unable to bring to life the personal side of the enterprise.

For these reasons, I adopted a strategy that allowed me to structure interviews flexibly according to the individual's experience and inclinations. I began not with a set list of questions, but with a list of topics that were worked out for each individual after the initial career history was completed. The topics were divided into three sections and were introduced in the same order for each informant. The first section included all questions about personnel matters: wage and bonus systems, hiring and disciplinary practices. These questions did not change much in the course of the research. The second section included questions about the aspects of factory organization that the informant experienced in daily routines—a "workplace ethnography." The informants were asked to reconstruct their duties, the daily routines of work and meetings, the organization of the immediate office or shop, and other aspects of plant administration with which they had become intimately familiar—plant accounting procedures, quality inspection systems, the procurement of supplies, and so forth. This section of the interview was rarely the same for any two individuals.

The last section was an oral history of the enterprise. The informant was asked to describe in concrete detail the events that surrounded each of the major political campaigns conducted during their work experience and any changes in plant administration that accompanied them. These questions varied according to the period of time the informant had worked. Throughout, care was taken to ask the informants only those questions that they could be expected to answer based on their personal experience. If they were not willing to discuss a topic, I did not press them (I found that they often would discuss these topics in subsequent weeks, as their trust in me grew).

I introduced each topic with a question and followed up the responses with requests for clarification or concrete examples. When new information was brought to light, I would probe in that direction until it no longer seemed fruitful. If information was introduced that did not appear relevant, I steered the informant back to the original topic. Generally speaking, I was able to reconstruct, in order, the person's occupational history, the personnel policies and reward practices of their factory, the aspects of enterprise organization with which informants were familiar through daily experience, and the political history of the enterprise. I took detailed notes by hand during each interview, translating into English as I went, and trying to retain the original wording and flavor as closely as possible. The collected transcripts total 579 pages of typed, single-spaced manuscript; these have been drawn upon for the quotations presented in the text of this book.

Characteristics of the Informant Pool

By selectively interviewing people with certain attributes, I was able to construct a sample of informants that represents a wide array of occupations, industries, and geographical regions. Of the 111 different positions held by the 80 informants, by far the most common were production worker (35) and department staff (37). I was also able to interview a total of 20 people who had occupied leadership positions at various levels:

Department Staff	37
Technical (24)	
Administrative (13)	
Production Worker	35
Workshop Technician	8
Staff Department Head	8
Workshop Office Staff	6
Factory Director's Personal Staff	5
Work Group Leader	4
Section Chief	4
Plant Director	2
Workshop Director	2

My informants came from a wide range of industries, enterprises, and geographical regions. Of the 96 different industrial enterprises in which the informants worked, by far the most common were machine-building and machine tool plants (22), but I also interviewed large numbers employed in chemical, rubber, and petroleum refining (14), and metallurgy and light machinery (7 each) (table A.2). Although I preferred to interview people who came from large enterprises, the informants worked in plants of all

Table A.2   *Informants' Work Experience, by Industrial Sector*

Industry	Number
Heavy machinery, machine tools	22
Chemicals, rubber, petroleum	14
Metallurgy	7
Light machinery	7
Auto, truck, and tractor building and repair	6
Textiles	6
Metal fabricating	5
Mining, ore processing	5
Food processing	5
Glass and cement	5
Miscellaneous light industry	5
Construction	3
Handicrafts	2
Wood and lumber	2
Electrical equipment	2
TOTAL	96

sizes (see table A.1). Of the 97 different geographical locations in which these people worked, only one-third (33) were in Guangdong Province, and large numbers came from the major industrial center of Shanghai in the east (11), and from the Beijing-Tianjin area in the north (17) (see map). If the pool of informants is unrepresentative, it is not because it relies heavily on a restricted number of occupations, industries, enterprise types, or geographical areas.

The pool of informants is atypical in two ways: as a group, they are considerably better educated than industrial employees in general, and they have had far greater exposure to the world outside China than most other citizens. Over one-half of the informants had formal schooling at the post-secondary level, and another one-quarter had attended high school. They are, as a group, much better educated than the average industrial employee. Many of the informants, further, were unusually familiar with life outside of China even before they emigrated. Of the 74 individuals who discussed their personal backgrounds, 24 had been born in Hong Kong or one of the overseas Chinese communities in Southeast Asia. They returned to China during the early and middle 1950s, part of a large group of ethnic Chinese actively recruited by the new government to help build socialism in the country of their ancestors. The ones from Hong Kong were often recruited by labor unions and student organizations that fronted for the Chinese

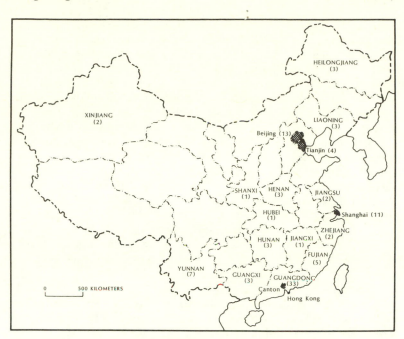

Appendix A Map. Location of Informants' Work Experience

Communist party; others were underground party members for years before repatriating. (An interesting historical sidelight to this period is that in
those years, the Hong Kong economy was depressed, while China's was
booming. Many said they went to China for jobs.)

Most of the overseas Chinese returned for patriotic reasons, some because ethnic Chinese in the emerging nations of Southeast Asia (especially
Indonesia) faced systematic discrimination in finding university places and
jobs. Often their youthful patriotism and ethnic identification with the new
China was closely linked with discrimination abroad. Another 10 informants were directly related to such people—they were either children born
to them in China, or married to them. Of the remaining informants, all of
whom had been born and raised in China, almost all had a close relative
living overseas—this is in fact the main criterion for granting an exit visa.
If the informants had not lived outside of China at one time, they at least
had relatives who did.

The cosmopolitan orientation of a large proportion of the informant
pool probably made their attitudes atypical, yet the group as a whole was
remarkable for the rarity of overt political hostility toward the regime they

had left. The criticisms of arrangements in China that informants occasionally volunteered were generally quite circumspect. They exhibited dissent over specific policies, disapproval of specific leaders (most often, like the current party line, of Mao and the leftist Gang of Four), and in some cases presented quite sophisticated critiques—but these views did not stray far from the self-critical mood of the party during those years. I did not interview people about their political attitudes, but the informants generally appeared to support the principles of socialist ownership and planning, and to accept communist party rule in China. Frequent comments on what some of them considered the economic insecurity, social instability, and degraded culture of Hong Kong sometimes gave the impression that many felt they had just left a social system that was, in many respects, superior. These were not escapees eager to denounce a system that had formerly oppressed them—only 2 of the 80 had ever been given a formal political punishment. These were emigrants who were weary of the rationing, shortages, and bureaucratic obstacles placed in the way of people with education and talent; they felt that life could offer more in the land of their often prosperous overseas relatives.

There were, in addition, several factors that tended to limit the expression of critical sentiments toward the regime. First, these people, as legal emigrants, were still Chinese citizens and holders of Chinese passports. They were able to return to China freely for visits any time after the first anniversary of their exit. Some returned to China to visit relatives during the course of their interviews with me. Others planned such trips in the future. Second, almost all of the informants had close relatives who still lived in China. Third, though these people were generally critical of some aspects of China's political system, they still harbored a strong sense of cultural loyalty to the Chinese nation and people. These factors limited the expression of critical views—in the first two instances, because of a desire not to jeopardize their own political status or that of their relatives with the Chinese government; in the last instance, because of a genuine sense that foreigners should not be party to the most negative information about their homeland. For some or all of these reasons, some individuals insisted on keeping strictly to nonpolitical topics (although in practice it was impossible to avoid them), and a few categorically refused to discuss such events as the Cultural Revolution.

The emigre population from which my informants were drawn was, therefore, part of a third wave of emigration from China. The first was in the years after 1949, the second the illegal emigration that began in large numbers in the early 1960s and continued into the late 1970s. This third wave does not have the same characteristics as earlier emigrants: they are neither dispossessed classes nor illegal escapees. And, unlike the Soviet emigres of recent decades, they are not considered defectors by their government. They did not risk political persecution by applying for an exit visa: thus, the level of political determination it took for them to leave China was not high. These people should be seen as part of the revival of China's historic ties with Chinese communities in Southeast Asia and beyond, as the nation opens up once again to the outside world.

Appendix B

List of Informants

General Work Experience

1. Carpenter in maintenance section of steel mill
2. Staff engineer in technical department of chemical products plant
3. Staff technician in design department of heavy machinery plant
4. Repair worker in auto repair plant
5. Assistant director of machine-building plant
6. Technician and laboratory head, chemical fertilizer plant
7. Staff technician, shop technician in lumber mill
8. Shop technician in machine tool plant
9. Staff time-quota specialist, labor and wages department of machine-building plant
10. Clerical worker, tractor-building plant
11. Staff technician in textile research institute
12. Technician, shift supervisor in production shop of synthetic fibers plant
13. Coal miner, assistant in mine office
14. Doctor in hospital attached to factory complex
15. Staff technician in technical department of machine-building plant
16. Worker in food processing plant
17. Repair worker in household articles plant
18. Worker in glass-making factory
19. Staff technician in technical department of wood products factory
20. Staff technician in construction design institute
21. Shop electrician in electric cell factory
22. Staff technician in technical department of agricultural machinery repair plant

23. Department head, production department of machine-building plant
24. Electrician and assistant shop director in machine tool plant
25. Staff technician in design department of tool-making factory
26. Staff technician in technical department of machinery plant
27. Painter for building construction company
28. Clerical worker in textile plant
29. Worker and group leader in rubber plant
30. Worker in chemical products plant
31. Staff technician in equipment department of machine-building plant
32. Repair worker, boat repair dock
33. Temporary worker; electrician in household articles plant
34. Worker and procuring agent for machinery plant
35. Worker on trucking crews of coal transport team
36. Technician in laboratory of glass-making factory
37. Staff technician, technical department of tractor factory
38. Worker in collective machine repair shop
39. Worker and group leader in collective auto parts shop
40. Welder in contact welding plant
41. Contract worker; worker and group leader in machinery repair plant
42. Staff technician in watch factory
43. Worker in electronics research institute
44. Personal assistant to mine director
45. Staff technician in technical department of glass-making factory
46. Factory doctor in clinic of textile factory
47. Clerical worker in motor-building factory
48. Staff technician in production department of tractor-building and repair plant
49. Staff technician in production department of sugar and paper mill
50. Repair worker for measurements institute
51. Staff technician, technical department of machinery plant
52. Worker in engine parts factory
53. Technician in geological survey team
54. Section chief in production shop of textile mill
55. Department head, finance department of steel mill
56. Staff technician, production department of food processing plant
57. Worker in communications equipment factory
58. Electrician in oil refinery

59. Temporary worker; clerical worker in steel mill
60. Staff technician, production department of food processing plant
61. Doctor in small hospital attached to local factories
62. Technician, assistant section chief in chemical fertilizer plant
63. Staff engineer in technical department of engine-building factory
64. Repair worker and group leader in automobile factory
65. Purchasing agent, supply and sales department of plastics factory
66. Worker in electrical equipment factory
67. Staff technician in production control department of petrochemical plant
68. Staff technician, technical department of auto assembly plant
69. Worker-prisoner, machine-tool factory
70. Staff technician, planning department of machine-building plant
71. Worker in chemical plant
72. Worker in petroleum refinery
73. Skilled worker, union official, procuring agent, head of sales and supply department, and vice-director in machinery plant
74. Staff accountant, head of accounting department in a cement factory
75. Skilled worker, assistant in shop office of a bicycle factory
76. Work section head, staff member of finance department of a construction company
77. Worker and group leader in chemical plant
78. Statistician in workshop office of a chemical plant
79. Worker in a textile mill
80. Staff member, technical design department of machine-building plant

Bibliography

Aird, John S. 1982. "Recent Demographic Data from China: Problems and Prospects." In *China Under the Four Modernizations*, Joint Economic Committee, U.S. Congress, pp. 172–223. Washington, D.C.: U.S. Government Printing Office.

Almond, Gabriel. 1983. "Corporatism, Pluralism, and Professional Memory." *World Politics* 35, no. 2 (Jan.): 245–60.

Aminzade, Ronald. 1981. *Class, Politics, and Early Industrial Capitalism: A Study of Mid-Nineteenth-Century Toulouse.* Albany: State University of New York Press.

Anderson, Eugene N., and Pauline Anderson. 1978. "Bureaucratic Institutionalization in Nineteenth-Century Europe." In *Political Corruption: Readings in Comparative Analysis*, ed. by Arnold J. Heidenheimer. New Brunswick, N.J.: Transaction.

Andors, Stephen. 1977. *China's Industrial Revolution: Politics, Planning, and Management, 1949 to the Present.* New York: Pantheon.

Arendt, Hannah. 1951. *Totalitarianism.* Part 3, *The Origins of Totalitarianism.* New York: Harcourt, Brace and World.

Bailes, Kendall. 1978. *Technology and Society Under Lenin and Stalin.* Princeton: Princeton University Press.

Bannister, Judith. 1985. *China's Changing Population.* Stanford: Stanford University Press.

Bao Lianzong. 1981. "Tichang gongchan zhuyi daode yu guanche anlao fenpei yuanze" [Promoting communist morality and implementing the principle of distribution according to labor]. *Huadong Shifan Daxue Xuebao* 2: 12–16.

Barber, John. 1980. "Labour Discipline in Soviet Industry, 1928–1941." Paper presented at the Twelfth Annual Convention of the American Association for the Advancement of Slavic Studies, Philadelphia, Nov. 5–8.

Barnett, A. Doak, with Ezra Vogel. 1967. *Cadres, Bureaucracy, and Political Power in Communist China.* New York: Columbia University Press.

Barton, Allen H., and Paul F. Lazarsfeld. 1969. "Qualitative Data as a Source of Hypotheses." In *Issues in Participant Observation*, ed. by McCall and Simmons, pp. 163–204.

Becker, Howard S., and Blanche Geer. 1969. "Participant Observation and Interviewing: A Comparison." In *Issues in Participant Observation*, ed. by McCall and Simmons, pp. 323–31.

Beijing Daily (*Beijing Ribao*). 1981. "Qunian benshi anzhi daiye qingnian shiba wan ren" [Last year city finds places for 180,000 youths awaiting work assignments]. March 6, p. 1.

Bendix, Reinhard. 1956 (1974). *Work and Authority in Industry: Ideologies of Management in the Course of Industrialization*. Berkeley and Los Angeles: University of California Press.

———. 1964 (1977). *Nation-Building and Citizenship*. Berkeley and Los Angeles: University of California Press.

———. 1967. "Tradition and Modernity Reconsidered." *Comparative Studies in Society and History* 9 (April): 292–346.

Berliner, Joseph. 1957. *Factory and Manager in the USSR*. Cambridge: Harvard University Press.

Bernardo, Roberto M. 1971. *The Theory of Moral Incentives in Cuba*. University, Alabama: University of Alabama Press.

———. 1977. *Popular Management and Pay in China*. Quezon City: University of the Philippines Press.

Bernstein, Thomas P. 1977. *Up to the Mountains and Down to the Villages: The Transfer of Youth from Urban to Rural China*. New Haven: Yale University Press.

———. 1984. "Stalinism, Famine, and Chinese Peasants: Grain Procurements during the Great Leap Forward." *Theory and Society* 13, no. 3 (May): 1–38.

Bialer, Seweryn. 1980. *Stalin's Successors: Leadership, Stability, and Change in the Soviet Union*. Cambridge: Cambridge University Press.

Bielasiak, Jack. 1981. "Workers and Mass Participation in 'Socialist Democracy.'" In *Blue-Collar Workers in Eastern Europe*, ed. by Triska and Gati, pp. 88–107.

Blau, Peter, 1954. *The Dynamics of Bureaucracy*. Chicago: University of Chicago Press.

———. 1964. *Exchange and Power in Social Life*. New York: Wiley.

Blauner, Robert. 1964. *Alienation and Freedom: The Factory Worker and His Industry*. Chicago: University of Chicago Press.

Brandes, Stuart. 1976. *American Welfare Capitalism, 1880–1940*. Chicago: University of Chicago Press.

Brugger, William. 1976. *Democracy and Organisation in the Chinese Industrial Enterprise, 1948–1953*. Cambridge: Cambridge University Press.

Brzezinski, Zbigniew. 1956. *The Permanent Purge*. Cambridge: Harvard University Press.

Burawoy, Michael. 1979. *Manufacturing Consent: Changes in the Labor*

Process Under Monopoly Capitalism. Chicago: University of Chicago Press.

———. 1983. "Between Labor Process and the State: The Changing Face of Factory Regimes Under Advanced Capitalism." *American Sociological Review* 48, no. 5 (Oct.): 587–605.

———. 1984. "Marx and the Satanic Mills: Factory Politics under Early Capitalism in England, the United States, and Russia." *American Journal of Sociology* 90, no. 2 (Sept.): 247–82.

Bureau of the Census, Department of Commerce, United States. 1982. *Statistical Abstract of the United States, 1982–83.* Washington, D.C.: Department of Commerce.

Cadre Department, Chinese Academy of Sciences, People's Republic of China. 1961. "Gei laodong bu gongzi ju 'Guanyu yanjiusheng jianxi qi manhou dingji wenti' de han" [Answer given to the wages department of the labor ministry "Concerning the question of setting wage grades for graduate students after their probationary period is completed"]. Cadre Office Doc. No. 151 (March 13). In Planning Commission 1973: 73–74.

Central Committee, Chinese Communist Party. 1959. "Guanyu zhaidiao youpai maozi de renyuan de gongzuo fenpei he shenghuo daiyu de guiding" [Provisions on work assignments and remuneration for personnel who have had their rightist labels removed]. In Planning Commission 1973: 137–38.

———. 1961. "Guoying gongye qiye gongzuo tiaoli (cao'an)" [Work regulations for state industrial enterprises (draft)]. In *Zhongguo gongye guanli bufen tiaoli huibian* [A partial compendium of Chinese industrial management regulations], ed. by Industrial Economics Research Institute, Chinese Academy of Social Sciences, pp. 216–43. Beijing: Dizhi Chubanshe, 1980.

———. 1964. "Guanyu zhigong tuizhi daiyu deng wenti de tongzhi" [Notice on various problems regarding severance pay for workers and staff]. No. 8 (March 25). In Planning Commission 1973: 467–77.

Chan, Anita, Richard Madsen, and Jonathan Unger. 1984. *Chen Village: The Recent History of a Peasant Community in Mao's China.* Berkeley and Los Angeles: University of California Press.

Chapman, Janet. 1979. "Recent Trends in the Soviet Industrial Wage Structure." In *Industrial Labor in the USSR*, ed. by Arcadius Kahan and Blair Ruble. New York: Pergamon.

Chesneaux, Jean. 1968. *The Chinese Labor Movement, 1919–1927.* Trans. by H. M. Wright. Stanford: Stanford University Press.

China Almanac [*Zhongguo baike nianjian*]. 1980. Beijing: Zhongguo Da Baike Quanshu Chubanshe.

———. 1981. Beijing: Zhongguo Da Baike Quanshu Chubanshe.

Chinn, Dennis. 1980. "Basic Commodity Distribution in the People's Republic of China." *China Quarterly* 84 (Dec.): 744–54.

Clark, Rodney. 1979. *The Japanese Company*. New Haven: Yale University Press.

Cocks, Paul. 1970. "The Rationalization of Party Control." In *Change in Communist Systems*, ed. by Johnson, pp. 153–90.

Cole, Robert E. 1971. *Japanese Blue Collar: The Changing Tradition*. Berkeley and Los Angeles: University of California Press.

————. 1979. *Work, Mobility, and Participation: A Comparative Study of American and Japanese Industry*. Berkeley and Los Angeles: University of California Press.

Comisso, Ellen Turkish. 1981. "Can a Party of the Working Class Be a Working-Class Party?" In *Blue-Collar Workers in Eastern Europe*, ed. by Triska and Gati, pp. 70–87.

Connor, Walter D. 1979. "Workers, Politics, and Class Consciousness." In *Industrial Labor in the USSR*, ed. by Arcadius Kahan and Blair Ruble, pp. 313–32. New York: Pergamon.

Cook, Linda J. 1985. "Political Mobilization Strategies and the Stalinist 'Revolution from Above.'" Ph.D. dissertation, Department of Political Science, Columbia University.

Dallin, Alexander, and George W. Breslauer. 1970. "Political Terror in the Post-Mobilization Stage." In *Change in Communist Systems*, ed. by Johnson, pp. 190–214.

Dalton, Melville. 1959. *Men Who Manage*. New York: Wiley.

Davis, Kingsley. 1975. "Asia's Cities: Problems and Options." *Population and Development Review* 1 (Sept.): 71–86.

Dawley, Alan. 1976. *Class and Community: The Industrial Revolution in Lynn*. Cambridge: Harvard University Press.

Dean, John P., and William F. Whyte. 1969. "How Do You Know if the Informant Is Telling the Truth?" In *Issues in Participant Observation*, ed. by McCall and Simmons, pp. 105–14.

Delaney, William. 1963. "The Development and Decline of Patrimonial and Bureaucratic Administration." *Administrative Science Quarterly* 7 (March): 458–501.

Denitch, Bogdan. 1981. "Yugoslav Exceptionalism." In *Blue-Collar Workers in Eastern Europe*, ed. by Triska and Gati, pp. 253–67.

DiFranceisco, Wayne, and Zvi Gitelman. 1984. "Soviet Political Culture and 'Covert Participation' in Policy Implementation." *American Political Science Review* 78, no. 3 (Sept.): 603–21.

Doeringer, Peter, and Michael Piore. 1971. *Internal Labor Markets and Manpower Analysis*. Lexington, Mass.: Heath.

Dore, Ronald. 1973. *British Factory–Japanese Factory: The Origins of National Diversity in Labor Relations*. Berkeley and Los Angeles: University of California Press.

Dyker, David A. 1981. "Planning and the Worker." In *The Soviet Worker*, ed. by Schapiro and Godson, pp. 39–75.

Economic Yearbook of China [*Zhongguo jingji nianjian*]. 1981. Shanghai: Jingji Guanli Zazhishe.
————. 1982. Shanghai: Jingji Guanli Zazhishe.
Edwards, Richard. 1979. *Contested Terrain: The Transformation of the Workplace in the Twentieth Century.* New York: Basic.
Eisenstadt, S. N., and L. Roniger. 1984. *Patrons, Clients, and Friends: Interpersonal Relations and the Structure of Trust in Society.* Cambridge: Cambridge University Press.
Elbaum, Bernard. 1984. "The Making and Shaping of Job and Pay Structures in the Iron and Steel Industry." In *Internal Labor Markets,* ed. by Osterman, pp. 71–107.
Emerson, John Philip. 1965a. *Nonagricultural Employment in Mainland China, 1949–1958.* International Population Statistics Reports, Series P-90, No. 21. Washington, D.C.: U.S. Government Printing Office.
————. 1965b. "Sex, Age, and Level of Skill of the Nonagricultural Labor Force of Mainland China." Foreign Demographic Analysis Division, U.S. Bureau of the Census (June). Mimeo.
————. 1973. *Administrative and Technical Manpower in the People's Republic of China.* International Population Statistics Reports, Series P-95, No. 72. Washington, D.C.: U.S. Department of Commerce.
————.1983. "Urban School-Leavers and Unemployment in China." *China Quarterly* 93 (March): 1–16.
Erickson, Kenneth. 1977. *The Brazilian Corporate State and Working Class Politics.* Berkeley and Los Angeles: University of California Press.
Falkenheim, Victor L. 1978. "Political Participation in China." *Problems of Communism* 27, no. 3 (May–June): 18–32.
Fehér, Ferenc. 1982. "Paternalism as a Mode of Legitimation in Soviet-type Societies." In *Political Legitimation in Communist States,* ed. by T. H. Rigby and Ferenc Fehér, pp. 64–81. New York: St. Martin's.
Feng Lanrui and Zhao Lukuan. 1982. "Urban Unemployment in China." *Social Sciences in China* 3, no. 1 (March): 123–39.
Field, Robert Michael. 1983. "Slow Growth of Labour Productivity in Chinese Industry, 1952–81." *China Quarterly* 96 (Dec.): 641–64.
————. 1984. "Changes in Chinese Industry Since 1978." *China Quarterly* 100 (Dec.): 742–61.
First Ministry of Machine Building, People's Republic of China. 1978. *Gongren jishu dengji biaozhun* [Worker technical grade standards]. Beijing.
Fitzpatrick, Sheila. 1978. "Cultural Revolution as Class War." In *Cultural Revolution in Russia, 1928–1931,* ed. by Sheila Fitzpatrick, pp. 8–40. Bloomington: Indiana University Press.
Frey, Frederick W. 1985. "The Problem of Actor Designation in Political Analysis." *Comparative Politics* 17, no. 2 (Jan.): 127–52.

Fried, Morton. 1953. *The Fabric of Chinese Society*. New York: Praeger.
Friedrich, Carl J. 1954. "The Unique Character of Totalitarian Society." In *Totalitarianism*, ed. by Carl J. Friedrich, pp. 47–60. Cambridge: Harvard University Press.
Friedrich, Carl J., Michael Curtis, and Benjamin R. Barber. 1969. *Totalitarianism in Perspective*. New York: Praeger.
Frolic, B. Michael. 1980. *Mao's People: Sixteen Portraits of Life in Revolutionary China*. Cambridge: Harvard University Press.
Fujian Province Labor Bureau, People's Republic of China. 1959. "Guanyu zhigong diaodong hou gongzi daiyu de chuli yijian" [Suggestion for handling the wages and remuneration of transferred workers and staff]. Labor and Wages Doc. No. 405 (July 23). In Planning Commission 1973: 37–39.
———. 1966. "Guanyu quxiao zonghe jiangli zhidu gaixing 'linshi fujia gongzi' de jidian yijian" [Some opinions concerning the abolition of the comprehensive bonus system and the switch to the "temporary supplemental wage"]. Labor Doc. No. 408 (Nov. 29). In Planning Commission 1973: 153–55.
Fujian Province Price Commission, People's Republic of China. 1966a. "Guanyu zhigong shenghuo butie de buchong tongzhi" [Supplemental notice on livelihood subsidies for workers and staff]. Doc. No. 85 (Sept. 15). In Planning Commission 1973: 222–24.
———. 1966b. "Guanyu tigao liangshi tongxiao jiage he dui zhigong shixing shenghuo butie de baogao (zhaiyao)" [Report on the rise in state grain prices and livelihood subsidies for workers and staff (abstract)]. July 29. In Planning Commission 1973: 219–21.
Fujian Province Revolutionary Committee, People's Republic of China. 1971. "Guanyu xin zhaoshou gongren de gongzi daiyu he dingji deng wenti de tongzhi" [Notice concerning various questions about wages and the setting of wage grades for newly recruited workers]. Provincial Political Department Doc. No. 63 (July 16). In Planning Commission 1973: 10–12.
———. 1973. "Guanyu zhigong zhuanzheng dingji deng wenti de tongzhi" [Notice on the setting of wage grades for workers and staff being given permanent status and related questions]. Provincial Political Department Doc. No. 166 (July 5). In Planning Commission 1973: 13–15.
Geng Weihai. 1956. "Guanyu 'zui qiang de ganbu dang changzhang'" [Regarding "the plant director as most powerful cadre"]. *Hubei Ribao*, October 14, p. 1.
Gerth, Hans, and C. Wright Mills. 1952. *Character and Social Structure: The Psychology of Social Institutions*. New York: Harcourt, Brace.
Gipouloux, Francois. 1981. "Les Problèmes politiques et sociaux en Chine à la fin du Premier Plan Quinquennal: Le Monde ouvrier et la Crise du Travail syndical en 1957" [Political and social problems in China at the

end of the First Five-Year Plan: The world of work and the crisis of trade unionism in 1957]. Ph.D. dissertation, Ecole des Hautes Etudes en Sciences Sociales [School of Advanced Study in the Social Sciences], Paris.

Gitelman, Zvi. 1977. "Soviet Political Culture: Insights from Jewish Emigrés." *Soviet Studies* 29, no. 4 (Oct.): 543–64.

―――. 1984. "Working the Soviet System: Citizens and Urban Bureaucracies." In *The Contemporary Soviet City*, ed. by Morton and Stuart, pp. 221–43.

Glaser, Barney G. 1969. "The Constant Comparative Method of Qualitative Analysis." In *Issues in Participant Observation*, ed. by McCall and Simmons, pp. 216–27.

Glaser, Barney G., and Anselm Strauss. 1967. *The Discovery of Grounded Theory*. Chicago: Aldine.

Goffmann, Erving. 1959. *The Presentation of Self in Everyday Life*. New York: Anchor.

Gold, Thomas B. 1980. "Back to the City: The Return of Shanghai's Educated Youth." *China Quarterly* 84 (Dec.): 55–70.

―――. 1984. "'Just in Time!' China Battles Spiritual Pollution on the Eve of 1984." *Asian Survey* 24, no. 9 (Sept.): 947–74.

Gordon, Andrew. 1985. *The Evolution of Labor Relations in Japan: Heavy Industry, 1853–1955*. Harvard East Asian Monographs, no. 117. Cambridge: Harvard University Press.

Gouldner, Alvin. 1955. *Patterns of Industrial Bureaucracy*. London: Routledge and Kegan Paul.

Granick, David. 1975. *Enterprise Guidance in Eastern Europe*. Princeton: Princeton University Press.

Gu Guichun. 1981. "Weihe chuxian 'tuixiu feng'?" [Why has there arisen a "wind of retirements"?] *Lilun yu Shijian* 2 (Feb.): 42–43.

Gusfield, Joseph R. 1967. "Tradition and Modernity: Misplaced Polarities in the Study of Social Change." *American Journal of Sociology* 72, no. 4 (Jan.): 351–62.

Hanagan, Michael. 1980. *The Logic of Solidarity: Artisans and Industrial Workers in Three French Towns*. Urbana: University of Illinois Press.

Haraszti, Miklos. 1979. *A Worker in a Workers' State*. Trans. by Michael Wright. New York: Universe.

Hershatter, Gail. 1986. *The Workers of Tianjin, 1900–1949*. Stanford: Stanford University Press.

Hoffmann, Charles. 1967. *Work Incentive Practices and Policies in the People's Republic of China, 1953–1965*. Albany: State University of New York Press.

―――. 1974. *The Chinese Worker*. Albany: State University of New York Press.

Honig, Emily. 1986. *Sisters and Strangers: Women in the Shanghai Cotton Mills, 1919–1949.* Stanford: Stanford University Press.

Hou Chi-ming. 1968. "Manpower, Employment, and Unemployment." In *Economic Trends in Communist China,* ed. by Alexander Eckstein, Walter Galenson, and Ta-ching Liu, pp. 329–96. Chicago: Aldine.

Hough, Jerry F. 1977. *The Soviet Union and Social Science Theory.* Cambridge: Harvard University Press.

———. 1978. "The Cultural Revolution and Western Understanding of the Soviet System." In *Cultural Revolution in Russia,* ed. by Fitzpatrick, pp. 241–53.

Howe, Christopher. 1971. *Employment and Economic Growth in Urban China, 1949–1957.* Cambridge: Cambridge University Press.

———. 1973. *Wage Patterns and Wage Policy in Modern China, 1919–1972.* Cambridge: Cambridge University Press.

———. 1974. "Labor Organization and Incentives in Industry, Before and After the Cultural Revolution." In *Authority, Participation, and Cultural Change in China,* ed. by Stuart Schram, pp. 233–56. Cambridge: Cambridge University Press.

Humphrey, John. 1982. *Capitalist Control and Workers' Struggle in the Brazilian Auto Industry.* Princeton: Princeton University Press.

Inkeles, Alex. 1950. *Public Opinion in Soviet Russia.* Cambridge: Harvard University Press.

Inkeles, Alex, and Raymond Bauer. 1959. *The Soviet Citizen: Daily Life in a Totalitarian Society.* Cambridge: Harvard University Press.

Jacoby, Sanford M. 1984. "The Development of Internal Labor Markets in American Manufacturing Firms." In *Internal Labor Markets,* ed. by Osterman, pp. 23–69.

Janos, Andrew C. 1970. "Group Politics in Communist Society: A Second Look at the Pluralist Model." In *Authoritarian Politics in Modern Society,* ed. by Samuel P. Huntington and Clement H. Moore. New York: Basic.

Jiang Zilong. 1979. "Qiao changzhang shangren ji" [Manager Qiao assumes office]. In *Qiao changzhang shangren ji,* pp. 1–49. Jiangsu: Jiangsu Renmin Chubanshe.

Johnson, Chalmers. 1970. "Comparing Communist Nations." In *Change in Communist Systems,* ed. by Chalmers Johnson, pp. 1–32. Stanford: Stanford University Press.

Jowitt, Kenneth. 1974. "An Organizational Approach to the Study of Political Culture in Marxist-Leninist Systems." *American Political Science Review* 68, no. 1 (Sept.): 171–91.

———. 1983. "Soviet Neotraditionalism: The Political Corruption of a Leninist Regime." *Soviet Studies* 35, no. 3 (July): 275–97.

Joyce, Patrick. 1979. *Work, Society and Politics: The Culture of the Factory in Later Victorian England.* New Brunswick, N.J.: Rutgers University Press.

Kahan, Arcadius. 1979. "Some Problems of the Soviet Industrial Worker." In *Industrial Labor in the USSR*, ed. by Arcadius Kahan and Blair A. Ruble, pp. 283–311. New York: Pergamon.

Kahn, Robert, and Floyd Mann. 1969. "Developing Research Partnerships." In *Issues in Participant Observation*, ed. by McCall and Simmons, pp. 45–51.

Kallgren, Joyce. 1968. "Aspects of Social Security in Contemporary China." Ph.D. dissertation, Department of Government, Harvard University.

―――. 1969. "Social Welfare and China's Industrial Workers." In *Chinese Communist Politics in Action*, ed. by A. Doak Barnett, pp. 540–73. Seattle: University of Washington Press.

Kassof, Alex. 1964. "The Administered Society: Totalitarianism Without Terror." *World Politics* 16 (July): 558–75.

Kirsch, Leonard Joel. 1972. *Soviet Wages: Changes in Structure and Administration since 1956.* Cambridge, Mass.: The MIT Press.

Klatt, W. 1983. "The Staff of Life: Living Standards in China, 1977–1981." *China Quarterly* 93 (Mar.): 17–50.

Kochan, Thomas A., and Peter Cappelli. 1984. "The Transformation of the Industrial Relations and Personnel Function." In *Internal Labor Markets*, ed. by Osterman, pp. 133–61.

Kornai, János. 1959. *Over-Centralization in Economic Administration: A Critical Analysis Based on Experience in Hungarian Light Industry.* Trans. by John Knapp. London: Oxford University Press.

―――. 1980. *The Economics of Shortage.* Amsterdam: North-Holland.

Kornhauser, William. 1959. *The Politics of Mass Society.* Glencoe, Ill.: The Free Press.

Korzec, Michel, and Martin K. Whyte. 1981. "Reading Notes: The Chinese Wage System." *China Quarterly* 86 (June): 248–73.

Köszegi, László. 1978. "Labour Turnover and Employment Structure in European Socialist Countries." *International Labour Review* 117, no. 3 (May–June): 305–18.

Kraus, Richard. 1981. *Class Conflict in Chinese Socialism.* New York: Columbia University Press.

Kravchenko, Victor. 1946. *I Chose Freedom: The Personal and Political Life of a Soviet Official.* New York: Scribners.

Lane, David. 1982. *The End of Social Inequality? Class, Status, and Power in State Socialism.* Boston: Allen and Unwin.

Lardy, Nicholas R. 1983. *Agriculture in China's Modern Economic Development.* Cambridge: Cambridge University Press.

―――. 1984. "Consumption and Living Standards in China, 1978–83." *China Quarterly* 100 (Dec.): 849–65.

Lawler, Edward E., III. 1973. *Motivation in Work Organizations.* Monterey, Calif.: Brooks-Cole.

Lee, Hong Yung. 1982. "The Personnel Dossier System in China." Unpublished paper.

Lewin, Moshe. 1977. "The Social Background of Stalinism." In *Stalinism*, ed. by Robert C. Tucker, pp. 111–36. New York: Norton.

———. 1978. "Society, State, and Ideology during the First Five-Year Plan." In *Cultural Revolution in Russia*, ed. by Fitzpatrick, pp. 41–77.

Lewis, John Wilson. 1963. *Leadership in Communist China.* Ithaca, N.Y.: Cornell University Press.

Li Xuefeng. 1956. "Jiaqiang dang dui qiye de lingdao, guanche zhixing qunzhong luxian" [Strengthen party leadership in enterprises, thoroughly implement the mass line]. *Tianjin Da Gong Bao*, Sept. 25, p. 1.

Liang Heng and Judith Shapiro. 1983. *Son of the Revolution.* New York: Knopf.

Lieberthal, Kenneth G. 1980. *Revolution and Tradition in Tientsin, 1949–1952.* Stanford: Stanford University Press.

Liebman, Robert. 1980. "Repressive Strategies and Working-Class Protest: Lyon, 1848–1852." *Social Science History* 4, no. 1 (Feb.): 33–55.

Lifton, Robert J. 1961. *Thought Reform and the Psychology of Totalism.* New York: Norton.

Lindqvist, Sven. 1963. *China in Crisis.* Trans. by Sylvia Clayton. London: Faber and Faber.

Lipset, Seymour Martin. 1983. "Radicalism or Reformism: The Sources of Working-Class Politics." *American Political Science Review* 77, no. 1 (March): 1–18.

Liu Binyan. 1983. *People or Monsters?* Ed. by Perry Link. Bloomington: Indiana University Press.

Liu Gang, Wang Guochang, and Xing Yichu. 1980. *Shanghai chengshi jiti suoyouzhi gongye yanjiu* [A study of municipal collective industry in Shanghai]. Shanghai: Shanghai Renmin Chubanshe.

Loh, Robert, and Humphrey Evans. 1962. *Escape from Red China.* New York: Coward-McCann.

Louie, Genny, and Kam Louie. 1981. "The Role of Nanjing University in the Nanjing Incident." *China Quarterly* 86 (June): 332–48.

Lowenthal, Richard. 1970. "Development vs. Utopia in Communist Policy." In *Change in Communist Systems*, ed. by Johnson, pp. 33–116.

McAuley, Alastair. 1981. "Welfare and Social Security." In *The Soviet Worker*, ed. by Schapiro and Godson, pp. 194–230.

McCall, George J. 1969. "Data Quality Control in Participant Observation." In *Issues in Participant Observation*, ed. by McCall and Simmons, pp. 128–41.

McCall, George J., and J. L. Simmons, eds. 1969. *Issues in Participant Observation.* Reading, Mass.: Addison-Wesley.

Martin, Roberta. 1981. *Party Recruitment in China: Patterns and Prospects.* Occasional Papers of the East Asian Institute. New York: East Asian Institute, Columbia University.

Merton, Robert K. 1968a. "Manifest and Latent Functions." In *Social Theory and Social Structure,* by Robert K. Merton, pp. 73–138. New York: The Free Press.

———. 1968b. "Continuities in the Theory of Reference Groups and Social Structure." In ibid., pp. 335–440.

———. 1968c. "The Bearing of Empirical Research on Sociological Theory." In ibid., pp. 156–71.

Meyer, Alfred G. 1970. "Theories of Convergence." In *Change in Communist Systems,* ed. by Johnson, pp. 313–41.

Ministry of Control, People's Republic of China. 1958. "Guanyu guojia xingzheng jiguan gongzuo renyuan de jiang cheng zhanxing guiding zhong jige wenti de jieda (zhailu)" [Answers to some questions about the provisions for reward and punishment of working personnel in state administrative organs (excerpts)]. June 12. In Planning Commission 1973: 139.

Ministry of Finance, Department of Financial Affairs for Cultural and Educational Administration, People's Republic of China. 1979. *Shehui wenjiao xingzheng caiwu zhaibian.* [Selected financial regulations for social, cultural, and educational administration]. Beijing.

Ministry of Internal Affairs, People's Republic of China. 1964. "Guanyu guojia xingzheng jiguan gongzuo renyuan de jiang cheng zhanxing guiding zhong ruogan wenti de jieda" [Answers to certain questions concerning the temporary provisions for reward and punishment of working personnel in state administrative organs]. April 22. In Planning Commission 1973: 140–42.

Ministry of Labor, People's Republic of China. 1953. "Laodong baoxian tiaoli shishi xize xiuzheng cao'an" [Revised draft of detailed rules for implementing labor insurance regulations]. Jan. 26. In Planning Commission 1973: 286–316.

———. 1964. "Laodong baoxian wenti jieda" [Answers to questions about labor insurance]. In Planning Commission 1973: 317–66.

Ministry of Labor and Personnel, People's Republic of China. 1983a. "Laodong renshi bu guanyu zhaogong kaohe zeyou luyong de zhanxing guiding" [Temporary regulations of the ministry of labor and personnel regarding the selective hiring of qualified new workers]. Feb. 25. *Zhonghua Renmin Gongheguo Guowuyuan Gongbao* 401 (April 30): 215–17.

———. 1983b. "Laodong renshi bu guanyu yi jiu ba san nian qiye tiaozheng gongzi he gaige gongzi zhidu wenti de baogao" [Ministry of labor and personnel notice regarding the 1983 wage readjustment in enterprises and the reform of the wage system]. April 4. *Zhonghua Ren-min Gongheguo Guowuyuan Gongbao* 410 (Aug. 20): 704–8.

Ministry of Metallurgy, People's Republic of China. 1963. "Kuangshan jingxia zhigong xiajing jintie shixing banfa" [Trial provisions regarding underground supplements for mine pit workers and staff]. Doc. No. 7266 (Oct. 21). In Planning Commission 1973: 166–67.

Mintz, Sidney. 1966. "*Pratik*: Haitian Personal Economic Relationships." In *Peasant Society: A Reader*, ed. by Jack Potter, George Foster, and May Diaz. Boston: Little-Brown.

Montgomery, David. 1979. *Workers' Control in America*. Cambridge: Cambridge University Press.

Morton, Henry W. 1980. "Who Gets What, When and How? Housing in the Soviet Union." *Soviet Studies* 32 (April): 235–59.

———. 1984. "The Contemporary Soviet City." In *The Contemporary Soviet City*, ed. by Morton and Stuart, pp. 3–24.

Morton, Henry W., and Robert C. Stuart, eds. 1984. *The Contemporary Soviet City*. Armonk, N.Y.: M. E. Sharpe.

Munro, Donald. 1977. *The Concept of Man in Contemporary China*. Ann Arbor: University of Michigan Press.

Nahirny, Vladimir. 1962. "Some Observations on Ideological Groups." *American Journal of Sociology* 67, no. 4 (Jan.): 397–405.

Nathan, Andrew J. 1973. "A Factionalism Model for CCP Politics." *China Quarterly* 53 (Jan.–March): 34–66.

———. 1985. *Chinese Democracy*. New York: Knopf.

National Labor Federation, People's Republic of China. 1965. "Guanyu zai 'siqing' yundong zhong chachulai de dizhu, funong fenzi de gongling ji-suan wenti de fuhan" [Reply to questions concerning the calculation of seniority for landlord and rich peasant elements uncovered during the 'four cleans' campaign]. Doc. No. 297 (May 24). In Planning Commission 1973: 542.

Nelson, Daniel. 1975. *Managers and Workers: Origins of the New Factory System in the United States, 1880–1920*. Madison: University of Wisconsin Press.

New China Daily (*Xinhua Ribao*). 1956. "Tigao ding'e shi gongren wan-bucheng jihua" [Raising of quotas makes it impossible for workers to finish the plan], July 22, p. 1.

Nie Mei. 1956. "Shenme shi zhongda wenti?" [What are major questions?] *Renmin Ribao*, Nov. 19, p. 1.

Nisbet, Robert A. 1966. *The Sociological Tradition*. New York: Basic.

———. 1969. *Social Change and History*. New York: Oxford University Press.

Oi, Jean C. 1983. "State and Peasant in Contemporary China: The Politics of Grain Procurement." Ph.D. dissertation, Department of Political Science, University of Michigan.

————. 1985. "Communism and Clientelism: Rural Politics in China." *World Politics* 37, no. 2 (Jan.): 238–66.

Oksenberg, Michel. 1970. "Getting Ahead and Along in Communist China: The Ladder of Success on the Eve of the Cultural Revolution." In *Party Leadership and Revolutionary Power in China*, ed. by John Wilson Lewis, pp. 304–47. Cambridge: Cambridge University Press.

Organization Department, Central Committee, Chinese Communist Party. 1983. *Dang de zuzhi gongzuo wenda* [Questions and answers on the party's organizational work]. Beijing: Renmin Chubanshe.

Orleans, Leo A. 1982. "China's Urban Population: Concepts, Conglomerations, and Concerns." In *China Under the Four Modernizations, Part 1*, Joint Economic Committee, U.S. Congress, pp. 268–302. Washington, D.C.: U.S. Government Printing Office.

Osterman, Paul, ed. 1984. *Internal Labor Markets*. Cambridge, Mass.: The MIT Press.

Parish, William L. 1981. "Egalitarianism in China." *Problems of Communism* 30, no. 1 (Jan.–Feb.): 37–53.

Parish, William L., and Martin K. Whyte. 1978. *Village and Family in Contemporary China*. Chicago: University of Chicago Press.

Parkin, Frank. 1971. *Class Inequality and Political Order: Social Stratification in Capitalist and Communist Societies*. New York: Praeger.

Parsons, Talcott. 1951. *The Social System*. Glencoe, Ill.: The Free Press.

People's Daily [*Renmin Ribao*]. 1956a. "Zhuyi wuren zeren xianxiang de mengya" [Be alert for the first signs of unclear responsibilities]. Oct. 27, p. 1.

————. 1956b. "Guanyu 'qinzi dongshou'" [On "personally getting the job done"]. Nov. 16, p. 1.

————. 1978a. "Jianqing gongchang de shehui fudan" [Lighten the social burdens of factories]. Oct. 27, p. 2.

————. 1978b. "Ping jiang yao yi kaohe shengchan chengji wei zhu, bu ying fujia qita tiaojian" [In bonus appraisals, assessment of production accomplishments is the chief consideration, other conditions should not be added]. Nov. 30, p. 3.

————. 1979. "Yige changzhang de xinli hua" [One factory director's words from the heart]. Nov. 25, p. 1.

————. 1980. "Chang kuang baowei jigou gui gong'an bu he ben bumen shuangchong lingdao" [Security organs in factories and mines returned to dual leadership by the ministry of public security and the industrial organs]. Feb. 12, p. 4.

Perkins, Dwight, ed. 1977. *Rural Small-Scale Industry in China*. Berkeley and Los Angeles: University of California Press.

Perlmutter, Amos. 1981. *Modern Authoritarianism: A Comparative Institutional Analysis*. New Haven: Yale University Press.

Planning Commission, Fujian Province Revolutionary Committee, People's

Republic of China. 1973. *Laodong gongzi wenjian xuanbian (gongzi, fuli, laodong baoxian)* [Selected documents on labor and wages (wages, benefits, and labor insurance)]. Fujian Sheng Geming Weiyuanhui.

Poggi, Gianfranco. 1978. *The Development of the Modern State.* Stanford: Stanford University Press.

Political Department, Fujian Province Revolutionary Committee, People's Republic of China. 1971. "Guanyu fujia gongzi de chuli wenti de guiding" [Resolution on problems in handling supplementary wages]. In Planning Commission 1973: 157.

Pollard, Sidney. 1965. *The Genesis of Modern Management.* Cambridge: Harvard University Press.

Powell, David E. 1977. "Labor Turnover in the Soviet Union." *Slavic Review* 37, no. 2 (June): 268–85.

Pravda, Alex. 1981. "Political Attitudes and Activity." In *Blue-Collar Workers in Eastern Europe,* ed. by Triska and Gati, pp. 43–69.

Qian Shiming. 1981. "Jiangjin jinjin shi chao'e laodong de baochou—yu Sun Keliang tongzhi shangque" [Bonuses are nothing more than remuneration for labor in excess of quotas—a discussion with comrade Sun Keliang]. *Xueshu Yuekan* 5 (May): 36–39.

Qiqihaer Daily [*Qiqihaer Ribao*]. 1957a. "Shei shi qiye de zhuren?" [Who is the master of the enterprise?] Jan. 17, p. 1.

———. 1957b. "Er ji chang shixing jishu ding'e ceding" [No. 2 machine plant implements technical determination of quotas]. March 10, p. 1.

Radcliffe-Brown, A. R. 1952. "On Social Structure." In *Structure and Function in Primitive Society,* by A. R. Radcliffe-Brown, pp. 188–204. New York: The Free Press.

Richman, Barry. 1969. *Industrial Society in Communist China.* New York: Random House.

Rimlinger, Gaston. 1968. "Social Security, Incentives, and Controls in the U.S. and U.S.S.R." In *State and Society: A Reader in Comparative Political Sociology,* ed. by Reinhard Bendix et al., pp. 391–402. Berkeley and Los Angeles: University of California Press.

Riskin, Carl. 1973. "Maoism and Motivation: Work Incentives in China." In *China's Uninterrupted Revolution,* ed. by Victor Nee and James Peck, pp. 415–61. New York: Pantheon.

Rohlen, Thomas P. 1975. "The Company Work Group." In *Modern Japanese Organization and Decision-Making,* ed. by Ezra Vogel, pp. 185–209. Berkeley and Los Angeles: University of California Press.

Roth, Guenther. 1968. "Personal Rulership, Patrimonialism, and Empire Building in the New States." *World Politics* 20, no. 2 (Jan.): 194–206.

Roy, Donald. 1954. "Efficiency and the Fix: Informal Intergroup Relations in a Piecework Machine Shop." *American Journal of Sociology* 60 (Nov.): 255–66.

Rudolph, Lloyd I., and Suzanne Hoeber Rudolph. 1964. *The Modernity of Tradition: Political Development in India.* Chicago: University of Chicago Press.

Rudolph, Jorg-Meinhard. 1984. "China's Media: Fitting News to Print." *Problems of Communism* 33, no. 4 (July–Aug.): 58–67.

Rustow, Dankwart. 1965. "Turkey: The Modernity of Tradition." In *Political Culture and Political Development*, ed. by Lucian W. Pye and Sidney Verba, pp. 171–98. Princeton: Princeton University Press.

Sabel, Charles. 1982. *Work and Politics: The Division of Labor in Industry.* Cambridge: Cambridge University Press.

Sabel, Charles, and David Stark. 1982. "Planning, Politics, and Shop-Floor Power: Hidden Forms of Bargaining in Soviet-Imposed State-Socialist Societies." *Politics and Society* 11, no. 4: 439–75.

Schapiro, Leonard, and Joseph Godson, eds. 1981. *The Soviet Worker.* London: MacMillan.

Schein, Edgar H., et al. 1961. *Coercive Persuasion.* New York: Norton.

Schmitter, Phillippe. 1981. "Interest Intermediation and Regime Governability in Western Europe and North America." In *Organizing Interests in Western Europe: Pluralism, Corporatism, and the Transformation of Politics*, ed. by Suzanne Berger, pp. 287–327. Cambridge: Cambridge University Press.

Schroeder, Gertrude. 1973. "Recent Developments in Soviet Planning and Incentives." In *Soviet Economic Prospects for the Seventies*, Joint Economic Committee, U.S. Congress, pp. 11–38. Washington, D.C.: U.S. Government Printing Office.

———. 1984. "Retail Trade and Personal Services in Soviet Cities." In *The Contemporary Soviet City*, ed. by Morton and Stuart, pp. 202–20.

Schurmann, Franz. 1968. *Ideology and Organization in Communist China.* Berkeley and Los Angeles: University of California Press.

Schwarz, Solomon. 1952. *Labor in the Soviet Union.* New York: Praeger.

Scott, John. 1946 (1973). *Behind the Urals: An American Worker in Russia's City of Steel.* Bloomington: Indiana University Press.

Second Ministry of Light Industry, People's Republic of China. 1966. "'Guanyu qing, shougongye jiti suoyouzhi qiye zhigong, sheyuan tuixiu tongchou zhanxing banfa' he 'Guanyu qing, shougongye jiti suoyouzhi qiye zhigong, sheyuan tuizhi chuli zhanxing banfa' de tongzhi" [Notice on "Temporary overall provisions for the retirement of workers, staff, and cooperative members of collectively owned enterprises in light industry and handicrafts" and "Temporary provisions for handling the severance of workers, staff, and cooperative members of collectively owned enterprises in light industry and handicrafts"]. Docs. No. 11 and 59 (transmitted concurrently, April). In Planning Commission 1973: 637–46.

Sewell, William H., Jr. 1980. *Work and Revolution in France*. Cambridge: Cambridge University Press.

Shenyang Daily [*Shenyang Ribao*]. 1957. "Weihe zheiyang duidai xin ding'e?" [Why are the new quotas handled in this manner?] April 2, p. 2.

Shils, Edward. 1957. "Primordial, Personal, Sacred and Civil Ties." *British Journal of Sociology* 8, no. 2 (June): 130–45.

————. 1965. "Charisma, Order, and Status." *American Sociological Review* 30, no. 2 (April): 199–213.

————. 1972. "Ideology." In *The Intellectuals and the Powers and Other Essays*, by Edward Shils, pp. 23–41. Chicago: University of Chicago Press.

Shirk, Susan L. 1981. "Recent Chinese Labour Policies and the Transformation of Industrial Organisation in China." *China Quarterly* 88 (Dec.): 575–93.

————. 1982. *Competitive Comrades: Career Incentives and Student Strategies in China*. Berkeley and Los Angeles: University of California Press.

Shorter, Edward, and Charles Tilly. 1974. *Strikes in France, 1830–1968*. Cambridge: Cambridge University Press.

Shue, Vivienne. 1984. "The New Course in Chinese Agriculture." *Annals of the American Academy of Political and Social Science* 476 (Nov.): 74–88.

Sirianni, Carmen. 1982. *Workers Control and Socialist Democracy: The Soviet Experience*. London: New Left Books.

Siu, Helen F. L., and Zelda Stern, eds. 1983. *Mao's Harvest*. New Haven: Yale University Press.

Skilling, H. Gordon. 1970. "Group Conflict and Political Change." In *Change in Communist Systems*, ed. by Johnson, pp. 215–34.

————. 1983. "Interest Groups and Communist Politics Revisited." *World Politics* 36, no. 1 (June): 1–27.

Skilling, H. Gordon, and Franklyn Griffiths, eds. 1970. *Interest Groups in Soviet Politics*. Princeton: Princeton University Press.

Smelser, Neil J. 1959. *Social Change in the Industrial Revolution*. Chicago: University of Chicago Press.

Starr, John Bryan. 1979. *Continuing the Revolution: The Political Thought of Mao Zedong*. Princeton: Princeton University Press.

State Council, People's Republic of China. 1953. *Labour Insurance Regulations of the People's Republic of China*. Peking: Foreign Languages Press.

————. 1957a. "Guanyu gongren, zhiyuan zai qiye zhijian diaodong gongzuo hou de gongzi he buzhu fei de zhanxing guiding" [Temporary provisions regarding the wages and allowances of workers and staff transferred between enterprises]. Doc. No. 35 (July 29). In Planning Commission 1973: 33–34.

―――. 1957b. "Guanyu chuli guojia jiguan, qiye, xuexiao zai sufan yundong zhong chachu de fangeming fenzi he qita huai fenzi de gongling he gongzi wenti de guiding" [Provisions concerning the question of the seniority and wages of counterrevolutionary elements and other bad elements in state organs, enterprises, and schools who were uncovered during the campaign to eliminate counterrevolutionaries]. Doc. No. 39 (Aug. 9). In Planning Commission 1973: 135–36.

―――. 1957c. "Guanyu gaodeng xuexiao he zhongdeng zhuanye xuexiao biyesheng zai jianxiqi jian de linshi gongzi daiyu de guiding" [Provisions on the temporary wages for graduates of institutions of higher learning and specialized secondary schools during their probationary period]. Doc. No. 57 (Oct. 25). In Planning Commission 1973: 65–69.

―――. 1958. "Guanyu gongren, zhiyuan huijia tanqin de jiaqi he gongzi daiyu de zhanxing guiding" [Temporary provisions on the length of home leave and leave pay for workers and staff]. Feb. 6. In Planning Commission 1973: 225–27.

―――. 1965. "Guanyu jingjian tuizhi de lao zhigong shenghuo kunnan jiuji wenti de tongzhi" [Notice on the problem of providing relief for old employees who are experiencing livelihood difficulties after being discharged during efforts to reduce payrolls]. No. 224 (June 9). In Planning Commission 1973: 459–61.

―――. 1966. "Zhaokai wu sheng jingjian anzhi gonggu gongzuo huiyi" [Five-province work conference held on cutting back on staff, making arrangements for those released, and consolidating organizations]. In Planning Commission 1973: 453–58.

―――. 1967. "Guanyu zhigong zhuanzheng dingji wenti de tongzhi" [Notice on questions regarding the setting of wage grades for workers and staff being given permanent status]. State Council Labor Department Doc. No. 382 (Dec. 29). In Planning Commission 1973: 1–2.

―――. 1971. "Guanyu tiaozheng bufen gongren he gongzuo renyuan gongzi de tongzhi" [Notice on the wage readjustment for a portion of the workers and working personnel]. Doc. No. 90 (Nov. 30). In Planning Commission 1973: 593–96.

―――. 1982a. "Guowuyuan guanyu yange kongzhi nongcun laodongli jincheng zuogong he nongye renkou zhuanwei fei nongye renkou de tongzhi" [State council notice on the strict control of the movement of the rural labor force into cities for work and the turning of agricultural population into nonagricultural population]. Dec. 30, 1981. *Zhonghua Renmin Gongheguo Guowuyuan Gongbao* 374 (Feb. 10): 885–87.

―――. 1982b. "Qiye zhigong jiang cheng tiaoli" [Regulations on the reward and punishment of enterprise employees]. April 10. *Xinhua Yuebao* 5 (May): 89–91.

State Labor Bureau, Policy Research Office, People's Republic of China. 1980. *Zhongguo laodong lifa, ziliao huibian* [Chinese labor law, a compendium of materials]. Beijing: Gongren Chubanshe.

State Statistical Bureau, People's Republic of China. 1959. *Weida de shi nian* [The ten great years]. Beijing: Renmin Chubanshe.

——. 1982. *Zhongguo Tongji Nianjian 1981* [China Statistical Yearbook 1981]. Hong Kong: Jingji Daobaoshe.

——. 1983. *Zhongguo Tongji Nianjian 1983* [China Statistical Yearbook 1983]. Hong Kong: Jingji Daobaoshe.

Statistics Bureau, Prime Minister's Office, Japan. 1982. *Japan Statistical Yearbook 1982*. Tokyo: Japan Statistical Association.

Stepan, Alfred. 1978. *The State and Society: Peru in Comparative Perspective*. Princeton: Princeton University Press.

Stinchcombe, Arthur. 1965. "Social Structure and Organizations." In *Handbook of Organizations*, ed. by James March, pp. 142–93. Chicago: Rand-McNally.

——. 1968. *Constructing Social Theories*. New York: Harcourt, Brace.

——. 1974. *Creating Efficient Industrial Administrations*. New York: Academic.

Stone, Katherine. 1975. "The Origins of Job Structures in the Steel Industry." In *Labor Market Segmentation*, ed. by Richard Edwards, Michael Reich, and David Gordon, pp. 27–84. Lexington, Mass.: D. C. Heath.

Sun Keliang. 1979. "Jiangjin jinjin shi chao'e laodong baochou ma?" [Are bonuses merely remuneration for labor in excess of quotas?]. *Jingji Yanjiu* 6 (June): 39–42.

Teckenburg, Wolfgang. 1978. "Labour Turnover and Job Satisfaction: Indicators of Industrial Conflict in the USSR? *Soviet Studies* 30, no. 2 (April): 193–211.

Theobald, Robin. 1978. "A Charisma Too Versatile?" *European Journal of Sociology* 19, no. 1: 192–98.

——. 1982. "Patrimonialism." *World Politics* 34, no. 4 (July): 548–59.

Thomas, Robert J. 1982. "Citizenship and Gender in Work Organization: Some Considerations for Theories of the Labor Process." In *Marxist Inquiries: Studies of Labor, Class, and States*, ed. by Michael Burawoy and Theda Skocpol, pp. 86–112. Supplement to *American Journal of Sociology* 88. Chicago: University of Chicago Press.

Thompson, E. P. 1966. *The Making of the English Working Class*. New York: Vintage.

Tilly, Charles. 1978. *From Mobilization to Revolution*. Reading, Mass.: Addison-Wesley.

——. 1981. "Proletarianization: Theory and Research." In *As Sociology Meets History*, by Charles Tilly, pp. 179–89. New York: Academic.

Tung Chi-ping and Humphrey Evans. 1967. *The Thought Revolution*. London: Leslie Frewin.

Turovsky, Fyodor. 1981. "Society Without a Present." In *The Soviet Worker*, ed. by Schapiro and Godson, pp. 156–93.

Triska, Jan F., and Charles Gati, eds. 1981. *Blue-Collar Workers in Eastern Europe*. London: Allen and Unwin.

Unger, Jonathan. 1982. *Education Under Mao: Class and Competition in Canton Schools, 1960–1980*. New York: Columbia University Press.

Unwin, George. 1957. *Industrial Organization in the Sixteenth and Seventeenth Centuries*. London: Cass.

VanMaanen, John. 1983. "The Fact of Fiction in Organizational Ethnography." In *Qualitative Methodology*, ed. by John VanMaanen, pp. 37–55. Beverly Hills, Calif.: Sage.

Vogel, Ezra F. 1965. "From Friendship to Comradeship: The Change in Personal Relations in Communist China." *China Quarterly* 21 (Jan.–March): 46–60.

———. 1967. "Voluntarism and Social Control." In *Soviet and Chinese Communism: Similarities and Differences*, ed. by Donald W. Treadgold, pp. 168–84. Seattle: University of Washington Press.

Walder, Andrew G. 1981. "Participative Management and Worker Control in China." *Sociology of Work and Occupations* 8, no. 2 (May): 224–51.

———. 1982. "Some Ironies of the Maoist Legacy in Industry." In *The Transition to Socialism in China*, ed. by Mark Selden and Victor Lippit, pp. 215–37. Armonk, N.Y.: M. E. Sharpe.

———. 1983. "Wage Reform and the Web of Factory Interests." Paper presented at the Workshop on Policy Implementation in Post-Mao China, Ohio State University, June 20–24.

———. 1984a. "The Remaking of the Chinese Working Class, 1949–1981." *Modern China* 10, no. 1 (Jan.): 3–48.

———. 1984b. "China's Industry in Transition: To What?" *Annals of the American Academy of Political and Social Science* 476 (Nov.): 62–73.

———. 1985a. "The Informal Dimension of Enterprise Financial Reforms." In *The Chinese Economy in the Eighties*, Joint Economic Committee, U.S. Congress, pp. 134–49. Washington, D.C.: U.S. Government Printing Office.

———. 1985b. "The Political Dimension of Social Mobility in Communist States: Reflections on the Soviet Union and China." In *Research in Political Sociology*, Vol. 1, ed. by Richard Braungart, pp. 101–17. Greenwich, Conn.: JAI Press.

———. 1986. "Communist Social Structure and Workers' Politics in China." In *Citizens and Groups in Contemporary China*, ed. by Victor Falkenheim. Michigan Monographs in Chinese Studies, No. 56, Ann Arbor: University of Michigan, Center for Chinese Studies.

Wang Hongding. 1956. "Shehui zhuyi qiye de zuzhi yuanze—minzhu jizhong zhi" [The organizational principle of the socialist enterprise—democratic centralism]. *Gongshang Jie* 10 (Oct.): 13.

Weber, Max. 1922 (1978). *Economy and Society: An Outline of Interpretive Sociology*, 2 vols. Ed. by Guenther Roth and Claus Wittich. Berkeley and Los Angeles: University of California Press.

White, Gordon. 1980. "The Politics of Demobilized Soldiers from Liberation to Cultural Revolution." *China Quarterly* 82 (June): 187–213.

White, Lynn T., III. 1978. *Careers in Shanghai: The Social Guidance of Personal Energies in a Developing Chinese City, 1949–1966*. Berkeley and Los Angeles: University of California Press.

Whyte, Martin K. 1974. *Small Groups and Political Rituals in China.* Berkeley and Los Angeles: University of California Press.

———. 1983. "On Studying China at a Distance." In *The Social Sciences and Fieldwork in China*, ed. by Anne F. Thurston and Burton Pasternak, pp. 63–80. Boulder, Colo.: Westview.

Whyte, Martin K., and William L. Parish. 1984. *Urban Life in Contemporary China.* Chicago: University of Chicago Press.

Wilbur, Martin C. 1970. "The Influence of the Past: How the Early Years Helped to Shape the Future of the Chinese Communist Party." In *Party Leadership and Revolutionary Power in China*, ed. by John Wilson Lewis, pp. 35–68. Cambridge: Cambridge University Press.

Wiles, Peter. 1981. "Wage and Income Policies." In *The Soviet Worker*, ed. by Schapiro and Godson, pp. 15–38.

Wittfogel, Karl A. 1957 (1981). *Oriental Despotism: A Comparative Study of Total Power.* New York: Vintage.

Wolfe, Bertram. 1956. *Communist Totalitarianism.* Boston: Beacon.

Workers' Daily [*Gongren Ribao*]. 1956. "Zhunbei kuoda he jianquan minzhu guanli zhidu" [Prepare, expand, and consolidate the democratic system of management]. Dec. 28, p. 1.

———. 1979. "Yao jianjue luoshi 'zhongzai zhengzhi biaoxian' de zhengce" [Resolutely implement the policy of "emphasis on political *biaoxian*"]. Feb. 28, p. 1.

———. 1981a. "Tan 'guanxi xue' de shehui genyuan" [On the social roots of "*guanxi*"]. Jan. 29, p. 3.

———. 1981b. "Yao bangzhu jiejue shiji wenti bu neng kao shuo jiao" [Don't rely on words, help solve real problems]. Feb. 7, p. 2.

———. 1981c. "Guanxin zhigong shenghuo, jiejue zhigong hougu zhi you" [Care for workers' livelihood, solve their household worries]. March 23, p. 1.

———. 1981d. "Woguo laodong jiuye gongzuo qude xianzhu chengjiu" [Our nation achieves outstanding results in employment of labor]. June 25, p. 1.

———. 1981e. "Yizhi shou huanying de 'zhigong shenghuo fuwu dui'" [A welcomed "workers household service brigade"]. July 18, p. 2.

———. 1981f. "Dao di yi xian qu guanxin zhigong shenghuo" [Go to the front lines, show concern for workers' livelihood]. July 22, p. 2.

————. 1982a. "Bu pa fengci, gan wei si hua" [Don't fear mockery, dare to stand up for the four modernizations]. Jan. 2, p. 1.

————. 1982b. "Zai fengci waku mianqian . . ." [In the face of mockery and sarcasm . . .]. Jan. 8, p. 2.

————. 1982c. "Jiejue jiuzheng guli daji xianjin de bu zheng zhi feng" [Check the unhealthy tendency of isolating and attacking the advanced workers]. Feb. 5, p. 1.

————. 1982d. "Dai changzhang de 'jinji tongzhi'" [Manager Dai's "urgent bulletin"]. Feb. 8, p. 1.

————. 1982e. "Qunian guoying qiye zichou daliang zijin jianzao zhuzhai" [Last year state enterprises raised large amounts of their own funds to build residences]. March 24, p. 1.

Wright, Tim. 1981. "A Method of Evading Management: Contract Labor in Chinese Coal Mines Before 1937." *Comparative Studies in Society and History* 23, no. 4 (Oct.): 656–78.

Xinhua News Agency. 1980. "Jueda duoshu zhigong jiating shouru xianzhu zengzhang" [Household income of vast majority of workers and staff increases markedly]. *Renmin Ribao*, Dec. 31, p. 1.

————. 1981. "Nongcun ren junnian shouru zengjia dao yibai qishijiu yuan" [Average annual income of rural people increases to 179 yuan]. *Renmin Ribao*, Jan. 3, p. 1.

————. 1982. "Guojia tongji ju de diaocha ziliao biaoming jin san nian chengshi zhigong jiating shenghuo shuiping xianzhu tigao" [State Statistical Bureau survey indicates standard of living of urban wage-earning households raised greatly in past three years]. *Xinhua Yuebao* 3 (March): 133–35.

————. 1983. "Quan dang nuli wancheng zhengdang weida renwu shixing dangfeng genben haozhuan" [The entire party strives to complete the great task of party rectification and bring about a basic improvement in the party's workstyle]. *Renmin Ribao*, Oct. 13, pp. 1–3.

————. 1984. "Central Committee Decision on Reform of the Economic Structure." *Daily Report, China*, Foreign Broadcast Information Service, Oct. 22: K1–K19.

Yuan Fang. 1956. "Wo guo laodong shengchang lü zengzhang yu gongzi zengzhang de bijiao guanxi" [The proportional relationship between the rate of increase in production and of wages in our country]. *Xin Jianshe* 99 (Dec. 3).

Zaslavsky, Victor. 1982a. "The Regime and the Working Class." In *The Neo-Stalinist State: Class, Ethnicity, and Consensus in Soviet Society*, by Victor Zaslavsky, pp. 44–65. Armonk, N.Y.: M. E. Sharpe.

————. 1982b. "Closed Cities and the Organized Consensus." In ibid., pp. 130–64.

Zelditch, Morris, Jr. 1962. "Some Methodological Problems of Field Studies." *American Journal of Sociology* 67, no. 5 (March): 566–76.

Zelnick, Reginald. 1971. *Labor and Society in Tsarist Russia: The Factory Workers of St. Petersburg, 1855–1870.* Stanford: Stanford University Press.

Zhang Zehou and Chen Yuguang. 1981. "Shi lun wo guo renkou jiegou yu guomin jingji fazhan de guanxi" [A tentative discussion of the relationship between China's population structure and the development of the national economy]. *Zhongguo Shehui Kexue* 4: 29–46.

Zhao Lukuan. 1983. "Lun laodong hetong zhi" [On the labor contract system]. *Renmin Ribao,* Sept. 7, p. 5.

Zhou Shulian and Lin Senmu. 1980. "Tantan zhuzhai wenti" [A discussion of the housing problem]. *Renmin Ribao,* Aug. 5, p. 5.

Zweig, David. 1978. "The Peita Debate on Education and the Fall of Teng Hsiao-p'ing." *China Quarterly* 73 (March): 140–59.

Index

Activists: attitudes of, 146, 147–153; and clientelism, 162–164, 164–165, 170–175, 220, 246–247; and instrumental-personal ties, 181, 185, 186, 210; interviews with, 257, 258–259; isolation of, 151–152, 164, 166–170; mobility of, 80–81, 247; and nonactivists, 166, 187, 193, 219, 244, 245; and the party, 89, 90, 96, 236, 248–249; and post-Mao reforms, 223, 224, 233–235, 238–239; and veteran workers, 151, 177–178; and work groups, 104, 105, 107. *See also* Political activism

Affectivity, 127–128, 178, 188, 189, 252

Anti-rightist campaign, 73, 119n31, 136, 137, 213

Ascription, 8, 128, 131

Authoritarianism, non-communist, 18, 19, 23, 85, 86, 87, 95

Authority, patterns of: and communist social structure, xiv–xv, 246, 248–249, 253; and ideology, 123–161; indulgent, 205–210; in industry, 1, 8–9, 11, 12, 242, 243, 249–251; and institutional culture, 23, 24; and interviews, 256; in non-communist societies, 18; and post-Mao reforms, 223, 239

Bargaining, hidden, 20, 239

Bendix, Reinhard, 23n21, 163, 233

Biaoxian: and activism, 152, 157, 184; and clientelism, 160–161, 162, 172, 173; and Maoist revitalization, 190,

191, 192, 212; and the party, 235, 237, 241, 248–249; and politics, 158–159; and post-Mao reforms, 223, 228, 230–231, 232, 233; and principled particularism, 132–143, 146–147

Blau, Peter, xiv

Bureaucracy: clientelist, 162–189; and commodity distribution, 60, 63–64, 67, 96; and ideology, 128; and industrial authority, 242–243, 249–253; and labor relations, 20–21, 34, 86, 87; and reform, 190, 220

Burawoy, Michael, 19n17, 96, 247

Capitalist society, xiv, 4, 8, 15, 243

Charisma, 125, 129–130

Chinese Communist party: and activists, 80–81, 148–149, 151–153, 159, 167, 233, 234–235; and *biaoxian*, 132, 134, 135, 137, 139, 140, 147, 160–161; and clientelism, 164, 169–175, 246–249; and employment, 36; and factions, 175, 176, 245; and factory organization, 84, 88–90, 96, 97, 98; and ideological orientation, 123, 124, 126, 127, 128, 162; and informants, 266–267, 268; and instrumental-personal ties, 180–181, 185, 186, 190; line changes of, 145–146, 156; and Maoist revitalization, 191, 192; and mass mobilization, 113, 116, 117, 121, 227; and nonactivists, 157, 179; and post-Mao reforms, 223, 224, 226, 229–232, 235–237, 239, 240, 241; and

Chinese Communist party (*continued*)
principled particularism, 131, 187;
and wages, 79, 118–120; and work
groups, 103, 105, 108, 111
Class: in communist society, 85, 242,
243, 245
Class background, 92, 126, 128, 131,
140, 142, 230
Clientelism, 6, 7, 8, 12, 161, 162–189,
242, 244; and authority patterns,
250–251, 253; causes of, 124, 192,
252; and legitimacy, 246–247; and
reform, 190, 224, 238. *See also*
Party-clientelism; Patronage
Cole, Robert E., 78, 179
Collective sector: activism in, 159;
benefits in, 54, 67, 68, 216; employment in, 57, 196; informants from,
262; and labor mobility, 69, 74n46,
75, 82; and state sector, 66, 98;
workers in, 43–48, 51, 52
Communist regimes, 19–20, 21–22,
85, 86–87, 88, 157, 244, 246–249
Communist society, xv–xvi, 1–8; clientelism in, 162–164, 170, 188; evolution of, 251–253; labor relations in,
xiv, 1–2, 12, 81, 83; and Leninist
organization, 187, 191; structure of,
242, 243–246; and totalitarianism,
2–3, 229, 240–241
Confucius, 109, 110, 145, 154
Consent, 23–24, 246–249
Cook, Linda, 121, 163
Corporatism, 86–87, 88, 95, 237
Criticism–self-criticism: and activism,
150, 152, 153; and political education, 121, 126; as punishment, 141,
142, 158, 159, 218–219, 231; in
work groups, 100, 108, 109, 110
Cuba, 132
Cultural Revolution: charges made during, 92n8, 201; consequences of, 79,
211; factions in, 175, 177, 245; informants on, 268; and labor discipline, 206, 216, 217, 218, 219; and
Mao, 130; policies during, 27, 112,
113; punishments after, 91, 205n8;

reaction against, 222, 223; as revitalization movement, 191–192,
220–221, 249

Dalton, Melville, xiv, 179
Demography, 30, 35–39, 82, 253
Deng Xiaoping, 109, 145, 154, 231
Dependence, xiii, xiv, xv, 8, 12, 242,
253; causes of, 30, 160; on the enterprise, 14–17, 31, 35, 68–75, 81–
84; on foremen, 20–22, 31, 97, 100,
102, 103; and institutional culture,
13, 14n13, 22–23; on management,
17–20; and reform, 193, 224, 237–
238; results of, 124n1, 157, 162,
163, 186, 188–189; and tradition,
9, 10, 35
Dossiers (*dang'an*), 91–92, 101, 131,
141, 230n6

Eastern bloc: activism in, 89n6, 157,
233; clientelism in, 162, 163, 164;
dependence in, 17, 30, 102, 242; labor in, xiv, 28n1, 75, 87n4, 102–
103. *See also* Hungary
Economic development: and industry,
33, 36–39, 65, 225; and reform,
190, 231, 233, 234, 236
Education: and class, 245, 246; of informants, 266; opportunities for, 14,
16, 59, 80, 81; political, 84, 121–
122, 123, 131, 143, 162, 192, 210;
technical, 58, 66, 117–118, 119,
234n8
Emigre interviews, xiii, xvi–xviii,
255–272
Employment: availability of, 14–15,
36–38; in collective sector, 46, 47,
57; and dependence, 11, 31, 59–68;
hereditary, 58, 67; lifetime, xiv; in
state sector, 56–59; structure of,
32–33, 39–40, 41, 196–197; and
wage structure, 79. *See also* Unemployment
Engels, Friedrich, 126
Europe, 10, 33–34. *See also* Eastern
bloc

Factions: and clientelism, 175–179, 187; in Cultural Revolution, 175, 177, 245; and labor discipline, 206, 212, 220; and reform, 193, 231, 236n9

Five-Year Plan, First, 27, 56, 65, 111; Soviet, 114, 117

Foremen: and activists, 151, 162, 164–165, 169–170, 171, 247; dependence on, xiii, 9, 11–12, 13, 20–22, 103, 242; and particularism, 124, 144; and post-Mao reforms, 224, 228–229, 233, 236, 237; power of, 95–102, 157, 160; traditional relationships with, 30, 31, 35, 189

Fried, Morton, 175

Gang of Four, 109, 145, 146, 154, 156, 222, 231, 268

Ganqing (feeling), 174, 175, 179, 181, 182–183, 211

Goffmann, Erving, 146

Gouldner, Alvin, xiv

Great Britain, 15, 31

Great Leap Forward: and *biaoxian*, 136, 137; and employment, 36, 37, 38, 42n12, 46, 69n40, 72, 116; and policy changes, 27, 119n31; and wages, 79, 111

Group theory, xv, 4–5, 7, 8, 18, 243–244, 245, 246

Guanxi, 26, 176, 179, 181–185. *See also* Instrumental-personal ties

Guomindang. *See* Nationalists

Haiti, 179

Haraszti, Miklos, 100n15, 102, 103n21, 157, 182n7

Hong Kong, 54n23, 55, 232; informants from, xiii, xvi, xvii, 53n22, 255, 259–269; working conditions in, 107, 213, 214, 248

Hou Chi-ming, 36

Housing: and *biaoxian*, 139, 148, 160; as employment benefit, 40, 42, 48, 60, 65, 67, 68, 81; and instrumental-personal ties, 166, 184, 185; and la-

bor mobility, 75, 82; leaders' control of, 98, 99, 100, 104, 113, 172; and paternalism, 14, 15, 248; and post-Mao reforms, 222, 226, 227, 238; shortage of, 193, 194, 196, 198, 200, 202, 210, 212; in Soviet Union, 102

Howe, Christopher, 49

Hundred Flowers period, 92n8, 136

Hungary, 29n1, 74n46, 75, 100n15, 102, 182n7, 223

Ideological orientation: and authority patterns, 23, 248; and clientelism, 6, 8, 25, 162, 187, 188, 247; and labor discipline, 206–209, 212, 220; and mobilization, 2, 12, 113, 114, 120, 121, 252; and personal ties, 7, 249; and principled particularism, 124, 130–132; and reform, 192, 229–232, 233, 235, 236, 239, 240; of social groups, 123, 125–130, 177

Incentives: and activism, 84, 144–147, 157, 160, 165; and clientelism, 162, 172–173, 181; and consent, xv, 6, 247; and divided workforce, 187, 219, 239; and instrumental-personal ties, 176, 210, 211, 251; and labor discipline, 208, 218–219; material, 111–113, 190, 191, 200, 229; moral, xiii, 122, 192, 193, 221, 231, 236; and post-Mao reforms, 222, 223, 224, 227, 228, 240; and principled particularism, 124, 130–131, 132–143, 220; and social structure, 245, 250; in Soviet Union, 116, 117; and wage distribution, 118–119, 120

Income, 49n18, 196–197, 200, 208, 243, 245; and family composition, 196, 198, 199, 202. *See also* Wages

Informal organization, 50, 166; and clientelism, xiii, xiv, 25, 165, 186–188, 251; and factions, 175, 176, 179

Institutional culture, 13, 14n13, 22–27, 238–241, 242

Instrumental-personal ties: in communist society, 6–7, 24, 26–27, 242,

Instrumental-personal ties (*continued*)
247–248, 249; and informal organization, 187, 188; and institutional
culture, 165–166, 179–186; and reform, 190, 193, 210–212, 218, 239;
traditional, 26, 189n12

Japan, 17, 26, 35, 60, 61, 62, 65n37,
186
Japanese industry: and Chinese industry, xiv, 10, 13n13, 14, 164, 188; dependence in, 15, 17, 21n20, 83, 84;
foreman control in, 96, 160, 237,
250; personal ties in, 25, 187; social
services in, 22, 23, 29; wages in, 76,
77, 78, 79, 96–97
Jiang Qing, 94
Jowitt, Kenneth, xv, 6n6, 9n9, 157,
251

Kornai, János, 11n11, 28

Labor: bureaus for, 35, 52, 53n22, 58,
59, 73, 74; contractors for, 30–31,
50; discipline of, 205–210; as fixed
capital, 11, 28–29, 43; markets for,
29, 40, 96, 252–253; mobility of,
13, 68–75, 82, 96, 115, 116, 159;
and modernization, 252–253; organized, 21, 31, 34, 85, 86, 88; productivity of, 37, 190, 205, 212, 229,
250; seasonal, 50–51, 53, 54, 55,
56, 75; and tradition, 30–31, 32, 34.
See also Employment; Workers
Labor insurance: in collective sector,
44–45, 46, 48, 68; in Soviet Union,
42n13, 83; in state sector, 42, 44–
45, 60, 63, 67, 73; for temporary
workers, 44–45. *See also* Sociopolitical services
Latin America, 85, 86, 87n1
Leninism, 126, 129, 187, 191, 251–252
Leninist parties, xv, 5, 121, 123, 127–
130, 175
Liberal-democratic regimes, 5, 18, 19,
85
Lin Biao, 109, 110, 145, 146, 154, 155
Lipset, Seymour Martin, 85

Liu Binyan, 222
Liu Xinwu, 184n8, 196n3
Living standards: and class, 243, 246;
and employment, 59–63, 69, 81;
and Maoist asceticism, 194–201,
212, 220; and post-Mao reforms,
222, 223, 224–227, 239, 240
Loyalty: of activists, 26, 149, 152, 170,
244, 248, 249; and *biaoxian*, 159,
160; and clientelism, xiv, 12, 25, 84,
165, 187, 246, 247; and factions,
176, 178; and instrumental-personal
ties, 179, 251; and Maoist revitalization, 191, 192, 193, 201, 220, 249,
251; and particularism, 124, 131,
181; to the party, 7, 25, 162, 175,
185, 252; and post-Mao reforms,
230–231, 233, 234, 235, 238, 239;
rewards for, 6, 80, 161, 172–173.
See also *Yiqi*

Management: and activists, 80, 233,
246; and *biaoxian*, 132, 135; and
clientelism, 24, 25, 84, 163, 181,
246; dependence on, 11–12, 13,
17–20; and divided workforce, 26,
167, 187; and foremen, 21, 22, 31;
and labor discipline, 119n31, 205–
210, 212; and the party, 235–237;
and post-Mao reforms, 226, 228,
230, 239; 240; power of, 23, 34, 70,
71, 78, 250; and principled particularism, 131–132; in Soviet Union,
116; and unions, 34, 76, 83; and
work groups, 103, 104, 105, 106,
108, 109, 120
Mao Zedong, 126, 129, 130, 146, 231,
268
Maoism: and asceticism, 190–221,
235, 249, 252; reaction against,
222–241
Markets: consumer, 17, 23, 26, 82;
farmers', 61, 64n36; labor, 29, 40,
96, 253; and living standards, 29, 40,
59
Marshall, T. H., 40
Marx, Karl, 126, 253
Marxism, 126. *See also* Leninism

Media, the, xvi–xvii, 246
Migration: controls on, 69n40, 82, 196; to Hong Kong, 260; rural-urban, 36–37, 38–39, 55n24
Military, the, 93, 116, 117
Mobility, upward, xvi; and activism, 148–149, 152–153, 247; and class, 243, 246; within enterprises, 76–81; and factions, 176, 177; and ideology, 131, 147–148
Mobilization, political: and communist society, xv, 3, 4, 8, 12, 86; decline of, 162, 163, 190, 251–252; and ideology, 123, 248, 249; and Maoist asceticism, 190, 191, 192, 193, 220; and post-Mao reforms, 222, 223, 227–229, 239; Stalinist and Maoist, 113–122, 164
Modernization, xv, 8, 10, 251, 252
Montgomery, David, 31
Munro, Donald, 122

Nahirny, Vladimir, 125, 129
Nationalists, 87n4, 92, 94
Nelson, Daniel, 21, 31
Neo-traditionalism, xv–xvi, 1–27, 31, 251, 253; defined, 9–13

Parsons, Talcott, 125–126, 127, 128
Particularism, xiii, 7, 179, 251, 252; and universalism, 8, 10, 128, 189. *See also* Principled particularism
Parties: communist, 6–7, 11, 13, 19–20, 22, 23, 163, 242; totalitarian, 2–3. *See also* Chinese Communist party; Leninist parties
Party-clientelism, xiii, xv, 24–25, 249; and informal organization, xiv, 179, 187–188; and personal ties, 165n2, 180–181, 189n12. *See also* Clientelism
Party-state, the, 1, 83–84, 85–122, 189, 253. *See also* State, the
Paternalism, 84, 97, 248, 249; early industrial, 15, 31, 83; and post-Mao reforms, 224–227, 239, 240
Patrimonialism, 25, 130, 251
Patronage, xiv, 132; Japanese, 187; traditional, 172, 175, 178. *See also* Clientelism
Pluralism, xv, 4–5, 7n7, 8
Political activism: and *biaoxian*, 132, 136–137, 138; and divided workforce, 153–159, 166–170, 244; in non-Chinese industry, 97, 116; and particularism, 124, 131–132, 144–145, 147–153; and the party-state, 84, 85, 86, 88, 161; and post-Mao reforms, 223, 224, 233–235, 239, 241; and wages, 112–113, 120; and work groups, 109–110. *See also* Activists
Political campaigns, 116, 212–213, 231–232, 245, 264. *See also* Mobilization, political
Population. *See* Demography
Principled particularism, 123–161, 181, 220, 242, 250; and clientelism, 25, 162, 163, 187. *See also* Particularism
Propaganda, 88, 114, 130; and activists, 150–151, 171, 234, 235, 236; and post-Mao reforms, 222, 224, 228
Punishment: and activism, 157, 158, 159, 169; of dissidence, 73–74; and foreman control, 100–102, 124; and labor discipline, 208, 210, 227; and principled particularism, 132, 140–143, 160, 220

Radcliffe-Brown, A. R., 244
Rationing: and activism, 172–174; and *biaoxian*, 139; and employment, 60, 61, 62, 63, 81, 248; and foreman control, 97, 98, 100, 102; and instrumental-personal ties, 183, 184, 210, 247; and population control, 37; and reform, 82, 200, 225, 238; in rural sector, 38, 52–53, 55, 56; and work groups, 104, 106
Reform: Maoist, 191–193, 220; post-Mao, 27, 222–241
Renqing (human sentiments), 174, 182
Roth, Guenther, 130
Rural sector: collectivization of, 36, 38;

Rural sector (*continued*)
  conditions in, 54, 194; decollectivization in, 223, 225; industry in,
  39, 54–56; population of, 35; in Soviet Union, 83; temporary workers
  from, 48–49, 50, 51, 52, 53, 55
Russia, Czarist, 19n17, 31n5, 35, 125.
  See also Soviet Union

Sabel, Charles, 239
Security departments, 88, 92–95, 101,
  141n5, 142
Seniority system: and benefits, 81, 99,
  100, 216; and wages, 78, 79, 80,
  177, 204, 228
Service sector, 65, 66, 68, 82, 225, 238
Shanghai, 47, 48n17, 50
Shils, Edward, 125, 129, 235
Shirk, Susan, 130, 153n7, 155n8
Social atomization, xv, 3, 4, 6, 7
Sociopolitical services: and dependence,
  14, 15, 16, 22, 23; and foreman control, 96, 97, 124, 163; and instrumental-personal ties, 185, 188; and
  labor mobility, 75, 82; and political
  loyalty, 84, 139–140, 160, 163, 248;
  and post-Mao reforms, 226–227,
  232, 237, 238; sectoral variations in,
  39, 40, 42–43, 44–45, 48, 54, 56,
  60–67, 81; in Soviet Union, 42n13,
  60, 64n36, 68, 74, 83, 102; and
  work groups, 104; and the workplace, 11, 29, 60, 250
Soviet Union: China's relations with,
  13; clientelism in, 162, 163, 164;
  corruption in, xv, 6n6; employment
  benefits in, 42n13, 60, 64n36, 68,
  74, 81, 82, 83, 102; incentives in,
  111, 190, 228, 229; instrumental-
  personal ties in, 165, 179, 186, 188,
  242; labor in, 28n1, 29, 30, 59n30,
  74–75, 82; labor relations in, xiv,
  9, 14, 14n13, 27, 34, 37, 85, 250;
  living standards in, 61, 62, 65nn; as
  model, 65, 78, 79, 80; the party in,
  89n6, 115–116, 117, 120–121,
  122, 147n6; pluralism in, 4n2; political loyalty in, 102, 147n6; politi-

cal mobilization in, 84, 88, 113–
  122; post-Stalin reforms in, 222,
  223, 224–225, 239, 240. *See also*
  Russia, Czarist
Stalin, Joseph, 114, 120, 129, 222, 223
Stark, David, 239
State, the: and charisma, 130; and
  groups, 5, 18–19, 39, 40; and labor
  policy, 12, 13; stability of, 1, 246–
  249; and the workplace, 16, 19, 20,
  21, 23, 29, 246, 253. *See also* Party-
  state, the
State sector, 28, 34–35; activism in,
  159; benefits and services in, 39,
  40–43, 44–45, 56, 60–67, 81, 216;
  and collective sector, 43, 46, 47–48;
  dependence in, 81–84, 238; employment in, 32–33, 56–59, 66–67,
  196; informants from, 261, 262; and
  labor mobility, 68, 69, 70, 72, 74–
  75; and post-Mao reforms, 224, 225,
  226–227; and rural sector, 55, 64;
  temporary workers in, 48–51, 66;
  wages in, 194, 195
Status groups, 39–56, 82, 83, 187
Stepan, Alfred, 85, 87nn1,3
Stinchcombe, Arthur, 15n14, 80

Temporary sector: benefits in, 44–45,
  67; employment in, 41, 48–54, 57;
  and labor mobility, 69, 74, 75, 82;
  rural residents in, 48–49, 50, 51, 52,
  53, 55; and state sector, 57–58, 66,
  68, 98
Tiananmen Incident, 73, 94–95, 145
Tönnies, Ferdinand, 125
Totalitarianism, xv, 2–3, 5–6, 7, 8
Tradition: and authority types, 125,
  251; Chinese, xiv, 31, 35n7; and clientelism, 25, 164, 172, 174–175,
  188–189; and mass mobilization,
  113, 122; and neo-traditionalism, 8,
  9–10; and particularism, 123, 178,
  252

Unemployment, 36, 37, 43, 47, 48n17,
  57, 67, 72
Unions: and activists, 80, 81, 116, 151,

153, 169, 171, 234, 235; and management, 34, 76, 83, 96; and the party, 126, 236; and the state, 84, 86, 87, 88; and workers, 108, 201

United States: conditions in, 60, 61, 62, 215; dependence in, 17, 22, 31, 188, 189; emigration to, 260; foreman control in, 21, 96, 97, 160, 237; industrial organization in, xiv, 13n13, 14, 29, 164, 247, 249–250; industrial revolution in, 33–34; informal organization in, 25, 176, 186, 187; labor mobility in, 74, 75, 82; paternalism in, 15, 19n17, 31, 83; wage grades in, 76, 77, 80

Universalism, 123, 188, 189, 240; and particularism, 8, 10, 128, 250, 252

Urbanization, 30, 35–37, 39, 65, 82

Virtuocracy, 130–131

Vogel, Ezra F., 127, 128, 144

Wages: and activism, 148, 164, 166, 172, 233; and *biaoxian*, 133, 134, 135–137, 160, 190, 232; and bonuses, 111–113, 137–139; and dependence, 14, 21, 31, 189, 237; and foreman control, 96, 97, 99, 100, 101, 124, 162, 163; as incentives, 116, 117, 118, 119, 190; informants on, 264; and instrumental-personal ties, 182, 185, 210, 211; and job classifications, 76–81; and labor discipline, 208, 210, 212, 213, 214, 215, 216, 220; and living standards, 59, 60, 61, 62–63, 68; management control of, 11, 34, 250; and Maoist revitalization, 192, 193, 194–201, 201–205; policies on, 9, 12, 35; and post-Mao reforms, 222, 225, 226, 228–229, 230, 236, 239–240, 241; sectoral variations in, 39–40, 41, 46, 55, 61, 68; and seniority, 78, 79, 80, 177, 204, 228; of temporary workers, 50, 52, 53, 54n23; and work groups, 103, 104, 106, 108–109, 120

Weber, Max, 9n9, 11n11, 14, 20n19,

29, 129, 252; on authority types, 23, 125, 250–251

Welfare benefits. *See* Sociopolitical services

Whyte, Martin K., 121, 150, 261

Women, 31, 143, 155, 196, 217; in collective sector, 43, 46, 47

Work groups, 102–113; and activism, 144, 149, 162, 167, 172; and *biaoxian*, 135, 137, 138, 139, 141; criticism in, 100; decline of, 212, 218–219, 220; and mass mobilization, 120, 190; politicization of, 191, 192, 193, 210; and post-Mao reforms, 228, 230

Workers: activist, 163–164, 233, 234, 244, 249; and *biaoxian*, 140, 141, 230; and clientelism, 164, 173, 224; in collective sector, 41, 43–48; dependence of, xiv, 11–12, 13, 14–17, 23, 35, 81, 83, 238; discipline of, 73, 90–95, 205–210, 212–219; divisions among, 26, 164, 166–170, 187, 238–239, 245, 246; and foreman control, 20–22, 31, 35, 100–102, 237, 242; and hidden bargaining, 239, 240; and ideology, 121–122, 123, 164; and instrumental-personal ties, 26, 27, 180–186, 189n12, 210–212, 247; and management, 17–20, 24, 34, 95n11, 250; and Maoist revitalization, 190, 191, 193, 194, 197, 201, 219; mobility of, 68–75; mobilization of, 88, 223; and the party, 5n4, 25, 89–90, 126, 237; and the party-state, 85, 86–88, 243, 246–249, 253; and post-Mao reforms, 223, 224, 226, 227, 230; and principled particularism, 131–132, 143–159; in rural sector, 41, 54–56; in state sector, 32–33, 40–43, 63–64; temporary, 41, 44–45, 48–54; veteran, 177–179; and wages, 76–81, 118–119, 120, 202, 204; and work groups, 103–113

Yiqi (personal loyalty), 172, 174, 175. *See also* Loyalty

Youths, 75, 231, 260; activism of,
130–131, 153n7; relocation of, 39,
57; in state sector, 56–57, 59, 66–
67; unemployed, 43, 47, 48n17, 67;
and wages, 78, 201–205, 210, 212
Youth league: activists in, 89, 90, 149–
151, 169, 171, 174, 234, 235; and

mobilization, 88, 108, 116; and upward mobility, 80, 81, 84, 105, 139,
148, 153, 228, 236
Yugoslavia, 87n4

Zhou Enlai, 73n45, 94

Designer:	Betty Gee
Compositor:	G & S Typesetters, Inc.
Text:	10/12 Sabon
Display:	Sabon
Printer:	Braun-Brumfield, Inc.
Binder:	Braun-Brumfield, Inc.